OLD TESTAMENT
INTERPRETATION

Gene M. Tucker

OLD TESTAMENT INTERPRETATION

Past, Present, and Future

Essays in Honor of Gene M. Tucker

EDITED BY

JAMES LUTHER MAYS,
DAVID L. PETERSEN,
AND
KENT HAROLD RICHARDS

Abingdon Press

Nashville

OLD TESTAMENT INTERPRETATION: PAST, PRESENT, AND FUTURE
ESSAYS IN HONOR OF GENE M. TUCKER

Copyright © 1995 by Abingdon Press

Library of Congress Cataloging-in-Publication Data

Old Testament interpretation: past, present, and future: essays in
   honor of Gene M. Tucker / edited by James Luther Mays, David L.
   Petersen, and Kent Harold Richards.
      p.   cm.
   Includes bibliographical references (p.).
   ISBN 0-687-13871-X (recycled alk. paper)
   1. Bible. O.T.—Criticism, interpretation, etc.   I. Tucker, Gene
M.   II. Mays, James Luther.   III. Petersen, David L.   IV. Richard
Kent Harold, 1939– .
BS1171.2.043   1995
221.6'09'045—dc20   95-20170
                                                             CIP

This book is printed on acid-free recycled paper.

95 96 97 98 99 00 01 02 03 04 — 10 9 8 7 6 5 4 3 2 1

MANUFACTURED IN THE UNITED STATES OF AMERICA

CONTENTS

PART 3: WRITINGS

PART 4: CONTEXT

PREFACE

The history of Old Testament study is a history of constant change. In every era critical interpreters have found and focused on dimensions and features of Old Testament literature that called for shifts in orientation and approach. What has been the case in the past holds for the contemporary era perhaps to a greater degree than ever before. Hypotheses and paradigms that have guided scholarly interpretation are being questioned, revised, and replaced.

This volume provides an introduction to the changing terrain of contemporary Old Testament study. It offers a road map to the course of the change and a fresh contact with the literature itself. Essays orient the reader to all the major sections of Old Testament study. Each essay attempts to discern the contours of the present and how present directions forecast the future of Old Testament study in the coming era. They are written, not only to acquaint the readers with directions in Old Testament study, but also to engage them in the work of its interpretation. As such the volume is designed to be a coherent and comprehensive resource for use in classroom and study.

The character of the volume reflects its cause. It is published to honor Gene M. Tucker in the year of his retirement from the chair of Old Testament in the Candler School of Theology at Emory University. The usual *Festschrift* composed of disparate academic contributions to professional agendas would not properly correspond to the quality and interest of his career. Professor Tucker's scholarship is marked by critical acumen and professional competence. But he has never lost focus in his teaching and writing on the vocation of interpreting the biblical literature for students, church, and world. The range of his scholarly and administrative work is amazing. Had a personal bibliography been prepared for this volume it would have included books, commentaries, essays, articles, interpretive writing for lectionary aids, and translations. His wisdom, foresight, and energy have been significant in the development and health of the Society of Biblical Literature. Many of his contributions are hidden from public view because they were made through the counsel, planning, and administrative services that benefited and supported others—his students and his colleagues.

For all these reasons, a volume that serves as a guide and textbook to the study of the Old Testament most appropriately extends collegial congratulations. The contributors intend by their essays to express their gratitude to a valued colleague. The editors, fellow members of the OTFS, offer the volume as a sign of a friendship whose worth outruns telling.

James Luther Mays
David L. Petersen
Kent Harold Richards

OLD TESTAMENT
INTERPRETATION

PART ONE
TORAH

Chapter 1
TORAH AS NARRATIVE AND NARRATIVE AS TORAH

Tamara Cohn Eskenazi

When, in time to come, your children ask you, "What mean the decrees, laws, and rules that YHWH our God has enjoined upon you?" you shall say to your children, "We were slaves to Pharaoh in Egypt and YHWH freed us. . . ." (Deut 6:20, TANAKH)

Poised ready to possess the promised land, Israel on the plains of Moab receives, again, the command to tell the story of its past: "We were slaves. . . ." The meaning of the "decrees, laws, and rules of YHWH" is disclosed through the *story,* the telling and re-telling of which is both remembering and re-membering.

> When all Israel comes to see the face of YHWH your God in the place where [God] will choose, you will read this Torah. . . . Gather the people, the men and the women and the little ones and the stranger within your gate, in order that they will hear and learn . . . and their children who did not know will hear and will learn. . . . (Deut 31:11-13)

The Torah is meaningful memory written explicitly for a purpose: to engage and teach a community (and each member within it) how to live in relation to God. The story is not a dispassionate report of what happened, merely told to satisfy curiosity. It seeks to promulgate a public memory of a shared past and define a common future. And the medium it uses, narrative, is inseparable from the messages it seeks to convey.

What, then, are the critical, responsible, effective ways to understand the Torah? Must one stand outside and gaze at it objectively or may one enter its universe as a participant? What skills must one have to analyze narrative, especially this one? And what does it mean "to understand" such a text? One of the major developments in biblical studies in the last twenty-five years is the emergence of responses to these questions in which literary, rather than historical, criteria predominate.

The Hebrew word Torah means "teaching" (note the singular). It refers in its narrower sense to the first books of the Bible, known also as the

Pentateuch or the Five Books of Moses (Genesis, Exodus, Leviticus, Numbers, and Deuteronomy). The translation of Torah as "Law" (as in "the Law and the Prophets") obscures the narrative nature of the Torah. Calling this collection Torah imposes a unity and designates a category. The term "Torah" has been used for the Pentateuch from around the fifth century BCE. The familiar story it relates spans events from the creation of the world to the formation of a people by God and Moses. It concludes just before the divine promises to ancestors are fulfilled, with Israel hearing Moses' "last will and testament" before entering the land.

For reasons no longer discernible, ancient Israel preserved its formal sacred traditions in prose narrative, in sharp contrast to the poetry that dominates the surviving ancient Near Eastern texts. Of course not all the material in the Torah is prose narrative; the Torah incorporates laws, songs, genealogies, and lists. But these are carefully embedded in narrative and receive their meaning from the narrative context. Why narrative? Was it a polemic against the epic Mesopotamian and Canaanite literature? Was it because narrative constitutes a specific form of communication best suited for forming and informing the kind of persons and community the Torah seeks to create or perpetuate? Literary critics conclude that the answer to both questions is yes.

Prose narratives or stories have distinct features that set them apart from other types of literature such as poems, proverbs, or philosophical treatises, all of which are equally familiar modes for transmitting traditions, sacred or otherwise. To use stories is to organize meaningful reality in a certain way: narratives endow structure, characters (i.e., particular persons), and time with significance. They also make certain modes of knowing possible, while bracketing other modes.

The choice of narrative is anything but irrelevant or haphazard. Yet for roughly two centuries, biblical narrative has been eclipsed in scholarly circles, although not outside such circles, by historical considerations. The emergence of literary approaches to the Bible thus signals a major shift. In what follows I review some newer methods, theories, and practices of literary approaches to the Torah that have mushroomed. To illustrate how they assist in interpretation, I show the variety of readings of Genesis 1–3 that result when the different literary lenses focus the analysis.

Torah as Narrative

Although the Torah is undeniably a composite of sources, reflecting different periods and concerns, it is also a coherent composition in which these sources were combined expressly to convey meanings. Literary critics therefore begin with the text in its final form as a unity whose meanings can

14

be discerned by attention to its literary features. Put simply, literary criticism analyzes *what* is said by looking at *how* it is said.

Biblical narrative, like all narrative, depends on certain necessary conventions. A story is told from at least one point of view by an implicit narrator (to be differentiated from an actual narrator or author), often to an implicit reader (again, to be differentiated from a real reader). Characters and plot develop through time in narrative. The specific arrangement of these components conveys the particular intention(s) of the text, and therefore must be examined skillfully.

There are, in addition, techniques and emphases distinct to biblical narrative. For example, the biblical narrator is typically anonymous. Later Jewish and Christian traditions assigned authorship to Moses whereas historical critics have suggested Ezra the scribe as possible author. The Torah does not make either claim. The identity of the reporter is not disclosed in the text. The narrator is also omniscient, reporting events that exceed ordinary human knowledge, such as the thoughts of God. Furthermore, this narrator often withholds explicit value judgments and leaves readers to reconstruct evaluations. While some messages are boldly proclaimed ("You shall have no other gods. . . .") others are subtle. Is Abraham lauded or criticized for pretending that Sarah is his wife (Genesis 12 and 20)? To uncover the possible answers encoded in the tale one must give close attention to the clues in the text, clues like shifts between first person reports by Abraham and those of the anonymous narrator. One must cultivate awareness of conventions such as type scenes and composite artistry that serve to communicate intention.

Repetition plays an inordinately important role in biblical narrative. Robert Alter observes that the repetition of keywords, motifs, themes, or type scenes is the most misunderstood aspect of biblical narrative. Far from being a mere relic from the past, repetition of words and events creates a network of meanings that demands acute attention. The leading keyword, often in several permutations, guides the attentive reader through the maze of complex ideas and narrative tensions.

The Joseph story illustrates how overlooking keywords lead scholars astray. Alter shows that repetition integrates the otherwise puzzling story of Judah and Tamar in Genesis 38. He shows how this story's keywords, themes, and motifs intimately link with the rest of the Joseph narrative and with the larger purposes of Genesis as a whole.

The leading word *nkr*, "recognize," plays a pivotal role. The word first appears when the brothers use clothing to deceive by presenting Joseph's bloodied tunic to Jacob: " . . . *Recognize* this please. Is this your son's tunic?" (Gen 37:32). Recognizing, Jacob reaches the wrong conclusions: "He *recognized* it and said. . . ." (Gen 37:33).

15

In the very next chapter clothing will deceive once again. Tamar uses clothing to disguise herself in order to get her father-in-law Judah to impregnate her. She uses clothing also as clues to compel recognition: "*Recognize* please to whom these belong . . ." she says, sending him items he had left in her possession when he lay with her. "And Judah *recognized* and said 'She is more right than I am!'" (Gen 38:25-26). The climax of this story comes when the brothers appear before Joseph. The text is buzzing with repetition: "And Joseph saw his brothers and *recognized* them and made himself *unrecognizable* [meaning also "a stranger"] to them" (Gen 42:7) and again, to emphasize the centrality of the issue, "And Joseph *recognized* his brothers and they did not *recognize* him" (Gen 42:10).

The delicate and vital task of "recognizing" not only shapes the story of Joseph, but also that of Judah and Tamar. It also constitutes a moral imperative to readers: the importance of cultivating knowledge. Biblical art is not simply about aesthetics; and literary sensibilities are not simply a luxury. On the contrary, the Bible displays "a complete interfusion of literary art with theological, moral, or historiographical vision, the fullest perception of the latter dependent of the fullest grasp of the former" (Alter, 19).

The relationship between the two creation stories in Genesis 1–3 illustrates the different approaches of the historical and the literary critic. The first creation story (Gen 1:1–2:4*a*) depicts symmetries and harmony: "God splits off the realm of the earth from the realm of the heaven. . . . Darkness and light, night and day, evening and morning, water and sky, . . . each moment of creation is conceived as a balancing of opposites. . . ." (Alter, 142-3). The second (Gen 2:4*b*–3:24) is more interested "in the complicated and difficult facts of human life in civilization" (145). But the accounts are not merely different; they also appear contradictory, most notably in their account of the creation of humanity. The first story states simply: "Male and female he created them" (Gen 1:27). The second story "on the other hand, imagines woman as a kind of divine afterthought, made to fill a need of man, and made, besides, out of one of man's spare parts" (141).

Source critics resolve the tension by designating different sources. They identify the first account as a Priestly source (P) and 2:4*b*–3:24 as the Yahwist (J). For the literary critic this explanation is insufficient. It fails to address the important question about the meaning of the final form. Why did someone choose to leave these contradictory accounts side by side without modifying them? What does this juxtaposition accomplish? A literary response explores what the text expresses through this arrangement of sources. One such conclusion is that the text creates a bifocal vision. It allows one to see a cosmic scale of events alongside a more human scale. Such a bifocal vision also coerces readers away from a single, monolithic perspective into a plurality and establishes a degree of indeterminacy. Like a postcubist painting that superimposes two perspectives in a single frame, it keeps in tension two realities that cannot be expressed linearly: there are paradoxical dimensions of man and woman. Complexity abounds with regard to God as both magisterially remote (Genesis 1) and intimately engaged with creation (Genesis 2). The story incorporates diverse perspectives by a montage. Monotheism is always caught in the need to make sense of the intersection of two incompatibles—the relative and the absolute, "human imperfection and divine perfection, the brawling chaos of historical experience and God's promise to fulfill a design in history" (154). The contradiction, therefore, is not accidental but an example of composite artistry expressing the paradoxical nature of the human experience within a divinely ordered universe.

Literary approaches to the Bible display a variety of positions concerning the role of history in interpreting biblical narrative. Some altogether dislodge narrative from historical context. Others, like Alter, and even more forcefully Meir Sternberg, underscore the need for historical sensibilities in interpretation. Sternberg, in fact, defends the historiographic character of biblical narrative. He reminds readers that "history-writing is not a record of fact—what 'really' happened—but a discourse that claims to be a record of fact" (Sternberg, 25). The Bible represents a new mode of historiography, emerging to convey certain distinctive messages that could not be conveyed by other available forms.

The role of author and the location of meaning also constitute a bone of contention in literary analysis of the Bible. While many biblical scholars avoid invoking an author, Alter and Sternberg refer to an author whose intentions are embedded in the carefully crafted narrative. The competent reader must discover these intentions. Sternberg also claims that in the Bible "foolproof composition" leads the "competent reader" on a journey from "truth to the whole truth," a view that provoked heated debates in which every one of these quoted expressions has been vociferously challenged.

By "foolproof composition" (unfortunately an inflammatory term), Sternberg asserts something more modest than at first appears. He means that biblical narrative is so constructed as to lead readers to definitively prescribed conclusions. Competent readers who respond to the clues—to what is in the text and what is deliberately omitted—will typically reach a consensus about meanings. The better the reader, the fuller the "truth" discovered.

Sternberg does not deny indeterminacy and ambiguity. On the contrary, they are in the text and they are plentiful. They are not subjective. The author put them there. For example, in the story of Joseph we cannot easily fathom Joseph's motivation in tormenting his brothers. Such inability is not accidental. It is deliberately controlled by the narrative, which is replete with explicit emotions, but leaves out the most important one. All of this serves specific ends. The biblical author has definite notions of truth and seeks to lead readers to them, sometimes explicitly and oftentimes by compelling one to tease out truths. Truth can be nuanced, ambiguous, or conflicted. What is the truth about Joseph's motives? Is he punishing, testing, teaching, or fulfilling dreams? The text deliberately keeps us in suspense because all four are at work (Sternberg, 285-308). Indeterminacy here is the product of foolproof composition. The untrained reader might only grasp a partial truth, such as the fact that Joseph teaches his brothers about true repentance by giving them a chance to relive scenes from their past and undo their original criminal behavior. The more sophisticated might discover two or more, such as the correspondence between the suffering that Joseph inflicts on his brothers and those they had inflicted on him. All of these readings are on a continuum. They are facets of the "whole truth" of this particular story. Sternberg adamantly rejects the notion that the Bible is elitist literature that gives one set of messages to the initiated "insiders," and a substantially different one to the "outsiders."

For Sternberg, Genesis 1–3, among other things, expresses with knowledge this unique concern of biblical narrative. Other ancient Near Eastern traditions dangle immortality before humanity as the lure for a quest. Gilgamesh journeys to find the elixir that will keep him from dying. In the Bible, however, knowledge takes this role. Trees and other features of the garden of Eden story recur in other mythologies, but the tree of knowledge is unique to the Bible. Medium and message coincide. Knowledge is not merely one of the subjects of biblical narratives. Nor is it merely an important quest that fundamentally defines humanity (hence the tree of knowledge). Knowledge also constitutes the very reason for the specific narrative form. The Torah casts reality as narrative and presents knowledge as a process that unfolds in time (rather than a set of rules or wisdom sayings).

Many contributions of literary analyses such as Alter's and Sternberg's have antecedents in scholarly circles going back to the turn of the century, and even in rabbinic traditions when one casts a wider net. Gunkel, Buber, Muilenburg, and this century's great commentaries on the Torah incorporate many of such readings and anticipate much of this work. Profound, new literary insights often echo Cassuto and Jacob commentaries on Genesis and Exodus; von Rad and Westermann on Genesis; Childs and Greenberg on Exodus; and Plaut on the Torah as a whole. Three important elements, however, differentiate the current literary approaches to biblical narrative. First, attention is given to theoretical underpinnings. Second, a unique synthesis reshapes earlier interpretive insights and practices into more self-conscious strategies of reading and speaking about biblical narrative (see also Bar Efrat, Fokkelman, and Robertson). Third, this widespread systematic literary analysis of biblical narrative in a modern idiom consolidates the inquiry and makes possible a new and urgent level of discussion.

Literary approaches also serve to reconnect in new ways the scholarly concerns with the wider culture. It helps nonspecialists reclaim the Bible as a communal, comprehensible text. Because the interpretation's starting point is the text's final form the novice can begin interpreting and go much further./

The emergence of feminist criticism of the Hebrew Bible offers an important example of the merging of literary issues and wider cultural concerns. Contemporary feminist criticism was launched in biblical studies as an effort to "depatriarchalize" biblical narrative. In her pioneering work, Trible claimed that important biblical texts have been distorted by patriarchal misreadings and need to be reclaimed for their egalitarian, liberating vision of womanhood and God.

Trible's approach is literary, which she initially defined as rhetorical criticism. She offers "close readings" of texts, focusing on surface meanings. Genesis 1–3 plays the crucial role in Trible's depatriarchalizing project. As a literary critic, Trible uses rhetorical analysis of narrative from a feminist perspective, paying attention to the structure of the story, characterization, word play, translation issues, and, above all, the relation between the sexes that the text inscribes.

She begins by drawing attention to the more complex meaning of the key term 'ādām, misleadingly translated as man.

> Ambiguity characterizes the meaning of 'ādām in Genesis 2–3. On the one hand, man is the first creature formed (2:7). . . . On the other hand, 'ādām is a generic term for humankind. In commanding 'ādām not to eat of the tree of the knowledge of good and evil, the Deity is speaking to both the man and the woman (2:16-17). Until differentiation of female and male (2:21-23), 'ādām is basically androgynous: one creature incorporating two sexes. (35)

Man and woman as gendered creatures come into being only after surgery (Gen 2:21-24). As Trible notes, only now do the distinctive words man ('îš) and woman ('iššāh) appear. "Before this episode the Yahwist has used only the generic term 'ādām. No exclusively male reference has appeared. . . . Male does not precede woman as female but happens concurrently with her" (37).

The so-called Fall, according to Trible, offers an astonishing portrait of a thoughtful woman and a thoughtless man. The woman takes up the theological problem posed by the serpent's question. She weighs the evidence and acts on the basis of three compelling reasons: the forbidden fruit is nutritious, attractive, and a source of wisdom. "If the woman be intelligent, sensitive and ingenious, the man is passive, brutish and inept. These character portrayals are truly extraordinary in a culture dominated by men. I stress their contrast not to promote female chauvinism but to undercut patriarchal interpretations alien to the text" (40)./

Feminist biblical criticism and Trible herself have come a long way from this initial, optimistic position to a more complicated range of assessments. Like other critical approaches to the Bible, feminist criticism ramified into multiple modes of analysis, theories, methods, and practices. Feminist studies typically combine with other critical perspectives (e.g., feminist-literary criticism to be distinguished, say, from feminist-historical criticism).

What unifies feminist approaches is the common concern with the relationship between gender and power. Feminists debate, however, whether feminism can merely investigate gender issues descriptively or must, prescriptively, advocate certain positions—either deliberately or inevitably— namely gender equality or the liberation of women.

The relation of biblical narrative to history often looms large in many feminists' analyses. Feminists concentrate on five related tasks: (1) retrieving images and voices of women in the Bible; (2) analyzing these representations of women and absence of women; (3) reconstructing lives of women; (4) analyzing the Hebrew Bible as a patriarchal construct; and (5) developing responses to these findings.

The role of reader takes a different form in feminist circles from the one emphasized by Alter's and Sternberg's approach. Since reading as a woman differs from reading as a man (men find themselves included, women excluded), feminist critics begin with a "hermeneutic of suspicion." They do not merely analyze underlying ideologies and tensions, but question them as well. They also pay attention to what is not there, especially the female presence. Feminist critics who position themselves within the biblical traditions of Judaism and Christianity have devised several different strategies for coping with androcentric, patriarchal, or sexist texts sanctioned by their communities as authoritative.

Some look for perspectives within the Bible to counteract those inimical to women. Yes, admittedly women are displaced in the text. Moses prepares the people to encounter God at Sinai by addressing only men, saying "Do not go near a woman". (Exodus 19). But this negative address can be contrasted and balanced by stories where women are prominent in Israel's other formative event, the Exodus itself. Women of different classes and ethnicity (the midwives Shiphra and Puah, Moses' mother and sister, and the daughter of Pharaoh) initiate nonviolent civil disobedience that saves baby boys, including Moses (Exodus 2) and makes the Exodus possible. They also have the final word: "And Miriam the prophetess, Aaron's sister, took a timbrel in her hand, and all the women went out after her, dancing with timbrels. And Miriam responded to them: 'Sing to YHWH. . . .' " (Exod 15:20-21)./

20

While some feminist critics reread texts in ways that revalorize women by claiming that this reading represents the narrative's point of view, others take issue with the narrative's perspective by reading *against* the grain. Some critics acknowledge the patriarchy in the text but separate the text's meanings from the historically contingent (as a product of its own time and place) and seek enduring messages in other portions of the Bible. Critics often relocate authority, shifting it from the early community responsible for the Bible (and subject to the conventions of its time) to the contemporary community of interpreters.

The question of where meanings reside is central to a number of new literary theories, but it takes on special urgency in feminist approaches. Feminists wrestle with the contradictions between biblical representations of women and archaeological information that reflects more participatory roles for women in culture (religious or secular). They often engage not only in the recovery of women, text, and tradition but also in an analysis of ancient and modern patriarchy with an eye towards change.

As a result, narratives in the Torah receive varied interpretation in feminist circles. Take again the story of Judah and Tamar (Genesis 38) where Tamar deliberately breaks a cultural taboo in order to coerce Judah to do his duty. Is this a story of a woman subverting patriarchal conventions or of transgression in the *service* of patriarchy? What is the force of Judah's conclusions about Tamar's breach of the tradition, "She is more right than I am!" (Gen 38:26)? Is Tamar's labor meant to encourage women to risk everything in order to produce male children or a mandate for women to refuse to be written out of history and take whatever measures are necessary to ensure their place? What about Miriam? Should feminists focus on her glorious role in the Exodus or in the stories that follow? What could be done with the narrative that shows how, when she stands up for equal public power, and not for maternal roles (Numbers 12), both God and the text silence her? How to process the fact that she is buried unceremoniously a few chapters later (Num 20:1), and Moses only recalls the sister who had saved his life by setting her as a warning (Deut 24:9)?

Feminist readings of biblical narratives and those of the Torah in particular, remain varied and provocative. No consensus is in view. Genesis 1–3 plays a prominent role in debates about biblical narrative and feminist perspectives.

Alter, for example, notes the linguistic correspondence between the two Hebrew words: "remembered" (*zākar*) and "male" (*zākār*).[1] The male is the one who remembers, whose memory is enshrined in the book. In patriarchy, "the only memory is the male memory, because the only members are male members" (Alter, 45). But the memory is not monolithic and within it are seeds that can flower into more inclusive models of self and others. Alter holds the two stories of the creation together, refusing to let either dominate. The first story (P source) depicts gendered humanity created as two varieties of a single species. "The creation precedes not by polarization but by differentiation within wholeness." Male and female, the two varieties of 'ādām, "embody diversity within similarity" (46). The second story (J source) is the birth of patriarchy, a process of opposition and partialization. "Adam in this story is a male individual and bears a curious resemblance to the motherless asocial resident of the state of nature posited by liberal political theory" (46). Woman has no independent being. Her very definition (woman, Heb. 'iššāh) is derivative from man ('îš) in Gen 2:23. Together they are the human and his woman (Gen 2:25). Genesis 2 is best understood as the creation of patriarchy, depicting "the patriarchs' inner experience— loneliness, and a sense of mutilation—and its attempt to recover the banished other through fusion. . . . An Eden founded upon a fantasy of obliterating the other is bound to be unstable" (46).

Pardes, however, refuses to disconnect Genesis 3 from the larger story of Genesis 1–11. To end with chapter 3 is to highlight the so-called Fall and distort the story. But Eve does not fade from view with her naming or with the expulsion. On the contrary, Pardes argues, Eve makes an impressive comeback: in the unfolding story she is not subjugated by either the man or by the narrative. She speaks more than the man, before and after the expulsion from the garden. In fact, only the woman speaks after that point (Gen 4:1 and 4:25). The names she chooses for her children claim a close connection with God. She defines motherhood as a partnership with God and boasts of her generative power in naming her son (Gen 4:1). "Through her naming of Cain, Eve rewrites Genesis 2 as a subversive comment on Adam's displacement of the generative power of the female body" (Pardes, 48). In her final appearance Eve, not the man who has been and will remain silent, comments on the tragic murder of Abel: " . . . she bore a son, and called his name Seth [šēt], for 'God had appointed [šāt] me another seed instead of Abel, whom Cain slew'" (4:25).

Bal recasts the questions. Reading Genesis 1–3, Bal accomplishes several different things, one of which will occupy us here. Bal offers a complementary perspective to Trible's (even if at times she contests Trible's views), seconding Trible's conclusions that the text depicts woman positively. She does not claim that this reading is the correct one but only one among several possible options. Bal wants to understand why sexist readings have dominated cultures from antiquity to the present when the positive readings of renditions of women in the text are as defensible.

She approaches the Bible as neither a feminist resource nor a sexist manifesto but as an influential text with cultural repercussions. In *Lethal Love* she demonstrates the relative arbitrariness of all readings, including sexist readings, by examining their emergence in biblical narrative. Her purpose is not to cancel "dominant readings" but to expose their relative position. She also examines the unacknowledged influence of popular culture upon scholarship.

Narrative as Torah

With the work of Bal we are already well within a second major development in recent biblical studies, one that can be organized loosely under the heading "Narrative as Torah." Since biblical narrative is Torah, that is a teaching, what does it teach by virtue of being narrative and how does it teach? Torah aims to persuade. Narrative as Torah seeks to impart teachings powerful enough to affect an entire people. What does that entail? Here the overarching question, "Where does meaning reside?" is refocused to examine some broader issues about language and culture as reflected and reproduced in biblical narrative. The overlap among many of these angles of visions, and their intimate connections to the approaches mentioned above, is inevitable and often salutary.

Bal herself deliberately uses several different sets of theories and practices in analysis of biblical narrative. With many postmodern critics she claims that the text is not an object to be interpreted but a subject who speaks to us. Interpretation is equally dependent on a reader's response. Her work, deliberately, stands at the intersection of several major tributaries of current biblical research on narrative. The critical task, not just the feminist task, is to account for the permanent interaction between social and individual processes.

Because all interpretations and critical analyses come from within several interdependent systems, unmasking presuppositions is necessary. The goal is neither to debunk theories or interpretations nor to plead for some Archimedean or purist stance. It is a necessary exercise for realizing the inevitable relativity of all interpretation, and therefore the relative status of any interpretive claims to authority.

Undergirding the critical perspectives that Bal and other postmodern critics represent is the recognition that biblical narrative presupposes a writer, a reader, a text, and a world. In recent decades scholars have reflected in new ways on how these elements intersect in the production of meaning(s). Although these approaches baffle the uninitiated with their technical, inbred vocabulary, they constitute a significant development in biblical studies in the ways they problematize the questions of meaning. They jar interpreters out of the naive assumption that what we mean by meaning is self-evident.

Structuralism locates meanings of narrative not in the vocabulary, plot, or characters of the text, but in its deep structures. Structuralists bracket individual features in favor of the linguistic, symbolic, or cultural codes embodied in the narrative through universal principles of communication. Genesis 1–3, for example, is replete with bipolar oppositions that must be held together, heaven/earth, night/day, man/woman, good/evil, death/life, and mortality/immortality. Structuralists chart the movements between these oppositions and analyze the transformations that follow.

Deconstruction (among other things) is the skeptic's challenge to structuralism and to any claims that meanings are stable entities. Meanings are not contained *in* any of the identifiable or identified elements in the text, but discerned in the perpetual processes of differentiation from what they are and what they are not. Therefore meanings are fluid and contextual, indeterminate in nature. It is an error to construe deconstruction as a nihilist denial of meaning. What it rejects is privileged claims on behalf of some essential meanings that persist through time in language or words. According to deconstruction, the futile quest for authoritative, original meaning or permanent meaning is a misapprehension of what meaning is and how it operates.

From a deconstructionist perspective, Genesis 1–3 exemplifies the ways meaning and identity emerge through a process of differentiation. The sea and the earth, for example, are not entities as much as differentiations. This is even clearer in the development of humans: first we find differentiation from earth to create the first human, *'ādām*. Then follows yet another differentiation in which first woman (*'iššāh*) and then man (*'îš*) are further distinguished, culminating in the case of woman with the name. The meaning of man or woman in these chapters is contextual and relative. They derive their identity through their differences and separation.

Speech-acts theory asks not what narrative *means* but what it *does*. Words create events. They do not merely lie inert on a flat surface; they shape history (not merely reflect history) and must be understood within the historical context they have modified. The Torah in the sense of the teachings embodied in the Pentateuch is not merely descriptive but also prescriptive. It intends consequence: "So that your children will learn . . ." (Deut 31:13). For speech-acts theory, Genesis 1 is the paradigm example of the creative power of speech. However, this approach also seeks to understand the more ordinary ways in which the mutuality between language and world takes place *in* biblical narrative and *through* biblical narrative.

Historical considerations of a different sort emerge in a variety of investigative models that examine ideological aspects of biblical narrative. Although Sternberg identifies the ideological nature of the Hebrew Bible, he retains a narrow definition of the ideology. The social-philosophical work by

Foucault, Jameson, and Eagleton illuminate texts as cultural products, serving a particular class, and exerting real socio-economic power on the world rather than a private intellectual experience of a reader. Materialist and new historicist investigations approaches to the Bible are among those that develop this line of investigation. Narratives are not only religiously "loaded" but economically charged. Decoding these dynamics is part of responsible interpretation. The reader may resist rather than assent to the forces embedded in the text. In biblical studies Gottwald stands out as pioneer in this line of interpretation. /

Genesis 2–3, for example, takes on different meanings when we contemplate the prominence of food in this text and examine the repercussions. The root meaning "eat" occurs fourteen times in nineteen verses (Gen 3:1, 2, 3, 5, 6 [3 times], 11, 12, 13, 14, 17, 18, 19)! Food is linked with knowledge and domination. Genesis 2–3 focuses on means of production, splits them along gender lines, and subordinates one (woman and her procreation of children) to the other (man and his production of food). One asks: who benefits from these constructions of reality? What class produced these narratives? Who was to read them and why? How does this story function in society? What social and economic powers does it serve? What positions can a responsible reader take vis-à-vis such a text, whether as a member of biblical religions or not? Like feminist analysis of gender issues, these analyses explore issues of class, race, and other overlooked ideologies in the text. The overarching assumption is that there are no texts or readers without ideologies. The question is always *what* they are, not *whether* they exist.

These perspectives, and others related to them, seek to discern or create commonly accessible responses to questions such as: Are meanings located in texts? If so how? What does it mean to interpret? Is meaning something stable, embodied in the words themselves or in the network of their specific or universal relations? Are the important relations on the surface or below it? And if it is in both, is there contiguity or tension between the two? What social forces and powers influence the creation and use of this text? How can we understand the world(s) of the text? How can it help us understand our world(s)? Given the significance that the Torah has been granted in religious and other cultural arenas, discussions about the very nature of meaning and its location remain consequential even when inconclusive.

Narrative theology, like speech-acts theory, attends to the impact of speech on the "real world" beyond the text. It focuses on the specific theological consequence of stories and on the ways this prescriptive literature functions. Like Alter's literary approach, narrative theology takes narrativity as a significant starting point but asks different questions. How are stories true? What does it mean really "to hear" a biblical story? What distinctive relations are there between stories and persons in communities?

Narrative theology does not ask whether Genesis 1–3 is true as an event that happened but what does it mean to be true to the story. This account is a living tradition that shapes communities and the individuals within them. Selves and communities are consolidated by stories. Biblical stories contributed to the means and mode of this consolidation in particular ways. Biblical stories, especially the Torah, seek to compel moral and practical assent not merely convey information.

Canonical approaches attend to the meanings of the Hebrew Bible as Scripture, i.e., as accepted (and in the case of the Torah also self-proclaimed), authoritative, and sacred teachings. Imputed sanctity is not just another ingredient superficially added after everything else has been done. It is a transformative category for the purpose of interpretation and must be investigated as such. Even before Alter's literary approach, canonical criticism insisted on examining the text in its final form. Before narrative theology, it also argued for the unique role of the biblical text in communities. Childs's canonical approach is especially decisive for the Torah. In contrast to the two approaches just mentioned, it puts historical criticism at the service of interpreting the final form of the text in the context of communities for whom the text is authoritative. Childs's layered exploration in his Exodus commentary exemplifies the depth and breadth of such possibilities. It also differs from other approaches listed above in originating uniquely in biblical studies.[2]

Torah as Torah

In theory and practice, the Torah had been the centerpiece of Jewish life for over two millennia and the subject of its most intensive analytic explorations. For Jews who lived mostly in exile, as a minority among host nations, the text became homeland. It was the most deeply and persistently probed reality. Because Hebrew remained the language of study and prayer, not merely the language of the subject matter (Torah), rabbinic interpretations accrued a vast treasury of insights especially attentive to linguistic nuances. The Jewish exegetical tradition came to influence scholarly readings once the similarities between rabbinic interpretive practices and certain contemporary approaches were noted. Buber helped bridge the rabbinic approaches to the Bible and the scholarly world in earlier decades. Indirectly Alter serves a similar role. A new synthesis is developing through the work of scholars grounded in contemporary biblical scholarship and also deeply immersed in Jewish exegetical practices.

Intertextuality, philology, polyvalent meanings, indeterminacy, and word play are some rabbinic hallmarks that overlap with recent approaches to biblical narrative. The rabbis revelled in multiplicity of meanings and the playfulness of the text long before these were discovered by modern critics. They said the Torah has seventy faces. And the revelation at Sinai had 600,000 different meanings, as many as the persons who heard it. In the Medieval period the term *Pardes*—a loan word and cognate of the English paradise—came to encapsulate exegesis. The four letters that form the Hebrew word, P, R, D, and S respectively designated levels or meanings: plain (*peshat*), allusive (*remez*), deep (*derash*), and secret (*sod*). Every text must be plumbed for these levels. An appropriate, multilevel reading is a paradise. It is not that the Torah guides you to paradise; it is paradise. You enter and inhabit it through the gates of exegesis.

Magonet's reading of Genesis 2–3 exemplifies such a synthesis.[3] The title of his essay, "Leaving the Garden: Did They Fall or Were They Pushed?" already hints at the conclusion and plants a measure of indeterminacy. It also reflects the sense of play that characterizes this most serious, holy task of rabbinic exegesis.

Magonet notes the different narrative structures implicit in Jewish and Christian readings. In the Hebrew Bible, the unit goes uninterrupted from Gen 2:4 to 3:21. In the Hebrew version, then, the story pauses at "And YHWH made skin clothings for Adam and his woman and dressed them." The encounter in the garden thus ends with divine compassion and practical provisions. "It is only the Christian chapter divisions, presumably because of the later importance attached to the story of the Fall, that make the artificial division at the beginning of chapter 3, thus isolating the episode of the snake" (113).

Magonet explores the pun on "naked" (*'ăûmmîm*) in Gen 2:25 and "cunning" (*'ārûm*) in Gen 3:1. What does "naked" mean? He concludes that sexual connotations are at most secondary because the philological study of the verb in other contexts shows that the term means "helpless" or "vulnerable." Elsewhere it describes captives dragged to war (Isa 20:2-4), a fugitive soldier (Amos 2:16), or a helpless baby (Eccl 5:14). As for sin, it only enters the picture with the story of Cain (115-18). The story of the garden is thus the story of God as an overprotective parent who tries to keep the children from the pain of knowledge but nevertheless gives them the impetus to explore. "So did they fall, or were they pushed? And is the 'Fall' the cataclysm that some theologies see it as—or is it a first, necessary step towards emancipation of humanity?" (115). Magonet concludes with the earlier rabbis that eating of the fruit and the expulsion from the garden "gave the 'children' in Eden the chance to grow up. God cut the strings of the puppets and let them walk erect upon the earth" (121-22).

Like the title of Magonet's book, which gently and humorously points a finger at God, (who else could have pushed them?), so too the conclusion challenges God even as it affirms. In this reading, as in other Jewish arguments with God, loving and wrestling flow together.

Future Directions

With newer approaches to Torah as narrative firmly established alongside historical ones, the most urgent task for the decades ahead is implementing, rigorously, the basic insights of such approaches. A vast number of excellent literary analyses of narratives in the Torah have been published, but the book of the Torah as a unified story remains largely unexamined. Scholars looking at trees have overlooked the forest. Since the parts and the whole are invariably interdependent, atomistic analyses lose anchorage as long as the Torah has not been studied as an integrated narrative. One can only point to Clines's *The Theme of the Pentateuch,* which uses literary analysis to understand the ways the promises to ancestors function in the multiple levels throughout the entire Torah and to Mann's *The Book of the Torah,* which uses Alter's literary approach to read the Torah as an integrated story. Plaut's *The Torah,* although it does not do so in a systematic fashion, nevertheless attempts to connect the parts with the whole. One still looks for studies that investigate in light of the new questions just how the five books of the Torah interact as "chapters" of the Torah. The literary significance of weaving poetry and laws into narrative still requires careful attention. Point of view studies are yet to appear. Polzin's pioneering analysis on the tension between the voice of Moses and those of the narrators in Deuteronomy[4] needs to extend to the Torah as a whole in order to understand how Moses is portrayed and what the undercurrents communicate. The development of characters such as God, Moses, Israel, or less prominent ones, in relation to plot, still awaits close scrutiny.

The dialogue between literary and historical issues needs to be revived in light of changing presuppositions and questions. Alter rightly claims that the Bible reflects "a complete interfusion of literary art with theological, moral, or historiographical vision, the fullest perception of the latter dependent of the fullest grasp of the former" (Alter, 19). It remains a future task to translate this assertion into studies of the Torah. At this stage literary critics largely pay lip service to traditional or postmodern historical questions and do not engage their findings. They wrestle more directly with theological issues, but shy away from exploring the moral implications of Torah narratives. Here contributions from other fields can assist the biblical scholar. Nussbaum's study of literature and the moral point of view[5] opens new perspectives for understanding how great literature shapes readers' morality by *complicating* their sympathies. Her insights shed light on the sympathetic treatment of Esau and other marginalized figures, and presses one to reformulate notions of morality. Pursuing these new directions demands greater collaboration among approaches and among critics. Like Israel at the end of the Torah, biblical scholars at the end of the millennium have heard the promises, have witnessed their potential, and have accepted obligations. Fulfillment belongs to the future.

Notes

1. "A Question of Boundaries: Toward a Jewish Feminist Theology of Self and Others," in *Tikkun* 3/6 (May/June) 1991 43-46 and 87.

2. See B. S. Childs, *The Book of Exodus: A Critical, Theological Commentary*, OTL (Philadelphia: Westminster, 1974), and *Introduction to the Old Testament as Scripture* (Westminster, 1979).

3. Jonathan Magonet, *A Rabbi's Bible* (London: SCM, 1991) esp. 111-22.

4. Robert Polzin, *Moses and the Deuteronomist: A Literary Study of the Deuteronomic History* (New York: Seabury, 1990) esp. 1-72.

5. See Martha C. Nussbaum, *Love's Knowledge: Essays on Philosophy and Literature* (New York and Oxford: Oxford University Press, 1990) esp. 230-44 and 335-64.

Selected Bibliography

Alter, Robert. *The Art of Biblical Narrative*. New York: Basic Books, 1981.

Bal, Mieke. *Lethal Love: Feminist Literary Readings of Biblical Love Stories*. Bloomington: Indiana University Press, 1987.

Bar-Efrat, Shimon. *Narrative Art in the Bible*. JSOTSup. 70. Sheffield: Almond, 1989 (orig. in Hebrew, 1979).

Buber, Martin. *Moses: The Revelation and the Covenant*. Atlantic Highlands, N.J.: Humanities Press International, 1988 (origin. 1946).

Clines, David J. A. *The Theme of the Pentateuch*. JSOTSup. 10. Sheffield: JSOT, 1978.

Fokkelman, Jan P. *Literary Art in Genesis: Specimens of Stylistic and Structural Analysis*. JSOT. Sheffield: JSOT, 1991. (origin. 1975).

Leibowitz, Nehamah. *Studies in Genesis*, 4th rev. ed. Translated by Aryeh Newman. Jerusalem: World Zionist Organization, Department of Torah Education and Culture in the Diaspora, 1981.

———. *Studies in Exodus*. Translated by Aryeh Newman. Jerusalem: World Zionist Organization, Department of Torah Education and Culture in the Diaspora, 1981.

———. *Studies in Leviticus*. Translated by Aryeh Newman. Jerusalem: World Zionist Organization, Department of Torah Education and Culture in the Diaspora, 1980.

———. *Studies in Numbers*, rev. ed. Translated by Aryeh Newman. Jerusalem: World Zionist Organization, Department of Torah Education and Culture in the Diaspora, 1981.

————. *Studies in Deuteronomy*. Translated by Aryeh Newman. Jerusalem: World Zionist Organization, Department of Torah Education and Culture in the Diaspora, 1981.

Mann, Thomas W. *The Book of the Torah: The Narrative Integrity of the Pentateuch*. Atlanta: John Knox, 1988.

Pardes, Ilana. *Countertraditions in the Bible: A Feminist Approach*. Cambridge, Mass. and London: Harvard University Press, 1992.

Plaut, Gunther, Bernard J. Bamberger, William W. Hallo. *The Torah: A Commentary*. New York: Union of American Hebrew Congregations, 1981.

Sternberg, Meir. *The Poetics of Biblical Narrative: Ideological Literature and the Drama of Ideological Reading*. Bloomington: Indiana University Press, 1985.

Trible, Phyllis. *God and the Rhetoric of Sexuality*. OBT. Philadelphia: Fortress, 1978.

Chapter 2
THE FORMATION OF THE PENTATEUCH

David L. Petersen

The title of this essay betrays one way of thinking about the Pentateuch, namely, a concern with its history, how it came to exist. To be sure, not all scholars today are interested in this issue. Some would prefer to talk about the literary configuration of the Pentateuch, its theme, canonical shape, or theological purport. In fact, the move away from questions about compositional history mark one major development in Pentateuchal studies during the twentieth century. Nonetheless, concern about Pentateuchal origins continues to generate important contributions to the field and regularly appears as a prime topic of interest for firsttime students of the Hebrew Bible. Moreover, theories about the formation of the Pentateuch serve as watermarks for the critical study of biblical literature.

In this essay, I will first address several introductory issues, followed by comments about theories concerning the formation of the Pentateuch. Then, after brief remarks concerning the literary and canonical approaches, I will take a specific case, the flood account, and examine it from the perspective of the current discussion as well as point to one potential mode for future research.

Introductory Issues

The first portion of this essay addresses four important introductory issues: (1) diversity in source-critical theories about the formation of the Pentateuch; (2) the impact of diverse methods on understanding the formation of the Pentateuch; (3) the problem of Deuteronomy as a part of the Pentateuch; and (4) ambiguity in the meaning of "literary."

First, when one reads general introductions to Hebrew Bible studies, one receives the impression that there is one general hypothesis, namely the source-critical theory, that scholars have used to explain the origins of the Pentateuch (or the Tetrateuch—Genesis through Numbers, or the Hexateuch—Genesis through Joshua). Such a judgment, however, does us a disservice to the extent that it masks the complexity of earlier discussions about these origins.

By the end of the nineteenth century, scholars in Europe had advanced three basic models for the formation of the Pentateuch. The source-critical model was only one of these, though its general contours are now the most widely known. Franz Delitzsch acted as a powerful spokesman for the notion that the Pentateuch is made up essentially of three narrative sources (P=Priestly; E=Elohistic; J=Yahwistic) and one embellished legal collection (D=Deuteronomy). A redactor or editor, spliced these documents together, resulting in the composition Genesis through Deuteronomy. Though Julius Wellhausen's name is routinely associated with this notion, Wellhausen was not responsible for identifying the four constituent documents. He inherited the idea of multiple sources from a long line of studies devoted to the Pentateuch. Wellhausen rang a change on the earlier theories by arguing that the relative age of the sources was different than had been supposed, namely, that P, instead of being the earliest, was the latest one, hence the well-known sequence, JEDP (one earlier theory had it PEJD). The source-critical answer to the question about how the Pentateuch was formed achieved such prominence and consensus that the Pentateuch could be divided, verse by verse, into these four sources (see, conveniently, the Appendix to Noth's *A History of Pentateuchal Traditions* and more recently, Campbell and O'Brien's *Sources of the Pentateuch*).

This source-critical hypothesis not only allowed the Pentateuch to be divided into three narrative strands (D is not really a narrative); it also involved theories about their respective relationships. Most scholars of this persuasion thought that there were at least three independent versions of Israel's early history. One version had it that J represented a version rooted in the Southern Kingdom, E a version native to northern soil, and P a document that, while not geographically distinctive, focused on a particular topic, the ritual implications of God's relation to Israel. All three arose somewhat independently, at least in their written versions, and were synthesized either by P or by a later redactor in the postexilic era.

However, two other models competed with the aforementioned source-critical or documentary one. The so-called fragmentary theory admitted that the Pentateuch was indeed made up of resources. But rather than extended narratives, Alexander Geddes, among others (e.g., Vater and De Wette), maintained that the ingredients were smaller, e.g., a few laws or a set of stories about one person. Documents or sources may have eventuated, but in the formative period much smaller literary units existed than those Delitzsch thought extended across several biblical books. By contrast, Geddes thought there were two primary series, characterized by the presence of the two different divine names, but these were redactional collections, not unified sources. They held nothing of the thematic or literary consistency claimed for a J or P by source critics.

A third model—the supplementary approach—attempted to combine the most compelling features of the two aforementioned ones, i.e., the notions of both source and fragment. Since there is a story line in the Pentateuch, some have thought that it should be attributed to a basic source, rather than to the final editor, which is the case with the fragment hypothesis. To this basic source, additions of various sorts—stories, genealogies, legal materials—have been added over time. Ewald, for example, argued early in his career that E was the basic source and had been supplemented by J material. Others, like Bleek, maintained that J was primary and had been supplemented by E. Unlike the source-critical hypothesis, however, the supplementary theory does not necessarily ascribe coherence to the various so-called E entries into the J document. If the criteria for identifying a source include coherence and significant scope, the supplementary theory allows for only one source, everything else is smaller-scale addition.

In sum, by the end of the nineteenth century, there were a number of models, each of which included the assumption that the Pentateuch resulted from a complicated history of literary developments. And though the models are conceptually distinct, each allowed the claim that the Pentateuch resulted from the integration of diverse texts and/or traditions. As we will see, all three models have their advocates in the late twentieth century.

Second, the pursuit of other methods, i.e., form criticism and tradition history, has created a challenge to the most common model, the source-critical hypothesis. Major turns may be associated with the names of Gunkel, Noth, and Rendtorff. One hallmark of the source-critical hypothesis was the notion of a long story narrated in several distinct literary traditions. Not only was there a narrative involving the family of Terah in Genesis, this story continued with the group known as Israel, in Egypt with Moses, and in the wilderness, with the people poised to return to the Promised Land. Moreover, the story had its beginnings in the so-called primeval period, in which the generational sequence involved all humans. The tale was virtually epic in scale. It moved from considering all people, to a family and its geographic movements and exile to the beginnings of a people, who migrated with difficulty from Egypt and stood, looking at the Promised Land from the plains of Moab.

Gunkel's investigations of Genesis narrowed the focus from that large narrative down to the individual stories, each of which appeared to have its own literary integrity. The stories within the story received pride of place.

These sagas (also termed "legends") themselves possessed the hallmarks of narrative, e.g., Gen 32:22-32, and, hence, could be studied as such. And since some of these stories could apparently occur in one or another context, e.g., Gen 12:10-20–20:1-18, the larger story line no longer seemed so important. The more scholars devoted attention to these smaller scenes, the less they attended to the longer sources. Still, most scenes were regularly deemed to have the characteristics of J (e.g., Gen 18:1-16), E (e.g., Gen 20:1-18) or P (e.g., Gen 17:1-14). Hence, even though form-critical work had focused on individual sagas, there was, initially, no perceived tension between that perspective and earlier source-critical work. Form criticism was typically understood to focus on the oral stage of Israel's literature whereas source criticism was treating a later, written form. Gunkel continued to use source-critical language, but for him the sources were more accretions of sagas rather than a carefully worked out narrative structure.

One should observe that the very model for understanding early Israelite literature had shifted. Whereas Wellhausen et al., had spoken about literary documents and written sources, Gunkel attended to the preliterary, predocumentary stages of Israelite literature. Though Wellhausen agreed that oral material lay behind the great sources, he maintained "this, however, is not the place to attempt a history of the development of Israelite legend" (296). Gunkel provided that place.

Martin Noth attempted to explain the process by means of which the small sagas emerged in larger literary compositions. Building on Gunkel's own judgments, Noth argued that the shorter narratives ("traditions") were combined around certain individuals and at discrete locations, e.g., Jacob at Shechem as opposed to Jacob in the Trans-Jordan. At a later stage, these localized traditions, which could include several narratives, coalesced around several "themes," e.g., "promise to the patriarchs," that make up the Pentateuch (Noth identified five such themes).

As had Gunkel before him, Noth, too, attempted to accommodate a source-critical approach to his so-called traditio-historical method. He continued to speak of J, E, and P. Noth understood P, the latest significant literary activity to be an editorial context into which the earlier J/E material was placed. However, behind J/E, Noth postulated a basic source ("G"— *Grundlage*) that presented the earliest form of the Israelite story extending across the Pentateuch. Noth offered this analysis at the outset of his *A History of Pentateuchal Traditions* and returned to it at the end, but the relation between the rest of the volume and this homage to earlier source-critical work was never entirely clear.

More impressive than the literary coherence of Israel's narrative was Noth's identification of a number of diverse collections of traditions within the Pentateuch.[1] The narratives in Genesis 12–37 seemed fundamentally different from those involving the wilderness, which in turn are different from those involving Sinai. In addition, Noth maintained that the narratives about each patriarch were originally unrelated, in large part because the individuals were geographically isolated. Some redactor had created their genealogical relationships as a late artifice. And the more one focused on those "themes" or even smaller collections (e.g., Jacob at Shechem), the more one is pulled away from studying the story line of an entire Pentateuchal source. Von Rad and Noth had intended to speak about the midrange stage in the evolution of Israelite literature. If the short sagas came first, and if the Pentateuch came last, then medium length collections, themselves of various levels of complexity (e.g., Jacob is made up of Jacob/Laban and Jacob/Esau), were a logical step. But how do the classical sources fit with form critically or traditio-historically defined literary units? For von Rad, the answer was more clear than it was for Noth.

To be sure, each of the methods treats a different entity and on a different scale, form criticism—the individual saga, tradition history—a collection such as that about Abraham and Sarah, and source criticism—the literary unit that extends throughout four books. And yet, if the genesis of the literature occurs in a manner like that proposed by Noth, the sources are really no longer sources. They are the results of a long process of literary formation, and far less the result of conscious redaction like the one von Rad proposed for J. In sum, one could say that both form criticism and tradition history challenge implicitly the claims of source criticism. With Noth one focuses on discrete "themes" or collections, not on consistent literary narratives that extend across the first four books of the Hebrew Bible.

What was implicit in Noth's work, R. Rendtorff made explicit. Rendtorff reviewed the aforementioned studies and sensed that Noth had posed a fundamental challenge to the classical source-critical hypothesis. If the literature began with the short sagas, which were later collected in smaller entities, and if these entities developed into even larger units (Noth's "themes"), Rendtorff wanted to know whether the sorts of continuities argued in the source-critical hypothesis were common to these larger units. Hence, he analyzed one of the mid-size complexes, the patriarchal stories, and, as well, assessed the nature of the connections between such complexes.[2] On the basis of that research, Rendtorff maintained that these "larger units" are remarkably independent and betray different histories of development as well as diverse theological perspectives. Only with the priestly tradition or redactor may one identify an integration of several (but not all of the) literary components that make up the Pentateuch. Rather than a narrative, "P" comprises a set of chronological notices (e.g., Gen 16:16; 17:24) and "theological passages" (e.g., Gen 17; 35:9-13). Rendtorff maintained, however, that P did not provide the overarching redaction that, in effect, created the Pentateuch. Rather, he discerned a number of texts that highlight the promise of land (e.g., Gen 22:16; 26:3; 50:24; Exod 13; 33:1-3*a*; Num 11:11-15), texts that Rendtorff attributes to some form of D. This D material occurs in every major unit in the Pentateuch except the primeval history. Still, Rendtorff and others have called the very notion of a Pentateuchal source fundamentally into question. The challenge is rooted in the methods at work, here form criticism followed by tradition history.

Third, the mention of D raises questions both about that source and the book of Deuteronomy itself. The book of Deuteronomy concludes the Pentateuch. And yet, its place in the Pentateuch as well as in discussions about the formation of the Pentateuch remain problematic. Since Deuteronomy ends with Israel outside the land, some scholars maintain that the first literary entity of the Hebrew is not the Pentateuch, but is rather the Hexateuch, namely, a body of literature ending with Joshua in which Israel enters the land. Only in this way are the promises made to the mothers and fathers of Israel about entering and possessing land brought to fruition. However, others have observed that Israel stands in roughly the same location at both the end of Numbers and Deuteronomy, viz., in the plains of Moab. When one takes seriously the Pentateuch in its final form, Israel is positioned outside the land (one might say in exile). Moreover, such an emphasis on life outside the Promised Land allows one to speak of a Tetrateuch that would have the same position on the fulfillment of promises concerning land as does the Pentateuch. The notion of a Tetrateuch with its own literary and theological integrity complements Noth's conception of a deuteronomistic history, of which Deuteronomy is the prologue. Hence, with the model either of the Hexateuch or the Tetrateuch, it is possible to maintain that Deuteronomy has a remarkably ambiguous role as the final literary component of the Pentateuch. According to such a reading, the Pentateuch may be understood as a late literary and theological construct, with Deuteronomy more integral to the deuteronomistic history than it is to the Pentateuch itself.

And there is a related question: To what extent is D, whether nuanced as deuteronomic or deuteronomistic (see the essay by D. Knight on this distinction), material present in Genesis–Numbers? If D is not present in the Tetrateuch, then the book of Deuteronomy looks even more unrelated to the initial portion of the Hebrew Bible. But if, on the other hand, D appears in Genesis through Numbers, then the Pentateuch would appear to have greater coherence.

Not surprisingly, scholars differ in their judgments about the measure of D in the Tetrateuch. It would probably be best to conduct such a discussion on a book by book, or major section by major section inventory. For example, there have been stronger arguments made on behalf of D in Exodus (e.g.,

Exod 13:3-16) than there have on behalf of D in Genesis. Noth apparently discerned nothing in Genesis that might reasonably be attributed to D. Others, e.g., Rendtorff, have identified D in all four Tetrateuchal books. Moreover, Rendtorff has identified critical instances in which linkages between the Tetrateuch and the deuteronomistic history occur when D material occurs in the Tetrateuch, e.g., Exod 1:6, 8 and Judg 2:8, 10. Blum has argued on behalf of an even more important D presence. For him, the first literary unit that crosses the boundaries of biblical books is a product of D (Blum's so-designated KD, D-Komposition), which reaches from the patriarchal literature to the narratives locating Israel in the desert (even for Blum, there is some evidence for an earlier and longer narrative, something akin to Noth's *Grundlage*). Since Blum and, more recently, Blenkinsopp have argued on behalf of D (or D-related) material throughout the Tetrateuch (e.g., Exodus 19–24), one might claim that there is a trend toward identifying greater and greater deuteronomistic redactional activity in the Tetrateuch, though the evidence for such D material in Genesis is less than assured (Blenkinsopp argues that Genesis 15 includes D-like material).[3]

To conclude this discussion about the place of D in the Pentateuch, one should raise a more formal question, which is relevant to literature beyond that normally ascribed to D: How are we to explain the place of legal material in the Pentateuch or Tetrateuch? Apart from the laws in Deuteronomy itself, there are legal collections in Exodus, Numbers, and Leviticus, the book of the Covenant (Exod 20:22–23:33), law of the Nazirite (Num 6:1-21), and Holiness Code (Leviticus 17–26), respectively. There has been a strong tendency to view these materials both to be the result of supplements and to be, themselves, supplemental additions to the more original narratives. And yet, if the speeches of Moses provide an intense soliloquy near the end of the Pentateuch, their purport must not be underestimated. Alternatively, some have appealed to the principle of literary symmetry and maintained that the prescriptions of Leviticus occupy the pivotal position in the Pentateuch. The key issue requiring further analysis, however, is the role that the laws play—whether in Exodus, Leviticus, or Deuteronomy—in their narrative setting.

Fourth, the previous pages presume a refined set of critical vocabulary, e.g., D and Dtr. Yet one term remains almost systematically ambiguous. During the twentieth century, the adjective "literary," when used in pentateuchal studies, has born a variety of meanings, a situation that bedevils those reading studies of the Pentateuch written in various decades. Earlier, scholars used the term literary criticism as simply another way of describing source criticism. This happened primarily because German scholars had used the term *Literarkritik* to label the source-critical endeavor (*Quellenforschung* and *Urkundenhypothese* were also part of the German vocabulary).

And, after all, the primary criteria for identifying the hypothetical sources were literary, variations in vocabulary, literary style, et al.

As is well known now, however, a sea of change in biblical scholarship occurred during the final third of the twentieth century. Scholars began exploring biblical texts using the analytical tools of literary studies, i.e., by attending to issues like imagery, theme, characterization, plot development, and the like. This exercise, too, was deemed literary criticism. But it was often fundamentally uninterested in questions of literary formation. Hence, the phrase literary criticism, when applied to the Pentateuch, may mean quite different things, an ambiguity that regularly perplexes newcomers to biblical studies.

Theories About the Formation of the Pentateuch

Many writers commenting recently on Pentateuchal studies have described the field as in crisis, in part because there have been such diverse proposals concerning the formation of that literature. To be sure, disagreements do run rife. But I would maintain that the current discussion about the Pentateuch's origins corresponds in considerable measure to earlier differing hypotheses. Whereas earlier vigorous disagreements often cut on religious lines (i.e., so-called liberal versus conservative positions), the dividing lines are now less religious and more methodological. One might, therefore, claim that there is no more of a crisis in pentateuchal studies than there ever has been.

One may review a number of recent, influential works in Pentateuchal studies and maintain that the three major alternatives within the critical paradigm are still before us. First, though sometimes deemed dated, most scholars adjudge that some form of the source-critical hypothesis still serves well to explain certain features of the Pentateuch, i.e., that there are at least two originally independent literary traditions of significant scale that have been combined in the Tetrateuch. In much of the current discussion, the debate has centered around whether P is truly a source or is simply a supplement. The former option has been advocated vigorously by, among others, Steck and Westermann.[4] So, even though the presence of E is ambiguous, the Pentateuch results from at least JDP.

The supplementary hypothesis probably has more adherents than might appear to be the case. Although such classifications are risky, it would appear that both Blenkinsopp's and Van Seters's work belongs in this vein. Van Seters has argued that the J source runs throughout the Pentateuch. Unlike the standard source-critical hypothesis, Van Seters deems the Yahwist to be a late, i.e., exilic, composition using earlier sources, and designed to function as a prologue to the deuteronomistic history. Since Van Seters denies the existence of E, his model is something like DJP (though D stands outside the Tetrateuch). Van Seters analysis results from a combination of explicit concern for form, "history writing," and more implicit (and traditional) source criticism. Blenkinsopp, too, uses fairly traditional source-critical perspectives, but, in his case, in dialogue with literary (new literary) observations. And, Blenkinsopp claims that P is primary, with J as a supplement.

Though presented in more programmatic than definitive fashion, Cross has articulated this position with considerable force. Cross maintains the primacy of a so-called poetic epic tradition, which evolved in two different prose forms; J in the south and E in Israel. In the Tetrateuch, at least, there is no evidence of D. And P, rather than an independent prose tradition, was a supplement or redaction to the J/N narrative. P structured the earlier material by introducing a system of covenants, formulaic references to generations (*tôlĕdôt*), e.g., Gen 5:1; 6:9, and station formulae (Exod 16:1). However, Cross identifies few if any P narratives (the cave of Macpelah episode, Genesis 23, is the primary exception). In sum, Cross, too, advances a perspective that may be viewed as consistent with the supplementary approach.

Rendtorff's analysis is, in my judgment, consistent with those whose work has been identified with the fragment approach. As had scholars in the nineteenth century, Rendtorff denied that any sources extended throughout Genesis, much less the Tetrateuch. Rather, as sketched above, Rendtorff argued on behalf of originally distinct collections of tradition that were placed into a story line only at a fairly late stage.

Literary and Canonical Approaches to the Pentateuch

Discussions about the form, if not formation, of the Pentateuch are, however, proceeding along other tracks as well, in part because some scholars have adopted a postcritical paradigm. And to this extent, contemporary scholarly discussions of the Pentateuch are indeed more complicated than they were at the end of the nineteenth century. As noted earlier, some scholars are interested in understanding the literary structures, themes, et al., and often uninterested in questions about the formation of the text. A similar ploy, though sometimes a more theologically motivated one, involves an interest in exploring the canonical shape of books or larger entities, such as the Pentateuch. Though quite different in their conceptual positions, those pursuing either a literary or a canonical approach may, in principle, be uninterested in pursuing questions about the origins of a text.

Both literary and canonical methods have achieved important results. As for the former, David Clines has argued that it is possible to speak about a primary theme at work throughout the Pentateuch. He provides the following definition:

> The theme of the Pentateuch is the partial fulfillment—which implies also the partial non-fulfillment—of the promise to or blessing of the patriarchs. The promise or blessing is both the divine initiative in a world where human initiatives always lead to disaster, and a re-affirmation of the primal divine intentions of man. The promise has three elements: posterity, divine-human relationship, and land.[5]

Such a judgment depends upon a carefully wrought definition of theme, which derives from the world of literary criticism. Moreover, such a judgment reflects in no consequential way considerations about the historical background of the literature in question or questions about the development of that literature. Instead, the reader treats the Pentateuch in its final form, without attending to genetic questions.

The latter mode, what has been termed by some as canonical criticism, also focuses on a given, the first five books of the Hebrew Bible. However, it is a given not simply as literature but because religious communities deemed it to be a Pentateuch, a controlling portion of the canon. For Childs, there is a "canonical shape" and shaping. Not only is there a conscious five-fold division, with the interior three books distinct from the surrounding frame, but also the very shape of the canonical story leaves Israel outside the land, a situation that emphasizes the prominence of Torah rather than territory.

> For the biblical editors, the first five books constituted the grounds of Israel's life under God and provided a critical norm of how the Mosaic tradition was to be understood by the covenant people.[6]

As the vocabulary of that sentence demonstrates, Childs is fully open to the notion of various authors and editors, i.e., the question of the Pentateuch's formation. Moreover, his canonical perspective is informed by the notion of editors shaping material. However, the canonical form presents testimony apart from reconstructions of the Pentateuch's formation.

There has been a tendency among some recent literary critics to pursue purely literary issues and then use their conclusions to address the problems of literary formation a la the source-critical hypothesis, without engaging the hypothesis directly. For example, it is not unusual to find an individual arguing that a biblical author is using the artifice of tension—different vocabulary and different literary style—to create a narrative, whereas such evidence would have been used by the source critic to maintain the presence of diverse traditions or sources. Similarly, evidence of a complicated plot or literary structure is often deemed as evidence for a sole author, rather than multiple traditions.[7] Such judgments may, on occasion, seem interesting, and yet rarely do they have the force necessary to offer an alternative to the various source-critical hypotheses.

The Flood Narrative

There are a number of parade examples for the classical form of the source-critical hypothesis. One that regularly appears in textbooks and introductory lectures is the flood story, Gen 6:5–9:17. During much of the twentieth century, most commentators agreed not only that these chapters could be allocated either to the J or P source, but they also held J to be the earlier version, which had later been supplemented by the P material (whether as independent source or redactional addition). The consensus was strong enough that the two versions were printed up separately in a standard volume such as von Rad's *Genesis*.

In thinking about these texts, it may prove useful to review the aforementioned recent proposals about the formation of the Pentateuch by articulating their respective positions, when evident, on the flood narrative. Blenkinsopp and Van Seters both argue that the flood story contains J and P material. Van Seters attributes the primary narrative to J and deems P to constitute a number of additions, chronology and the like, but P offers no different narrative elements. Blenkinsopp posits a diametrically opposed notion, namely, that P provides the primary story line and that J constitutes a series of additions, most notably the bird-sending scene. Here, two scholars, both working with source-critical perspectives, develop positions that stand in stark contrast. Cross appears similar to Van Seters, namely, maintaining the primacy of J and the supplementary character of P. Finally, Rendtorff, who would not admit a J source extending beyond the primeval history, does identify "two different literary strata" in the flood narrative.[8] However, he offers no explicit judgments about the primacy of one over the other, nor does he allow the status of either one as an independent narrative. Instead, he is inclined to speak of a narrative that has been supplemented. Especially interesting here is the prominence of "supplementary" vocabulary in most of these positions.

Few scholars who work on the flood narrative dispute the multiple voices in that material, i.e., the sorts of arguments adduced in typical source-critical discussions. However, at the moment, there are at least three unresolved questions: (1) Are both traditions narratives, or is one only a supplement, i.e., not a full narrative? (2) Is it possible to determine which version is basic or primary? and (3) Is either tradition connected to or a part of a tradition outside the primeval history?

The third question lies beyond the scope of this essay. However, the first two questions, which are of fundamental importance to an assessment of the flood narratives' origins, may be addressed here. And in so doing, I offer one suggestion about the manner in which future study of these narratives (and more generally the Pentateuch) might proceed. Specifically, it would seem appropriate to use literary critical perspectives to address some of the issues that have arisen in the source-critical discussion.

The first question requires us to identify what we mean by a narrative. A narrative is more than a chronicle or annal. A chronicle may report events in a sequence, but it is not a narrative per se. A chronicle or annal does not present the literary dynamics typically associated with a story. Some literary critics speak of narrative structure that presents three primary components: an initial platform, followed by a complication and then a resolution. Others speak of rising and then falling action. Still others refer to the beginning, middle, and end of a narrative. All this language constitutes different ways to conceptualize what we mean by plot.

The notion of plot is of pivotal importance in addressing the first afore-mentioned question. If a body of textual material that has been attributed to one of the classic sources does not possess plot structure, then one might assume it to have the character of a supplement, and not that of a basic story.

If one reviews the flood texts attributed to J and P, it should, in theory, be possible to determine if either one or both embodies a plot.[9] Without making the exercise too arcane, one might ask specifically: does each of the accounts present a beginning, middle, and end? To address this question, we must make a tentative judgment about where the respective flood stories begin. The answer for P seems clear: with Gen 6:9. And most readers working from a source-critical perspective would point to Gen 6:5 for the J material. Yet, there is something peculiar about this beginning of the J flood account. Genesis 6:5-8 are a prologue to the story like that preserved in the Atrahasis epic, namely, that a deity wanted to destroy humankind. In that epic, the deity (Enlil) attempted drought and disease before turning to a flood. Genesis 6:5-8 does not refer specifically to a flood, only that God will "blot out humanity." And then J, in Gen 7:1, jumps to orders according to which Noah is to load and enter the ark. A major early portion of the flood story (as told in Atrahasis, Gilgamesh, and P) is not present in J, namely, the specific decision by the deity to effect a flood and the interaction with a human that results in the creation of an ark.

From this perspective alone, one might begin to argue that J presents only a partial narrative, a skeleton for the flood story as we know it elsewhere. It is important to note the methodological move, namely, to utilize a literary-critical category, narrative structure, to address a source-critical problem. In so doing, one is able to achieve leverage of a new sort on the topic of the literature's formation. In this case, the P version of the flood appears to present a more complete beginning of the narrative. J appears fragmentary when compared with the more complete narrative structure of P. Moreover, J seems to supplement that P narrative, for example, by introducing more detail regarding the bird-sending scene. But in no way does J present major new narrative moments. Such a judgment suggests that P has provided the basic narrative and that J works as a supplement to it. And these are the sorts of judgments that classical source criticism entailed, but could not readily resolve.

Such blending of critical perspectives should prove useful in addressing some of the basic questions vexing those interested in the formation of the Pentateuch. And, more generally, it may be possible for critical and postcritical perspectives to engage in fruitful dialogue, rather than to stand in an either isolated or antagonistic posture.

Directions for Future Research

This overview of theories about the formation of the Pentateuch suggests that the basic positions adumbrated by earlier scholars will continue to reappear. Theories articulated in the nineteenth century have achieved prominence in the twentieth century as well. Hence, one should expect to see the source, fragment, and supplementary theories in various forms. Vigorous debate between the various critical positions will continue. And, in the postcritical vein, some scholars with special interest in literary matters will be inattentive to questions about the Pentateuch's formation. Others will utilize newer literary perspectives to argue that the Pentateuch was not so much formed—out of diverse traditions and at different times—but was created by a primary author. What one may hope for is a crossover, namely, that some scholars with expertise in literary matters will broach the question of the Pentateuch's formation and will be conversant with the vigorous contemporary discussion about Pentateuchal formation. In that way, new perspectives might be brought to bear upon a nodal problem in Hebrew Bible studies.

Scholars will also struggle with even broader questions: Is the Pentateuch a meaningful entity in its own right? What is the primary early Israelite story—is it presented in Genesis through Numbers, Genesis through Deuteronomy, or Genesis through Joshua? If the first, then the covenant at Sinai, particularly as understood from a ritual perspective, seems primary. If the second, then the promulgation of Mosaic Torah has been highlighted. And if the third, then accession of the land is the primary point of resolution.

These various judgments are essentially literary. However, the issues they raise will broaden to include social-world problems. For example, it will be necessary to ask: In what social environment would any of these literary works have been important? Some scholars maintain that the Pentateuch was elicited by the religious and social needs of Persian period Judah, particularly as that community was encouraged to codify its own "native" religious traditions by the Achaemenid empire. How would this community view the Pentateuch's story of Israel outside the land? These topics are best suited to the social-world approach, a fact that emphasizes the need both for methodological clarity and the complementary use of various perspectives in the future.

Notes

1. At this point in the argument, Noth depended decisively on von Rad's articulation of the various literary moments that make up the Pentateuch. And von Rad, even more than Noth, honored the source-critical perspective. For von Rad, the Yahwist was *the* author of the Pentateuch—both as writer and as redactor.

2. For Rendtorff, important "larger units" in the Pentateuch are: the primeval story, the patriarchal story, Exodus 1–15 (Moses and Exodus), Exodus 19–24 (Sinai), Exodus 16–18 and Numbers 11–20 (wilderness), and occupation of the land.

3. There is, of course, a related issue, namely, even if the Tetrateuch were deemed not to contain D material, it may have been composed to serve as a prologue to the deuteronomistic history.

4. For example, O. Steck, "Aufbauprobleme in der Priesterschrift," *Ernte, was man sät: Festschrift für Klaus Koch zu seinem 65 Geburtstag*, ed. D. Daniels et al. (Neukirchen-Vluyn: Neukirchener, 1991) 28-308; C. Westermann, *Genesis 1–11* (Minneapolis: Augsburg, 1984), 588-600.

5. D. Clines, *The Theme of the Pentateuch*, JSOTSup 10 (Sheffield: JSOT, 1978) 29.

6. B. Childs, *Introduction to the Old Testament as Scripture* (Philadelphia: Fortress, 1979), 131-32.

7. In that regard it is interesting to compare two articles that appeared in 1978: B. Anderson, "From Analysis to Synthesis: The Interpretation of Genesis 1–11," *JBL* 97 (1978), 23-39; G. Wenham, "The Coherence of the Flood Narrative," *VT* 28 (1978) 336-48. The respective authors made a very similar argument about literary structure and yet diverged on the issue of literary formation.

8. R. Rendtorff, *The Old Testament: An Introduction* (Philadelphia: Fortress, 1986) 133.

9. Much in the analysis depends upon the specific divisions of the textual material. It is instructive to compare von Rad's divisions with those of Van Seters.

Selected Bibliography

Blenkinsopp, J. *The Pentateuch: An Introduction to the First Five Books of the Bible.* ABRL. New York: Doubleday, 1992.

Blum, E. *Studien zur Komposition des Pentateuch.* BZAW 189. Berlin: Walter de Gruyter, 1990.

Campbell, A., and M. O'Brien. *Sources of the Pentateuch: Texts, Introductions, Annotations.* Minneapolis: Augsburg, 1993.

Clines, D. *The Theme of the Pentateuch.* JSOTSup 10. Sheffield: JSOT 1978.

Cross, F. "The Priestly Work." In *Canaanite Myth and Hebrew Epic.* Cambridge, Mass.: Harvard University Press, 1973, 293-325.

de Pury, A. *Le Pentateuque en question: Les origines et la composition des cinq premiers livres de la Bible à la lumière des recherches récentes.* Le Monde de la Bible. Geneva: Labor et Fides, 1989.

Gunkel, H. *The Legends of Genesis: The Biblical Saga and History.* New York: Schocken, 1964.

Noth, M. *A History of Pentateuchal Traditions.* Englewood Cliffs, NJ: Prentice-Hall, 1972.

Rendtorff, R. *The Problem of the Process of Transmission in the Pentateuch.* JSOTSup 89. Sheffield: JSOT 1990.

Seters, J. Van. *Prologue to History: The Yahwist as Historian in Genesis.* Louisville: Westminster/John Knox, 1992.

von Rad, G. "The Form-Critical Problem of the Hexateuch." In *The Problem of the Hexateuch and Other Essays.* New York: McGraw-Hill, 1966, 1-78.

Wellhausen, J. *Prolegomenon to the History of Ancient Israel.* New York: Meridian, 1957.

Whybray, R. *The Making of the Pentateuch: A Methodological Study.* JSOTSup 53. Sheffield: JSOT 1987.

Chapter 3
PERSPECTIVE AND CONTEXT IN THE STUDY OF PENTATEUCHAL LEGISLATION

S. Dean McBride, Jr.

How are we, as contemporary biblical interpreters, to take appropriate account of the extensive blocks of legal and cultic lore that comprise the bulk of the Pentateuch after Exodus 19? Can these detailed, repetitive, and yet also ostensibly disparate nomistic traditions be understood in cogent relationship to one another? What are their principal functions and collective significance within the broader literary scope of the Pentateuch?

These questions are basic for understanding the shape of the Pentateuch as we know it. It is important to acknowledge from the outset, however, that the issues posed by the questions are also fractious. Consideration of them throughout the centuries since late antiquity has divided the hermeneutical household of scripture, usually along but sometimes also even within the confessional boundaries of Judaism and Christianity. At stake in the perennial debate has been not only the compositional integrity and intention of the Pentateuch but the viability of its theological claims for the communities of faith that have preserved, interpreted, and relied on it.

Divergence of Traditional Views

At least in large measure, the crux of the matter is conceptual. We can discern it already with respect to the sense that the Hebrew term "Torah [*tôrâ*]" makes as the chief designation for what became the initial five books of the Bible, traditionally ascribed by Jews and Christians alike to the work of Moses.[1]

With specific reference to Mosaic scripture, but elsewhere as well, Torah has usually been translated "law" (and by *nomos* in Greek). In spite of objections, often voiced to defend the Pentateuch against the charge that it evinces a harsh religious legalism, this translation is neither inaccurate nor pejorative. Although in particular contexts "polity," "charter," "oracular guidance," and the like are reasonable alternatives to the rendering "law," the Hebrew term in its full range of usage refers to prescriptive knowledge. Torah is closer in meaning to decree than to edifying discourse, mandatory instruction than to insightful counsel; the differences in nuance are important. In specific instances the term can connote a judicial decision formally rendered (Deut 17:11), a sacred ritual divinely prescribed (Lev 7:1), a priestly directive (Hag 2:11), a parental testament (Prov 3:1), or an edict bearing the weight of inspiration and divine sanction (Isa 2:3; Lam 2:9). The feature shared by these examples is authoritative pronouncement, command. Individual and collective proclamations of Torah expect faithful observance as well as the immediate attention of those to whom they are addressed (see also Exod 16:4; Josh 1:7-8; 2 Kgs 17:13; Hos 4:6; 8:1; Ps 78:10). Similarly, Torah incorporated into Mosaic scripture was not only taught but publicly promulgated and implemented with the force of law under royal auspices (cf. Deut 17:18-20; 31:9-13; 2 Kgs 23:24-25; 2 Chr 17:7-9; Dan 9:11-14; Ezra 7:14, 25-26).

To be sure, there is much in the Pentateuch that does not well suit the category "law" in either a technical or a general sense. The narrative richness of the work comes immediately to mind, as does its notable poetic components. Historiography, etiological folklore, genealogy, patriarchal blessing, and hymnic praise all have prominent place in the Pentateuch, around and alongside the formal segments of law. Still, the traditional title "Torah/Law of Moses" apparently comprehended the composite whole with particular reference to the prescriptive traditions understood to form its principal revelatory content. In the perceived relationship between literary sum and nomistic substance lies the conceptual crux that differentiated traditional Jewish and Christian views of Pentateuchal scripture.

For the major intellectual currents of Judaism whose developments can be traced through the Hellenistic and Roman periods, the "primacy" and "efficacy" of Mosaic Torah are defining concepts. These fundamental tenets of Jewish religious identity function as theological corollaries. They require no proof, other than the axiomatic testimony of scripture itself to ancient Israel's unique, intimate, transformative experiences of God's purposeful and compassionate rule (e.g., Deut 4:32-40; Neh 9-10; Psalms 78; 105; 145). "Primacy" denotes the claim that the various statutes, judicial rulings, and cultic instructions transmitted to Israel through the agency of Moses are unprecedented and insuperable. No clearer revelation needed to be sought, since what was already in hand constituted a trustworthy, definitive articulation of God's sovereign will for the life of Israel (e.g., Exod 19:9; 33:7-11; Num 12:1-9; Deut 4:1-8; 30:11-14; Mal 3:22 [Eng 4:4]; Ps 103:6-18). "Efficacy" means that, in addition to being reliably promulgated, the Torah authorized through Moses is an enduring medium of divine grace and wisdom: it provides a sufficient revelation of all that Israel will ever need to know and to do in order to sustain its corporate existence as God's people (e.g., Lev 26:3-13; Deut 6:20-25; 30:15-20; Josh 1:6-9; 1 Kgs 2:1-4; cf. Psalm 1). In short, the two corollaries establish a hermeneutical position that treats the sum and the substance of the Pentateuch as fully complementary. From this perspective, the various components of Torah—whether descriptive of formative events and redemptive institutions or prescriptive in character, setting forth the protocols, rites, and requirements of divine government—together present a blueprint for the perennial relationship between God and the discrete community of God's people.[2]

By and large, early Christian sources reaffirm the authority of "the Law and the Prophets" as clear witnesses to God's involvement in human history (e.g., Acts 13:13-41; 2 Tim 3:16-17). It is not surprising, however, that the new confessional perspective of the gospel compromises Jewish views of Mosaic scripture. While the corollaries of Torah's primacy and efficacy are never categorically denied in New Testament writings, they are relativized in order to accommodate claims for the preeminence and efficacy of Jesus' redemptive work. Such primacy is qualified especially by treating Moses' achievement as proleptic rather than insuperable (John 5:39-46; Acts 3:11-26; cf. Deut 34:10-12). Thus, in early Christian retrospect, Mosaic revelation inaugurated an interim dispensation of divine rule that prepared for the fuller disclosure and advent of God's kingdom in the authoritative teaching and personal witness of Jesus as the Christ (e.g., Matt 11:7-15; Luke 24:44; Acts 28:23; cf. John 14–16). The Gospels adumbrate this view when they depict Jesus' uncanny ability to expound Torah in ways that purport to clarify the divine intention of the law or to extend and complete it (cf. Matt 5:17-48; Mark 10:2-12; 12:24-34; Luke 16:14-18; John 8:3-11). This supersessionist position is drawn most boldly in the Epistle to the Hebrews, which develops the argument that Christ's heavenly assumption of the high priesthood and his expiatory self-sacrifice have overwhelmed the limited efficacy of the old Israelite covenantal cultus. What was revealed through Moses at Sinai has been rendered obsolete by the "new covenant" mediated to the faithful through the ministry of Jesus (Heb 12:24; cf. also 7:18-19; 8:13).

Ambivalence toward Mosaic Torah, exhibited through much of the New Testament and later patristic literature, already approaches paradox in Paul's epistles to the fledgling churches of Galatia and Rome. On the one hand, Paul declares that Torah was received by Israel as a spiritual gift; as such it is both "good" and upheld by those who profess faith in Christ (cf. Rom 3:31; 7:7-25). On the other hand, Paul treats fragile fidelity to Torah's prescriptions as inimical to the righteousness now shared by authentic heirs of Abraham, which has come as a gift of the Spirit through faith (cf. Rom 3:1-26;

Gal 3:1-29). In Gal 4:21, the antithesis is sharply posed: Paul contrasts "the law [*ho nomos*]" as scriptural witness to divine providence with life "under law [*hupo nomon*]" (cf. also Gal 3:23-26; 4:5; 5:18). The latter, which means the traditional discipline of Jewish faith as prescribed in Torah, Paul characterizes as "a yoke of slavery" (Gal 4:22–5:1); it is a debilitating burden that Gentile Christians should not take upon themselves, because it did not and cannot save them from the wrath of God (see Rom 1:18–3:30; cf., e.g., *m. 'Abot* 3.5).

The hermeneutical strategy inchoate in these Pauline epistles severs the Pentateuch's nomistic traditions from the themes of divine presence, guidance, and blessing that bind them together into a coherent whole. As a result, divine prescription is subordinated to promise, communal norm to narrative. In broader theological effect, however, the approach sketched by Paul rends asunder the congruent twofold sense of Torah. This development, in turn, shaped a traditional Christian perspective that views the Pentateuch as essentially an historiographical work that, despite the nomistic impediments, points with confidence well beyond itself to denouement in the messianic reconciliation between the God of creation and all of humankind.[3]

Criticism of the Law

Critical study of Jewish and Christian scriptures, which emerged in the later seventeenth and early eighteenth centuries, owed much, not always acknowledged, to medieval Jewish philology and exegetical method. But the principal forces that sustained the new approach and continued to shape its agenda were generated by Renaissance antiquarian humanism, Reformation iconoclasm, and Enlightenment rationalism. Questions about the Pentateuch's authorship and varied literary components loomed large in this discussion from the outset. One effect of such inquiry was to encourage anew the antinomian tendency of traditional Christian interpretation.

An important early witness to the confluence of intellectual currents that produced modern criticism of Mosaic Torah is Baruch (Benedict de) Spinoza's *Tractatus theologico-politicus*, published as an anonymous work in 1670.[4] Through his own unfettered, rational investigation of scriptural traditions, Spinoza wanted to differentiate between what was of enduring value and what should be regarded either as false or otherwise of limited worth because of its heavy cultural conditioning. Although Spinoza appreciated the humanitarian politics and social ethics that he discerned especially in the Decalogue and Deuteronomy, he relegated pentateuchal traditions of "ceremonial law" (rules pertaining to cultic institutions and sacrificial rites, dress codes, food taboos, and the like) to the realm of primitive Israelite superstition. Once again, as Paul had done many centuries before, the problem of the Mosaic law was attributed to its historical particularity; the peculiarities of cult and custom that set ancient Israel apart from other nations were no longer defensible. Spinoza's historizing hypothesis about the composition of the Pentateuch—that Ezra, the postexilic scribe empowered by the Persian court, had a much stronger claim than Moses to authorship of the work—both presaged the course of critical scholarship and gained the *Tractatus* a place on the list of works proscribed in the papal index of 1677.

During the eighteenth century, critics such as J. Astruc and J. G. Eichhorn made considerable progress in identifying putative Pentateuchal literary strands (or documentary sources) on the basis of characteristic terminology and themes. Moreover, W. M. L. de Wette, at the beginning of the nineteenth century, discerned some important implications of this work for historical study of ancient Israelite literature, law, and religion. In particular, de Wette receives major credit for making the case that associates Deuteronomic legislation, in whole or significant part, with "the Book of the Torah"—or, as it is alternatively named, "the Book of the Covenant"—reported to have been recovered from the Jerusalem Temple and vigorously implemented in the reforms of King Josiah during the later seventh century BCE (2 Kgs 22:3–23:25). This correlation became the cornerstone for subsequent critical efforts to determine the likely provenances of Pentateuchal sources and to establish their relative dates and literary relationships.

The contributions of de Wette, as they were further developed by the generation of Pentateuchal scholarship that followed him, reached epochal synthesis near the end of the nineteenth century in Julius Wellhausen's beguilingly simple reconstruction of ancient Israel's religious history. Wellhausen not only announced in the initial sentence of his introduction what the *Prolegomena* is about but also signaled his principal conclusion:

> In the following pages it is proposed to discuss the place in history of the "law of Moses;" more precisely, the question to be considered is whether that law is the starting-point for the history of ancient Israel, or not rather for that of Judaism, i.e., of the religious communion which survived the destruction of the nation by the Assyrians and Chaldaeans.[5]

Wellhausen's self-styled "criticism of the law" involved correlation of three major Pentateuchal literary strata with consecutive phases in the development of Israelite religious thought and institutional practice. In this scheme, the "golden age" of preexilic kings and prophets, otherwise well attested in scriptural literature, was represented in the Pentateuch by the "Jehovistic work," an editorial composite of older "J" and "E" materials. Although essentially a narrative account of Israel's protohistory, the Jehovistic work incorporated some segments of legislation into its review of the Israelite

sojourn at Mount Horeb in the wilderness of Sinai. The nomistic components are, specifically, the familiar Decalogue of Exod 20:1-17 followed by
the longer and shorter versions of the "Book of the Covenant" in Exodus
20–23 and 34 (cf. Exod 24:7). Because these traditions already presuppose
an agronomous society, they could not in Wellhausen's view derive immediately from the presettlement era of Moses' leadership. He understood the
"law-book" of Deuteronomy 12–26 to be a transitional document, which
originated as an elaborated revision of the Jehovistic "Book of the Covenant."
Composed rather than genuinely rediscovered early in Josiah's reign, the
Deuteronomic code was designed to legislate—under the pretended authority and prophetical inspiration of Moses—a radical centralization of Judaean
worship, as a last-ditch defense against the assault of pagan religious and
political ideology during the Assyrian period. Finally, according to Wellhausen's analysis, the Pentateuch was considerably distended under
"Priestly" auspices during the postexilic period of Judaean restoration. The
work became a repository for multiple corpora of sacerdotal legislation and
cultic lore, which further revised and supplemented the Jehovistic and
Deuteronomic laws. This culminating triumph of theocratic traditions over
the pristine narrative themes of divine promise and gracious providence
transformed the Pentateuch into Torah, the putative "Law of Moses." Moreover, Wellhausen considered this literary development, completed during
the Persian period, to mark the demise of ancient Israelite religion and the
inauguration of its successor, Judaism.

Not without reason, Wellhausen's developmental scheme has been seen
by some as programmatic Christian antinomianism, an apology for the
Pauline and Lutheran positions proffered in the form of critical-historical
scholarship.[6] But in spite of hermeneutical biases, and even serious flaws and
omissions in his interpretation of specific data, the skeletal structure of the
reconstruction has proven to be remarkably resilient. While continuing to
debate matters of chronology and provenance, critical scholarship has in the
main sustained Wellhausen's view that the awkward burgeoning of legal
corpora in the stratified literary setting of the Pentateuch is a relatively late,
secondary phenomenon, reflecting the peculiar nomistic concerns of Deuteronomic and Priestly traditionists.

Wellhausen's basic claim brings us back to the basic questions, posed at
the beginning of the essay, pertaining to the hermeneutical coherence of
Pentateuchal laws and narrative. Before addressing them, however, at least
brief note must be made of two broad, interrelated developments that have
influenced the most substantial contributions to the study of Pentateuchal
legislation made during the present century.

Scholarship since Wellhausen has employed methods of form-criticism
and tradition-history in tandem to classify Pentateuchal laws according to

their principal stylistic types and to identify their ostensible social settings and functions in the life of ancient Israel. This research, whose agenda was formulated brilliantly by Albrecht Alt in 1934, has shed light especially on the cultural origins, distinctive theological character, and institutional shaping of the various traditions of Israelite law prior to their incorporation into the Pentateuchal text.[7] Appropriate restraint as well as progress in these matters has been greatly facilitated by the second major development: the recovery and publication since 1902 of substantial exemplars of both cuneiform law and international treaties and loyalty oaths.[8]

Compositional Design of the Pentateuch: Covenant and Cultus

The following section offers programmatic judgments and suggestions that are designed to enable the reader to understand Pentateuchal narrative and legal material in a more integrated manner. In addition, they suggest future directions in which integrative discussion might move.

1. *Literary structure.* The Pentateuch centers on the revelation assuring God's continuing presence with Israel and the closely related exaltation of Moses as executor of divine authority. Still, the Pentateuch is clearly a composite work, comprised of several narrative strands and incorporating traditions of various dates and provenances. The work also evinces a purposive structure that is broadly historiographic.

After a primordial prologue and a tracing of Israel's ancestral lineage, one may discern a coherent, symmetrical arrangement of materials that fill out the central drama of Israel's deliverance from servitude in Egypt, institutional formation in the wilderness of Sinai, and guidance toward possession of a national homeland:

Prologue	*From Egypt to Mount Sinai*	*Sojourn at Sinai*	*From Sinai to Plains of Moab*	*Recapitulation*
Genesis	Exod 1–18	Exod 19–Num 10:10	Num 10:11–36:13	Deut

Embedded in this sequence is a series of five, interconnected Pentateuchal covenants, also exhibiting symmetry.[9] This series centers on the extended episodes of covenant-making at Sinai.

"Noahic" Covenant	*Covenantal Grant to Abraham*	*Sinai/Horeb Covenant*	*Covenantal Grant to Phinehas*	*Covenant in the Land of Moab*
Gen 9:9-17	Gen 17:1-14; cf. 15:1-21	Exod 19:1–34:28	Num 25:11-13	Deut 29:1–32:47

Each covenant includes or is connected with the enactment of divinely authorized "law." And, the last of these covenants is particularly concerned with the written transmission and observance of authoritative Mosaic Torah (cf. Deut 30:6-14; 31:9-13, 24-26). The Pentateuchal narrative has, in its final stages of redaction, been designed to frame or support this series of five covenants.

2. *The legal corpora.* As conventionally identified in recent scholarship, the principal corpora of Pentateuchal law are the following: (a) the Decalogue or "Ten Words" in Exod 20:2-17 (cf. Exod 34:28; Deut 4:13; 5:6-21), sometimes referred to as the "Ethical Decalogue"; (b) the "Book of the Covenant" in Exod 20:22–23:33 (cf. Exod 24.7); (c) revelatory description of the Tabernacle complex and associated rites in Exod 25:1–31:17, with a parallel account of how the plans were closely implemented in Exod 35:1–40:33; (d) the stipulations epitomizing the renewed covenant in Exod 34:11-17, sometimes supposed to comprise a "Cultic Decalogue" or "Dodecalogue"; (e) the "Priestly" or "Sinaitic Code" of Leviticus 1–26 (incorporating an earlier or variant stratum of Priestly legislation, evident primarily in Leviticus 17–26 and often referred to as the "Holiness Code") with supplements attached in Leviticus 27 and episodically thereafter throughout the book of Numbers; (f) and the so-called Deuteronomic Code or Mosaic "Book of the Law [Torah]" in Deut 4:44–28:68 (cf. 30:10; 31:26).

The primary function of the Pentateuchal narrative is to undergird the authority of these laws by identifying them as divine will articulated through the agency of Moses (Lev 26:46; cf. Neh 9:13-14; 10:30 [Eng 29]). Covenantal laws and cultic prescriptions together define Israel as a theocratic community, constituted and sustained by the indwelling presence of God.

3. *Sinai pericope.* Underlying the present shape of the so-called Sinai pericope (Exodus 19–Numbers 10)—the central panel in the Pentateuchal literary structure—is the two-part agenda still clearly exhibited in Deuteronomy 5–28. Specifically, the older traditions of covenantal legislation consist of the Decalogue (the "covenant document" proper) and the additional laws promulgated through Moses (the Book of the Covenant in Exodus, revised and supplemented in Deuteronomy 6–28 and probably also in another clerical version in the so-called Holiness Code of Leviticus). The Priestly work of redactional supplementation has also substantially rearranged earlier materials so as to produce the broader contrapuntal design, the main purpose of which was to incorporate the Tabernacle cultus as the necessary completion and high point of the Sinaitic revelation. Whereas the older "covenant" traditions established the formal relationship between God and Israel, the cultic traditions of "P" instituted the presence of God in the midst of Israel (resolving in a particular way the issue raised in Exodus 33–34 and resolved differently in the Deuteronomic legislation).

The intentionality of the larger Priestly design is attested in its symmetrical arrangement of (mostly) older materials to frame the "Sinai pericope" (with its counterpoints of covenant and cult):

[A] Defeat of Pharaoh's Army (Exod 14:1–15:21)
　　[B] Conflict in the Wilderness (Exod 15:22–18:27)
　　　　[C] Institution of Covenant and Cult (Exod 19:1–Num 10:10)
　　[B'] Conflict in the Wilderness (Num 10:11–20:29)
[A'] Conquests in Transjordan (Numbers 21–32)

While the symmetry of the B-B' segments could be shown in much more detail (e.g., the theme of three-days journey, the parallel manna-quail-water episodes), it is more important to observe the closer structure of C, where covenant and cult are made to intersect:

[a] Covenant enacted, with legislation promulgated (Exodus 19–24)
　　[b] Design of Tabernacle Cultus revealed (Exodus 25–31 [note Sabbath law in 31:12-17])
　　　　[c] Covenant documented (Exod 31:18)
　　　　　　[d] Covenant broken (Exodus 32)
　　　　　　　　[e] Mosaic intercession gains divine commitment to be present with Israel (Exodus 33)
　　　　　　[d'] Covenant restored (Exodus 34)
　　　　[c'] Covenant documented (Exod 34:28)
　　[b'] Design of Tabernacle Cultus implemented (Exodus 35–40 [note Sabbath law in 35:2-3, resumptive of 31:12–17])
[a'] Cultus activated, with relevant legislation promulgated (Leviticus–Num 10:10)

This symmetry presents clear evidence that the narrative and legal material are integrally related at this pivotal Pentateuchal moment.

4. *Narrative setting of the legal corpora.* The Pentateuch is an archive of sacral traditions that define Israel as the peculiar people of God. The several narrative strands identified by critical-historical scholarship do more than trace Israel's ostensible ancestry from primordial times and give multifarious account of its proto-history among kindred peoples and other nations. The episodes that comprise these strands focus attention consistently on theological politics, specifically on the maturing though often strained relationship between the emergent community of Israel and its sovereign God. There are several obvious ways in which the narrative framework affects interpretation of the laws. First and foremost, it marks them as legislation, enacted by Israel's divine king at the time when sovereignty was decisively

asserted. Second, by providing contextual knowledge of both this God and the people formed into the nation Israel, the framework personalizes and particularizes the laws: they are presented not as general principles of morality or as codifications of Near Eastern common law but as the express, articulate decrees of God for Israel's well-being and identity. The laws are addressed to a specific community, which has experienced God's deliverance and nurture and anticipates continuing benefactions in a national homeland. Moreover these laws will keep Israel distinct from the inhabitants of the land being disenfranchised in Israel's favor as well as the nations round about. Third, the narrative setting makes Moses the preeminent mediator, the norm—implicitly over against other conflicting claims to authority (see Numbers 14–16; Ezekiel 40–48; Malachi).

What seems to be an overabundance of repetitious collections of law exhibits signs of ordering/cogent arrangement, which associates two institutions as the principal matters revealed to Israel at Sinai/Horeb. These two—cult and covenant—separately but especially together consolidate and substantiate the relationship between the people Israel and its divine deliverer. The Pentateuch associates authoritative jurisprudence as well as cultic praxis with the covenant established between God and Israel at Sinai. Covenant and Tabernacle cultus become overlapping and, to a certain extent, reciprocal institutional means for defining and preserving the relationship between Israel and its divine deliverer.

The final form of the Pentateuch represents, essentially, the contribution of editors associated with the Priestly school. They restructured and supplemented already existing materials that portrayed covenant-making as the central "event" between the Exodus from Egypt and conquest of the national homeland west of the Jordan River. The conspicuous repetition of the Tabernacle texts in Exodus 25–31 and 35–40 points to the broader "ring composition" (often called chiasm—see above) that is used elsewhere to structure source materials (e.g., in the cycle of Abraham stories in Genesis 12–22). The effect of this for "P" is to identify the Tabernacle cultus as the central and crucial component of the Sinaitic revelation—since it is the mechanism that enables the presence of the cosmic God to cohabit with Israel. In effect, "P" resolves the crisis posed by the calf episode and the consequent discussion between Moses and God: How will God accompany the people and keep them distinct from the nations?

The biblical corpora have in their setting acquired the character of legislation—authoritatively promulgated law meant to be observed and enforced by sanctions of divine promise and threats. Even so, the tensions and developments within as well as between the several collections of laws indicate that law had not become a static or stagnant legalism. The corpora defined the covenantal character of Israel's identity and a dynamic understanding of what covenantal obedience required. Arrangement acknowledges a developmentalism within the traditions of covenantal law. What is "fixed" is not so much the letter of the law, but its normativeness as revelation received through Moses.

This dynamic aspect owes much to the Deuteronomic jurists, who can most easily be identified with the Levitical priests claiming succession from Moses; they appear as guardians and interpreters of Mosaic/covenantal law in Deuteronomy 17 and 33. Priestly traditions, on the other hand, while affirming and even exalting Moses, emphasize the cultus as the dynamic center of Israel's life as the people of God. Cultus, as detailed in Exodus through Numbers, refers to the institutions of Tabernacle and consecrated clergy, together with the associated rites of sacrifice, expiation, ordination by means of which Israel can sustain the presence of God in its midst, imparting blessing to the community and—in appropriate, mediated measure—to all earth's families.

Law in narrative setting is meant not only to ground enactments of law and covenant in specific events but to establish a paradigm that informs later history. The history of God's people is supposed to be intelligible on the basis of the covenantal commitments given in the past. What is necessary for success has been given through Moses; all Israel needs to do is to adhere to the program revealed in Torah. Such are the implications of the Pentateuch when understood as both norm and story.

Notes

1. The Hebrew Bible already attests "Torah [Law]" in designations for Mosaic scripture, e.g., Josh 8:31; 1 Kgs 2:3; 2 Kgs 14:6; Ezra 3:2; Neh 8:1-3; Dan 9:11, 13; Mal 4:4 [Heb 3:22]; cf. "the Book of Moses" (2 Chr 25:4; Ezra 6:18; Neh 13:1). Cf. also Matt 5:17; Acts 28:23; the prologue to Sirach; *Ep. Arist.* 45; Josephus *The J. W.* (*Bellum Judaicam*) 2.229; and *b. Ketubot* 50*a*.

2. The following sources effectively illustrate the emergence of this hermeneutical perspective: Sir 24:1-22; Philo *Life of Moses* 2.12-58 (cf. *Abraham* 6; *Special Laws* 2.165-167); and Josephus *Ag. Ap.* 1.37-43. For overviews of the early development of traditional Jewish interpretation, see the essays by Y. Amir, L. Feldman, and R. Kasher in *Mikra*, ed. M. Mulder, Compendia Rerum Iudaicarum ad Novum Testamentum 2/1 (Assen/Maastricht: Van Gorcum; Philadelphia: Fortress, 1988) 421-53, 455-518, 547-94.

3. Overviews of New Testament and patristic exegesis of the Old Testament are provided in the essays by E. Ellis and W. Horbury in Mulder, ed., *Mikra*, 691-725, 727-87. Also useful is R. Greer, "The Christian Bible and Its Interpretation," *Early Biblical Interpretation*, ed. J. Kugel and R. Greer, Library of Early Christianity (Philadelphia: Westminster, 1986) 107-208, especially 126-54.

4. A reprinted English translation is available in Benedict de Spinoza, *A Theologico-political Treatise and a Political Treatise*, trans. R. Elwes (New York: Dover, 1951).

5. Julius Wellhausen, *Prolegomena to the History of Ancient Israel*, trans. A. Menzies and J. Black(Edinburgh: A. & C. Black, 1885 [*Prolegomena zur Geschichte Israels*, Berlin: Georg Reimer, 1883]) 1.

6. For perspectives on and assessments of Wellhausen's contributions, see the essays in D. Knight, ed., *Julius Wellhausen and His Prolegemona to the History of Israel*, Semeia 25 (Chico,Calif.:

Scholars Press, 1982). Cf. also R. J. Thompson, *Moses and the Law in a Century of Criticism Since Graf,* VTSup 19 (Leiden: E. J. Brill, 1970).

7. Albrecht Alt, "The Origins of Israelite Law," *Essays on Old Testament History and Religion* (Garden City,N.Y.: Doubleday, 1968) 101-71. See W. Clark, "Law," in *Old Testament Form Criticism,* ed. J. Hayes, Trinity University Monograph Series in Religion 2 (San Antonio: Trinity University Press, 1974) 99-139 for a review of preliminary results. See also D. Knight, "The Pentateuch," in *The Hebrew Bible and Its Modern Interpreters,* ed. D. Knight and G. Tucker (Philadelphia: Fortress, 1985) 263-96 for a summary and assessment of the work of H. Noth and G. von Rad.

8. On the legal material, with special emphasis on character as "codes," see M. Greenberg, "Some Postulates of Biblical Criminal Law," in *Yehezkel Kaufmann Jubilee Volume,* ed. M. Haran (Jerusalem: Magnes, 1960) 5-28, and S. Greengus, "Biblical and Ancient Near Eastern Law," in *The Anchor Bible Dictionary,* ed. D. Freedman et al. (New York: Doubleday, 1992) 4: 242-52. As for treaties, see the studies of Mendenhall, Baltzer, and Hillers as cited in the bibliography.

9. Cf. F. Cross, "The Priestly System of Covenants," in *Canaanite Myth and Hebrew Epic* (Cambridge, Mass.: Harvard University Press, 1973) 295-300.

Selected Bibliography

Alt, A. "The Origins of Israelite Law." *Essays on Old Testament History and Religion.* Translated by R. Wilson. Garden City, N.Y.: Doubleday [Anchor], 1968, 101-71.

Baltzer, Klaus. *The Covenant Formulary in Old Testament, Jewish, and Early Christian Writings.* Translated by David E. Green. Philadelphia: Fortress, 1971.

Blenkinsopp, J. *The Pentateuch: An Introduction to the First Five Books of the Bible.* ABRL. New York: Doubleday, 1992.

Boecker, H. *Law and the Administration of Justice in the Old Testament and the Ancient East.* Translated by J. Moiser. Minneapolis: Augsburg, 1980.

Clark, W. "Law." In *Old Testament Form Criticism.* Edited by J. Hayes. TUMSR 2. San Antonio: Trinity University Press, 1974, 99-139.

Coats, G. *Moses: Heroic Man, Man of God.* JSOTSup 57. Sheffield: JSOT, 1988.

Cross, F. *Canaanite Myth and Hebrew Epic: Essays in the History of the Religion of Israel.* Cambridge, Mass.: Harvard University Press, 1973.

Damrosch, D. *The Narrative Covenant: Transformations of Genre in the Growth of Biblical Literature.* San Francisco: Harper & Row, 1987.

Greenberg, M. "Some Postulates of Biblical Criminal Law." In *Yehezkel Kaufmann Jubilee Volume.* Edited by M. Haran. Jerusalem: Magnes/Hebrew University Press, 1960, 5-28.

Greengus, S., R. Sonsino, and E. Sanders. "Law." In vol. of *The ABD.* Edited by D. Freedman et al. New York: Doubleday, 1992, 242-65.

Hillers, D. *Covenant: The History of a Biblical Idea.* Seminars in the History of Ideas. Baltimore: Johns Hopkins University Press, 1969.

Knight, D. "The Pentateuch." In *The Hebrew Bible and Its Modern Interpreters.* Edited by D. Knight and G. Tucker. Philadelphia: Fortress, 1985, 263-96.

Levenson, J. *Sinai and Zion: An Entry into the Jewish Bible.* Minneapolis: Winston (Seabury), 1985.

———. "The Theologies of Commandment in Biblical Israel." *HTR* 73 (1980) 17-33.

Mann, T. *The Book of the Torah: The Narrative Integrity of the Pentateuch.* Atlanta: John Knox, 1988.

McBride, S. "Biblical Literature in Its Historical Context: The Old Testament." In *Harper's Bible Commentary.* Edited by J. Mays et al. San Francisco: Harper & Row, 1988, 14-26.

Mendenhall, G. "Ancient Oriental and Biblical Law" and "Covenant Forms in Israelite Tradition." *BAR,* vol 3. Edited by E. Campbell and D. Freedman. Garden City, N. Y.: Doubleday [Anchor], 1970, 3-53.

Noth, M. *The Laws in the Pentateuch and Other Studies.* Translated by Duidon Ap-Thomas. Philadelphia: Fortress, 1966.

Patrick, D. *Old Testament Law.* Atlanta: John Knox, 1985.

Tuell, S. *The Law of the Temple in Ezekiel 40–48.* HSM 49. Atlanta: Scholars Press, 1992.

Westbrook, R. "Biblical and Cuneiform Law Codes." *RB* 92 (1985) 247-64.

———. "Cuneiform Law Codes and the Origins of Legislation." *ZA* 79 (1989) 201-22.

Chapter 4
DEUTERONOMY AND
THE DEUTERONOMISTS

Douglas A. Knight

T he literature with which we are here dealing occupies nearly a quarter of the Hebrew Bible and describes some six or seven centuries of Israel's history. The book of Deuteronomy, cast as Moses' last three addresses to the people and concluded by an appendix, includes a reiteration of the laws according to which the Israelites are to live after they inhabit the Promised Land. The book of Joshua chronicles the military conquest of the land of Canaan by Joshua, Moses' successor, and the allotment of the land among the twelve tribes. The settling of the land, which, as it turns out, had not been as completely conquered as Joshua portrays, is detailed in the book of Judges. The books of Samuel describe the career of Samuel, his anointing of Saul as the first king over Israel, and the rise and eventual rule of David as the second king. The books of Kings pick up the story at the point of the struggle for succession to David's throne and follow the monarchic history from Solomon's reign on to the division of the kingdom into northern and southern states, the fall of the North in 722 BCE, and the demise of the South in 586 BCE, ending with the assassination of the appointed governor and with the leaders of the people in Babylonian exile.

The Deuteronomistic Problem

On its face, this story line seems coherent enough. A complication emerges, however, upon closer analysis of the books, both individually and above all collectively. There is overwhelming evidence that the text was reworked by an editor or editors employing distinctive styles, language, perspectives, themes, and intentions. These redactors did not passively collect and reproduce the old traditions that came down to them, but often recast them substantially by inserting editorial comments and organizing them according to a schematic plan, such that it can truly be said that the whole turned out to be greater and markedly different from its parts.

The deuteronomistic problem, then, is to identify the redactional linkage among the books of Deuteronomy, Joshua, Judges, 1–2 Samuel, and 1–2 Kings, to describe the stylistic and ideological characteristics of the redactional layer(s), and to associate this compositional work with its historical context(s). Furthermore, it is important to pursue the traces of these redactors in other parts of the Hebrew Bible, for their editorial marks appear also in the Tetrateuch (Genesis–Numbers), in the book of Jeremiah, and perhaps elsewhere as well.

For the purpose of this discussion, we will use the following conventional terms and abbreviations for various aspects of the deuteronomistic problem:

Deuteronomy (Deut)—the fifth book of the Hebrew Bible.

Deuteronomic (Dt)—pertaining to the tradition or source underlying Deut, especially its pre-Dtr legal core in chaps. 12–26.

Deuteronomistic (Dtr)—pertaining to the editorial activity inspired by the Dt tradition and generally dated anywhere from the Josianic to the late exilic period, ca. 630-540 BCE. The siglum D, long regarded as one of the four classical sources of the Pentateuch/Hexateuch, has now been generally reconceived: Dt for the source or original form of Deut, and Dtr for the redaction of Genesis–Numbers.

Deuteronomistic History (DtrH)—the historical account introduced by Deut and encompassing the books of Joshua, Judges, 1–2 Samuel, and 1–2 Kings as produced by the Deuteronomists.

We should note that these terms are not consistently used in this fashion by all scholars. Thus, "deuteronomic" is occasionally used in the above sense of "deuteronomistic." Also, "deuteronomist" frequently occurs in the singular form; we will use it here in the plural because it is likely that more than one individual was involved, whether two or more in sequence or a number in a group or "school." Because of the indications of multiple redactional stages, a plethora of abbreviations now prevails throughout current studies, each new investigator often creating a variation on the terminology. For the sake of simplicity we will limit ourselves to the primary categories just enumerated. We will also construe the Dtr work as primarily editorial or redactional; the emphasis by some on authorship, while appropriately highlighting the substantial compositional work done by the Deuteronomists, has the net effect of underplaying the significant amount of traditional materials received and reworked by the Dtr editors.

To assess the Dtr problem, we will in the following engage two interrelated areas: first, the compositional history of DtrH; and second, the historiographical implications of DtrH. In the process, special issues associated with each of the biblical books constituting DtrH will be addressed.

Composition

Discussion of the compositional history of Deut and DtrH is more complex than that of almost any other part of the Hebrew Bible. At first glance it would appear simple: one needs primarily to describe the work of the Deuteronomists. But the history of research on this long block of material reveals a series of intricate questions that have been debated relentlessly and yet still remain largely unresolved. If anything, in fact, they are now more complicated and troubling than ever before. We will focus our attention on the issues of redactions, pre-Dt/Dtr sources, characteristic phraseology, and regional and institutional contexts.

Compilers and Redactors

The point of departure for modern DtrH studies lies in the work of Martin Noth, whose *Überlieferungsgeschichtliche Studien* first appeared in 1943 and was finally translated into English in 1981.[1] Prior to his study, the prevailing opinion among scholars held that the sources J, E, and P continue on into the book of Joshua, providing thereby the fulfillment to the promises, expressed beginning with Genesis, that the Israelites would inherit the land. According to this view, one should thus speak of a Hexateuch, not a Pentateuch, as the first large literary block of the Hebrew Bible. Moreover, many source critics argued that J and E also extend into Judges, and even into 1–2 Samuel and 1–2 Kings, resulting in a grand historical account stretching from creation to the fall of the kingdom. In opposition to these notions, Noth argued that P does not include a conquest narrative at all, is found in Deut only in slight references to Moses' death (parts of Deut 32:48-52; 34:1, 5, 7-9), and is thus effectively limited to the books of Genesis through Numbers. J and E may well have told of the conquest, but that part of their narrative became omitted when J and E were incorporated into the framework of P. Concerning these sources, then, we have to do essentially with a Tetrateuch and not more.

The ground was thus cleared for Noth to offer a fundamentally new hypothesis.[2] For him, the books of Joshua, Judges, 1–2 Samuel, and 1–2 Kings constitute a separate and distinct composition, based on the book of Deut but otherwise independent of the Pentateuch. He called this composition the "Deuteronomistic Work," and the one responsible for producing it he named "the Deuteronomist." In Noth's view, the Deuteronomist was one man, not a group or a series of individuals, and he emphasized that this Deuteronomist's role in composing DtrH was so significant that he should be called an author, not a redactor. To be sure, the Deuteronomist gathered together old traditions and incorporated them into his historical narrative, but he normally did so with a heavy hand, casting the Joshua story as a grand, divinely guided conquest, organizing the disparate stories of the judges into a rebellion–salvation cycle, and depicting the history of the monarchy as a recurring disaster due to disobedience of God. Some accretions and glosses also postdate DtrH. According to Noth, the Deuteronomist's traces in the narrative are evident in the distinctive language and the theological tone, a homiletic style that stands out especially in transitional commentaries and in editorializing speeches placed in the mouth of key characters—Joshua twice (in Joshua 1 and 23), Samuel (1 Samuel 12), and Solomon (1 Kgs 8:14ff.). The laws of Deut ground the theological principles followed by the Deuteronomist, and the first three chapters of Deut (perhaps also chap. 4) should be regarded not merely as the introduction to Deut but as the Deuteronomist's introduction to the entire DtrH. Noth dated the Deuteronomist to the mid-sixth century BCE, and he thought it most likely that the Deuteronomist was not among the deportees but rather had remained in the land of Palestine and sought with his historical narrative to help his compatriots understand the religious and moral reasons for the fall of Jerusalem. Noth's ground-breaking analysis of DtrH, like other of his studies, reveals a painstakingly constructed and tightly reasoned argument, an explanation of the origin and intention of DtrH that has become normative for many subsequent investigators.

As cogent as Noth's thesis may appear, it has been disputed from two directions, either by positing a major redaction *prior to* Noth's Dtr edition or by finding evidence of additional redactional layers *after* it. According to the former, the theory of a double redaction, DtrH was first composed in the late monarchic period during Josiah's reign, and then in the Exile, i.e., at the time corresponding to Noth's DtrH, this text underwent a new editing. The hypothesis of a two-stage redaction stems from the nineteenth-century great, Abraham Kuenen, and was supported by Julius Wellhausen and numerous others in coordination with the source-critical approach described above. Noth disputed the idea explicitly at several points because of his conviction that DtrH was a unity (except for the post-Dtr insertions). In recent times, however, the hypothesis—absent the source-critical dimension—has resurfaced with new force at the hands of F. Cross and several of his students.[3] In Cross's view of the compositional process, DtrH[4] was written during the time of Josiah as a part of his reform. Two themes characterized this history: one of judgment as a result of the history of apostasy initiated with Jeroboam's sin of setting up two calf-idols for the people to worship;

and the other of hope issuing from David's faithfulness, the promise to his dynasty, and the reforms now begun by the good king Josiah. By contrasting these themes with each other, DtrH[5] managed to articulate an affirmative program for the reform in Judah and for the good times that were surely to follow. After the fall of Jerusalem and the deportation of many Judeans, however, the historical narrative needed to be revised to take the new circumstances into consideration. DtrH[6], produced ca. 550 BCE (roughly the same date named by Noth), incorporates only slight modifications—adding the events after Josiah's reign, attributing the defeat to the evil done especially by Manasseh, and enjoining the exiles to repent and hope for a return to the land. Unlike Noth, Cross attributes the bulk of the composition to the Josianic writer. Unlike Kuenen and others advocating a double redaction, however, Cross joins Noth in regarding DtrH as a grand historical narrative separate and distinct from the sources underlying the Tetrateuch.

The other counterproposal to Noth's thesis of the unity of DtrH focuses on the opposite point in time. Rudolf Smend[7] has maintained that the unevenness, diversity of viewpoints, and different intentions evident within DtrH are best explained not by positing a Josianic edition but by looking to redactional layers in the exilic period. He agrees with Noth that an exilic compiler living in Palestine wrote DtrH, but he moves Noth's mid-sixth-century BCE dating somewhat earlier, to about 560 BCE, i.e., after Jehoiachin was restored to favor. Smend's contribution to the debate comes in identifying a redaction that was especially concerned to emphasize the law; hence Smend's siglum DtrN, the nomistic Deuteronomist (or perhaps more than one such nomistic redaction, if Smend is correct in suggesting that DtrN is also not a unity). Set in the final decades of the Exile when mingling with neighboring peoples threatened the continuation of the Jewish identity, DtrN advocated obedience to the law as the necessary means for survival, a point already present in Deut and DtrH but now driven home by DtrN at numerous junctures in the narrative. Walter Dietrich has refined this picture further by proposing yet another redactional layer, named DtrP because of its interest in the prophets and situated at some point after DtrH but before DtrN. Most of the prophetic narratives were inserted into DtrH by DtrP, and its characteristic rhetoric shares much with the language of the book of Jeremiah.[8]

As indicated at the outset, the debate over the composition of DtrH has become extremely complicated and shows little sign of abating. Only one thesis can be said to have won the day: that DtrH originated as a literary entity independent of the Tetrateuch (what some call the Priestly Work) on the one hand and from the Chronicler's History on the other. Beyond that, most scholars would associate all or at least some of its redactional layers with the Exile and the special theological and political circumstances of the period;

some, e.g., Engnell, date it to the early postexilic years but indicate that it is directly influenced by the exilic experience. And most would also connect the Deuteronomist, of whichever of these periods, to a redactional reworking of both the Tetrateuch and the book of Jeremiah. But any unanimity on these points belies the deep differences over DtrH's compositional or redactional history. One wonders if there might be better approaches, but before we can pursue this question other issues need consideration.

Sources

In addition to such redaction-critical work, one other part of the compositional process has preoccupied researchers, namely, the identification of Dt/Dtr sources. Noth drew special attention to the importance of this problem, even though he chose to refer to the Deuteronomist as an author rather than an editor. According to him, the Deuteronomist did not create much of the laws, narratives, lists, and poetry that DtrH comprises; rather, the Deuteronomist collected them from diverse corners and wove them into a comprehensive history by means of a chronological framework and interspersed commentary. These sources, often rather lengthy and many but not all in written form by the time of the Deuteronomists, possess, in some cases, considerable antiquity. It may be useful at this point to survey, albeit cursorily, some of the prominent sources for each book, even though many others will, for lack of space, need to be omitted from the list.

Deuteronomy. Modern scholarship on Deut dates back to Wilhelm Martin Leberecht de Wette, who in 1805 suggested that Deut, or at least part of it, was the "book of the law" that Josiah found during repair of the Temple and used as the basis of his reforms, according to 2 Kings 22–23. This lawbook is now conventionally limited to the core of Deut, the bulk of the laws in chaps. 12–26. Whether it was actually written during Josiah's time or earlier is subject to debate. For that matter, the story in 2 Kings 22–23 appears suspiciously Dtr in flavor, throwing into question the historicity of the event itself. On the other hand, many of the individual laws antedate the collection, whenever it may have been drafted. The part of Deut 5–26 available to the Deuteronomists was probably limited to the passages in singular in Hebrew (see below). Other parts, such as Moses' blessing (Deuteronomy 33), are also likely to be early material.

Joshua. A series of old narratives about the conquest of the land west of the Jordan River stands behind Joshua 2–11. It is a matter of conjecture how old they are and in what form they existed when the Deuteronomists inserted them in the book. Joshua 13–22, describing the distribution of the land among the tribes, is similarly based on largely pre-Dtr traditions.

Judges. For the period of the judges, the Deuteronomists could draw on a collection of stories about military leaders (the Deuteronomists were responsible for calling them judges) who helped to save the people in battle. Originally these stories were probably loosely connected narratives about tribal heroes. The Song of Deborah (Judges 5) is often thought on philological grounds to be especially ancient.

1–2 Samuel. The traditions about Samuel's early years and Hannah's song (1 Samuel 1–3) as well as the ark narrative (1 Samuel 4–6) were available to the Deuteronomists. Similarly, the Saul narratives (1 Samuel 9:1–10:16; 11; 13–15) stem from an early time. The pre-Dtr history of David's rise to power (1 Samuel 16–2 Sam 5) sought to legitimate David's right to the throne. The succession narrative (2 Samuel 9–20; 1 Kings 1–2), with its superb depictions of the troubled years of David's reign, has often been dated—although certainly too optimistically—to Solomon's reign.

1–2 Kings. The remainder of the account of the monarchy may be based on assorted court annals, or more popular versions of them. DtrH, at any rate, suggests something of the sort by frequently citing sources: the "Book of the Acts of Solomon" (1 Kgs 11:41) and the "Book of the Annals of the Kings of Israel" (e.g., 1 Kgs 14:19) or " . . . of Judah" (e.g., 1 Kgs 14:29). In addition, many of the prophetic narratives must clearly be pre-Dt/Dtr.

All of the texts just mentioned as sources contain secondary materials; they did not reach the Deuteronomists in a form fixed from the beginning. Moreover, virtually none of the sources could be imported into DtrH without being reworked, often quite substantially. The Deuteronomists took the traditions at hand, brought them together into a continuous whole, and altered or added to them as necessary to reflect the Dtr point of view and to attain the effect desired for this monumental history.

Secure dating of these various sources eludes our best efforts. Often the stories reflect the conflicts, dilemmas, customs, and other details of everyday life in ancient Israel and could therefore fit in many different times and diverse contexts. Just because they are considered pre-Dt/Dtr implies in no way that they stem from the period that they describe; in fact, in no instance is it possible to establish the date of origin. The primary point of importance for us is that DtrH is not a free creation of the late monarchic or exilic period—if by that is meant that its contents first saw the light of day in that era. DtrH is the end product of a long process of development, and the Deuteronomists deserve the credit for turning the previously independent pieces into a new and coherent whole.

Terminology and Style

How does one distinguish between an older source and an editor's addition or between one editor's interpretations and another's? The Dtr

style has generally been described as homiletic or didactic. Such characterization should not conjure up the modern image of a preacher, for the
carriers of the Dtr tradition did not have a regular "pulpit" from which to
admonish and counsel their congregations. Nonetheless, there is some basis
for regarding the stereotypical Dt/Dtr style as homiletic: repeated phrases,
jargon, fervent appeals—in short, a style that seems to have developed and
continued in the context of public, oral presentations designed to exhort
the people to understand their situation in a specific manner and to pursue
a certain course of action. Long ago, August Klostermann suggested that the
Dt laws were collected not for the purpose of literary archiving but for public
recital,[9] and others have referred to the Dt laws as "preached law." In a
much-quoted article, Georges Minette de Tillesse has expanded and demonstrated the not unrelated thesis, proposed previously and supported by
Noth, according to which the Hebrew singular forms of address in Deut 5–26
are Dt (or pre-Dt), distinguishable from the later plural forms which the
Deuteronomist used to redirect the tradition in such a manner that all of
Israel would hear it.[10] The term "parenesis" has also occurred frequently in
the literature as a means of describing the addressive, exhortatory tone in
Deut as well as in DtrH. Whatever the public context might have been for
such presentations, the Dt/Dtr literary style evinces the stylistic marks that one
would normally not expect to have originated at a purely literary stage, although
such devices can also have a persuasive effect in written form as well.

Various researchers have compiled lists of the recurring phrases and
terms in Deut/DtrH corresponding to the Dtr ideology and intents. Such
characteristic terminology, it must be noted, is also used to identify the Dtr
sections in Jeremiah as well as the Dtr revision of the Tetrateuch. Weinfeld's
very useful catalogue, complete with Hebrew and English renderings and
biblical references, includes 203 phrases plus variations, all distributed
among ten different categories.[11] Some key examples from Weinfeld's inventory
provide a sense both of the rhetoric and the subject matter typical of Dt/Dtr:

> The Struggle against Idolatry: "to follow/worship foreign gods"; "to burn
> incense to . . ."; "to burn/pass the son/daughter in fire"; idolatry as
> "abomination"; "detestable things."
> Centralization of Worship: "the site/city that YHWH will choose/has cho-
> sen"; "to make his name dwell there."
> Exodus, Covenant, and Election: "to ransom"; "the house of bondage";
> "the iron-furnace"; "to choose"; "to be a people to him"; "a strong
> hand and outstretched arm."
> The Monotheistic Creed: "know that YHWH alone is God"; "in the heaven
> above and on earth below"; "you alone are the God."

Observance of the Law and Loyalty to the Covenant: "to fol-low/serve/fear/love YHWH"; "to walk in the way/ways of YHWH"; "with all the heart and all the soul"; "to do that which is right/good in the eyes of YHWH"; "to keep the commandments/testimonies/judgments"; "to do that which is evil in the eyes of YHWH"; "to turn away/aside."

Inheritance of the Land: "which YHWH, your God, is giving you as an inheritance"; "the land which you come in to possess"; "to dispossess nations"; "the good land/ground"; "be strong and resolute."

Retribution and Material Motivation: "to prolong days"; "in order that YHWH may bless you"; "live/life" (in the sense of prosperity); "was incensed"; "to destroy/perish/put an end to/uproot."

The Fulfillment of Prophecy: "establish the word of YHWH"; "as at this day"; "behold, I will bring evil upon."

The Davidic Dynasty: "for the sake of David, my/his servant"; "did that which is right . . . as David/not as David."

Rhetoric and Parenetic Phraseology: "hear, O Israel"; "pour/lay upon/fill with innocent blood"; "know therefore."

Such phrases and terms, indicative of Dt or Dtr style, generally occur in statements and sections that stand out as editorial reworking of earlier material. To distinguish between two or more Dtr compositions or redactions depends above all on the themes and ideologies attributed to each. One such theme is the stance toward the monarchy: the promonarchical levels are generally associated with the monarchic period, whether in the early sources themselves or in a Josianic composition, while the antimonarchical position is normally connected with exilic criticisms, although some scholars trace it back to earlier prophetic or popular reactions against the ways in which the royal regimes operated. Again, centralization of worship often serves as a barometer: it is asserted in Dt but assumed in the Dtr layer, or perhaps left vague in Dt and associated explicitly with Jerusalem in DtrH. Or again: is the Dtr threat of doom conditional or absolute? Opinions have varied widely on these and other matters, although each scholar has tried to be consistent in applying a set of criteria to the Dtr layers. One can at times be left with the uneasy suspicion, however, that distinctions, as also phraseology, are applied mechanically and arbitrarily to the narrative and that the Dtr historians may have operated with more nuanced, even conflictual attitudes than a presumption of consistency would allow.

Regional and Institutional Base

Redaction-critical work on DtrH appears often to be overly nuanced and speculative. Of perhaps more interest, though, is the question of the gional, institutional, or intellectual base for the Dt/Dtr tradition. Is it possible to identify the ideological leanings of the group or groups that stand behind the book of Deut and the rest of DtrH? Not surprisingly, opinions differ on this matter as well. Note the following hypotheses, not all of which are mutually self-exclusive:

(1) The legal core of Deut, chaps. 12–26, is often associated with the Northern Kingdom—in part because of its affinities with both Hosea and the Elohist and in part because of the absence of distinctive Jerusalem traditions, notably the Zion theology, the Holiness Code, and the cultic heritage retained in P. It is conceivable that, when Samaria and the whole northern region were conquered by the Assyrians in 722 BCE, some of the people fled southward, bringing with them their traditions and ideologies, among which were their laws and social norms. Perhaps after living in the South for some time, these displaced northerners sensed that their heritage was on the verge of disappearing and that it could have a positive effect on the South, and they compiled their laws into a collection that eventually formed the substance of Deut 12–26, which served as the impetus, or the legitimation, for the Josianic reform.[12] In this manner Dt, the deuteronomic tradition reaching back to the eighth century or earlier in the North, became transformed into Dtr, the deuteronomistic school continuing in the South from as early as Josiah on down through the Exile. Ironically, DtrH, which is so critical of the northern kings and their willing subjects, was itself inspired by some of the moral and religious principles stemming from the North.

(2) Rural Levites, according to Gerhard von Rad, served as the carriers of this tradition. Functioning in public as "preachers," they developed a homiletic style characterized by exhortation and formulaic language, passionately urging religious and moral unity and revitalization. They were familiar with the Dt sacral traditions and quite at ease in reinterpreting them for the people's new circumstances. Ronald Clements has added that these Levitical priests, drawing on their northern heritage, wrote Deut specifically in order to reform the cult in Jerusalem.[13]

(3) The prophets have also been proposed as the originators of the Dt/Dtr stream of tradition. Ernest Nicholson, following previous scholars who had suspected the same, points to numerous Dt/Dtr features in favor of a prophetic provenance: the antimonarchical critique, the opposition to apostasy and idolatry, the interest in the old amphictyonic traditions of covenant, holy war, charismatic leadership, and the portrayal of Moses as a prophet and covenant mediator. Again, the connection with Hosea in the North plays an important role in this argument. The Dt group escaped to the South after the fall of Samaria and compiled Deut as a reform program for Jerusalem.[14]

(4) Jerusalem court scribes, with their strong interest in wisdom, have also been identified as the group responsible for the production of Deut and subsequent Dtr literature. Moshe Weinfeld, in the aforementioned study, finds grounds for this attribution at several points: both the structure and content of Deut resemble ancient Near Eastern treaties, with which scribes in Judah's capital would have been familiar; not being attached to the cult, the scribes had an interest in curtailing its importance, especially in the rural regions, and sought instead to encourage a secularization of the legal system; and the scribes were steeped in the venerable Israelite and Near Eastern wisdom tradition, which promoted the "humanism" evident in the Dt laws. Deut and DtrH betray a distinctive didactic tone, underscoring the consequences of moral behavior and tying wisdom to the fear of God—both central tenets of the wisdom school. In Weinfeld's opinion, these scribal circles began their work before Josiah with the composition of Dt, and their exilic successors continued in this same spirit with the editing of DtrH and the prose sermons in Jeremiah.

Assessment

Northern, southern? Josianic, midexilic, late-exilic, postexilic? Palestine, Babylon? Priests, prophets, scribes? Extent and date of any sources? There have been other proposals in addition to those reviewed above, which are only the main ones that have enjoyed some favor among specialists. Everyone agrees that DtrH is not made of whole cloth, but there is no consensus about how the quilt has been stitched together. The Deuteronomists' distinctive terminology and themes have been isolated, but more research is necessary before we can with some surety assert that we understand the compositional process to any reasonable degree. It seems likely that an extensive version of DtrH emerged during the monarchic period, whether in Josiah's time or not. But to that assertion we must also add that the work of the exilic redactor was certainly more far-reaching than some adherents of the double-redaction theory have thought.

Frankly, the search for redactors and sources brings to mind a haunting melody. The source-critical work on the Hebrew Bible during the nineteenth and early twentieth centuries reached a level of absurdity that in the end discredited the whole enterprise, at least so in the minds of many: Can the text really be dissected into such minute fragments without exceeding the limits of plausibility? DtrH scholarship needs to be cautioned against repeating some of the same excesses of Pentateuchal (Hexateuchal, etc.) source criticism if it wishes to remain credible. Overly precise and overly confident determinations, while aimed at constructing a plausible hypothesis, can belie the extent of the judgment. Such preoccupations can also distract us from other important tasks, which we can highlight, however, only after reviewing the historiographical significance of DtrH.

History

At a fundamental level, the Dtr problem touches on the very task of writing the history of Israel. Every historian, ancient and modern, necessarily operates with personal presuppositions and agendas. Objectivity is a chimera—a worthy ideal according to many, yet nonetheless fanciful, illusive, and impossible to achieve. We must always remember that our own history books, though often deceptively straightforward and fair, cannot fail to reflect the perspectives of their authors, not only in the editorializing comments but also in the very selection of events, contexts, individuals, and groups to be described in the historical narrative.

What, then, are we to make of DtrH? We have no comparable historical account closer in time to the events it describes. The Chronicler's History, i.e., the books of Ezra, Nehemiah, and 1–2 Chronicles, covers some of the same period and more, but it most probably postdates DtrH by a couple centuries and, in fact, depended on it as one of its primary sources. Non-biblical inscriptions referring to events, places, or names mentioned in DtrH have sporadically yielded themselves to the archaeologist's spade: e.g., the earliest allusion to some entity called "Israel" on Egyptian Pharaoh Merneptah's stela from ca. 1220 BCE; the naming of certain Israelite towns in the tenth-century inscription by Pharaoh Shoshenq I (Shishak) on the Aton temple at Karnak; the mention of "the house of Omri" on the ninth-century stone of Mesha, king of Moab; the ninth-century portrayal of King Jehu on the Black Obelisk of Shalmaneser III, the Assyrian emperor; the eighth-century Siloam inscription's account of the building of the water conduit in Jerusalem, probably the same water channel attributed to King Hezekiah in 2 Kgs 20:20; the ostraca from various periods at Arad; the military letters from Lachish during the time of the Babylonian conquest of Judah; and various other Assyrian and Babylonian descriptions of their military campaigns against southwestern Asia, including specific references to certain kings and places in Israel and Judah.[15] The archaeological picture is more detailed than this meager list would suggest, for numerous excavations throughout the land have revealed much about settlements, economic conditions, domestic patterns, cultic sites, and the like.

One cannot escape the fact that DtrH remains essentially our only source of information about most of Israel's political history, institutions (e.g., prophecy, priesthood, judiciary), and leading individuals. If one removed

DtrH as a source, our history of Israel from 1200 to 550 BCE would be so sparse as to be unrecognizable—and probably unusable for modern religious, moral, or other ideological ends as well. In fact, it would be as thin in detail as are the histories of many of its surrounding countries during this period. For example, we would not even know of the existence of Saul, David, or Solomon, none of whom is named in any early non-biblical text[16] despite the supposed extent and impact of their "empires" in southwestern Asia.

It is thus jolting to realize that some of the most dynamic narrative material in the Hebrew Bible stands on its own with largely no external textual support, and that in its present form it is the product of the end of the monarchy—at the very earliest. Moreover, its producers were guided by an agenda so pronounced, self-serving, and even tendentious that it colors much of the narrative itself. The Dtr editors were looking back at premonarchic and monarchic Israel from the perspective of the events transpiring between 625 and 550 BCE or even later, and they sought to write a history that would cause their own contemporaries to understand better their current situation. Particularly the experience of exile was vexing to the survivors, who would understandably have wondered why this defeat had happened to them and what they were to make of their lives in the future. DtrH presented them with a well-considered and carefully developed answer: The Israelites had repeatedly been rebellious ever since Joshua brought them into the land, and with few exceptions the kings continued this path of religious infidelity and moral depravity. Josiah (640-609 BCE), the last good king, offered a ray of hope, but his successors reverted—according to DtrH—to past practices and brought about the fall of Jerusalem in 586. Thus the colonization of Israel/Judah by first the Assyrians and then the Babylonians represented not the power politics of emperors but the moral judgment of YHWH, the God who had chosen, guided, sustained, and now punishes Israel. The Dtr historiographical principle can be depicted as a theology of the two ways: do good and be blessed; do evil and be cursed. It is, as one historian describes it, a "devotional" picture[17]—but, more than this, also a moralistic, controlling, and opportunistic interpretation that favors the groups in power or in search of power over the people.

From a modern critical historical perspective, a more realistic and plausible judgment about these events would attribute Israel's and Judah's fall externally to the westward expansion of the Assyrian and later the Babylonian empires and internally to the policies of the elites—the royal house, the wealthy, the merchants, the priesthood, the military officers, and others holding national power. The vast majority of the population, probably some 95 percent of the people, were peasants or hirelings—no threat to Asshur or Babylon, although this class could and did represent a source of taxation, labor, and military strength. In fact, for this sector of the populace, the defeats meant merely that their compatriot rulers were to be replaced by distant rulers, a circumstance that many of the peasants might have seen as a possibility for relief from economic exploitation, as it perhaps was for a time after the Babylonian conquest of the land. Such an interpretation of the course of history omits the action of God; that is the purview of DtrH.

The historian's difficulties run even more deeply than already suggested. (1) How are we to understand the very enterprise of history-writing in the ancient world, a problem that has long been an issue of debate? Two excellent treatments have appeared in recent years. John Van Seters casts his net broadly over Greece and the ancient Near East in an effort to capture the differences that existed among the various historiographical projects, including DtrH. Departing from the views of others, he disputes the presence of lengthy pre-Dtr source collections but not of chronicles or popular stories, and in the exilic DtrH he sees a coherent, integrated, wide-ranging history work designed to articulate nothing less than the Israelites' own sense of their identity. For all his differences from Van Seters at individual points, Baruch Halpern presents an equally high estimation of the historians, the one Josianic and the other exilic, who produced DtrH. For him, in fact, these historians sought diligently to write a credible account by separating fact from fiction as best they could and by employing editorial comments, not the censor's erasure, to temper materials not congenial to their ideology. In both studies ancient historiography is acknowledged to be different from modern history-writing in certain ways, but the ancient ways are no less worthy.[18]

(2) Why are there essentially no royal inscriptions from the Israelite kings when surrounding lands have yielded numerous such examples? One historian, Giovanni Garbini, has speculated that later Israelites practiced a policy of *damnatio memoriae,* a deliberate effort to purge the record by destroying all such inscriptions, whether out of hatred for the monarchy or because of a desire to remove information conflicting with the re-written history, i.e., DtrH.[19] In other words, did the biblical historians "cook" the data, not only making the information about the past fit their own purposes but also eliminating records that might have challenged their theses?

(3) Is the usual Josianic or exilic dating of DtrH much too early, perhaps by several centuries? Several recent investigators have regarded the literary texts and sources, e.g., those of the Pentateuch, as much younger than previously argued. Some would date the writings of the Hebrew Bible to the Persian period or even the Hellenistic period.[20] If DtrH was written in the fourth or third century BCE, then what occasioned it, and what was its intention?

(4) Might DtrH be of virtually no use in the reconstruction of premonarchic and monarchic history? Could its account of the monarchy be fully unreliable, just as is its depiction of the conquest of the land in Joshua? It has recently been argued, for example, that the monarchy did not begin ca. 1000 BCE, that David and Solomon and their empires are imaginary, that there never was a united monarchy, that the northern state with Samaria as its capital was founded in the tenth-ninth centuries, and that the Judean state with Jerusalem as its capital did not emerge until the seventh century.[21] Scholarly discussion has not yet engaged these issues enough for a consensus to be forged, but it is clear that the historical veracity of DtrH is under fire now to a greater extent than ever before. As an Egyptologist who has examined the record supporting certain parts of premonarchic and monarchic Israel and found for David and Solomon, for example, little that would rank them as more than legendary figures, Donald Redford offers this counsel: "Let us learn to live with ambiguity. Some day evidence may be produced on Solomon's trade in horses or on his marriage to Pharaoh's daughter. Until then these must remain themes for midrash or fictional treatment."[22]

Other Agendas

As indicated above, the study of ancient literature and the reconstruction of ancient history often meet with exceptional difficulties, beyond which it is difficult if not impossible for the modern investigator to move. Much of our work amounts to a pyramid of speculations and hypotheses. Unfortunately, we often fail to realize how tenuous is our grasp on ancient realities.

One alternative pursued by some recent scholars involves a text-oriented approach that seeks neither the compositional process that produced the text nor the events and allusions to which the literature may refer. Instead, the literary critic analyzes the text *qua* text, i.e., in terms of its artistic features and its rhetorical devices, according to highly refined methods well practiced in other fields of literary studies. Such strategies, which tend to downplay the historical-critical or referential approaches to the literature in favor of a concern for asking *how* a text means, have proven increasingly attractive and promising in the many recent studies that have emerged, including analyses of portions of DtrH. As a result, we have gained new appreciation of the narratives about Deborah, Samson, Jephthah's daughter, the Levite's concubine, David, Bathsheba, among others.[23] An unlimited number of possibilities await the literary critics who will be turning to the DtrH texts in the future.

DOUGLAS A. KNIGHT

There is quite another type of approach that promises to draw an increasing number of disciples in coming years. Like literary criticism, it is attentive to the ideological dimensions of the text. Like historical-critical methods, it recognizes that the Hebrew Bible is a product of another time and deserves to be interrogated about its relation to that context. Unlike both, its primary concern is for the social dynamics operating through the text at each stage in its development. The method is sociohistorical criticism, an approach that looks for evidences of social structures, institutions, and values in the literature, generally through heavy reliance on the contributions sociology, anthropology, and archaeology can make to our understanding of this literature and its social world. Attention is drawn especially to matters of propaganda, ideology, and social location, which have the effect of radicalizing the analysis in the direction of politics and economics and pulling the focus away from religion and morality, the ostensible concerns of the text. Thus the Josianic DtrH may be regarded not simply as an effort to persuade Josiah's court of the importance of right rulership, but as a tactic to safeguard the governing class's regained hold on power by highlighting the past mistakes that brought down previous monarchs. Or for the exilic Deuteronomists, DtrH is not merely a document to convince the exiles of Israel's long history of guilt and to bring new resolve for reform, but is a ploy of the elites to secure again their position in society, during and after the Babylonian exile. Inadvertently, DtrH may have painted a bleak picture of the centralized power, for too often the narrative depicts the Israelite subjects suffering from the machinations of their rulers—evidence which the social historian can use to reconstruct the situations in which the non-elites must have found themselves. Actually, further sociohistorical and ideological investigations may disclose that this literature is not so sharply oriented toward the elites, or at least that the pre-Dtr sources are rooted in the popular culture and portray the social dynamics just as much on the local level as on the national level. Much more work will be needed before such questions can be adequately answered.

Several studies applying these methods to DtrH have already appeared. Note, for example, N. Steinberg's interpretation of Deut 19–25, in her view a collection based on tenth-century laws that were "aimed at weakening local political boundaries in order to strengthen the authority of the central government under the united monarchy."[24] Patricia Dutcher-Walls focuses on the social location of the Deuteronomists, whom she identifies as "a coalition of elite professional groups, joined in a political alliance so necessary for power in the factionalized politics of aristocratic states."[25] According to R. Carroll's assessment, the myth that the land was emptied by the Exile, just like the myth that the land was polluted centuries earlier by the Canaanites and insufficiently cleansed by Joshua and the people, was a device to control membership in the community.[26] Ken Stone demonstrates how certain stories in DtrH dealing with women can actually be instances in which male honor or shame are played out through the patriarchal customs of trafficking in women.[27]

Such studies indicate a new angle from which DtrH and other biblical texts are being approached, and some of the more exciting and illuminating work to come in future years will proceed along the line of seeking to identify the social and ideological moorings of the literature, its relation to the workings of Israelite society, and its role in articulating the Israelite ethos and identity. If past research on DtrH serves as a guide, the debate will be lively and the insights substantial, even if consensus remains elusive.

Notes

1. Martin Noth, *Überlieferungsgeschichtliche Studien: Die sammelnden und bearbeitenden Geschichtswerke im Alten Testament* (Halle: Max Niemeyer, 3d ed.; Tübingen: Max Niemeyer, 1967). English translation in two parts: *The Deuteronomistic History*, trans. J. Doull et al., Foreword by E. Nicholson, JSOTSup 15 (Sheffield: JSOT, 1981; 2d ed., 1991); and *The Chronicler's History*, trans. and with an Introduction by H. Williamson, JSOTSup 50 (Sheffield: Sheffield Academic , 1987). Only the first part concerns us here.

2. The Swedish scholar I. Engnell also advocated the integrity of DtrH and its separation from the Tetrateuch, noting that he came to these conclusions independently of Noth. See Engnell, *Gamla Testamentet: En traditionshistorisk inledning, I* (Stockholm: Svenska Kyrkans Diakonistyrelses Bokförlag, 1945) 210 n. 3, 231-47.

3. See F. Cross, *Canaanite Myth and Hebrew Epic: Essays in the History of the Religion of Israel* (Cambridge: Harvard University, 1973) 274-89. Among those who have been influenced by this proposal are R. Friedman, *The Exile and Biblical Narrative: The Formation of the Deuteronomistic and Priestly Works*, HSM 22 (Chico: Scholars Press, 1981), and B. Peckham, *The Composition of the Deuteronomistic History*. HSM 35 (Atlanta: Scholars Press, 1985). A helpful discussion of the hypothesis is found in R. Nelson, *The Double Redaction of the Deuteronomistic History*. JSOTSup 18 (Sheffield: JSOT, 1981).

4. See note 1 above.

5. See note 1 above.

6. See note 2 above.

7. Rudolf Smend, "Das Gesetz und die Völker: Ein Beitrag zur deuteronomistischen Redaktionsgeschichte," *Probleme biblischer Theologie: Gerhard von Rad zum 70. Geburtstag*, ed. H. W. Wolff (Munich: Chr. Kaiser, 1971) 494-509; and *Die Entstehung des Alten Testaments* (Theologische Wissenschaft, 1; Stuttgart: W. Kohlhammer, 1978) 111-25.

8. W. Dietrich, *Prophetie und Geschichte: Eine redaktionsgeschichtliche Untersuchung zum deuteronomistischen Geschichtswerk*, FRLANT 108 (Göttingen: Vandenhoeck and Ruprecht, 1972). Further efforts to distinguish these redactors have been made by T. Veijola, *Die ewige Dynastie: David und die Entstehung seiner Dynastie nach der deuteronomistischen Darstellung* (Helsinki: Suomalainen Tiedeakatemia, 1975); and *Das Königtum in der Beurteilung der deuteronomistischen Historiographie: Eine redaktionsgeschichtliche Untersuchung* (Helsinki: Suomalainen Tiedeakatemia, 1977).

9. August Klostermann, *Der Pentateuch: Beiträge zu seinem Verständnis und seiner Entstehungsgeschichte* (Leipzig: A. Deichert, N.F. 1907) 347.

10. Georges Minette de Tillesse, "Sections 'tu' et sections 'vous' dans le Deutéronome," *VT* 12 (1962) 29-87.

11. Moshe Weinfeld, *Deuteronomy and the Deuteronomic School* (Oxford: Clarendon, 1972) 320-65.

12. A. Alt argued that Deut, except for its later additions, was already written in the North and then brought to Jerusalem; "Die Heimat des Deuteronomiums," *Kleine Schriften zur Geschichte des Volkes Israel*, 3 vols. (Munich: C. H. Beck, 1953) 2:250-75.

13. Gerhard von Rad, *Studies in Deuteronomy*, trans. David Stalker, SBT 9 (Chicago: Henry Regnery, 1953) 60-69; Clements, "Deuteronomy and the Jerusalem Cult Tradition," *VT* 15 (1965) 300-12.

14. Ernest Nicholson, *Deuteronomy and Tradition* (Oxford: Basil Blackwell, 1967); *Preaching to the Exiles: A Study of the Prose Tradition in the Book of Jeremiah* (Oxford: Basil Blackwell, 1970). In the latter study, Nicholson argues that the Dtr activity during the Exile occurred in Babylon, not in Judah where most other scholars place Dtr.

15. For translations of many of these texts, see *ANET*; and for general discussion see K. Smelik, *Writings from Ancient Israel: A Handbook of Historical and Religious Documents*, trans. G. Davies (Louisville: Westminster/John Knox, 1991). The value of these inscriptions for the enterprise of writing the history of Israel is scrutinized in G. Ahlström, *A History of Ancient Palestine* (Sheffield: Sheffield Academic; Minneapolis: Fortress, 1993).

16. In 1993 excavators at Tel Dan, in northern Israel, unearthed an inscription in paleo-Hebraic script, dating probably to the ninth century BCE, containing the word *bytdwd*, translated by the archaeologists as "the house of David," i.e., the dynasty of David. This interpretation is presently under considerable scrutiny, with other scholars proposing quite different solutions that do not involve David at all. However this matter will be resolved, one is nonetheless left with the fact that the inscription, even if it does name David, says nothing at all about him but at most only refers to a dynasty after him.

17. G. Ahlström, *The History of Ancient Palestine*, 770.

18. John Van Seters, *In Search of History: Historiography in the Ancient World and the Origins of Biblical History* (New Haven and London: Yale University, 1983); Baruch Halpern, *The First Historians: The Hebrew Bible and History* (San Francisco: Harper & Row, 1988).

19. Giovanni Garbini, *History and Ideology in Ancient Israel*, trans. J. Bowden (New York: Crossroad, 1988) 18.

20. See the arguments and references to other studies in N. Lemche, "The Old Testament—A Hellenistic Book?" *JSOT* 7 (1993) 163-93; and P. Davies, *In Search of "Ancient Israel*," JSOTSup 110 (Sheffield: Sheffield Academic, 1992).

21. See especially T. Thompson, *Early History of the Israelite People: From the Written and Archaeological Sources*, SHANE 4 (Leiden: E. J. Brill, 1992).

22. Donald Redford, *Egypt, Canaan, and Israel in Ancient Times* (Princeton: Princeton University Press, 1992) 311.

23. Exemplary book-length studies using literary methods include: M. Bal, *Death and Dissymmetry: The Politics of Coherence in the Book of Judges* (Chicago and London: University of Chicago Press, 1988); R. Polzin, *Moses and the Deuteronomist: A Literary Study of the Deuteronomic History, Part I: Deuteronomy, Joshua, Judges* (New York: Seabury, 1980); and Polzin, *Samuel and the Deuteronomist: A Literary Study of the Deuteronomic History, Part II: 1 Samuel* (San Francisco: Harper & Row, 1989).

24. N. Steinberg, "The Deuteronomic Law Code and the Politics of State Centralization," *The Bible and the Politics of Exegesis: Essays in Honor of Norman K. Gottwald on His Sixty-Fifth Birthday*, eds. D. Jobling, P. Day, and G. Sheppard (Cleveland: Pilgrim, 1991) 161-70.

25. P. Dutcher-Walls, "The Social Location of the Deuteronomists: A Sociological Study of Factional Politics in Late Pre-Exilic Judah," *JSOT* 52 (1991) 77-94.

26. R. Carroll, "The Myth of the Empty Land," in *Ideological Criticism of Biblical Texts*, ed. D. Jobling and T. Pippin, *Semeia* 59 (1992) 79-93.

27. Stone, "Sexual Practice and the Structure of Prestige: The Case of the Disputed Concubines," SBLSP (1993) 554-73.

Selected Bibliography

Graham, M., and S. McKenzie, eds. *Martin Noth and the History of Tradition.* JSOTSup 182. Sheffield: Sheffield Academic Press, forthcoming.

Mayes, A., *The Story of Israel between Settlement and Exile: A Redactional Study of the Deuteronomistic History.* London: SCM, 1983.

Mullen, E., *Narrative History and Ethnic Boundaries: The Deuteronomistic Historian and the Creation of Israelite National Identity.* SBLSS 24. Atlanta: Scholars Press, 1993.

Peckham, B., *History and Prophecy: The Development of Late Judean Literary Traditions.* ABRL. New York: Doubleday, 1993, 518-655.

PART TWO
PROPHETS

Chapter 5
THE FORMER PROPHETS:
READING THE BOOKS OF KINGS

Robert R. Wilson

The books of Joshua, Judges, 1 and 2 Samuel, and 1 and 2 Kings have traditionally been viewed as a single block of material, although the major interpretive traditions have characterized this material in different ways. In Jewish tradition, these books are known collectively as the Former Prophets, a designation presumably based on the observation that the activities of prophets play a central role in many of the narratives, particularly in Samuel and Kings. Furthermore, many of these prophets are thought to have lived before the time of Amos (ca. 786-746 BCE), who is the earliest of the so-called Later Prophets and the first to have had collections of his oracles preserved in a book bearing his name.

Among Christian interpreters, the books are often called the Historical Books, since the narratives in them are arranged roughly in chronological order and thus form a history of Israel from the time of its entry into the land of Canaan (Joshua 1) to the time of the capture of Jerusalem and the exile of its inhabitants to Babylon (2 Kings 25). In scholarly circles, on the other hand, there is a tendency to refer to the books as the Deuteronomistic History and to stress the degree to which they reflect the themes and theological views of the book of Deuteronomy. Seen in this light, the books are taken together as an account of Israel's history that illustrates the deuteronomic principle that disobedience to God's law, as it is expressed in Deuteronomy, inevitably brings punishment and the revocation of God's gift of the land that had been promised to Israel's ancestors.

Although there is clearly textual warrant for understanding the Former Prophets as a single literary unit, these various ways of characterizing the books suggest that their contents can be viewed in more than one way and that no single designation adequately describes the diversity of themes and literary genres found in them. For this reason it is not surprising that contemporary biblical scholars have normally stressed the independent origins and purposes of the individual books rather than dealing with their overall unity. This approach to the Former Prophets began late in the nineteenth century, when scholars trained to identify and analyze the original documents used to form the Pentateuch began to wonder if traces of the same documents could be found in the Former Prophets. Various attempts were made to uncover Pentateuchal documents in Joshua and Judges, and even in Samuel and Kings, but these attempts were generally not convincing and were soon abandoned.

More influential was the form-critical approach, pioneered by Hermann Gunkel and his disciples. Under Gunkel's influence, scholars began to focus on individual literary genres in the narratives of the Former Prophets, and as a result began to lose sight of the overall structure of individual books and of the Former Prophets as a whole. This atomistic tendency reached its height in studies of the book of Judges, which was increasingly seen as a loose collection of tales about the exploits of individual heroes. Few attempts were made to talk about the overall literary structure of the book or to describe its literary themes.[1]

In recent biblical scholarship, however, a new trend has developed. In keeping with contemporary interest in literary approaches that focus on whole literary works rather than on their individual components, interpreters have recently made a series of attempts to read the books of the Former Prophets as whole, individual books. These efforts at holistic reading have been most fruitful in 1 and 2 Samuel, where the originally independent literary units have been woven together skillfully enough to be treated as a coherent narrative. Recent studies focusing on the literary artistry of the final product are a great improvement on earlier studies that concentrated solely on the tensions existing among the various sources employed in creating the present book. Efforts to apply these same techniques to Joshua and Judges have been less successful because of the diverse literary genres employed in Joshua and the overt anthological style of Judges. To date, no one has attempted a holistic reading of all of the Former Prophets. Indeed, the most successful treatments of individual books suggest that each component of the collection has its own point of view and distinctive themes and that the unity of the collection, if it exists at all, is due primarily to the rough chronological order in which the books have been arranged. Nevertheless, the holistic approach to the books of the Former Prophets seems firmly established in current scholarship and is bringing readers a renewed appreciation of the artistry of biblical narrative.[2]

However, one of the major anomalies in recent study of the Former Prophets is that research on 1 and 2 Kings seems to be running counter to the general trends evident in the interpretation of other books in that corpus. While a growing number of scholars are rejecting older form-critical and tradition-critical approaches in favor of reading texts in their literary or theological integrity, students of Kings are moving increasingly away from the notion that the book can be approached as a single literary unit. In spite of a long history of holistic interpretations of the book, which saw it as a chronologically ordered literary unit, and in spite of Martin Noth's influential arguments that the bulk of the work comes from the hand of a single exilic author,[3] scholars today are increasingly treating Kings as a composite document made up of two or more literary layers.[4] This acceptance of a more or less complex editorial history for Kings in turn influences the way that scholars read it literarily and analyze the points that the ancient authors wanted to make.

Although there is nothing intrinsically wrong with the current redaction-historical approach to Kings, unless pursued with caution it runs the risk of overlooking or relegating to secondary status the overall interests of the book as a whole. In the quest to delineate the themes and interlocking features of the individual units and layers that make up the book, there is always the danger of ignoring the investigation of the book's final form, the overall message conveyed by the last editor(s) to work on the material.

Of course, it is always possible that, as a composite work, Kings makes no general points and has no overarching themes. The book could be understood simply as an antiquarian document, intended to preserve originally independent narrative and archival material illuminating the history of Israel's monarchy. However, even the most enthusiastic proponents of literary analysis rarely push the argument this far, and almost all scholars see the book as tied together by a complex of overarching themes or motifs. The most frequent account of this thematic unity points to the evaluations made by the editors in the formulaic statements used to introduce and to conclude the reigns of individual Israelite and Judean kings. On the basis of these formulas, scholars have usually concluded that the book's final editors were interested in making a theological evaluation of the contrasting fates of the Northern and Southern Kingdoms. From their standpoint, the Northern Kingdom was doomed from the very beginning because all of its rulers "walked in the ways of Jeroboam son of Nebat, who made Israel to sin" (1 Kgs 15:26, 34; 16:25, 30; 22:52-53; 2 Kgs 3:2; 13:2, 11; 14:24; 15:9, 18, 24, 28; 17:2). In contrast, the Southern Kingdom was relatively blessed because the majority of its rulers "walked in the way of their father David," for whose sake the kingdom was preserved, even though individual kings did what was evil and ultimately the whole nation was punished, presumably temporarily, through the Babylonian exile (1 Kgs 15:4-5, 11; 22:43; 2 Kgs 8:18-19, 27; 14:3-4; 15:3, 34; 16:2-3; 18:3; 21:2, 20; 22:2; 23:32, 37; 24:9, 19-20).

To be sure, the themes found in the formulas do play an important role in giving Kings literary and theological cohesion, but do they exhaust the points that the final authors or editors wanted to make? That they do not is suggested by the simple observation that the book includes much more than the formulas. In addition, there are numerous narratives, and one might fairly expect that whatever their origin, these materials too would reflect the interests of the final editors. In order to explore the question of the book's general overarching themes, then, it is important to take into account the narrative material and the way in which the narratives are related to each other and to the formulas. This exploration will certainly not exhaust the thematic material in the book, but it may help highlight material that has not yet been duly considered.

If one looks particularly at the narratives, then, what is the book of Kings about? What occupies the attention of the authors? One of the earliest answers to this question, and one that bears further examination by modern scholars, is that the book of Kings is about prophets. The book is, after all, part of a block of literature traditionally called the "Former Prophets;" and rabbinic sources believed the text to have been authored by a prophet, Jeremiah. So close is the association between prophecy and monarchy in the book that many modern readers see in it a portrayal of the archetypical relationship between prophet and king. Unlike the prophetic books themselves, which only occasionally describe a prophetic encounter with the king, the stories in Kings are so full of such encounters as to give the impression that confrontation was the normal prophetic style. All prophets are thereby cast into the mold of Elijah, single-handedly challenging the worship of Baal in the Ephraimite court. In fact the close intertwining of prophetic and royal activities in Kings has led some scholars to suggest that the two institutions of prophecy and monarchy were so tightly linked in Israel that one could not survive without the other. Prophecy arose in Israel with the establishment of the monarchy and declined at about the same time the monarchy came to an end.[5]

In the scholarly discussion of the book of Samuel, where prophetic stories are similarly prominent, the interest in prophecy that the book displays has often been explained by assigning the prophetic stories and references to a prophetic author or editor. However, one seldom finds this thesis in studies of Kings, at least in modern times. Although a few scholars have posited prophetic sources as fundamental editorial layers, and others, following Gerhard von Rad, have pointed to the importance of the prophecy/fulfillment schema in the book, until recently most scholars have followed the lead of Martin Noth and argued for the basic literary cohesion of the book and suggested that this cohesion is based primarily on deuteronomistic theological themes, none of which are particularly prophetic.[6] The claim that the book's author had little interest in prophecy has also been accepted by scholars who see the book as having undergone two distinct editings but who follow Noth in omitting prophecy from their list of the book's major themes.[7]

A slightly different situation exists in the case of scholars advocating a three-redaction theory. The primary work has been done in this area by Rudolph Smend, Walter Dietrich, and their followers. In the form in which Dietrich articulates the thesis, the basic text of Kings was created early, around 580 BCE, by a Deuteronomist whom Dietrich labels DtrG. Slightly later a second Deuteronomist, this one having prophetic interests and therefore designated DtrP, added a number of passages dealing with prophecy. Finally, about 560 BCE a Deuteronomist with legal interests (DtrN) made some further additions, thus giving the book its final form.[8] In this version of the editorial history, prophetic interests become a secondary feature of the book rather than part of its foundational structure.

Swimming against the critical tide that deemphasizes the importance of prophecy in Kings has been Antony F. Campbell, who has used careful literary analysis to uncover what he calls a "prophetic record," which he takes to be a late ninth-century document, created in Ephraim, and later used as the basic text for much of the present book of Kings (1 Kings 1–2 Kings 10).[9] While there are a number of problems with Campbell's literary analysis, it is becoming increasingly clear that the role of prophecy in Kings must be reassessed. Could it be that this part of the "Former Prophets" really deals with the prophets in some meaningful sense? A new assessment of this issue will require more careful and extensive literary analysis than is possible in a brief paper, but the task can begin by asking a fundamental question and then by making some simple descriptive observations about the role of prophecy in the narratives and in the formulas that tie them together. First, the question: If scholars wanted to look for evidence of a prophetic substratum or editorial layer in the present book of Kings, what would they look for? This seems to be an obvious question, but it is one that has been largely overlooked.

In the past, scholars have tended to isolate prophetic editorial material first by applying various literary-critical tools to the text in order to separate its various literary layers. These layers are assumed to be coherent (although this is not always demonstrated, and, indeed, cannot always be demonstrated) and to exhibit consistency in the use of themes, ideology, vocabulary or the like. An attempt is then made to determine the setting or the authorship of the literary layer by linking it in some way with a known person or group. It is not important at this point to engage in a critique of the way in which scholars have traditionally uncovered editorial layers in the text. However, it is crucial to look briefly at the grounds for labeling a particular literary layer "prophetic." In the past, several criteria have been used for this purpose. First, characteristic vocabulary has been employed. A particular layer of Kings is shown to contain terms or expressions thought to be peculiarly prophetic. The difficulty with this approach is that prophecy in Israel was not confined to a particular social group, and prophets were not isolated in any special way from the society as a whole. The distinctive vocabulary of any given prophet was, therefore, shared with other members of the prophet's social group, with the result that the appearance of that vocabulary in a text does not necessarily point to prophetic authorship. In the case of Kings, the situation is even more complicated, since much of the book uses a deuteronomic vocabulary that makes further distinctions on the basis of language difficult to support. How does one separate a prophetic Deuteronomist from a nonprophetic Deuteronomist when both use the same idioms and vocabulary? This problem is sometimes solved by appealing to a second criterion for identifying prophetic editorial layers: the use of peculiar prophetic speech forms. Both Campbell and Dietrich, for example, note the appearance of forms such as the invective-threat ("because you have done thus-and-so, therefore the following will happen"). When Campbell and Dietrich find these forms in Kings, they assume them to be a sign of prophetic authorship. The flaw in this line of reasoning, however, is that many of the so-called prophetic speech forms appear in their pristine purity only in the book of Kings and not in the writings of the prophets themselves. It is not at all clear, then, that these speech forms are truly prophetic. They might simply be deuteronomistic literary conventions, or they might point to deuteronomistic notions of how prophets talked. Even if the forms are prophetic, their use in the narrative does not necessarily point to prophetic authorship. All writers frequently use speech that is not part of their normal vocabulary.

Similar problems exist when prophetic theology or ideology is used to identify editorial layers as prophetic. Just as Israelite prophets did not share a common "prophetic" vocabulary, so they did not share a particular "prophetic" theology. Their views on power and politics and what God required of Israel at a particular time were widely diverse and capable of changing without warning. Even though it is popular in some circles today to talk about a prophetic stance on this or that issue, the danger of stereotyping the prophetic message is always present and must be resisted. Certainly the diversity of content within the prophetic corpus makes content criteria for identifying prophetic sources difficult to apply.

Finally, some scholars have identified prophetic sources in Kings on the grounds that they deal primarily with prophets. This criterion has the virtue of being objective, but like the other criteria we have considered, it is thoroughly flawed. Non-prophetic authors were certainly capable of writing about prophets, so the mere appearance of prophets in the narrative does not necessarily indicate prophetic authorship. In short, then, there seem to be no firm criteria for identifying a particular editorial layer in Kings as prophetic, unless that designation is used simply for the sake of scholarly convenience. Rather than pursue the question of prophetic sources in Kings any further, then, it might be more fruitful to ask three more general questions concerning the role of prophets in the book. First, what role do the prophets play in the narratives of the book of Kings? Second, are there any patterns to be found in the placement of the narratives involving prophets? Third, do these patterns throw any light on the question of the book's overarching themes?

For descriptive purposes, the narratives about prophetic activity may be divided into two types.[10] First, some prophetic stories are part of the prophecy-fulfillment schema that von Rad identified as a major structural feature of the book.[11] Second, there are narratives concerning prophetic activity that are not directly related to the prophecy-fulfillment schema. Both types of material sometimes contain prophetic oracles, but the oracles themselves do not seem to be separable from their narrative matrix. (The division of the material in this way is only for the sake of analytical convenience and is not intended to imply anything about a separate origin for the two types.)

Although the motif of prophecy and fulfillment is sometimes thought to be a major structural and thematic feature of Kings, in fact its use is highly restricted. Outside of the famous (and probably secondary) prophecy against the altar at Bethel (1 Kgs 13:1-10), which is not fulfilled until the account of Josiah's reforms in 2 Kgs 23:15-18, the explicit prophecy-fulfillment notices in Kings are applied only to the reigns of northern kings from the time of Jeroboam I (1 Kgs 14:7-16) to the end of the Omride dynasty (2 Kgs 10:17). In all but one case, the prophecy involves the end of the king's reign or dynasty and is grounded in unspecified sins, presumably of a religious nature. Thus, Ahijah of Shiloh prophesies the end of Jeroboam's line in 1 Kgs 14:1-16; this prophecy is fulfilled in 1 Kgs 15:27-30. A similar oracle is given against Baasha's line in 1 Kgs 16:1-4 and fulfilled in 1 Kgs 16:11-14. As part of the narrative of prophetic opposition to the Omrides, the motif appears two more times. In 1 Kgs 21:20-24 Elijah condemns Ahab and Jezebel specifically because of their murderous plot to seize Naboth's vineyard. This prophecy is fulfilled in three stages: 1 Kgs 22:37-38 (against Ahab), 2 Kgs 9:36-37 (against Jezebel), and 2 Kgs 10:17 (against Ahab's dynasty). Finally, in 2 Kgs 1:2-4 Elijah prophesies the death of Ahaziah, a prophecy that is fulfilled in 2 Kngs 1:17-18.

At the end of the story of the Omride wars, the prophecy-fulfillment pattern is modified and extended when God personally (and unexpectedly) places a limitation on Jehu's dynasty, and the fulfillment of this divine oracle is duly noted in 2 Kgs 15:12. However, strictly speaking, no prophet appears in this case. Later in Kings, in the theological retrospectives on the fall of

Samaria (2 Kgs 17:13) and the fall of Jerusalem (2 Kgs 24:2), there are references to prophetic warnings that might have helped to avert the judgment against the two cities, but the narratives contain no examples of such warnings, and they seem to be part of a larger deuteronomic picture of idealized prophetic activity. In summary, then, the prophecy-fulfillment schema seems restricted to the accounts of northern kings' reigns and to be a part of a collection of prophetic stories dealing with the fall of the north. The schema is not connected with Judah and is, therefore, absent from the latter part of 2 Kings, which deals only with Judah. If the prophecy-fulfillment motif is a structural theme in Kings, then it is a restricted one and at most can only be part of a larger collection of such themes.

The second group of references to prophetic activity lies outside of the prophecy-fulfillment schema and is found in various narratives dealing with the interaction between prophets and the Ephraimite kings. These stories are often focused on political rather than strictly religious issues, although some of them have to do with the aggrandizement of the prophet or the prophetic office rather than with either politics or religion.

These stories begin with Ahijah's role in the anointing of Jeroboam and the legitimation of the Northern Kingdom (1 Kgs 11:29-39), an act which is interpreted as a judgment on Solomon for allowing the worship of foreign gods in Israel. The legitimacy of the establishment of the north is further reinforced by Shemaiah's oracle to Rehoboam (1 Kgs 12:22-24), just as the oracles rejecting Jeroboam and all that he stands for (1 Kgs 13:1-10; 14:1-16) are reinforced by the narrative of the old prophet at Bethel (1 Kgs 13:11-32). The remaining stories of prophetic activity in Kings all have to do with the overthrow of the Omrides. Most of this material is found in the Elijah/Elisha stories, which often focus on the direct involvement of the prophet with the workings of the government, either on the side of Israel (1 Kgs 20:13; 2 Kgs 3:1-27) or against it (1 Kings 17–20; 21; 22).

All of this general prophetic material is northern in its interests and reinforces the impression given by the use of the prophecy-fulfillment motif. The part of Kings that deals with the north seems to have an extraordinary interest in prophecy, and prophetic themes and motifs seem to have a structural function in the ordering of this material. This observation, however, still leaves unanswered the question of the overarching themes in that part of Kings dealing with the south and therefore does not help to identify the themes of the book as a whole. Although the stories of northern prophetic activity occupy a great deal of space, the book of Kings in its present form is ultimately the story of the fall of Jerusalem and the Exile. In the final part of the book, which focuses on Judah alone, there seems to be little interest in prophecy. Outside some general references, the only two prophets to appear in the Judean material are Isaiah, who delivers a long oracle as part of the Hezekiah narratives (2 Kings 18–20), and Huldah, whose oracle to Josiah foretells the destruction of Jerusalem (2 Kings 22–23).

What, then, are the overarching themes of the Judean material? One answer to this question has recently been supplied by Iaian Provan, who argues on the basis of the accession formulas that the Judean narratives are interested primarily in the question of whether or not the southern kings removed the high places, which Provan understands as outlying shrines of Judah's God. Judean kings who engage in actual idolatrous worship, usually because they have some sort of connection with the north, are condemned outright by the historian, while the majority of the southern kings are given positive evaluations, with the historian noting only that they nevertheless failed to remove the high places. This theme continues in the evaluation formulas until the reign of Hezekiah, who is said to have been the first king to remove the high places and to centralize worship in Jerusalem. These two acts earn for Hezekiah the unqualified praise of the writer of Kings. Provan then uses these observations to suggest that there was once an edition of Kings that reached its climax in the account of Hezekiah's reforms. This edition was unified by the primary theme of the importance of removing the high places and by a secondary theme, the theme of God's promise that David's line would be eternal. Because of this promise, even the evil Judean kings who preceded Hezekiah were not destroyed, as evil kings routinely were in the north. The theme of the dynastic promises was later modified in order to accommodate the judgment that finally fell on the city in 586.[12] Provan's analysis is useful so far as it goes, but it is still based solely on an analysis of the Judean evaluation formulas. He does not consider any of the narratives that focus on the Judean kings themselves. However, when this narrative material is brought into the discussion, a somewhat different picture of the thematic interests of the final authors or editors begins to emerge.

When the stories that Kings tells about the southern kings are examined carefully, two thematic interests become clear. First, there are a surprising number of accounts about religious reform, although none deal with the removal of the high places. Asa is credited with such a reform (1 Kgs 15:11-15), as is Joash (2 Kgs 12:1-16). The Chronicler mentions additional reforms that do not appear in Kings, including one credited to Manasseh (2 Chr 33:15-17). However, even though these events might have been of interest to the people who compiled the stories about the Judean kings, they were clearly of no interest to the author of the evaluation formulas, who never gives a king special credit for religious reform unless the high places are removed.

However, a second focus of the Judean narratives provides a stronger clue to the thematic interests of the authors. These narratives seem especially concerned about whether or not Judean kings made foreign alliances and what price was paid to maintain them. Interest in this question first surfaces in the historian's evaluation of Jehoshaphat (1 Kgs 22:41-44). Although the king is said to have done what was right in the sight of the Lord, his praise is typically qualified by the note that he did not remove the high places. Then the historian adds an additional negative note. Jehoshaphat made a peace treaty with the king of Israel (1 Kgs 22:44). Now this comment may simply reflect the historian's general antipathy toward anyone who has anything to do with the Northern Kingdom and its apostate worship, but there is little evidence in the narratives themselves that Jehoshaphat was influenced by Israelite religious practices, and, even more important, the writer of the evaluation formulas gives no such evidence either. However, the narratives do provide ample evidence that Jehoshaphat was a political vassal of the Israelite king. In fact the immediately preceding story of the abortive attempt to recapture Ramoth-gilead portrays the Judean king fulfilling military obligations to his suzerain (1 Kgs 22:1-4).

The issue of political alliances arises again in the historian's comments on Jehoram and Ahaziah, both of whom are evaluated negatively. Jehoram is said to have walked in the way of the northern kings because he had married into the family of the Israelite king, Ahab, perhaps to seal a treaty between Judah and Israel (2 Kgs 8:16-19). Ahaziah also was a son-in-law of Ahab's, and the only story told about him describes a joint military venture with Ahab's son (2 Kgs 8:25-29).

After the Athaliah interregnum, Joash, who is credited with a major renovation of the Temple and who is evaluated positively by the historian, is said to have bought the safety of Jerusalem by becoming a vassal of Hazael, the king of Syria. To seal the agreement, Joash took all of the votive gifts that Jehoshaphat, Jehoram, and Ahaziah had collected, along with all the gold in the royal and temple treasuries, and gave it to the Syrian king (2 Kgs 12:17-18). The description of this payment bears a striking similarity to the later narrative of Hezekiah's payment of tribute to the Assyrians (2 Kgs 18:13-16).

Joash's son, Amaziah, also tried to force the king of Israel to conclude a vassal treaty with him, although the attempt backfired when the offended Israelite king raided Judah, broke down the wall of Jerusalem, and seized all of the gold and silver in the royal and temple treasuries. It may be for this reason that the historian pointedly does not compare Amaziah to David but rather to Joash his father: "He [Amaziah] did what was right in the sight of the LORD, yet not like his ancester David; in all things he did in all things he did as his father Joash had done" (2 Kgs 14:3; 14:1-14).

The narrative's interest in political alliances becomes even more explicit in the account of Ahaz's reign, and, for the first time, they clearly become an issue in the evaluation formulas as well. Ahaz is evaluated negatively by the historian, and this evaluation seems to be based on two factors: a wide range of apostate cultic activities and a treaty that he concluded with the Assyrian king Tiglath-pileser in order to obtain Assyrian help during the Syro-Ephraimitic war (2 Kgs 16:1-20).

All of these Judean narratives, when taken together, indicate that as the book of Kings proceeds it manifests an increasing interest in the issue of foreign alliances, an interest that finally invades the evaluation formulas themselves when the Assyrians become involved in the political picture.[13] It can hardly be irrelevant, then, that at the end of the positive evaluation of Hezekiah the historian notes that this king rebelled against the king of Assyria. In this way Hezekiah forms a sharp contrast with Ahaz, who concluded a treaty with the Assyrian monarch.

If the author of Kings had been interested in the question of Judean political alliances as well as in the attitude of the kings toward religious reform, then some of the redactional problems posed by the Hezekiah narratives become more amenable to solution. While the complex narrative of the Assyrian invasion in 2 Kgs 18:13–19:37 does not seem interested in Hezekiah's religious policies, it does appear concerned with his foreign policies. The whole narrative has a complex history and has traditionally been analyzed as follows:

(A) 18:13*b*-16	an annalistic account that seems generally to agree with Sennacherib's own account of events in his royal annals.
(B1) 18:17–19:9*a*, 36	a narrative of the confrontation between the messengers of Hezekiah and the Rabshakeh. The Rabshakeh's long speech focuses on Hezekiah's political stance, which is interwoven with comments about God's power. The Judean king in this narrative acts in a way that is consistent with the deuteronomic prescriptions for the conduct of kings. When faced with a threat to his rule, he consults the prophet Isaiah and receives from him an oracle of reassurance and promises of Yahweh's protection.
(B2) 19:9*b*–35	a second account of the same event, in which the sequence of events and the conduct of the king are somewhat different. Hezekiah rather than Isaiah is the central figure, and the king himself prays to Yahweh for aid. The issue in the second account is no longer Hezekiah's foreign policy, as

it is in the first account, but the focus is on Yahweh's ability to save the city. Lying behind this
account is clearly the Jerusalem royal theology, as
articulated in 2 Samuel 7 and expressed often in
Isaiah (e.g., chap. 7).[14]

In recent years some scholars have argued that (B1) and (B2) are in fact
a single unified narrative, but even if this could be shown to be true, the
fundamental literary problem in the passage would not be solved. As the text
now stands, (A) and (B) appear to be two accounts of the same event,
although they are obviously written from two very different perspectives.
After Hezekiah's initial payment of tribute, the sudden appearance of the
Rabshakeh makes no sense and has even led some scholars to propose that
Sennacherib made two campaigns against Israel.

Some of these difficulties would be resolved if it is assumed that the editor
is in fact arranging the traditional accounts in order to comment on
Hezekiah's foreign policy and, by so doing, to hold up Hezekiah as a model
for later Judean kings, who also had to address the problems of political
alliances with the Assyrians, Babylonians, and Egyptians. From this perspective, the sequence of events in the text would be these: At the beginning of
his reign, Hezekiah did what all good kings should do in the opinion of the
historian. He rebelled against the king of Assyria (18:7). This rebellion quite
naturally led to a reprisal by Sennacherib, who invaded Judah and threatened Jerusalem. However, instead of maintaining the appropriate policy of
trust in Yahweh's ability to save the city, Hezekiah capitulated and paid a
heavy tribute to the Assyrians, thus depleting the treasuries of both the palace
and the temple. This capitulation, however, achieved nothing. Sennacherib
still threatened to lay siege to Jerusalem, and it is clear that nothing had been
gained by Hezekiah's policy. The Rabshakeh's speech is designed, among
other things, to cast doubt on the wisdom of trusting in Yahweh and resisting
the Assyrians. Treaties with the Assyrians are portrayed as the reasonable
thing to do, and the follies of any other course, including alliances with
Egypt, are stressed. Hezekiah appears not to know how to respond to these
arguments and turns appropriately to Isaiah for advice. The prophet gives
the king an oracle of reassurance, and when the Rabshakeh reappears
Hezekiah remains firm in his policy of rebellion. For taking this stance he is
rewarded when God miraculously delivers the city.

If this analysis of the Hezekiah narratives is correct, it would suggest that
one of the major themes of the Judean material in Kings is the question of
foreign policy, particularly toward the Assyrians. It would also be clear where
the editor or author stood on this issue. He favored a policy of nonalliance
and supported some version of the Jerusalemite royal theology, which

stressed God's eternal and unqualified promise of protection for the city. This stance is not normally associated with the Deuteronomists, and its appearance in Kings raises questions about the traditional scholarly notion that the book is part of a Deuteronomistic History, although in this connection it is important to note Deuteronomy's frequent exhortations against making treaties with the inhabitants of Canaan. However, at the same time, the point of view being taken in Kings is very close to what is found in Isaiah, who also opposed foreign alliances of all sorts and advocated trust in Yahweh as an adequate foreign policy. These similarities between Kings and Isaiah raise again old questions about the relationship between these two books, as well as some new questions about the origins of deuteronomism. For this reason, a comprehensive view of the overarching themes of the book of Kings not only enhances the reader's understanding of the book as a whole, but also invites the reader to explore more deeply the links between Kings, the Pentateuch, and the prophetic books themselves.

Notes

1. For a brief survey of early critical scholarship on the Former Prophets, see R. Clements, *One Hundred Years of Old Testament Interpretation* (Philadelphia: Westminster, 1976) 31-50.

2. Surveys of recent approaches to the Former Prophets are provided by B. Childs, *Introduction to the Old Testament as Scripture* (Philadelphia: Fortress, 1979) 229-301; and P. Ackroyd, "The Historical Literature," in *The Hebrew Bible and Its Modern Interpreters*, eds. D. Knight and G. Tucker; (Philadelphia: Fortress, 1985), 297-305. As examples of holistic readings, note particularly R. Polzin, *Moses and the Deuteronomist* (New York: Seabury, 1980); *Samuel and the Deuteronomist* (San Francisco: Harper & Row, 1989); *David and the Deuteronomist* (Bloomington: Indiana University Press, 1993); D. Gunn, "Joshua and Judges," in *The Literary Guide to the Bible*, eds. R. Alter and F. Kermode (Cambridge, Mass.: Harvard University Press, 1987) 102-21; J. Rosenberg, "1 and 2 Samuel," in *Literary Guide to the Bible*, 122-45; G. Savran, "1 and 2 Kings," in *Literary Guide to the Bible*, 146-64; B. Webb, *The Book of Judges* (Sheffield: JSOT, 1987); and L. Klein, *The Triumph of Irony in the Book of Judges* (Sheffield: Almond, 1988).

3. M. Noth, *The Deuteronomistic History*, JSOTSup 15 (Sheffield: JSOT, 1981).

4. For a survey of recent treatments of the editorial history of 1 and 2 Kings, see S. McKenzie, *The Trouble with Kings* (Leiden: Brill, 1991) 1-19. Attempts at a more unified reading of the books are provided by R. Nelson, *First and Second Kings* (Atlanta: John Knox, 1987); and B. Long, *1 Kings with an Introduction to Historical Literature*, FOTL (Grand Rapids: Eerdmans, 1984); *2 Kings*, FOTL (Grand Rapids: Eerdmans, 1991).

5. See, for example, the comments of F. Cross, *Canaanite Myth and Hebrew Epic* (Cambridge, Mass.: Harvard University Press, 1973) 223-29; and D. Petersen, *Late Israelite Prophecy* (Missoula, Mont.: Scholars Press, 1977) 2-5.

6. A. Jepsen, *Die Quellen des Königsbuches*, 2d ed. (Halle: Niemeyer, 1956), 76-101; G. von Rad, *Studies in Deuteronomy* (London: SCM, 1953) 74-91.

7. See, for example, Cross, *Canaanite Myth*, 274-89; R. Nelson, *The Double Redaction of the Deuteronomistic History* (Sheffield: JSOT, 1981) 119-28; and McKenzie, *The Trouble with Kings*, 81-100, 147-50.

8. W. Dietrich, *Prophetie und Geschichte* (Göttingen: Vandenhoeck & Ruprecht, 1972).

9. A. Campbell, *Of Prophets and Kings* (Washington: The Catholic Biblical Association of America, 1986); cf. M. O'Brien, *The Deuteronomistic History Hypothesis: A Reassessment* (Freiburg: Universitätsverlag, 1989).

10. For a more detailed literary analysis of the stories, see A. Rofé, *The Prophetical Stories* (Jerusalem: Magnes, 1988).

11. Von Rad, *Studies in Deuteronomy,* 74-91.

12. I. Provan, *Hezekiah and the Books of Kings: A Contribution to the Debate* (Berlin: Walter de Gruyter, 1988).

13. For an elaboration of this point, see C. Hardmeier, *Prophetie im Streit vor dem Untergang Judas* (Berlin: Walter de Gruyter, 1990).

14. For a judicious analysis of these narratives, see B. Childs, *Isaiah and the Assyrian Crisis* (London: SCM, 1967) 69-111.

Selected Bibliography

Alter, R., and F. Kermode. *The Literary Guide to the Bible.* Cambridge, Mass: Harvard University Press, 1987.

Campbell, A. *Of Prophets and Kings: A Late Ninth Century Document (1 Samuel 1–2 Kings 10).* CBQMS 17. Washington: The Catholic Biblical Association of America, 1986.

Childs, B. *Introduction to the Old Testament as Scripture.* Philadelphia: Fortress, 1979.

Long, B. *1 Kings with an Introduction to Historical Literature.* FOTL 9. Grand Rapids: Eerdmans, 1984.

———. *2 Kings.* FOTL 10. Grand Rapids: Eerdmans, 1991.

McKenzie, S. *The Trouble with Kings: The Composition of the Books of Kings in The Deuteronomistic History.* VTSup 42. Leiden: Brill, 1991.

Nelson, R. *The Double Redaction of the Deuteronomistic History.* JSOTSup 18. Sheffield: JSOT, 1981.

Noth, M. *The Deuteronomistic History.* JSOTSup 15. Sheffield: JSOT, 1981.

O'Brien, M. *The Deuteronomistic History Hypothesis: A Reassessment.* OBO 92. Freiburg: Universitätsverlag, 1989.

Provan, I. *Hezekiah and the Books of Kings.* BZAW 172. Berlin: Walter de Gruyter, 1988.

Rofé, A. *The Prophetical Stories.* Jerusalem: Magnes, 1988.

Chapter 6

THE WORLD AND MESSAGE
OF THE PROPHETS:
BIBLICAL PROPHECY
IN ITS CONTEXT

Patrick D. Miller, Jr.

C alled of God and sent to address a word from the Lord to leaders and/or to the people, the prophets of ancient Israel found their reason for being in declaring the divine word in particular and broader human situations. They addressed injustice and social oppression, crises of military invasions and the barbarities of war, creation of political alliances, religious apostasy, monarchical pretensions and tyranny, people lamenting their exile or directionless in trying to start a new life. All these—and other situations—as the focus of prophetic words mean that the prophets and their message are only intelligible in the context of an understanding of the social, political, and religious conditions and circumstances of their prophecy. The need to understand that context and that world is less a requirement of a particular methodology or mode of interpretation than it is an inherent demand of the material under study—the prophets and their prophecies.

Israelite Prophecy in Its Ancient Near Eastern Context

We have become increasingly aware that the phenomenon of biblical prophecy, which has been so central to the interpretation and assessment of the Old Testament, was not peculiar to ancient Israel. Before that nation came into being and while prophecy was at its peak, the nations and states of the ancient Near East had their own oracular speakers,[1] whom we may, for convenience sake, consider prophets. As in Israel, they took various forms and titles and presented different sorts of messages. There are some significant differences in emphasis—differences that may be an accident of archaeological discovery— but the analogies are sufficiently clear that we must speak of prophecy as a part of the ancient world and not simply a part of Israel's history.

That such is the case is already suggested from within the Old Testament itself where we find reference to prophets of Baal.[2] References—in more or less detail—to prophets (male and female) occur throughout Syria-Palestine, in such places as Emar on the Middle Euphrates River, Phoenicia, Aram, and Ammon, as well as in Anatolia and especially in Mesopotamia in the second millennium texts discovered at Mari and in first millennium Neo-Assyrian texts.[3] The distinction between divination and prophecy, as well as the possible overlap and confusion of the two, is evident in other cultures as well as in Israel. In the Mari texts, however, the claims of oracular speakers may be confirmed by technical or divinatory processes, a move forbidden in Old Testament texts though possibly practiced on occasion. The terms for prophecy that were most common in Israel—$nābî'$/$nĕbîāh$ (is prophet [masc. and fem.]), $ḥōzeh$ (is seer), and $'îš$ $(hā)$ $'ĕlōhîm$ (is "man of God"), or their equivalents—were to be found in other societies as designations of prophetic-type figures, although a number of other terms were used, especially in the Mari literature where four or five different terms appear.[4] The diversity of prophetic-type figures may have been greater in the Old Babylonian culture than in Israel, but there are clear signs of distinctions in Israel also where conflicts arose between the $nĕbî'îm$ or prophetic groups and other individual prophets and where some distinction is recognized between $ḥōzeh$ and $nābî'$ (1 Sam 9:9), though the same person may be designated by either term. While the biblical literature does not have a separate term for an ecstatic prophesier, as does Mari, it knows that form of prophesying both in Israel (1 Sam 10:5) and outside Israel (1 Kings 18). One notes also that Amos's identification of himself as a lay person rather than a prophet or a member of the prophetic guild has an analogy in the prominence of lay folk as prophets at Mari. The distinction between these lay prophets and those who perform in the temple is similar to Amos's differentiation of himself from any prophets who might be under the supervision of Amaziah, the chief priest of Bethel (Amos 7:10-17). While we do not have elsewhere the conflict between prophets that is so prominent in some of the biblical texts, the differentiation between professionals and those who are not is evident. So also the need for authentication of a prophecy, accomplished at Mari by checking a lock of hair and a hem belonging to the prophetic figure, is clearly a major feature of the prophetic conflicts in ancient Israel. It is reflected in the various discussions about what is a true (i.e., valid and authentic) prophecy from Yahweh. The frequent call accounts also served to provide some legitimation and authority for the prophet whose oracles were being communicated or preserved.

One notes further the number of women among the lay prophets at Mari and the possible references to "prophetesses" at Emar and wonders if there were not more of these in Israel than the brief story of Huldah (a lay prophet?) in 1 Kngs 22:14-20 might indicate. This story, in which several officials including the priest Hilkiah, went to inquire of Huldah and then reported the prophetic oracle back to the king is reminiscent of the frequent report of oracles to kings or queens at Mari by third parties who received the oracle from the prophet and then passed it on, though in these cases the oracle was usually unsolicited. Ezekiel's condemnation of the women prophets (Ezek 13:17-23) also suggests more women engaged in prophetic activity than we are accustomed to think. While at Mari there were occasionally prophecies directed toward non-royal recipients there and elsewhere outside Israel, the prophetic oracle was usually addressed to the king. The royal oracle dominated the oracular activity of the prophetic figures, a fact that is probably more the case among Israelite prophecies than is usually acknowledged. It is not simply that court prophets such as Nathan, Gad, Ahijah, and Isaiah worked in direct relation to the king, but the prophetic words generally were more likely to have been directed toward the ruler of the land and the royal court.[5]

A number of things suggest that Amos was accused of prophesying against Jeroboam. More significant is the work of the prophetic groups, the *nĕbi'îm*, who Jeremiah condemns as the prophets of peace. That is, they were salvation prophets, prophets who brought words of assurance to the king about defeat of the enemy and the god's protection. A classic instance of such prophetic activity is found in the report of the kings of Israel and Judah inquiring of the deity through the *nĕbi'îm*—some four hundred—and then through Micaiah. The oracle of salvation that the four hundred gave is like the later "peace" prophecies of the *nebi'îm* whom Jeremiah called false. That his judgment was vindicated does not vitiate the fact that such oracles of salvation, directed primarily to the king but, by association and extension to the people also, were the norm at Mari and among the Neo-Assyrian prophecies. The argument has been made that the oracles of salvation of Deutero-Isaiah were royal oracles now adapted for the people in exile who were without a king.[6] While the basic form of prophetic oracle among the prophecies preserved from preexilic Israel in the prophetic books of the Old Testament was the judgment speech, the actual basic form of prophetic speech, in and outside Israel, was likely to have been the oracle of salvation or assurance.[7] Indeed the oracles against the foreign nations, which are so prominent in a number of the prophetic books, are anticipated among the ancient Near Eastern prophets by their oracles assuring victory to the king. The many judgment speeches of the major prophets of the Old Testament were against the grain of typical prophecy. The preservation of these speeches may have had as much to do with the resistance to their message as their negative content.[8] In the world in which Jeremiah and Hananiah prophesied, Hananiah's message of assurance to Zedekiah was more likely to have been the true, that is, the typical and expected prophetic word than that of Jeremiah despite Jeremiah's words to the contrary (Jer 28:8). It is only when the cautionary voices of those who remembered the judgment speeches of Micah intervened that Jeremiah was not executed for his words against Zion (as in fact his prophetic colleague Uriah was [Jeremiah 26]).

Other types of oracles could, of course, occur. They frequently had to do with cultic matters or cultic requests on the part of the gods. This is especially true at Mari. The reprimand for cultic failures is, in some ways, different from what one encounters in ancient Israelite prophecy, but it has some analogue in the prophetic condemnation of the cult of those who did not practice justice. And, as some scholars have noted, there are occasional prophecies at Mari that reflect the kind of ethical concern for justice and attention to the marginal that is so much a part of Israelite prophecy.[9] In some instances, oracles were spoken in a more public forum, whether at the door of the palace or in the hearing of the elders or general populace. The move from royal to popular prophecy in Israel is reflected here also, at least in the sense that the populace may be addressed indirectly even if the king is the primary recipient.

In various ways, therefore, Israelite prophecy is finding its place as an oracular phenomenon of the ancient world whose peculiar character is found more in the content of prophetic words to pre and postexilic Israelite (including Judean) communities than it is in some special office or vocation that was *sui generis* to the people who preserved the biblical prophetic collections.

The Prophetic Role

Awareness of the larger prophetic world drives us, however, toward further definition of the prophetic role(s) and the social setting in which the prophets "played out" their role(s). Increasingly, the prophet has come to be understood more functionally than psychologically, more in terms of prophetic activity and its purpose(s) than in terms of the prophetic experience. That is, we do not think of prophets first and foremost in terms of their peculiar relation to the deity or their religious experience, as has been more characteristic of earlier generations of scholarship, but more in relation to their vocation and roles in the society of which they were a part, whether centrally or peripherally.[10]

This approach, however, cannot ignore the religious character of prophetic activity that is consistently presented as a mediation of a divine word. And when the personal experience of the prophet comes into view, that usually represents some kind of engagement with the reality of the divine.

100

So one of the primary definitions of the prophetic role that continues to maintain its place when prophetic oracles and narratives are investigated is that of *messenger*.[11] Both formally and conceptually, the prophetic oracle is a message, not simply from the deity but from the divine world, from the divine assembly where the decrees of God are set forth and transmitted as a divine proclamation or message by the prophetic herald: "Thus says the Lord." Prophetic activity, therefore, cannot be understood simply in terms of its social, religious, or political world. It has to be understood from a frame of reference outside the realia of social existence though never separated from them. Prophetic oracles and prophetic narratives attest to a starting point for prophetic activity in a transcendent world identified by the image of the council of the Lord, the heavenly assembly (e.g., 1 Kngs 22:19-23; Isaiah 6; and Jer 23:16-22).[12] This is so persistently a feature of prophecy that it must be understood as a more determining factor in understanding it than defining a particular position for prophecy vis-à-vis society. That prophetic activity took place within a society, whether critically or supportively, whether in critique of existing reality or envisioning a new reality, is clear. But the word of the prophet to that society is rooted firmly in a relationship to the divine effecting a mediation of the divine word to the contemporary community of the prophet. The socio-political, indeed religious, character of prophecy is not simply due to the particular concerns of the prophet in addressing the human world. It arises out of a socio-political transcendent world that is understood to be the source of governance for what happens in the royal court and the law court, in battle and exile, in the streets and the sanctuaries. Heaven speaks through the prophet; earth listens in anticipation. The social world of the prophet is to be found in heaven as much as on earth.

Such an understanding of the prophetic role does not rule out other definitions or understandings. Sufficient complexity is discernable within the prophetic texts of the Bible that one is not surprised to find varying definitions or multiple dimensions. The long-recognized association of prophecy with ecstasy, or possession, a phenomenon attested in other cultures, Near Eastern and otherwise, perdures as a significant feature of prophecy and may be a fundamental dimension of the encounter with the deity and the vision of the divine council. Yet possession may take many forms, from the frenzy of the prophets who met Saul (1 Samuel 10) to the self-mutilations of the Baal prophets (1 Kings 18), to the strange acts of Ezekiel, which, in their reports of them, are thoroughly rationalized as obedience to divine commands to carry out symbolic actions.

The form-critical study of the prophets that began with Hermann Gunkel focused upon their activity as speakers and poets whose oracles became literature in a complex process. Gunkel recognized that prophetic speaking could range from the passionate, ecstasy-impelled to the more quiet and reflective.[13] But his focus on the mode of communication and his emphasis on their poetic speech continues to be a significant part of the understanding of prophecy.[14] Strong voices in contemporary scholarship have sought to place particular weight on the poetic character of the prophetic oracles and less on their prophetic character, suggesting that the association of the central figures of Amos, Hosea, Micah, Isaiah, Jeremiah, and Ezekiel with prophecy is the result of later more reflective and redactional moves in the composition of the books of the Former and Latter Prophets.[15] Until a relatively later stage in the history of prophecy, the time of Jeremiah and Ezekiel, the prophets were "poetic critics" who "come across not as men of the word but as craftsmen with words."[16] They were intellectuals and ideologues more than intermediaries of a divine communication.[17]

This separation of "poetic" prophets from "prophetic" prophets would have astonished Gunkel. It may seem to reflect some of the redactional layers of the prophets and the historical books. It is less likely to reflect the prophetic reality than the often-noted conflicts between prophets and other prophets, what has come to be identified with true and false prophecy, although that understanding may be too simple a label. The multiplicity of prophetic voices and thus the tension between different words seems to have been a significant part of the context in which the biblical prophets, named and unnamed, operated.

Thus the issue of prophetic authority rises constantly within the stories and implicitly within the prophetic oracles. The call stories and the accounts of prophetic disputations represent an effort to establish the credentials of the prophets. It may be the case that these narratives were contributions more from the prophets' disciples and the redactors of their oracles than that they were actually set forth by the prophets to certify their authority. But it is clear that the world of the prophets assumed the presence of the prophets and the significance of their word. Kings sought them and responded to their message. Individuals and groups within society reacted strongly—both positively and negatively—to their message.

Credibility, however, was never to be assumed, and conflicting voices undermined the authority of any individual prophet, as the biblical prophets from Micaiah to Amos to Jeremiah could testify. The authority of the prophet rested on intangible bases. It was to be found in the prescience of the prophet as demonstrated by the correspondence between prophetic announcement about the future and what actually happened. Yet acquiescence to the prophetic word did not depend upon waiting to see what happened. The elders in Jerusalem remembered Hezekiah's repentance in response to Micah's judgment oracle, a response that evoked a change of mind on the part of the deity (Jer 26:16-19). Even less tangible a ground of authority was

102

the locus of Yahweh's prophet in the divine council. There are various indications of the vision of the heavenly assembly as the source of the prophetic word (Jer 23:16-22; Amos 3:7) or the locus of the prophetic call (Isaiah 6). But claims to have stood in the divine assembly seem not to have succeeded in settling the inner-prophetic debate more than any other word or act. That is indicated by the narrative in 1 Kings 22, however it is to be dated, where the single voice of Micaiah is identified as the accurate prophecy when he proclaims his vision of the Lord in the heavenly assembly. The response is one of rejection by other prophets and the king, although the rest of the episode suggests that the king of Israel had some fear of the accuracy of the prophetic announcement (as indicated by his attempts at disguise). We probably also have in this story further indication of the primacy of oracles of salvation as a basic form of speech among prophets generally and resistance to the "basic form of prophetic speech" of the major biblical prophets, that is, the judgment speech.

Prophecy in Its Israelite Context

If we ask after the relation of prophets to *society* as a whole and, more specifically, to the *state* or the ruling power(s) and to the *cult,* that is, to the social, political, and religious institutions, the picture is complex. Careful sociological and anthropological work has pointed us to issues of the specific social location of the prophet in his or her role. Indeed the conflicts among prophets often seem to arise from different social locations, though one must be careful not to assume that as a simple explanation. Conflict may arise within shared social locations. It may indeed reflect differences with regard to the content of the prophetic message or its source, as we have suggested above. But the story of Micaiah ben Imlah in 1 Kings 22 suggests that the conflict between his message and that of the four hundred prophets, while being couched in terms of the question of who has stood in the council of the Lord, may also represent the opposition between what Robert Wilson has designated central prophets, such as the four hundred prophets to whom the kings naturally turn for a word from the Lord, and peripheral prophets, such as Micaiah, who has to be brought in from outside and is not one to whom the king regularly and naturally turns. The same may be the case for the conflict between Amaziah and Amos. The priest of Bethel assumed and presumably had power and authority over the various *nĕbi'îm* in ancient Israel who were in some way responsible to religious and political leaders. Amos, a lay figure who was peripheral to these structures, rejected any central authority over him (Amos 7:10-17). The question of the social location(s) of the prophet(s) remains a persistent one in understanding the prophetic role. It will have to be held in relation to the prophet's self-understanding and the constant intimations of the prophet's own conviction that the religious and theological location was more important than the social location. Scholarship on the prophets may weigh these issues in a manner that reflects their own social and theological location, the present writer included.

In any event, prophets spoke a divine word when besought by individuals, whether official or not, but also often proclaimed a divine word when directed to by the deity through an oracle or vision not precipitated by human inquiry. Prophets were figures to be consulted as intermediaries, but also to be listened to whether or not consulted. In the tenth and ninth centuries, prophetic oracles were primarily directed to the court, Elijah being a notable partial exception. This is consistent with the data from other societies in the ancient Near East. Prophecy was not exclusively directed toward the king, but the connections of kingship and prophecy were intimate. Many have argued that the rise and decline of prophecy are to be directly associated with the rise and decline of kingship. That particular thesis is less in vogue, but future study of the prophets needs to direct itself toward the analysis of the interrelation between these two institutions of ancient Israel. If the monarchy had a profound effect upon the whole character of Israelite society and politics as well as upon its theological foundations, it is to be expected that a, if not the, primary focus of the prophets would be upon the state, its leader and its influence. Thus prophecy moves from oracular call to attack the enemy and assurance of victory to condemnation of royal misconduct and on to the very conduct of war by the state.

The political context of prophetic activity is thus indicated not only theologically, that is, by the place of the prophet in the politics of the divine government centering in the divine assembly, but by the prophet's direct involvement in the human political scene. Prophets gave divine oracles to the king about the outcome of wars and whether to go into battle. But in their words and acts as the emissaries of Yahweh, they appointed and deposed kings—so Samuel, Ahijah, Elijah, and Elisha, for example, as well as the royal oracles in the book of Isaiah, and the postexilic oracles and visions of Haggai and Zechariah. Amos's confrontation with Amaziah, in which the chief priest attempted to ban the prophet from the land, arose out of the priest's reaction to the prophet's announcement that the king, Jeroboam II, would die by the will of the deity. Amaziah properly saw the political dynamite in such preaching and sought to stop it quickly. His accusation of "conspiracy" against Amos, whether accurate or not, reflects something of the political involvements of the prophets. As agents of the divine rule, they also called kings to account for their failure to carry out righteousness and justice in the community they ruled—as in Nathan's judgment speech against David for his acts of adultery and murder (1 Samuel 12), Elijah's condemnation of Ahab and Jezebel for the judicial murder of Naboth (1 Kings 21), and Jeremiah's condemnation of Jehoiakim for his unjust exploitation of his people for the sake of his extravagant style of life (Jer 22:13-19). Prophetic oracles were directed toward kings about their participation in military alliances and how they should respond to the threats of hostile neighbors (Isaiah, for example). In Israel, such political matters were always ultimately theological, reflecting in the prophet's judgment the degree of faithfulness and trust in Yahweh on the part of king and court.

At least by the eighth century, prophetic oracles came to be directed against *various segments of society* or against the *society as a whole*. From Amos to Isaiah, from Micah to Jeremiah and Ezekiel, the words of the prophets identified particular groups—leaders such as elders, priests, and other prophets, women, upper class elements of society, landholders, and the like—as the ones against whom words of future judgment were directed. In specific instances, the prophet moved to a center of the community and spoke to the larger whole, Elijah at Mount Carmel, Amos at Bethel, Jeremiah at the Temple in Jerusalem. With the data at hand, this move to a kind of popular prophecy, which one scholar has associated with developments in Assyrian statecraft, cannot be claimed to be unique in Near Eastern prophecy, but its dominance in biblical prophecy represents a development not attested elsewhere.[18] The prophet came to speak not simply as a messenger from the deity to the king but as an emissary of the heavenly assembly to the covenant people who were in league with the deity Yahweh. As many have pointed out, prophecy in Israel can hardly be understood apart from a long tradition that was drawn upon constantly, a tradition reaching back to the formation of Israel, assuming their creation as a people belonging to the deity Yahweh, bound together and to him in fidelity, and responsible for manifesting a particular mode of existence in the world. The character of the prophetic word to the larger society varied depending upon the circumstances. That it was largely in the form of judgment speech in the prophetic writings from the preexilic period has been established. We have also noted that oracles of salvation played a significant role in the proclamation of many of the prophetic groups and later in the "literary" prophecy of Second Isaiah.

As to the social situation and the social issues that evoked the prophets' oracles, that has been well-analyzed in various studies. The prophetic insistence on justice and righteousness was rooted in the covenant traditions of Yahwism and addressed a society that, according to those traditions and standards, was in crisis, although the crisis was hardly self-evident to many within the community of Israel. Indeed, there were plenty of signs of social well-being and prosperity in ninth- and eighth-century Israel and in eighth-

and seventh-century Judah. The prophets perceived the reality differently and so called for a measure of justice in society that was largely absent. One interpreter has aptly characterized the social situation in which prophetic judgment speeches were announced:

> The problem was the ownership of land and the benefits and rights that went with it in Israelite society. Land was being accumulated in estates and used as a basis for status and to generate surplus wealth. Those who lost their land were deprived of status and material support. They had to become slaves or wage laborers to live. The leverage employed was the administrative apparatus of the monarchy and of the courts, where all social conflict in Israel was settled. The rights of the widow, the fatherless, and the weak to protection against the economic process were widely ignored. The result was a growing differentiation between rich and poor.[19]

The issue of justice was not the only concern of the prophets about what was happening in society. The proper worship of the Lord of Israel was a central feature of their proclamation, and indeed it often overlapped with the call for justice and the announcement of judgment against the society that grew by economic oppression. The relation of the prophets, individuals and groups, to *the cult*—both in terms of attitude and social location remains an issue of continuing debate. There are many intimations of varying cultic involvements on the part of prophets. The *nĕbi'îm,* may have been particularly associated with cultic centers and under some supervision of priestly types, such as Amaziah at Bethel (Amos 7:10-17; cf. Jer 29:26). In various texts, they are to be found at cultic sites, such as Bethel (2 Kgs 2:3) and Gilgal (2 Kgs 4:38). Some would see these groups as largely cultic functionaries. Whether or not such a depiction is too simple, as with some of the individual prophets, formal links to the temple or cultic complex and participation in cultic acts belonged to prophetic activity.[20] Samuel and Elijah are both depicted engaging in sacrifice (along with the *nĕbi'îm,* of Baal in 1 Kings 18). Other prophets, such as Isaiah, Jeremiah, and Ezekiel seem to have had links to the temple and its cult.[21]

The stance of the "classical" prophets vis-à-vis the practices of the cult was not uniform. Their condemnation of cultic activity is fairly frequent and indeed thematic in the prophetic oracles attributed to such prophets as Amos, Isaiah, and Jeremiah. While Amos may go far, however, in denouncing the cult altogether (e.g., Amos 5:25), the problem seems to have been less a dissociation from and rejection of practices of worship than it was an insistence upon social practices that were as consistent with the covenant requirements as were the practices of worship. The prophetic indictments were less against cult per se than they were against the apparent assumption

106

that the relation to Yahweh was so centered in the activities of worship that one could freely betray the requirements for righteousness and justice as long as proper worship was carried out in the sanctuary. Time and again, prophets denounced that assumption and placed the social sphere as prominently to the fore as the sanctuary as the locus of right relation to Yahweh.

The Future of Prophecy

If prophecy is about the future, it is also the case that the future will involve considerable discussion and reassessment of prophecy. In the light of where we are at the present in our understanding of prophecy, some of the issues that belong to that discussion include the following:

(1) One is the relation of prophetic oracles to the actual prophetic activity of identifiable prophets. We are well aware of many particular prophets in ancient Israel, and we also have a great many prophetic oracles—in prophetic books and in narrative contexts. A true understanding of prophecy is more likely if one can make many connections between the prophets whose actions are described and the oracles that are ascribed to them. But there is much uncertainty about those connections (see Carroll, Auld, etc.). Indeed, even the stories of the prophets may be largely the work of later redactors. So Carroll speaks of the prophets being invented. Ability to speak with detail about particular prophetic deeds and words is a major point of departure for drawing conclusions about the nature and character of prophecy generally. To the degree that we are forced to disconnect particular acts and particular oracles from prophets whose identities are preserved in Scripture, the more uncertain becomes the characterization of the prophetic role and function.

Even if the picture now preserved is a later one, not to be directly ascribed to particular known prophetic figures, we will still learn something of how prophets were perceived or remembered as acting and what people thought prophets did and said. That is, the "invented" picture may still have much to do phenomenologically with the actuality of prophecy, even if it is not a historical reflection of the work and words of a particular prophet.[22]

(2) The first part of this essay has sought to press the importance of the ancient Near Eastern world of prophecy and mediation for understanding Old Testament prophecy. If scholarship should take us further from the biblical prophets themselves and their work [see (1) above], this larger context remains a fruitful avenue for continued efforts to comprehend the phenomenon of prophecy. Cross-cultural studies will continue to provide comparative data for studying biblical prophecy, but the geographical, historical, and linguistic contexts of the ancient Near East are closer to what

we encounter in ancient Israel. Such comparative study will incorporate the analysis of other forms of mediation that existed alongside prophecy in Israel as well as elsewhere.

(3) The tension between idealistic and functional or materialistic interpretations of Israelite prophecy, between essentially theological understandings of prophecy and those that root prophecy thoroughly in social contexts, is by no means settled, nor will it necessarily be resolved in the future. Indeed it is reflected within the pages of this essay and the perspective of this author. To what extent is the prophet a fundamentally theological vocation, with an identity and ascribed role that has to be understood and characterized with reference to religious activity and a transcendent source (even if one regards that source as mediated by hallucinations, visions, and the like)? To what extent is the definition of the prophet as a messenger of *Yahweh* the primary datum for understanding prophecy, in at least its central character? Or must one understand prophecy primarily in relation to interests and groups that it represents within the human society, the social and economic forces at work in the community, the power struggles reflected in political, religious, and economic life? The divine message would then be understood essentially as a reflection of those interests and values, which are themselves shaped by the location and role of the prophet. The degree to which the prophet is intimately a part of the court and the religious establishment or peripheral to its life and associated with minority elements, oppressed groups, parties in disfavor with the royal establishment, and the like would be decisive for his message.

These two positions, described here in much too simple a form, do not have to be in mortal combat, but the future discussion will probably weight the general understanding of prophecy more in one direction than the other, drawing primary attention to the presumed transcendent source of the prophet's message or to the presumed social context of the prophet's activity. One interpreter, with reference to the issue of prophetic conflict, has sought to characterize the kind of model that is needed to draw these perspectives into a whole:

> What is required is a model of prophecy in which the prophet interacts with both God and people and in which the people have their own relationship with God apart from the prophetic channel of communication. Both prophet and people are, therefore, active in the coming into being of the divine word. The function of the prophet is to realize and to articulate the will of God in the context of his or her (charismatic) relationship with a particular group.[23]

(4) Developments in biblical and theological scholarship generally suggest that insufficient attention has been given to the role of women in

prophecy. While the data, as we have noted, are not extensive, there are several indications of groups of women prophets and individual named or unnamed female prophets. Comparative materials, as we have noted, reinforce the picture of prophecy as a female as well as male activity. The role of women in Israelite religion is sufficiently particular and distinctive that the study of prophecy should not overlook or subsume the women prophets in its general focus on prophecy as a largely male phenomenon. The particular social location of women and how that may have affected the function and activities of female prophets needs some sustained scholarly attention.[24] Both the study of prophecy and feminist interpretation of biblical literature will probably give a closer look in the future to the women prophets of ancient Israel.

(5) The rhetoric and speech of the prophets remain a focus of attention, not simply because rhetorical criticism and the study of stylistics are in vogue today but because the authority and effectiveness of the prophet in society was affected by the skill and power with which he or she communicated. So also the study of prophetic rhetoric may have much to tell us about *what* the prophets were trying to say. A signal example of this is the work of Vanlier Hunter on the meaning and function of the exhortations in several of the preexilic prophets. See, for example, his comment:

> The form critical observation that every exhortation but one is related integrally to a judgment speech leads to the conclusion that the primary function of the exhortations is to render service to the prophetic task of reproaching and accusing.[25]

Here the form-critical work that has been so fundamental to the modern study of prophecy continues with particular attention to the modes of expression, the intentions of the prophetic proclamation, and the effects of prophetic speech on the audience.[26]

Notes

1. The term "oracular speaker" is a more general and neutral one that Robert Wilson adopts from Herbert Huffmon with particular reference to the Mari "prophets," but it may be used broadly to speak of the varieties of prophetic-type figures in the ancient Near East. See R. R. Wilson, *Prophecy and Society in Ancient Israel* (Philadelphia: Fortress, 1980) 99, n. 27.

2. 1 Kgs 18:19 refers to "prophets of Asherah," but this reference is suspect for several reasons. In this context, to assume its accuracy would simply reinforce the point being made.

3. A concise survey of this material is conveniently and capably presented by Herbert Huffmon in the essay "Prophecy (ANE)" in *The ABD*, 5:477-82. Among the more recent and important studies of this material are Robert Gordon, "From Mari to Moses: Prophecy at Mari and in Ancient Israel," *Of Prophets' Visions and the Wisdom of Sages: Essays in Honour of R. Norman Whybray on His Seventieth Birthday*, eds. Heather A. McKay and David J.A. Clines. JSOTSup 162 (Sheffield: JSOT, 1993) 63-79; Abraham Malamat, "A Forerunner of Biblical Prophecy: The

Mari Documents," in *Ancient Israelite Religion: Essays in Honor of Frank Moore Cross*, eds. P. D. Miller, P. D. Hanson, and S. D. McBride (Philadelphia: Fortress, 1987) 33-52; S. B. Parker, "Official Attitudes toward Prophecy at Mari and in Israel," *VT* 43 (1993) 50-68; and M. Weippert, "Aspekte israelitischer Prophetie im Lichte verwandter Erscheinungen des Alten Orients," in *Ad bene et fideliter seminandum: Festgabe für Karlheinz Deller zum 21 Februar 1987*, ed. G. Mauer and U. Magen (Neukirchen-Vluyn: Neukirchener Verlag, 1988) 287-319. All of these articles contain extensive further bibliography on prophetic activities in the ancient Near East. The presence of prophecy in Egypt as a phenomenon comparable to Israelite prophecy is less certain.

4. For a convenient listing of these designations, see Huffmon, "Prophecy (ANE), 478-79. None of the biblical terms is standard elsewhere in the Near East, as far as available evidence indicates. The term *nābî'* may be present in the texts from Emar and is now found as a title at Mari in a plural form referring to a group of *nabû*, though we are told nothing about their functions. The translation "man of God" is an approximate translation for a Hittite term referring to one who receives a divine communication. *Hōzeh,* "seer" has its parallels as a designation for Balaam in the Deir Alla Balaam text as well as in the Zakkur inscription in the plural for those who bring a divine word of assurance of victory to the king.

5. On the shift from court prophecy (to the king) to popular prophecy (to the people) see J.S. Holladay, Jr., "Assyrian Statecraft and the Prophets of Israel," in *Prophecy in Israel,* ed. D. L. Petersen (Philadelphia: Fortress, 1987) 122-43.

6. M. Weippert, "Aspekte israelitischer Prophetie," 312-13; idem, "Assyrische Prophetien der Zeit Asarhaddons and Assurbanipals," in *Assyrian Royal Inscriptions: New Horizons in Literary, Ideological and Historical Analysis,* ed. F. M. Fales (Rome: l'Oriente, 1981), 108-11.

7. See Claus Westermann, *Basic Forms of Prophetic Speech* (Philadelphia: Westminster, 1967; reprinted, 1991).

8. One recalls in this connection the argument of Ernst Würthwein that Amos moved from being a prophet who gave typical oracles of salvation, as reflected in the oracles against the nations in the first two chapters, to being a prophet of judgment, as reflected in the judgment speeches against Israel that make up much of the rest of the book. See E. Würthwein, "Amos-Studien," *ZAW* 62 (1949-50) 10-52.

9. For example, Gordon, "From Mari to Moses," 77-78.

10. For particular attention to the prophets as either central or peripheral intermediaries in Israelite society—as well as elsewhere—see especially R. R. Wilson, *Prophecy and Society in Ancient Israel,* where anthropological data are drawn upon to define and characterize the possible relationships to the larger society. At one point, he notes the difficulty of isolating particular *psychological* characteristics of intermediaries, Wilson's primary term for the prophets, while arguing that it is much clearer what *social* characteristics intermediaries shared (*Prophecy,* 46).

11. For representative articulations of this understanding, see Westermann, *Basic Forms of Prophetic Speech*; J. F. Ross, "The Prophet as Yahweh's Messenger," in *Prophecy in Israel,* ed. D. L. Petersen (Philadelphia: Fortress, 1987) 112-21; and Holladay, "Assyrian Statecraft."

12. For the connections of Mari prophecy and the Balaam text from Deir Alla to the divine council, see Gordon, "From Mari to Moses," 71-75.

13. H. Gunkel, "The Prophets as Writers and Poets," *Prophecy in Israel* 25.

14. In Gunkel, such attention to the poetic character of prophetic speech was not separated from an understanding of their role and vocation as Yahweh's messenger. See "The Prophets as Writers and Poets," 49.

15. See the symposium of articles, and the literature cited there, in *JSOT* 27 (1983) 3-44: A. Graeme Auld, "Prophets Through the Looking Glass: Between Writings and Moses," 3-23; Robert Carroll, "Poets Not Prophets," 25-31; H. G. M. Williamson, "A Response to A. G. Auld," 33-39; and A. G. Auld, "Prophets Through the Looking Glass: A Response," 41-44. Cf. Robert P. Carroll, "Prophecy and Society," in *The World of Ancient Israel,* ed. R. E. Clements (Cambridge, Mass.: Cambridge University Press, 1989) 203-25. For a critical response to the work of Auld and Carroll, see Thomas W. Overholt, "Prophecy in History: The Social Reality of Intermediation," *JSOT* 48 (1990) 3-29, and the appreciative but ultimately critical essay of Hans M. Barstad, "No Prophets? Recent Developments in Biblical Prophetic Research and Ancient Near Eastern Prophecy," *JSOT* 57 (1993) 39-60.

16. So A.G. Auld, "Word of God and Word of Man: Prophets and Canon," in *Ascribe to the Lord: Biblical and Other Studies in Memory of Peter C. Craigie*, eds. L. Eslinger and G. Taylor, JSOTSup 67 (Sheffield: JSOT, 1988) 246-50.

17. So R. Carroll, "Poets Not Prophets," 26-27. Carroll recognizes approvingly the connections between this perspective and the earlier work of Max Weber on the nature of prophecy (See M. Weber, *Ancient Judaism* [Glencoe, Ill.: The Free Press, 1952]).

18. So Holladay, "Assyrian Statecraft and the Prophets of Israel."

19. James L. Mays, "Justice: Perspectives from the Prophetic Tradition," in *Prophecy in Israel* 148.

20. The several texts that associate priests and prophets in the same breath have been seen as indicating the cultic location of the prophetic groups, e.g., Isa 28:7; Jer 4:9; 6:13; 14:18; 18:18; Mic 3:11; Zech 7:3. Some of these texts seem to point in that direction more than others (e.g., Zech 7:3), and the situation may have changed over a period of time. At several points, Chronicles indicates that prophecy became a part of the second temple worship in the form of the Levitical singers (1 Chr 25:1-8; 2 Chr 20:14; 29:25; 35:15). The association of prophecy with music is indicated for a much earlier time also (1 Sam. 10:5).

21. See the summary statement of Lester Grabbe:

> Isaiah seems to have functioned in conjunction with the temple and monarchy at least part of his life (or so the tradition: Isa 6–7; cf. 2 Kgs 19:20–20:19). Jeremiah was of a priestly family and spent much of his career in close association with the temple, even when some (but not all) of the temple personnel opposed him. Ezekiel was also a priest (Ezek 1:3). Several of the written prophets have been widely accepted as cult prophets (Nahum, Zechariah, Haggai, perhaps Joel and Habakkuk).

"Prophets, Priests, Diviners and Sages in Ancient Israel," in *Of Prophets' Visions and the Wisdom of Sages*, 55.

22. Cf. Hans M. Barstad, "No Prophets? Recent Developments in Biblical Prophecy Research and Ancient Near Eastern Prophecy," *JSOT* 57 (1993) 39-60.

23. A. D. H. Mayes, "Prophecy and Society in Israel," in *Of Prophets' Visions and the Wisdom of Sages*, 39-40.

24. Note, for example, that the only mention of Isaiah's wife as a prophet is in regard to Isaiah having intercourse with her to beget a son who will bear a symbolic "prophetic" name (Isa 8:3). Also, Huldah, a prophet whose significance in the Josianic reform is clear from 2 Kgs 22:14-20, is identified at length by her husband and his lineage.

25. A. Vanlier Hunter, *Seek the Lord! A Study of the Meaning and Function of the Exhortations in Amos, Hosea, Isaiah, Micah, and Zephaniah* (Baltimore: St. Mary's Seminary and University, 1982) 277.

26. A further example of the sort of stylistic and rhetorical work that may lie ahead can be found in the author's stylistic and theological study of the way in which the prophets correlated sin and punishment, an analysis that has significant implications for the prophetic understanding of retribution and judgment. See P. D. Miller, *Sin and Judgment in the Prophets*. SBLMS 27 (Chico, Calif.: Scholars Press, 1982).

Selected Bibliography

Blenkinsopp, Joseph. *A History of Prophecy in Israel: From the Settlement in the Land to the Hellenistic Period*. Philadelphia: Westminster, 1983.

Brueggemann, Walter. *The Prophetic Imagination*. Philadelphia: Fortress, 1978.

Carroll, Robert P. "Prophecy and Society." In *The World of Ancient Israel*. Edited by R. E. Clements. Cambridge, Mass.: Cambridge University Press, 1989, 203-25.

Culley, R. C., and T. W. Overholt, eds. *Anthropological Perspectives on Old Testament Prophecy. Semeia* 21. Chico, Calif.: Scholars Press, 1982.

Huffmon, Herbert B. "The Origins of Prophecy." In *Magnalia Dei: The Mighty Acts of God.* Edited by Frank M. Cross, Werner E. Lemke, and Patrick D. Miller, Jr., Garden City, N.Y.: Doubleday, 1976, 171-86.

Huffmon, Herbert B., John J. Schmitt, John Barton, and M. Eugene Boring "Prophecy." In vol. 5 of *The ABD.* New York: Doubleday, 1992, 477-501.

Kselman, John S. "The Social World of the Prophets: A Review Article." *ReSRev* 11 (1985) 120-29.

Mays, James L., and Paul J. Achtemeier, eds. *Interpreting the Prophets.* Philadelphia: Westminster, 1987.

McKay, Heather, and D. J. A. Clines, eds. *Of Prophets' Visions and the Wisdom of Sages: Essays in Honour of R. Norman Whybray on His Seventieth Birthday.* JSOTSup162. Sheffield: JSOT, 1993.

Petersen, David L., ed. *Prophecy in Israel.* Philadelphia: Fortress, 1987.

Tucker, Gene M. "Prophecy and the Prophetic Literature." *The Hebrew Bible and Its Modern Interpreters.* Edited by Douglas A. Knight and Gene M. Tucker. Chico, Calif.: Scholars Press, 1985, 325-68.

Wilson, Robert R. *Prophecy and Society in Ancient Israel.* Philadelphia: Fortress, 1980.

Chapter 7
FORMATION AND FORM IN PROPHETIC LITERATURE

Marvin A. Sweeney

Principles for Interpreting Prophetic Literature

For most of the twentieth century, form-critical study of the prophetic literature has proceeded on the basis of the methodological guidelines laid down by Hermann Gunkel. Gunkel argues that the prophets were primarily speakers, not writers; consequently, research on the prophetic writings must focus on the typical oral speech forms (*Gattungen,* "genres") employed by the prophets and the social settings (*Sitz im Leben,* "settings in life") in which these speech forms functioned. Because he views the Israelites and Judean prophets as primitive shamanistic figures, who generally blurted out their messages in a state of uncontrolled ecstatic frenzy, Gunkel maintains that they were incapable of writing the long, well-reasoned compositions that are characteristic of modern thinkers. He therefore argues that the basic forms of prophetic discourse are short, self-contained speech units, formulated according to standardized speech patterns, that are easily memorized, recorded, and gathered by the prophet's followers into much larger collections of the prophet's sayings. The exegete's goal in interpreting the prophetic books is to identify and isolate these short speech units in order to reconstruct the original message of the prophet.

The short prophetic speech unit is therefore the primary object of exegesis in most form-critical research on the prophetic literature during the twentieth century. In such a conception, the prophetic book therefore stands as an obstacle to the interpreter. According to early form critics, its function is archival in that it is designed to record and preserve the sayings of the prophet. The later writers and editors who recorded and arranged the prophetic literature added a great deal of additional material to the original prophetic speeches, either deliberately or inadvertently, in order to clarify or modify their meanings. In many cases, early form critics maintain that later writers misunderstood the meanings of the original prophetic speeches and thereby added material that distorts the prophets' meanings. In other cases, they maintain that copyists erred in transcribing the original speeches because they did not understand them in the first place.

Consequently, the first task of the interpreter according to the early form critics is to identify and strip away the extraneous materials added by later writers and to correct their errors. Only after this step is completed can the interpretation of the true prophetic message begin. The material deemed to be added by later editors is generally given very little attention in early form-critical studies because exegetes believe that it has very little to do with the original prophetic speakers. Redaction criticism, the study of the editorial formation of biblical literature, is deemed to have little theological or interpretative significance. It therefore becomes a sort of exegetical afterthought in the minds of many early form critics, because it deals primarily with the extraneous material that was added by later writers to the original prophetic speeches. Once redactional material has been identified and removed, it can be safely discarded and ignored.

Although this has been the dominant paradigm for the form-critical study of prophetic literature throughout the twentieth century, the years since World War II have seen major changes in the study of history and literature that have major implications for form- and redaction-critical methodology in general and for the interpretation of the prophetic books in particular. Much of the early form-critical methodological discussion presupposes the romanticist conceptions of history and literature that were prevalent throughout the late-nineteenth and early-twentieth centuries. Such conceptions prompt scholars to focus almost exclusively on the roles played by the most visible or dominant elements of human culture, such as the great personalities or individual leaders who left their marks on the major events of world history and wrote the important works of literature. With regard to the study of prophetic literature, such conceptions motivate interest in understanding the personalities and ideas of the individual prophets whose words were recorded in the prophetic literature.

Morgan and Barton relate how the experience of the twentieth century, including two World Wars, the Cold War, the rise of social movements, and the emerging importance of many previously ignored cultures and nations throughout the world, demonstrates the need to examine the social dimensions of human history and literature. A focus on great personalities and leaders does not prepare scholars to understand the social forces that lead both to conflict and the establishment of new nations during the course of the twentieth century. Likewise, a focus on individual authors does not prepare scholars for the role that cultural perspectives, values, and ideologies play in the composition of literary works and the means by which they influence the presentation of their subjects. Consequently, the twentieth century has seen a rise in interest in both the social sciences and literary theory.

These interests have a tremendous impact on the study of prophetic literature in that they focus attention on the literary character and social dimensions of prophetic books. Therefore, they motivate a reconceptualization of the role of redaction criticism in relation to the form-critical study of the prophetic books. Because redaction criticism is the study of the editorial formation of biblical literature it is necessarily a literary discipline, but like form criticism, it also requires consideration of the social dimension of the formation of biblical literature. Clements shows how scholars now recognize that redactors are not just literary technicians or archival collectors lacking in literary or ideological agendas. Rather, redactors act as authors who compose prophetic books according to their own purposes or theological agendas. Redactors choose the earlier materials included in the book, add their own writings or modifications as they deem fit to suit their purposes, and arrange the entire composition into its present form. Because the final forms of the biblical books come to us from the hands of their respective redactors, they reflect the perspectives, ideologies, interpretations, and concerns of the redactors in relation to their own later historical settings. Therefore, the redactors of the final form of a prophetic book determine the presentation of the prophet's words and shape that presentation to fit their understanding of the prophet and the prophet's message. In this manner, redactors employ prophetic writings to address concerns of their own times.

Knierim shows how this has important implications for establishing exegetical procedure in the interpretation of prophetic texts. As a result, scholars can no longer consider the short, self-contained prophetic speech to be the primary basis for the interpretation of prophetic literature. Exegesis can no longer begin with the literary dissection of a prophetic book; this only produces an artificial text. Instead, interpreters must begin with the largest literary unit available, that is, the final form of the prophetic book as a whole, in order to understand the significance of the smaller texts that constitute the book; after all, the complete prophetic book is the only form in which the prophetic texts are available. This means that interpreters must consider not only the *Sitz im Leben* or "setting in life" of prophetic texts, but the *Sitz im Literatur* or "literary setting" as well.

Essentially, redaction critical questions must be addressed at the outset in that the final form of the prophetic book as a whole is the only means to understand the outlook and purposes of the redactors as revealed in the literary presentation of the prophet. This requires the interpreter to establish several dimensions of the prophetic book. The structure or arrangement of the book reveals the final redactor's overall perspectives and conceptualization of the prophet's message in that the sequence of texts within the final form of the book points to those aspects of the prophetic message that the redactor wishes to emphasize. The overall genre of the book is likewise important in that the typical linguistic or rhetorical forms employed in the book point to the purpose of the composition. An archival text designed merely to preserve the prophet's words is very different from an exhortational text that employs the prophet's words as a means to motivate or persuade people to adopt a specific course of action or set of beliefs. The historical, social, and literary setting of the text is essential to its interpretation. For example, an eighth-century setting for the book of Isaiah reveals a prophet who interpreted the significance of the Assyrian invasions for the future of Israel and Judah, but it does not account for the addition of later materials in chapters 40–66 and elsewhere throughout the book. In contrast, a fifth-century setting for the book of Isaiah reveals a hermeneutical perspective that demonstrates the theological dynamism of the prophetic tradition: Isaiah ben Amoz emerges as a prophet who is relevant to later times as well, in that his statements made during the eighth century were believed to be addressed to the situation of postexilic Judaism and motivated Jews to rebuild Jerusalem and Judah during this period. All of these factors are relevant to establishing the intention of the redactors in composing the final form of the prophetic book.

Once the interpreter has established the interpretation of the final form of the prophetic book according to its structure, genre, setting, and intention, she or he may then proceed to determine earlier layers that might appear within the composition. In general, this may be accomplished by employing the standard tools of literary-critical exegesis, such as inconsistencies in forms of expression, clearly anachronistic references, changes in perspective, or other factors that point to the presence of more than one hand in the composition of a text. But the interpreter must always keep Barton's warnings concerning the "disappearing redactor" firmly in mind. At times, the redactor may do his or her work so well that it is very difficult or even impossible to detect the presence of more than one hand in a prophetic composition. Furthermore, the interpreter cannot assume the presence of an earlier composition behind the final form of the text. In all cases, the presence of earlier text forms must be demonstrated, but at times, it may be impossible to do so.

Finally, the interpreter may wish to examine the function of the prophetic book in relation to settings following the time of its final composition. For example, the book of Zephaniah appears to have been composed in relation to the seventh-century reform program of King Josiah of Judah, but its presentation of a scenario of worldwide judgment and restoration of Jerusalem certainly is relevant to the postexilic Jewish community that attempted to restore Jerusalem and Judah during the fifth-third centuries when conflict racked and eventually toppled the Persian empire. Although this requires an examination of the history of exegesis, it demonstrates the continuing vitality of prophetic tradition that is evident in the redactional reinterpretation of the original prophetic compositions.

Interpreting Amos

The principles outlined above are best illustrated when they are applied to the interpretation of a specific prophetic book. The book of Amos provides an ideal basis for such an illustration. It is generally regarded as one of the earliest examples of a prophetic book since the prophet is dated to the middle of the eighth century BCE, a period earlier than that of any of the other writing prophets. Furthermore, the presence of a narrative formulated in a third-person objective reporting style in Amos 7:10-17 and the similarly formulated superscription in Amos 1:1 demonstrate that someone other than the prophet assembled the book into its present form. Finally, its relatively small size in relation to larger books such as Isaiah, Jeremiah, or Ezekiel, makes it possible to discuss the form and formation of a prophetic book within the limits of the present essay.

Past interpretation of Amos tends to place greater importance on reconstructing a portrayal of the man and his message rather than understanding the literary character of the book and its function in periods after the lifetime of the prophet. To be sure, scholars address the literary formation of the book; both Wolff and Mays identify various stages of redaction subsequent to the original words of the prophet. But they do so primarily in order to eliminate later material and to understand the prophet Amos in relation to the eighth-century context of his life and activities. The result is a portrayal of Amos as a Judean herdsman and agriculturalist who received a call from YHWH to speak as a prophet against the Northern Kingdom of Israel in the middle of the eighth century BCE. He speaks at the height of the power of the kingdom during the reign of King Jeroboam II (786-742 BCE), and pays particular attention to issues of social justice in that the poor continue to suffer greatly despite the wealth of the kingdom. He is portrayed as an opponent of both the monarchy and the cultic establishment of the Temple at Beth-El, which are seen to be the primary beneficiaries of the social abuses described in the book. Consequently, he announces the coming destruction of Israel, the monarchy, and the Temple as a punishment brought about by YHWH for mistreatment of the poor and violation of the covenant between

God and the people. Of course, the agent of divine punishment must be the Assyrian empire, which destroyed the Northern Kingdom in the course of several campaigns during the years 735-721 BCE, presumably after the life-time of the prophet. Although debated, elements of the text that call for the repentance of the people (Amos 5:6) and the restoration of the Davidic monarchy (Amos 9:11-15) are frequently regarded as later additions that do not reflect the message of the prophet. The book of Amos was preserved because his message of judgment against Israel was taken to be a paradigm for the later judgment against Judah and its destruction by the Babylonian empire in the sixth century BCE.

A consideration of the literary formation and form of the book of Amos, including consideration of its structure, genre, setting, and intention, sheds considerable light on the function of the book of Amos in periods sub-sequent to the prophet's lifetime. Furthermore, it has the potential to alter some aspects of the commonly accepted reconstruction of the prophet and his message.

The first step in interpreting the book of Amos as a whole is to define the major textual building blocks that constitute the structure of the book. Auld's survey of literary issues in Amos demonstrates that a number of proposals have already been put forward. But although there is considerable agreement in defining most of the major textual subunits of Amos, there is still wide disagreement as to how they function together within the book as a whole.

The first major subunit of the book of Amos is the superscription and motto that introduces the book in Amos 1:1-2. This text is defined by its third-person objective reporting style that identifies Amos as the author of the words found within the book in v. 1, and provides a statement in v. 2 that serves as a summary of his message. The superscription provides the reader with the details of Amos's profession (shepherd), hometown (Tekoa in Judah), the subject of his discourse (Israel), and the historical period in which he spoke (during the reigns of Kings Uzziah of Judah and Jeroboam ben Joash of Israel, two years before the earthquake). The motto provides a summary of the book's message that employs the metaphor of a roaring lion, the symbol of the tribe of Judah, to express YHWH's anger and power. It states that YHWH roars from Zion or Jerusalem, the capital of Judah and home of the royal House of David, and that the pastures of the shepherds and the top of Carmel, the rich fertile coastal hills of the Northern Kingdom of Israel, will mourn and wither. Superscriptions, particularly those that stand at the beginning of a book, always stand apart from and introduce the material that follows. In this case, the reader learns something of the historical circum-stances of Amos's activity, but she or he also learns that his message pertains to issues that divided the Northern Kingdom of Israel and the Southern Kingdom of Judah.

The second major subunit of the book of Amos is the oracles against the nations in Amos 1:3–2:16. This text is defined by the relatively consistent formulation of a series of oracles directed against various nations, including Damascus or Aram (1:3-5), Gaza or Philistia (1:6-8), Tyre or Phoenicia (1:9-10), Edom (1:11-12), Ammon (1:13-15), Moab (2:1-3), Judah (2:4-5), and finally Israel (2:6-16). Each is introduced with the so-called "messenger formula" *kōh 'āmar* YHWH, "thus says YHWH," which indicates that the prophet's role is to convey a message from YHWH, and many conclude with a YHWH speech formula, *'āmar* YHWH, "says YHWH," (1:5, 15; 2:3) or a variation (1:8; 2:16). Furthermore, each employs a graduated numerical formula to describe the transgressions of the nations that justify their punishment, "for three transgressions of XX, and for four, I will not revoke the punishment (lit., 'cause it to return')." Each oracle then specifies the crimes of the nation addressed and continues with a first-person singular statement by YHWH that specifies the punishment to be brought against the nation for its crimes.

Commentaries on Amos note the rhetorical impact of listing a series of similarly formulated oracles against foreign nations that lead ultimately to a lengthy climactic oracle against Israel at the end of the series. The audience is drawn into acceptance of the prophet's assertion that YHWH will punish the various nations that surround Israel, and it identifies with his supposed intention to condemn nations. But the climactic condemnation of Israel takes them by surprise and reveals the prophet's true intention to condemn Israel and the audience that is addressed. Although Judah is also condemned in the penultimate oracle of the series, the size and position of the oracle against Israel indicates that the primary purpose of this text is to charge the Northern Kingdom of Israel with wrongdoing and announce its punishment.

The third major subunit of the book of Amos is the sermon addressed to Israel (i.e., *běnê yiśrā 'ēl*, "the people [lit., 'sons'] of Israel") in Amos 3:1–4:13. The identification of this subunit is disputed, especially since it is composed of a number of disparate elements that seem to lack logical coherence. It is identified by the introductory "call to attention" in 3:1, "Hear this word that YHWH has spoken against you, O people of Israel, against the whole family that I brought up out of the land of Egypt," which is parallel to a similar call to attention that introduces the following sermon in Amos 5:1. Although a similar call directed to the women of Samaria (the capital of the Northern Kingdom) appears in Amos 4:1, Koch demonstrates that it does not introduce a new subunit, but simply a component of the present text that includes the women of Samaria in the overall purpose of Amos 3:1–4:13. That purpose appears to be to warn the kingdom of Israel that it will be punished for its wrongdoing and to establish that YHWH is the cause of the troubles that are beginning to afflict the nation. It begins by stating that YHWH's special relationship with the people established during the Exodus from Egypt is the reason that they are being singled out for punishment (3:2). The prophet makes the analogy that when trouble comes, YHWH is revealed through the prophets as the cause (3:3-8). The balance of the subunit outlines the troubles that will befall Israel (3:9–4:3). It emphasizes the people's wrong-doing at Beth-El and Gilgal, the locations of the cultic sites in the Northern Kingdom (4:4-11), including statements of YHWH's actions for and against the people that did not prompt them to return. Finally, it concludes with statements that YHWH will punish the people for their wrongdoing (4:12-13).

The fourth major subunit of the book of Amos is the sermon directed to Israel in Amos 5:1–6:14. It begins with an introductory call to attention, formulated similarly to the one that introduces the preceding subunit: "Hear this word that I take up over you in lamentation, O house of Israel (*bêt yiśrā'ēl*)." Like the previous subunit, this sermon is composed of formally disparate elements, but it is held together by thematic factors and its overall concern with the punishment of Israel. It also differs in that it includes exhortational elements in 5:4-6 and 5:14-15 that call upon the people to change their ways, seek YHWH and live, lest the punishment come upon them. This changes the character of the subunit considerably in that it demonstrates that its purpose is to convince the people to change their actions and thereby to avoid the punishment decreed by YHWH. It does this by mixing statements of Israel's coming demise with exhortational elements and a statement of YHWH's cosmic power in 5:2-17, followed by warnings, formulated as "woe" speeches in Amos 5:18–6:14, that further describe the upcoming punishment.

The fifth and final major subunit of the book of Amos is the vision reports in Amos 7:1–9:15. The subunit is defined by its relatively consistent first-person autobiographical formulation in which Amos is the speaker, and by its thematic focus on reporting the visions that apparently prompted him to speak as a prophet. It reports a total of five visions, but similarities in formulation and content indicate that they are grouped into two pairs followed by a concluding climactic vision.

The first two vision reports, concerning the locusts in Amos 7:1-3 and concerning fire in Amos 7:4-6, both indicate warnings of upcoming punishment against Israel. Both begin with the formula, *kōh hir'anî 'ădōnāy yhwh wĕhinnēh*, "This is what the Lord YHWH showed me, and behold. . . ." In each case, the prophet states that YHWH showed him a vision from the natural world that symbolizes God's decision to destroy Israel: the locusts that were devouring the land and the fire that consumed the water and the land. Both visions pertain to Amos's agricultural and pastoral background; locusts are a cyclical threat in the land of Israel and fires commonly break out in the fields during the dry summer season. Each time, the prophet objects to YHWH's intention by pleading with YHWH to rescind the judgment because Jacob (i.e., Israel) is too small to withstand it. In each case, YHWH relents.

The second two vision reports, concerning the plumb line in Amos 7:7-17 and the basket of summer fruit in Amos 8:1-14, assert that YHWH's punishment against Israel is inevitable. Like the first pair of visions, these begin with the formula *kōh hir'anî 'ǎdōnāy yhwh wěhinnēh* (8:1) or the variant *kōh hir'anî wěhinnēh* (7:7). Again, the visions presuppose Amos's experience as a pastoralist and agriculturalist and symbolize the upcoming punishment. The plumb line is a weighted cord used in the building of walls to insure that they are built straight so that they will not collapse. When Amos sees YHWH employing the plumb line, he concludes that YHWH has measured Israel and found that it is morally crooked. Like an improperly built wall, it will collapse under the weight of its own flaws. The basket of summer fruit is a common sight during the harvest season. This vision employs a play on the words *kělûb qāyiṣ*, "basket of summer fruit." When Amos sees it, he concludes that YHWH has shown him that the "end" (*qēṣ*) has come upon the people Israel. Both *qāyiṣ* and *qēṣ* employ the same basic Hebrew consonants, and thereby establish the pun that stands as the basis of the vision's message. In neither case does Amos protest YHWH's decision as before. These visions serve as the basis of a lengthy speech, like that of Amos 2:6-16, that condemns Israel for its wrongdoing.

The climactic vision concerns the destruction of the sanctuary at Beth-El and the reestablishment of the fallen House of David in Amos 9:1-15. Obviously, this constitutes the climax of both the vision reports and the book as a whole. It differs formally from the first four vision reports in that it does not begin with the customary formula stating that YHWH showed Amos a vision; it begins simply with the statement, "I saw the LORD standing beside the altar, and he said. . . ." The vision then relays YHWH's statements concerning the upcoming destruction of the altar at Beth-El and reiterates YHWH's power over the earth and intention to punish Israel (9:1-10). It concludes with a statement that in the future, once the punishment is complete, YHWH will restore the fallen booth of David, i.e., the Davidic dynasty, and the people of Israel to their land. Again, the vision of Beth-El's destruction may well have been motivated by Amos's own experience. The customary view of a working altar in ancient times would include the bloodied carcasses of the sacrificial animals and the fire and smoke of the sacrificial fires that consumed them. Clearly such an image could also represent an image of Israel's destruction in the mind of the prophet. More importantly, the altar at Beth-El symbolized the Northern Kingdom's rebellion against the Temple of YHWH in Jerusalem and the ruling House of David and provided the basis for the condemnation of the Northern Kingdom in Deuteronomistic History (cf. 1 Kings 12–13; 2 Kings 17). Essentially, the climactic vision of both this subunit and of the book as a whole calls for the destruction of the Beth-El sanctuary and the restoration of Davidic rule over the Northern Kingdom of Israel.

The second step in interpreting the book of Amos as a whole is to determine its genre. Certainly, the above discussion identifies a variety of generic elements that appear in the text, including the superscription and motto (Amos 1:1-2); the oracles against the nations that announce judgment against them (Amos 1:3–2:16); a sermon directed to Israel that likewise announces judgment by YHWH (Amos 3:1–4:13); an exhortational sermon directed to Israel that announces judgment but in a context that offers the possibility of life after repentance (Amos 5:1–6:14); and a series of vision reports that announce judgment against Israel in general and Beth-El in particular, together with the future restoration of the House of David (Amos 7:1–9:15). Elements of judgment clearly interact with the possibility of future restoration in the book, which indicates that the genre of the book of Amos cannot be limited only to an announcement of judgment. As the sequence of movement in the structure of the text and the generic elements identified above indicate, the book of Amos views the punishment of Israel and destruction of Beth-El as preparatory to the restoration of the House of David. Consequently, the exhortational elements identified in Amos 5:1–6:14 take on special importance in defining the genre of the book. The book of Amos as a whole must be considered as an exhortation in that it employs the scenario of judgment and destruction as a means to motivate its audience to accept a specific point of view and to pursue a course of action to realize that view. In this case, the book of Amos is designed to persuade its audience that the restoration of Davidic rule is the necessary outcome of the punishment of Israel and the destruction of the Beth-El altar. The exhortation to "Seek YHWH and live" (Amos 5:6; cf. 5:4-5, 14-15) must be understood in relation to the restoration of the royal House of David. In this context, seeking YHWH means to accept the restoration of Davidic rule.

The third step is to establish the historical and social setting of the book. As is the case with the discussion of the genre of the book, an examination of the individual subunits that constitute the book indicate more than one potential setting.

The superscription and motto (Amos 1:1-2) clearly stem from a period later than that of the prophet in that they identify the prophet and his historical context retrospectively, i.e., they are able to look back on the period of Amos and place him in relation to the reigns of two well-known monarchs, Jeroboam ben Joash of Israel (786–746 BCE) and Uzziah of Judah (782–742 BCE). Furthermore, the emphasis on YHWH's roaring from Zion indicates the potential for a Judean or Jerusalemite setting among circles that would have an interest in transmitting the message of Amos.

The oracles against the nations (Amos 1:3–2:16) appear to presuppose Assyrian invasion strategy for the conquest of the Syro-Israelite region. Scholars have debated the significance of the order of the nations without success, but the sequence appears to suggest a strategy of invasion from the north by an army that attacks Aram first and then proceeds immediately to Philistia in order to eliminate the possibility of aid from Egypt. Afterwards, the invader is free to mop up resistance in Phoenicia, the Trans-Jordan, and Israel itself. This general strategy was employed consistently by the Assyrians throughout their eighth-century campaigns and by Hazael of Aram in the ninth century (see 2 Kgs 12:17-18). Nevertheless, there is no evidence that the sequence of nations in Amos corresponds to any actual campaign of the Assyrians. Assyria did not invade Ammon, Edom, or Moab, although the Assyrians did impose tribute on these countries. Consequently, it appears to be a projection of a potentially successful strategy that was later employed in principle but not in its entirety. This is confirmed by another dimension of these oracles. All of the nations listed in Amos 1:3–2:16 were subject to the rule of Israel under King Jeroboam II, who is described as asserting his rule "from Lebohamath as far as the Sea of the Arabah" (2 Kgs 14:25). All of the nations listed here were opponents of Israel during the period of the collapse of the Omride dynasty that ruled Israel during 876–842 BCE and the rise of the dynasty of Jehu that ruled Israel in Amos's time, including Aram (2 Kgs 13:3-9; 10:32-33; 8:28-29), Philistia (2 Kgs 12:17; cf. 8:22), Phoenicia (2 Kgs 10:28), Edom (2 Kgs 8:20-24), Ammon (cf. 2 Kgs 10:32-33), Moab (cf. 2 Kgs 10:32-33), and Judah (2 Kgs 12:17-18; 13:10-13). By pointing to the punishment of these nations, the author identifies Jeroboam's successes as the means to carry out well-deserved punishment against Israel's various enemies, prior to turning the condemnation against Israel itself. The most likely author for such a sequence would be Amos himself.

The two sermons directed to Israel in Amos 3:1–4:13 and 5:1–6:14 appear generally to presuppose an eighth-century setting. In both cases, the message of judgment against Israel and Beth-El and the exhortation to seek YHWH appear to be consistent with what would be expected of Amos, an eighth-century Judean prophet who travels to Beth-El to condemn the Northern Kingdom (cf. Amos 7:10-17).

Finally, the autobiographical style of the vision reports in Amos 7:1–9:15 suggests the possibility that Amos is the author of this material, but the presence of a third-person narrative about the prophet's encounter with Amaziah at Beth-El demonstrates the presence of later redaction. The message would appear to be that of Amos, insofar as the prediction of Jeroboam's death by the sword never took place. But the narrative writing style and the interest in preserving a prediction of Israel's exile demonstrate an interest by a later writer in writing this account and including it in the present context. The concluding oracle promising the restoration of Davidic rule and the restoration of the land of Israel likewise points to redactional activity. Paul demonstrates that it is not impossible that Amos would support the restoration of Davidic rule over both Israel and Edom (n.d., see 2 Kgs 8:20-24, which reports Edom's revolt against Judah), but it is unlikely that Amos would envision a scenario that would depend so greatly on a Judean alliance with Assyria and an Assyrian assault on Israel.

A scenario that envisions the destruction of the Beth-El altar together with the restoration of Davidic rule over Israel and Edom would fit well in relation to the seventh-century program of religious reform and national restoration attempted by King Josiah of Judah (639–609 BCE). Josiah ruled Judah during the period of the collapse of the Assyrian empire that had destroyed Israel in the latter part of the eighth century BCE and dominated Judah and the surrounding region through the middle of the seventh century. The demise of the Assyrians enabled Josiah to pursue a program of religious reform and national restoration that was designed to reestablish the old Davidic-Solomonic empire that ruled the Syro-Israelite region during the tenth century BCE. The account of Josiah's reign in 2 Kings 22–23 concentrates primarily on the religious aspects of the reform, including the renovation of the Temple in Jerusalem, the discovery of a book of Torah (presumably Deuteronomy) on which Josiah's actions were based, the purging of pagan religious elements throughout the land, the reinstitution of the celebration of the Passover festival, and the closing of all worship sites other than the Jerusalem Temple, especially the altar at Beth-El. This last act is of particular importance in that it underscores the political dimension of Josiah's program to restore the territory of the former Northern Kingdom of Israel to Davidic rule. Beth-El had always served as the royal sanctuary of the Northern Kingdom and its existence was a challenge to both the Temple in Jerusalem and the royal House of David that sponsored the Jerusalem Temple (see 1 Kgs 12:25-33; cf. 1 Kgs 13, which states that Josiah will destroy the Beth-El altar). The destruction of this Temple by Josiah was an important statement of the reinstitution of Davidic rule over the north.

In such a scenario, the intention of the present form of the book of Amos would be to support Josiah's policies. Indeed, the structure of the book is designed to provide the reader with a progressively focused perspective, starting with a worldwide view of YHWH's activities among all the nations, to a focus on YHWH's punishment of Israel, and finally to an announcement of YHWH's destruction of the Beth-El altar and restoration of Davidic rule over Israel. This observation is buttressed by the observation of many scholars that the oracle against Judah in Amos 2:4-5, which is formulated somewhat differently from other oracles against the nations in Amos, may well be the product of a later hand. Certainly, the accusation that Judah had rejected YHWH's Torah would fit well with Josiah's program based on the premise of a return to YHWH's Torah that had previously been neglected.

In order to achieve their aim, the Josianic redactors of the book employed the statements of the prophet Amos made against Israel, Jeroboam II, and the Beth-El altar in the mid-eighth century BCE. From what is known of the prophet Amos, his statements would provide an ideal basis for presenting the restoration of the Josianic/Davidic rule over Israel as the logical outcome of the punishment suffered by the Northern Kingdom at the hands of the Assyrian empire. Amos's opposition to the northern monarchy and the royal sanctuary at Beth-El, together with his sense of prophetic commission, led him to announce the future exile of the Northern Kingdom, the death of its king, and the destruction of its main sanctuary. At the same time, the exhortations in chapter 5 seem to indicate that at some point, he held out the hope for some form of repentance or return. Amos may have conceived such repentance to be a return to Davidic rule; the uncertainties concerning the dating of Amos 9:11-15 certainly leave this open as a possibility. But regardless of whether Amos looked for a return of the Northern Kingdom to Davidic rule or not, clearly the Josianic redaction of the book of Amos saw such a return as the fulfillment of the prophecy of Amos.

These considerations demonstrate how the redactional formation of the book of Amos enable the prophet's message to speak to a period much later than his own. Even after the Josianic period, the message of destruction and restoration continued to speak when the postexilic Jewish community continued its efforts at restoration after the conclusion of the Babylonian exile.

Selected Bibliography

Auld, A. G. *Amos.* OT Guides. Sheffield: JSOT, 1986.

Barton, John. *Reading the Old Testament: Method in Biblical Study.* Philadelphia: Westminster, 1984.

Clements, Ronald E. "The Prophet and His Editors," in *The Bible in Three Dimensions.* Edited by D. J. A. Clines, et al. JSOTSup 87. Sheffield: JSOT, 1990, 203-20.

Gunkel, Hermann. "The Prophets as Writers and Poets." In *Prophecy in Israel.* Edited by David L. Petersen. Philadelphia: Fortress; London: SCM, 1987. 22-73.

Knierim, Rolf P. "Criticism of Literary Features, Form, Tradition, and Redaction." In *The Hebrew Bible and Its Modern Interpreters.* Edited by Douglas A. Knight and Gene M. Tucker. Phildelphia: Fortress; Chico, Calif.: Scholars Press, 1985. 123-65.

Koch, Klaus, et al. *Amos. Untersucht mit den Methoden einer strukturalen Formgeschichte.* AOAT 30. Kevelaer: Butzon and Bercker; Neukirchen-Vluyn: Neukirchener, 1976.

Mays, James L. *Amos: A Commentary.* OTL. London: SCM, 1969.

Morgan, Robert, with John Barton. *Biblical Interpretation.* Oxford Bible Series. Oxford: Oxford University Press, 1988.

Paul, Shalom. *Amos. Hermeneia.* Minneapolis: Fortress, 1991.

Sweeney, Marvin A. *Isaiah 1–39: With an Introduction to Prophetic Literature.* FOTL 16. Grand Rapids: Eerdmans, forthcoming, 1995.

Tucker, Gene M. *Form Criticism of the Old Testament.* Philadelphia: Fortress, 1971.

Wolff, Hans W. *Joel and Amos. Hermeneia.* Translated by Waldemar Janzen, S. Dean McBride, Jr., and Charles A. Muenchow. Philadelphia: Fortress, 1977.

Chapter 8
LITERARY PERSPECTIVES ON PROPHETIC LITERATURE

Katheryn Pfisterer Darr

ncient Israel's prophetic poetry presents readers with many of the Bible's crowning literary achievements. It also proffers conundrums to translators and interpreters. Reading texts in the original Hebrew, rather than in translation, alleviates some problems, but discloses others that translators smooth out. How can we competently construe Hebrew verse when its characteristics are nowhere explained, the meanings of many attested poetic terms (e.g., *maśkîl*) uncertain? What features of Hebrew poetry distinguish it from the prose that also appears in prophetic texts?

We should not be surprised that comprehending ancient prophetic poetry is an arduous, as well as gratifying, task. After all, these texts reflect ancient times, alien societies, distinctive literary conventions, and worldviews far removed from our own. Even setting these formidable obstacles aside, we recognize that this poetry, no less than much modern verse, demands labor for reward: poetry, after all, stretches both language and the imaginations of those reading or hearing it. Adele Berlin points to the important role readers play in construing the terse lines of Hebrew poetry:

> The lines, by virtue of their contiguity, are perceived as connected, while the exact relationship between them is left unspecified . . . such contiguity creates the impression of connectedness and forces the reader to "consider their relations for himself" and to "invent a variety of reasons to explain the relationship." (1985:6)

Can we, modern readers of ancient poetry, hope to understand its distinctive formal features, culturally determined figurative uses of language, e.g., metaphor and simile, as well as other, sophisticated signatures of the venerable poets' craft? We must try, for meaning inheres in the vehicles of prophetic utterance—words and the worlds they create. To revive an old cliché, the medium is the message. The ability to read a poem in its original language naturally enriches our experience of it. Consider, for example, the following verses:

(7a) For a brief moment I abandoned you,
(7b) but with great compassion I will gather you.
(8a) In overflowing wrath for a moment I hid my face from you,
(8aβ) but with everlasting love I will have compassion on you,
(8b) says YHWH, your Redeemer. (Isa 54:7-8)

These lines portray YHWH, Israel's God, as an estranged and even culpable husband entreating his wife, personified Zion, to believe that reconciliation is possible. Their poignancy transcends the limitations of translation. Moreover, English readers can recognize certain of the poem's features: vv. 7a and 8a on the one hand, and vv. 7b and 8aβ on the other, express a similar thought, while vv. 7a and 7b, like 8a and 8aβ, stand in stark contrast to each other. They cannot see, however, that alliteration intensifies the effect of the Hebrew phrase translated "overflowing wrath" (bĕšeṣep qeṣep) in v. 8a, or that other poems, e.g., Isa 57:3-13, are thick with polyvalent vocabulary and wordplay.

Language limitations notwithstanding, careful study of ancient prophetic poems, and of scholarly works devoted to their elucidation, recompenses all readers with a wealth of information, insight, and enhanced appreciation for Israel's prophetic literature. In this essay, we shall look back to some earlier literary critical work on the prophetic corpus, look over the contemporary scholarly scene, and look toward future literary approaches to prophetic literature.

Looking Back: "Remember These Words"

Many nineteenth-century biblical scholars regarded ancient Israel's prophets as the true pioneers of its faith. Breaking with earlier beliefs and cultic practices, they averred, these prophets/theologians championed an innovative religion built upon moral values and ethical ideals. Bernhard Duhm's *Die Theologie der Propheten* (1875), clearly influenced by nineteenth-century moral idealism, championed this view of the prophets as religious rebels.

Just seventeen years later, a fresh appraisal of significant issues concerning Israel's prophets and their literature appeared in Duhm's commentary on Isaiah (1892). On the one hand, his earlier emphasis upon the prophets as theologians was superseded by intense interest in those ecstatic experiences through which they had received their messages. On the other hand, he focused upon the prophets as poets.

The relationship between prophecy and poetry was already a subject of long-standing debate in Duhm's day. In his famous *Lectures on the Sacred Poetry of the Hebrews* (1815), Robert Lowth had asserted the poetic nature of prophetic utterance, identifying parallelism of various types (synonymous, antithetic, synthetic) as the principle feature of Hebrew verse. Primary among Duhm's contributions to this debate, however, was his investigation of metrical patterns of prophetic speech. Lowth's aforementioned lectures had addressed that topic as well, albeit somewhat obscurely. But Duhm was convinced that metrical analysis enabled him to distinguish between individual units in a prophetic text, to identify authentic prophetic utterances, and to distinguish them from subsequent redactional embellishments. The latter task was particularly essential since, to Duhm's mind, one could not interpret what a prophet meant without first knowing what that prophet had actually said.

Duhm's approach set the agenda for much ensuing scholarship. Indeed, his search for a prophet's own words continues to occupy many a critic, while his concomitant awareness that the prophetic literature attained final form only at the end of a complex literary process presaged the need for yet another critical approach to Israel's prophetic literature, redaction criticism. To be sure, his views on Hebrew meter have been both refined and vigorously challenged over the following century. Unlike Duhm, the majority of contemporary critics are reluctant to excise part of a poem on the basis of metrical considerations alone (see below). Moreover, both he and subsequent scholars too often overlooked the importance of redactional supplements. To adapt an account of sculpting attributed to the great Italian artist, Michelangelo, Duhm and others carved into a textual block until they reached the prophet's "skin" and then stopped. The emerging prophetic figure might look remarkably as they had anticipated, but littered around its base lay chunks and shards of discarded text. Contemporary redaction critics, by contrast, recognize that every textual shard contains information potentially vital to a thorough understanding of how earlier prophecies were later reoriented and reinterpreted by redactors in light of subsequent events, perspectives, and interpretive strategies.

Thus far, we have noted both Lowth's identification of parallelism as the principle feature of Hebrew verse, including prophetic poetry, and Duhm's emphasis upon metrical analysis as a tool for identifying "authentic" prophetic utterances and distinguishing them from later, ostensibly "spurious" additions. The contributions of yet another scholar, Hermann Gunkel (1862-1932), belong in our brief historical retrospect as well, for his "form-critical" method focused attention upon texts as literary types, or genres, with original settings in community life, characteristic features (beginnings, endings, patterns), and functions.

Gunkel also shared Duhm's interest in those ecstatic experiences by which God's words were revealed to the prophets. In his view, the earliest prophetic oracles consisted primarily of compact, future-oriented utterances—revealing, but also mysterious. Over time, however, the prophets—hoping to explain and justify God's imminent actions—began supplementing these terse oracles with additional elements, e.g., threats, reproaches, disputations. They drew from secular as well as religious literary reservoirs, adapting, e.g., drinking, mocking, and battle songs, in order to enthrall, convince, and convict their audiences.

Gunkel explored these conventional genres in ways that Duhm had not, isolating them from their larger literary contexts, identifying their characteristic constitutive parts, comparing them with other texts exhibiting identical or similar features, tracing their original settings in life, and describing the specific content and functions of the particular text at hand. Consider, for example, Isa 44:1-5, an oracle of salvation. Like many other such oracles, this unit begins with a declaration of YHWH's past dealings with Israel (vv. 1-2a); continues with promises of future intervention on its behalf (vv. 2b-3), introduced by the typical "fear not" formula (v. 2b); and describes the results of YHWH's intervention (vv. 4-5). (Not every oracle of salvation contains all of these elements, but they characterize the genre.) Originally, such oracles likely functioned in ritual situations where sufferers uttered laments, seeking assurances of divine healing and justification. Within its Deutero-Isaian context, however, this oracle functions to reassure the Babylonian exiles of YHWH's ability and desire to rescue them, restoring Israel to its appropriate place within God's unfolding, worldwide plan.

Gunkel's investigation of the literary forms utilized by Israel's prophets (and other biblical authors) have earned him the title "father of form criticism." As with Duhm, his method and the conclusions he drew from its application were but the beginning of a major scholarly movement with its attending challenges, changes, and growth. Form criticism has taught us much about ancient Israel's literature. True, for all its emphasis upon literary types and characteristic formulas, form criticism has often served largely historical ends. Indeed, we conclude this retrospective with the frank acknowledgement that early critical work on biblical prophetic literature was largely preoccupied with recovering history, that is, identifying the actual words of Israel's prophets against their earliest historical settings. More recently, reconstructing the redaction history of prophetic collections has taken its place alongside this primary concern. But recovering ancient Israel's *literary* history has played a crucial role in these endeavors. Moreover, some critics have brought to their historical-critical task exceptional literary skills and insights that enhance our appreciation of prophetic poetry *qua* poetry. Nevertheless, study of biblical prophetic literature, using the methods of current literary criticism as practiced in the study of poetry in English and other languages, is a recent addition to our analysis and interpretation.

Looking Around: "Inquire About Ancient Paths"

The introduction of new methods inevitably enriches a field of investigation. After all, our presuppositions and methods shape the questions we bring to texts; and our questions inevitably influence the answers we discern there. So long as historical-critical concerns dominated biblical scholarship, literary methods of analysis have taken a second seat. Specialists are increasingly aware, however, that literary approaches can illumine heretofore overlooked or neglected features of biblical texts, increasing our understanding of, and appreciation for, Hebrew poetry and prose and the world whence they came. Of course, embracing a fresh method does not necessarily entail the rejection of others. The literary critic may choose to set aside certain traditional agendas, such as distinguishing between "authentic" and "inauthentic" (i.e., later) prophetic materials, seeking to associate each prophecy with a specific historical situation. But historical criticism and literary criticism need not be antithetical. To the contrary, they can be mutually enriching.

Turning to contemporary literary analyses of Hebrew poetry, including prophetic poetry, we observe that formal features rediscovered by eighteenth- and nineteenth-century scholars (e.g., parallelism, meter) remain topics of intense scrutiny and debate. Recent investigations benefit, however, from new understandings gleaned from fields such as linguistics.

Parallelism

Earlier, we noted Robert Lowth's identification of parallelism as the dominant feature of Hebrew verse. Lowth spoke about three types of parallelism, or correspondence, between cola: synonymous, antithetic, and synthetic. By synonymous parallelism, he referred to those poetic cola in which "the same sentiment is repeated in different, but equivalent terms" (1847:210; quoted in Petersen and Richards 1992:25). Consider the following bicolon:

> Listen, and hear my voice;
>> Pay attention, and hear my speech. (Isa 28:23)

In this example, both the first colon and the second express similar sentiments.

Antithetic parallelism, by contrast, "is not confined to any particular form; for sentiments are opposed to sentiments, words to words, singulars to singulars, plurals to plurals" (1847:215; Petersen and Richards 1992:25). Isa 1:27-28 exhibits what Norman Gottwald has called "external antithetic parallelism" (1962:833). That is, internal synonymous parallelisms in v. 27 and v. 28 are juxtaposed to create a contrast. The contrastive relationship between vv. 27 and 28 is rendered explicit in English by the word "but":

> Zion shall be redeemed by justice,
>> and those in her who repent, by righteousness.
> But rebels and sinners shall be destroyed together,
>> and those who forsake the LORD shall be consumed.

Another example of external antithetic parallelism between bicola appears in vv. 19-20 of the same chapter:

> If you are willing and obedient,
>> you shall eat the good of the land; (v. 19)
> but if you refuse and rebel,
>> you shall be devoured by the sword; (v. 20ab)
>> for the mouth of the LORD has spoken. (v. 20$a\beta$)

Again, the first bicolon (v. 19) and the second (v. 20ab) express opposing sentiments.

Consider, however, the relationship of the two cola within each of these verses. The thought of the first colon in v. 19 ("If you are willing and obedient") is completed by the second ("you shall eat the good of the land"); the two cola of v. 20 (ignoring the closing formula) repeat this pattern. Viewed individually, each of these bicola illustrate Lowth's third type of parallelism, viz., synthetic, in which "sentences answer to each other, not by the iteration of the same image or sentiment, or the opposition of their contraries, but merely by the form of construction" (1847:216; Petersen and Richards 1992:25). Isa 3:8 consists of an initial, synonymous bicolon ("For Jerusalem has stumbled/and Judah has fallen"; v. 8a), followed by a second bicolon (v. 8b) exhibiting synthetic parallelism both with v. 8a, and between its first and second cola:

> because their speech and their deeds are against the
> LORD, defying his glorious presence. (v. 8b)

In this example, v. 8b is linked to the preceding bicolon causally (note the English "because"). But the link between cola in v. 8b involves neither restatement of the same idea, nor the opposition of contrasting ideas. Rather, the thought begun in the first colon is completed by the second.

Lowth's "synthetic parallelism" category served an important function, for he realized that many units of Hebrew verse exhibit neither semantic synonymy nor antithesis, but may be similar in length, share a trope, or (as in the present example) correspond in the sense that the meaning of an initial line is further developed by the following colon or cola. The task of identifying what justifies claims of "parallelism" between synthetic lines has occupied scholars since Lowth's time.

This brings us to certain limitations of Lowth's pioneering work. First, scholars now recognize that the presence of parallelism does not inevitably signal poetry; parallelisms appear in Hebrew prose as well, though they generally are more frequent in the former than in the latter.

Second, parallelisms exist at levels other than the semantic level of the colon, bicolon, or tricolon. New insights from linguistics, in particular, enable scholars to move beyond the meaning of lines to correspondences of other sorts and at different levels: e.g., grammatical forms, syntax, individual words and word pairs, fixed formulaic expressions.

In this context, the following examples can only begin to suggest the variety of such parallelisms. Consider Isa 1:3:

> The ox knows (*yāda'*) its owner,
>> and the donkey its master's crib; (v. 3a)
> but Israel does not know (*yāda'*),
>> my people do not understand. (v. 3b)

On first reading, the two cola in v. 3a may seem simply synonymous ("the same sentiment . . . repeated in different, but equivalent terms"). James Kugel, however, points to subtle differences between them and to their import for construing the bicolon that follows (v. 3b):

The ox was hardly considered the most praiseworthy of beasts: nevertheless "ox" is in several significant respects considered superior to its frequent pair, "ass": More important, parallel to the "owner" of the first is "masters trough" in the second. The cumulative effect of these differences is the establishment of a climactic descent: "An ox knows its owner, and *even* an ass"—who may not be very obedient or attentive—at least knows where to stand to be fed, i.e., "knows his masters' trough"; but "Israel does not know,"—or obey, even this much; in fact—"my people do not understand at all." (1981:9, 102)

A. Berlin further observes the effect of verb "gapping," or ellipsis in this verse: the verb "to know" (*yādá*), present in the first colon, is missing (i.e., gapped) in the second, and reappears in the third without an object, "hinting that its object is nothing—'Israel doesn't know (anything)'" (1985:97-98).

Finally, W. G. E. Watson's translation of Isa 1:27 highlights the additional "balance" between synonymous cola created by reversed gender parallelism:

> Zion [fem.] by justice [masc.] shall be redeemed
> and those [masc.] in her who repent, by right [fem.].

We see, then, that examining correspondences between elements in parallel cola—nuances of words (e.g., "ox"/"ass") and grammatical variations (e.g., the presence or ellipsis of certain words like "to know" in Isa 1:3; the balancing of gender), enhances our awareness of the ancient poet's skill and creativity.

Meter and Rhythm

The first-century CE Jewish historian and apologist, Flavius Josephus, claimed that Hebrew verse, like Greek poetry, was composed according to certain metrical patterns. And in the nineteenth century, as we have already seen, Duhm believed that metrical analysis enabled him to restore prophetic poetry to its original form, freed from subsequent expansions. Hence, the presumption of Hebrew meter and attempts to recover its various patterns have a long history. Nevertheless, many contemporary researchers find little textual support for the claim that ancient Israel's poets were governed by rigid metrical schemes. Since Duhm's day, scholars have tackled and clarified certain issues germane to metrical analysis; E. S. Gerstenberger acknowledges (1985:413), however, that ". . . the material condition of our sources and the lack of any reliable information make it altogether inadvisable to hope for clear-cut solutions." Prosody, the study of rhythmic or dynamic aspects of speech, properly applies to both poetry and prose. Metrics, by contrast, focuses upon poetry. In their chapter on "Meter and Rhythm," Petersen and Richards define meter as a "subspecies of rhythm":

> . . . we understand rhythm to be "a cadence, a contour, a figure of periodicity, any sequence perceptible as a distinct pattern capable of repetition and variation." . . . On the other hand, meter may be construed as "more or less regular poetic rhythm; the measurable rhythmical patterns manifested in verse, or the 'ideal' patterns which poetic rhythms approximate. . . . If meter is regarded as the ideal rhythmical pattern, then 'rhythm' becomes meter the closer it approaches regularity and predictability." Meter may be viewed as a subspecies of rhythm, one that occurs within the poetic provenance. (1992:37-38)

Rhythm, they claim, is present in Hebrew poetry; meter is not. Counting is integral to both metrical and rhythmic analysis. But what, in Hebrew verse, does one count? Scholars have answered this question in at least two ways: one may count stressed and unstressed syllables, or one may count stressed syllables only. These approaches can yield quite different results. Consider Isa 9:20: the first bicolon contains fifteen plus eight syllables, the second seven plus seven. Counting stressed syllables alone, however, reveals a four plus three, three plus three pattern.

Of course, the matter is more complex than this example suggests: major developments in the Hebrew language affected how words were accented over time; the marking of stressed syllables in the Masoretic Text is much later than the poetry itself; and modern as well as some ancient versions and translations disagree concerning the correct delineation, or stichometry, of poetic lines. Despite these and other difficulties, however, counting stressed syllables, rather than both stressed and unstressed ones, appears the more fruitful approach to understanding poetic rhythms. Scanning poetry according to this principle, we discover that ancient Israel's poets tended to compose lines of roughly equal length: "this similarity of line length," Petersen and Richards explain, "created parallel lines, the regularity of which is based on regular occurrences of stress. . . . A two-accent bicolon is one sort of . . . pattern, and a three-accent tricolon is a different kind. . . ." (1992:44). However, such patterns do not constitute meter as defined above, because they need not be rigid and regular. Some poems exhibit greater rhythmic consistency than others; one part of a poem may be more regular than its other parts. "Hebrew poetry," Petersen and Richards remind us, "is marked by a delicate balance between regularity and variation" (44; 46). Speaking of rhythm, rather than meter, permits appreciation of both.

Numerous factors assist biblical scholars in determining where a unit begins (e.g., introductory formulae, the onset of a new subject) and ends (e.g., concluding formulae, distinctive forms of words occurring at the end of a poetic line). Semantic and other forms of parallelism assist the task of dividing verses into monocolons, bicola, tricola, and multicolon units beyond the tricolon.

The Masoretes marked the end of each verse with a major break, further dividing poetic verses into what they deemed the appropriate number of cola. They then subdivided cola into as many parts as, in their opinion, syntax demanded. In Isa 40:13 (a bicolon), for example, they indicated a pause by placing a punctuation mark, called an 'atnāḥ, beneath the stressed syllable of the word ending the first colon; its presence is represented in English translation by a comma: "Who has directed the spirit of the LORD, ..." At the end of the second colon they placed punctuation indicating a full stop, represented in English by a period or, in this example, a question mark: "or as his counselor has instructed him?" In v. 15 (a tricolon), a minor pause appears at the end of the first colon, the *'atnāḥ* at the end of the second. In English translation, the first colon ends with a comma, the second with a semicolon:

> Even the nations are like a drop from a bucket,
> and are accounted as dust on the scales;

The final colon ends with a full stop, indicated in English by a period: "see, he takes up the isles like fine dust."

Hence, Masoretic punctuation, though postdating the poems by centuries and not infallible, is a potentially valuable aid for determining the correct stichometry of parallel lines, dividing verses into the appropriate number of cola, and identifying their rhythmic patterns.

In sum, contemporary analysis of Hebrew poetry includes, but also goes beyond, earlier study of those formal features recovered by scholars of the nineteenth century: parallelism, form criticism, and poetic rhythm. Methods and insights drawn from other fields are enhancing our understanding of compositional techniques utilized by ancient Israel's poets. But are other stylistic features also fruitful areas of investigation?

Prophetic Makers of Metaphor

The oracles of Israel's prophets teem with figurative uses of language. To borrow from Aristotle's definition of metaphor, the prophets were forever giving a thing (person, or place) a name belonging to something else: foundling Jerusalem grows to become YHWH's adulterous wife (Ezekiel 16); Israel's leaders are prattling toddlers (Isa 28:9); Tyre, a handsome and heavily laden trade ship, suddenly sinks beneath the waves (Ezekiel 27).

Despite their abundance, figurative uses of language have not been the focus of ongoing research and debate in Hebrew Bible studies. (The situation is different in New Testament studies, owing to keen interest in the parables of Jesus.) Patrick Miller has urged biblical scholars to avail themselves of contemporary philosophical and literary theories of metaphor and related tropes in exploring this potentially fruitful field of investigation:

> Our contemporary focus on formal characteristics, figures of speech more than figures of thought, and parallelism has served to obscure the role of figures in biblical poetry. . . . Considerable work has been done in the analysis and categorization of metaphors in general that is capable of being applied to the metaphors of biblical poetry. . . . [t]he figurative language of biblical poetry should be—and of course is—able to tell us much about Israel's experience and how they assimilated and understood it. (1983:103-5)

Contemporary scholars are filling this major lacuna, or gap, in biblical scholarship. Witness, for example, recent monographs by K. Nielsen (1989), M. Brettler (1989), and J. Galambush (1992). My own study of the Isaiah scroll traces how two recurring metaphors—Israel as YHWH's rebellious children, and Zion as YHWH's wife and Israel's mother—not only enrich their immediate poetic contexts, but also bridge major sections (First, Second, and Third Isaiah), contributing to the reader's understanding of Isaiah as a unified literary work.

Figurative Uses of Language and Contemporary Theory

Metaphor and simile are important to many fields of inquiry—literary criticism, philosophy, mathematics, science, and social and cultural anthropology. Three of the many tasks and topics germane to metaphor studies are of special importance for investigating poetic uses of figurative language: (1) identifying a theory of metaphor that grounds our discussion; (2) describing ways by which we can recover, to the extent possible, ancient Israel's associations with the terms in figurative utterances (information necessary for its competent construal); and (3) highlighting the significance of metaphors and similes as strategic speech, i.e., invitations to a different perception of reality.

Numerous definitions of metaphor and theories of how it functions appear in philosophical literature. Theologian J. Soskice groups these theories under three headings:

> . . . those that see metaphor as a decorative way of saying what could be said literally [substitution theories]; those that see metaphor as original not in what it says but in the affective impact it has [emotive theories]; and those that see metaphor as a unique cognitive vehicle enabling one to say things that can be said in no other way [incremental theories]. (1985:24)

Soskice defines metaphor as "that figure of speech whereby we speak about one thing in terms which are seen to be suggestive of another" (1985:15). According to her preferred theory of metaphor, we should:

> regard metaphor neither as a simple substitution for literal speech nor as strictly emotive. Metaphor should be treated as fully cognitive and capable of saying that which may be said in no other way. It should explain how metaphor gives us "two ideas for one," yet do so without lapsing into a comparison theory. . . . Ideally, a theory of metaphor should go even further and discuss . . . the hearer's reception of it, how the hearer decides that the speaker is speaking metaphorically rather than nonsensically. (44)

Soskice's work builds upon I. A. Richards's famous remarks about how metaphors create meaning: "when we use a metaphor," Richards wrote, "we have two thoughts of different things active together and supported by a single word, or phrase, whose meaning is a resultant of their interaction" (1936:93). Richards went on to distinguish between the "tenor," or underlying subject of a metaphor, and the "vehicle," or utterance conveying that subject.

Many literary critics deny simile the impact of metaphor, since a simile's simple comparison cannot rival metaphor's richer interactive meaning. Soskice contends, however, that "the most interesting similes" function like metaphors: the presence of "like" [or "as"] is but "an aspect of superficial grammar" (59). By "most interesting similes," she refers to "modelling similes," i.e., those which, like metaphor, "use a subject that is reasonably well known to us to explain or provide schematization for a state of affairs which is beyond our full grasp." "Illustrative similes," by contrast, point to similarities between the two entities. The former function works well, Soskice notes, if one "wishes to produce an exploratory schema," the latter when precision is the goal (60).

Yet another difference between certain similes (and metaphors) and others is the presence or absence of an explicit "secondary predicate," that is, "the complex of concepts, assumptions and ideas that, correctly or incorrectly, but usually is linked to the secondary subject and can be derived from it" (M. S. Kjärgaard 1986:86; see 84-105). *Implicit* secondary predicates do not specify those associations crucial to certain similes (and metaphors); *explicit* secondary predicates do. Consider, for example, YHWH's use of the travailing woman simile in Isa 42:14 (Like a travailing woman I shall shout, I shall gasp and pant; author's trans.; see Darr 1987a; 1994). There, explicit secondary predicates ("shout," "gasp," and "pant") tell the reader just those features of a travailing woman's behavior by which the poet illumines God's powerful, impending acts (vv. 14-17).

Identifying Associated Commonplaces

Knowledge of culturally defined associated commonplaces is essential, especially in the case of implicit secondary predicates, for construing figurative uses of language. Competent North American readers encountering an "A is B" metaphor like "time is money," for example, are able mentally to sift through associations with both "time" and "money," to determine which are appropriate: unlike U. S. currency, time is not associated with green paper rectangles or round pieces of metal, but it can be "spent" or "wasted," and its use or misuse has economic consequences.

How can we recover those ancient, complex webs of associations with words that informed the ancient reader's interpretive task? Unlike modern anthropologists doing fieldwork in extant cultures not their own, biblical scholars cannot ask ancient Israelites to explain the meaning and function of their metaphors and similes. Only ancient Near Eastern texts, including biblical texts, assist us. Our efforts suffer from incomplete or unrecoverable data. They benefit, however, from the biblical authors' penchant for traditional imagery.

Israel's literary artists did not share modern critics' taste for novel tropes. To the contrary, they used established metaphors and similes to demonstrate knowledge of their tradition, to imbue new verses with the authority accruing to earlier ones, to assist audiences in interpreting new works, and to enrich fresh contexts with the meanings and associations borne in earlier sources. The prophets' repeated embrace of traditional tropes aids interpretation, because it enables us to examine how they function in various literary contexts, thus giving us some sense of their normal spectrum of associations. Helpful too are examples of Kjärgaard's "explicit secondary predicate" (see above), such that the trope specifically directs readers or hearers to its pertinent associations. Against those averring that historical and literary methods are antithetical, recovering ancient Israelite society's webs of associations with a given trope's terms entails the reconstruction of historical knowledge.

Investigations of ancient Israel's tropes must be undertaken with care, of course, lest we too facilely assume that they enable us to grasp the "essence" of Israel's society and culture. Cultures are, anthropologist J. C. Crocker reminds us, too filled with "contradictions, ambiguities, and befuddlements" to be apprehended by even the most popular tropes (1977:66). With that warning in place, however, study of figurative uses of language can shed light not only on Israel's literary conventions, but also on its "worldview."

Reading Prophetic Tropes

Focusing upon prophetic metaphors and similes not merely as medium, but as an inextricable part of meaning, enriches our experience and interpretation of those words the prophets claimed to speak for God. Consider, for example, Ezekiel's invitation (29:1-5) to perceive Egypt's Pharaoh as *hattannîn haggādôl* (MT *hattannîn haggādôl*)—the "great crocodile," most commentators agree, although mythological associations undoubtedly cling to *hattannîm* ["sea monster"] in this context as well. When he depicted Pharaoh as a crocodile, Ezekiel was not breaking new metaphorical ground. W. Zimmerli quotes an Egyptian hymn to Thutmose III in which Amun says of Pharaoh's foes: "I have made them see thy majesty as a crocodile, Lord of fear in the water, unapproachable" (1983:111). Casting Pharaoh as a proud crocodile basking in his Nile canals foregrounds fearsome associations: he is menacing, cunning, the predator before whom others flee.

What is Pharaoh's sin? Hubris, commentators agree. Redoubtable in his Nile, proud of his control over the mighty river, the crocodile boasts, "My Nile is my own; I made it for myself" (v. 3). His illusion of absolute sovereignty and safety is destroyed in two swift strokes, however, when YHWH, the mighty hunter, hooks him, pulls him from the Nile, and tosses his body, along with the fish clinging to it, into the desert. Ezekiel has perceived the established metaphor's soft underbelly. For all its ostensible strength and security, the crocodile is surrounded by death, since that is the certain fate awaiting water-dependent creatures when cast onto dry, desert ground.

Crocodiles by the thousands inhabited the Nile region. Moreover, the cult of Sebek, the great crocodile deity, flourished in ancient Egypt for centuries; like Pharaoh, the crocodile was both revered and feared. Clearly, then, Ezekiel selected a metaphor commanding immediate assent: it was familiar, appropriate, economical, and packed an emotive punch. His trope is not complex. Understanding it requires little more than the recognition that the prophet was not speaking nonsense (i.e., that he did not actually believe that Pharaoh is a crocodile). However, an historically informed audience familiar with the Egyptian metaphor, and with the enormous waterworks systems built by Egyptian pharaohs to regulate the inundation of the Nile as it flowed north, might make more of the metaphor than those knowing little about this background. After all, the degree of knowledge that ancient hearers or readers brought to metaphors or other tropes (i.e., their "extratextual repertoire"; J. Darr 1992:22) played a determinative role in the depth of their understanding. The same is true today. Again, historical data enrich the reader's understanding of figurative uses of language.

But anyone who realizes that Ezekiel's words are intended metaphorically, and who attempts to grasp their meaning, accepts an offer of communication of a special sort. All communication draws speaker and hearer closer together: the former issues a kind of invitation; the latter expends effort to accept that invitation; and this transaction constitutes the acknowledgment of community. But when communication involves figurative uses of language, the intimacy created between the maker and the appreciator of metaphor is enhanced.

Will Ezekiel's audience draw back in dismay? The answer depends, of course, upon its identity. Judeans advocating an anti-Egyptian foreign policy, believing that Egypt is indeed a slender reed upon which to learn, will find Ezekiel's oracle pleasing, the intimacy initiated by the metaphor like the intimacy experienced by two friends sharing a joke. If, on the other hand, the audience is Egyptian or, more likely, Judeans hoping for Egyptian assistance in Jerusalem's struggle for survival, then Ezekiel's invitation to intimacy is dangerous, since its denouement means death for Pharaoh *and* those clinging to him. Like Ehud, who ostensibly approached Eglon to share a secret, but instead planted a sword in his stomach (Judg 3:15-22), Ezekiel's crocodile metaphor invites pro-Egyptian hearers near in order to deal a deadly thrust. Exploiting the weakness implicit in a familiar image and matching metaphor and mode of punishment with deadly perfection, the prophet depicts YHWH's utter destruction of a presumptuous monarch.

Looking Forward: "Tell Us the Former Things . . . Tell Us What Is to Come Hereafter"

As this essay suggests, features of Hebrew poetry that caught the attention of critics during the previous century remain topics of analysis and debate. Doubtless they will stay on the scene for years to come, as scholars increasingly make use of various resources, including poetic texts composed elsewhere in Israel's ancient Near Eastern world, and analytic tools from other fields. Our understanding of poetic parallelism has been expanded and refined far beyond the three types identified by Lowth. If scholars are more pessimistic than was Duhm about recovering metrical patterns of composition, their understanding of rhythmic patterns—regular, but also variable—has grown considerably. Moreover, much work remains to be done in analyzing figurative uses of language, as well as many other stylistic features not treated in this essay.

Some students of Hebrew verse choose to interpret biblical poetry using contemporary methods of analysis, yet ignoring a poem's origins—its social and cultural context. I believe, however, that the richer approach combines contemporary tools developed to study the poetry of many peoples and times, with knowledge of relevant socially and culturally specific data (e.g., associations with words appearing in figurative utterances). Bringing, as best we are able, the ancient audience's extratextual repertoire to bear enables us to recover the meaning and import of poems for its earliest audiences.

Earlier, I mentioned my work on recurring Isaian metaphors. In *Isaiah's Vision and the Family of God,* I presuppose the modern critical view that the book of Isaiah is the product of many hands over centuries. I likewise presuppose that redactors, no less than authors, played a crucial role in shaping the scroll in its final form. Yet I bracket out these issues, accepting the text's invitation to read Isaiah as what it purports to be—the vision that the eighth-century prophet saw in the days of Uzziah, Jotham, Ahaz, and Hezekiah, kings of Judah, but that was not limited to events transpiring during those reigns. Positing a first-time, highly literate reader who moves through the scroll from beginning to end, I trace the unfolding of Isaiah's vision, focusing upon selected, recurring female and child tropes. Future interpreters may profitably undertake similar readings of other prophetic books. Consider, for example, the book of Ezekiel with its chronologically ordered sections and dates. A sophisticated, sequential reading of this prophetic work and of others promises to shed new light on elements of narrativity present in the final arrangement of originally discrete poetic units.

For those who esteem ancient Israel's prophetic literature primarily as a window back on history, its transparency (enabling scholars to see through the text to prior events and conditions clearly and without distortion) constitutes its greatest value. Literary perspectives on prophetic poetry remind us, however, that the text is not a window, but a painting whose every stroke was purposefully placed. Literary perspectives permit us to study these strokes—figures, rhythms, structures, and composition—creations of an ancient world, images of another world, glimpses of a future world that Israel, in faith, claimed as God's creation.

Selected Bibliography

Berlin, Adele. *The Dynamics of Biblical Parallelism.* Bloomington: Indiana University Press, 1985, 6.

Brettler, M. *God Is King: Understanding an Israelite Metaphor.* JSOTSup 76. Sheffield: JSOT, 1989.

Croker, J. Christopher. "The Social Functions of Rhetorical Forms." In *The Social Use of Metaphor: Essays on the Anthropology of Rhetoric.* Philadelphia: University of Pennsylvania Press, 1977, 33-66.

Darr, John A. *On Character Building: The Reader and the Rhetoric of Characterization in Luke–Acts. Literary Currents in Biblical Interpretation.* Edited by D. N. Fawell and D. M. Gunn. Louisville: Westminster/John Knox, 1992.

Darr, Katheryn Pfisterer. *Isaiah's Vision and the Family of God. Literary Currents in Biblical Interpretation.* Edited by D. N. Fewell and D. M. Gunn. Louisville: Westminster/John Knox, 1994.

Duhm, Bernhard. *Die Theologie der Propheten als Grundlage für die innere Entwicklungsgeschichte der israelitischen Religion.* Bonn: Adolph Marcus, 1875.

———. *Das Buch Jesaia.* HKAT 3.1. Göttingen: Vandenhoeck and Ruprecht, 1892.

Galambush, J. *Jerusalem in the Book of Ezekiel: The City as Yahweh's Wife.* SBLDS 130. Atlanta: Scholars Press, 1992.

Gerstenberger, Erhard S. "The Lyrical Literature." In *The Hebrew Bible and Its Modern Interpreters*. Edited by Douglas A. Knight and Gene M. Tucker. Philadelphia: Fortress, 1985, 409-44.

Gottwald, Norman K. "Poetry, Hebrew." In vol. 3 of *The Interpreter's Dictionary of the Bible*. Nashville: Abingdon, 1962, 829-38.

Kjärgaard, M. S. *Metaphor and Parable*. ATDan XI. Leiden: E. J. Brill, 1986.

Kugel, James. *The Idea of Biblical Poetry: Parallelism and Its History*. New Haven and London: Yale University Press, 1981.

Lowth, Robert. *Lectures on the Sacred Poetry of the Hebrews*, 1815. Reprint, London: S. Chadwick and Co., 1847.

Miller, P. D. "Meter, Parallelism and Tropes: The Search for Poetic Style." *JSOT* 28:99-106, 1984.

Nielsen, K. *There Is Hope for a Tree: The Tree as Metaphor in Isaiah*. JSOTSup 65. Sheffield: JSOT, 1989.

Petersen, David L., and Kent Harold Richards. *Interpreting Hebrew Poetry*. Guides to Biblical Scholarship. Minneapolis: Fortress, 1992.

Richards, I. A. *The Philosophy of Rhetoric*. Oxford: Oxford University Press, 1936.

Soskice, J. M. *Metaphor and Religious Language*. Oxford: Clarendon, 1985.

Watson, W. G. E. *Classical Hebrew Poetry: A Guide to Its Techniques*. JSOTSup 26. Sheffield: JSOT, 1984.

Zimmerli, Walther. *Ezekiel 2*. Edited by Paul D. Hanson. *Hermaneia*. Philadelphia: Fortress, 1983.

PART THREE
WRITINGS

Chapter 9
PAST, PRESENT, AND
PROSPECT IN PSALM STUDY

James Luther Mays

The course of the study of the psalms can be read as a story of shifting concentrations on their various features in the search for the best answer to the question, "What is a psalm?"

Critical interpretation in the course of its explorations has selected different aspects of the psalms as the central clue to the answer. The feature taken to be crucial has tended to organize the interpreter's approach and evaluate the relative significance of the various aspects.

The psalms confront the interpreter with an array of features. In the Hebrew Bible there are one hundred and fifty psalms. All are composed according to the conventions of Hebrew poetry, which include using various rhetorical devices to achieve effect and unity. Many of them are introduced by superscriptions made up variously of classifications, including directions for performance and attribution to authors or patrons. The attributions are mostly to David and to guilds of singers associated with him by tradition, the Korahites and Asaphites. The psalms are composed to serve three general purposes: prayer, praise, and instruction; in some psalms the functions are combined. Many of the psalms appear as the voice of an individual, others of a group; in some both individual and corporate styles appear. Except for a few duplicates, each psalm presents distinct differences. Yet continuities of vocabulary, themes, and arrangement run through many of them. Moreover, psalms refer to certain institutions of Israel's religious life: temple, king, sacrifice, processions, and pilgrimage. The book of Psalms is divided into five "books" by doxologies at the end of Psalms 41, 72, 89, and 106; beyond that there is no obvious arrangement of the collection except for the predominance of prayers toward the beginning and of hymns of praise toward the end.

147

The Background of Our Century

Traditional interpretation took the attributions to David and his musicians as the decisive clue to the identity of the psalms. The psalms were read largely as the expression of the piety of David in the many situations of his life as narrated in the books of Samuel. Thirteen of the superscriptions refer to such situations, and these connections were taken to be paradigms for all the other psalms of David. For centuries the connections with David sponsored a rich and useful interpretation. The traditional approach did not think of David as a strictly historical figure. Rather, David was a paradigm and prototype in a canonical context. In the psalms he exemplified prayer, praise, and piety for Israel. He was the anoited king, the once and future Messiah. The psalms as his prayer and praise provided instruction and prophecy. The best of traditional interpretation drew on the psalms for spiritual and theological purposes that enriched the life of Judaism and Christianity. The psalms' identity as scripture controlled their identity as expressions of David's piety.

In the latter part of the nineteenth century, historical criticism called the Davidic identity of the psalms into question. Historical critics began to look at the incongruities between the details in many psalms attributed to David and the account of David's career in Samuel as well as at the connections between many psalms and biblical literature from times later than the period of David. The individual and corporate experiences described in the prayers and hymns were considered from a historical rather than from spiritual and theological perspectives. The psalms were regarded as the voice of some historical person or occasion. But lacking the occasion and/or person supplied by the Davidic connection, interpreters were left to search through the record of Israel for other plausible times and people as a context in which to read the psalms. The tendency was generally to locate them later rather than early in Israel's religious history. The results of this venture were largely inconclusive, especially since the poetic language of the psalms supplied almost no details that could be linked with particular historical contexts. The psalms did not seem to be defined by the individuality and particularity of time, place, and event.

Psalm Study in This Century

Around the turn of the century form criticism emerged as a corrective to the historical approach to Psalms. The preeminent figure in the shift was Hermann Gunkel. In his work he employed two principal concepts, *Gattung* (genre, type) and *Sitz im Leben* (setting-in-life, social context). Gunkel concentrated on the very features that had frustrated historical criticism, the general, formulaic, and repetitious character of the language in which the psalms are composed. He concluded that elements psalmic language refers to is typical rather than historical, i.e., it refers to types of persons and situations. The psalms could be sorted out into categories of types, a limited list of genres, on the basis of common vocabulary, themes, and arrangements. The various types had emerged from and belonged to various occasions in Israel's religious practice. Each type derived from a setting-in-life, the verbal dimension of a religious performance. So the psalms were not texts rooted in unique historical circumstances, but instances of a genre that belonged to occasions that occurred again and again in the course of Israel's religion.

The genres identified by Gunkel have provided a standard instrument for the interpretation of psalms in this century. Refinements of his list have been proposed but hardly a work on Psalms has appeared in this century that does not employ some version of Gunkel's types. The major genres into which he incorporated most psalms are these (the cited psalms are paradigmatic instances of the types):

(1) Hymns, songs of praise for festival occasions (Psalm 100), including two smaller genres identified by particular themes: Songs of Yahweh's enthronement (Psalm 47) and Songs of Zion (Psalm 48).

(2) Laments of the Community, songs of appeal to Yahweh in a time of national distress (Psalm 44).

(3) Laments of the Individual, psalms of appeal by an individual in a time of personal distress (Psalm 13).

(4) Thanksgiving Songs of the Individual, songs of witness and gratitude for answered prayer (Psalm 30).

(5) Royal Psalms, psalms of various functions that belonged to ceremonies centering in the anointed king (Psalm 2).

(6) Wisdom Poetry, psalms composed under the influence of the wisdom tradition to instruct in piety (Psalm 37).

Besides these major genres, Gunkel created a list of minor genres to account for formulaic features in some of the psalms and to account for the few beyond his major genres.

For Gunkel's interpretation of psalms, the notion of genre was more important than setting-in-life. Through the genres derived from cultic practice, many of the actual psalms were, in his opinion, "spiritual songs," personal songs from the religious life of the pious individual. The truly cultic songs were earlier, he thought, and the spiritual songs later.

In contrast to Gunkel and his followers, e.g., Claus Westermann, other form critics have placed more emphasis on the importance of setting-in-life for the interpretation of particular psalms. The most influential name here is probably Sigmund Mowinckel. These critics have tended to identify most psalms as agenda for performance in cultic ritual. They have searched the Psalms, other Old Testament books, and the literature of other peoples in the ancient Near East for evidences of festivals and ceremonies that might plausibly constitute the settings in which types of psalms were used. More psalms were judged to be early cultic pieces. The liturgy for festivals with themes such as the kingship of Yahweh and Zion and covenant renewal was reconstructed as the setting for congregational psalms. A much greater role was assigned to the king as a major figure in the cult. Attempts were made to determine the specific problems referred to in the individual laments and to reconstruct the ceremonies in which they were used. Nevertheless, no general agreement has emerged that would determine the specific cultic setting-in-life of each psalm. Still, this effort—the cult-functional approach— has focused attention on the relation of psalmic literature to the religion of ancient Israel.

During the late nineteenth and throughout the twentieth centuries, an impressive body of literature from ancient Egypt, Sumeria, Babylonia, and Assyria, the other national cultures contiguous to Israel, has been discovered and translated. The discoveries include hymns, prayers, royal literature, and wisdom texts, all of which have recognizable similarities to the psalms. This material has made it possible to view the canonical psalms as part of the religious literature of the ancient Near East. Similarities between the vocabulary, motifs, and elements of Israelite hymns and prayers and those of other national cultures provide confirmation of genres and their characteristics as features of a general religious culture. The poetic character and language, particularly in the texts from Ugarit, have been used to analyze and translate psalmic tests. Possible dependence of Psalms like 29 and 19 on earlier texts has been explored. This collateral literature constitutes the primary source for data used in reconstructing cultic occasions and ceremonies as settings for Israel's psalms.

Psalm 3 can illustrate these diverse interpretive perspectives. Psalm 3 is introduced by a superscription identifying the psalm as a psalm of David when he fled from Absalom. The psalm is a prayer of an individual who laments the opposition of many enemies, professes trust in Yahweh, appeals to Yahweh for deliverance, and asks for blessing on the people of Yahweh.

(A) The traditional approach would be guided by the superscription and point to the details in the psalm that correspond to features of the story in 2 Samuel 15. It might dwell on David's confident faith in the Lord in the face of insuperable odds and commend his concern for the people of the Lord in the midst of his personal trouble.

(B) The historical-critical approach might seek a context in the Maccabean period and attribute the psalm to a leader caught in the partisan battles and struggles of that time.

(C) The form-critical approach could view the military language in the psalm as metaphorical and interpret the psalm as a prayer composed for an individual in some indefinite but overwhelming trouble.

(D) Those who emphasize the importance of cult might conclude that Psalm 3 was composed for use by a king of Judah in ceremonies during which he professed his dependence on Israel's God using the reference to many enemies as hyperbole to enhance his profession.

In all these instances, a general hypothesis about the character of the psalms affects decisively its interpretation. (The interpretations listed above report the conclusions of representative scholars, but do not exhaust the possibilities of a particular approach and are given only for heuristic purposes.)

Though they are employed in different ways by different scholars who reach quite varying conclusions, the concepts of genre and setting-in-life and the body of literature comparable to the psalms from the ancient Near East are important features of contemporary psalm interpretation. They are certain to play a role, however qualified, in the future study of the psalms. But there is a growing dissatisfaction with these approaches. Among the important difficulties are these:

(A) Many psalms do not correspond exactly to the standard profiles of the genres to which they are assigned. They include extra elements that go beyond the ideal type or are composed of a mixture of elements from several genres. Neat lists of psalms that simply classify them according to genre ignore this reality.

(B) Form-critical descriptions necessarily concentrate on what is typical in a psalm. But the psalms also are compositions that incorporate distinctive literary elements important to their meaning. Focus on the typical may depreciate or ignore the individuality of a psalm.

(C) The reality of the psalms as a book and the possibility that the location of a psalm in this literary context allows for an important interpretive perspective are not items on the agenda of approaches that only deal with the psalms singly and in groups created by genre.

(D) Comparison of Israel's psalms with apparent counterparts from other religions may lead to the conclusion that similarities in form and language may involve similarities in meaning and purpose. An interpretation that too easily equates the two misses the defining context of different cultural contexts and religions.

Gunkel was aware of these problems and referred to them in his magisterial work. Concern with them and their implications is currently shaping much that is developing in the study of psalms. Approaches and perspectives that transcend and supplement form-critical and comparative methods are being tested. No one "method" is gaining dominance. Instead different experiments are being tried out in the attempt to cope with these problems.

Changes in Direction

Past research on psalms has characteristically focused on psalms grouped according to categories and on the setting for which psalms were originally composed. The leading questions have been: What are the genres of psalmic literature? To which genre should a particular psalm be assigned? What purpose did it serve in Israel's religion? In current scholarly work attention is shifting to concern with individual psalms, to psalms as products of a process of preservation, reuse, and collection, and to psalms as part of a book. The earlier questions are not discounted. But there is a growing recognition that the psalms as we have them have been influenced by contexts other than the setting-in-life of their apparent genres and have undergone changes of meaning, purpose, and sometimes content. There is also significant interest in the book of Psalms as the final and sole directly available context of the psalms. Samples of what is afoot will illustrate the features of the psalms receiving emphasis and furnish examples of what is being made of them.

A Psalm as an Individual Literary Composition

Though psalm criticism has tended to focus on the typical and to group psalms on the basis of their shared features, there is a renewed interest in the literary features that constitute a psalm's distinctive individuality. The conventions of a genre are not the only factor in the shaping of a psalm. Various modes of literary analysis allow the reader to discern and describe the poetic, stylistic, and rhetorical character of particular psalms.

Although Psalm 3 can be analyzed in terms of the typical elements of the individual lament, it constitutes a distinctive composition. It is composed of invocation and complaint (vv. 1-2), affirmation of confidence (vv. 3-6), petition (v. 7), a concluding sentence of praise of Yahweh (v. 8a), and blessing on Yahweh's people (v. 8b). Nonetheless, this typical structure involves a distinctive literary work-up. The threefold repetition of "many" unites and enforces the complaint. The affirmation of confidence balances statements about what Yahweh is and does for the psalmist with statements about the psalmist's enactment of trust in the face of the "many." The psalm as a whole turns on the repeated theme of help (v. 2), deliver (v. 7), and deliverance (v. 8—all the same word in Hebrew); the psalm moves from a denial that God will save through an appeal for Yahweh to save to a declaration that salvation belongs to Yahweh.

The literary shaping of the typical elements creates the individuality and theological substance of this psalm.

A Psalm as a Product of Israel's Religious Tradition

Although psalm criticism has been concerned primarily with the form in which and the use for which a psalm was first composed, more attention is now being given to the contribution of the transmission and continuing use of psalms to their identity and meaning. Features of the psalms not accounted for by generic criteria provide clues to a richer complex identity of the psalms. In the process of their transmission, psalms were used in settings different from the one for which they were composed. Psalms written for individuals were put to corporate use and the elements of individual experience cited in prayers and thanksgivings became metaphors for corporate life. Some psalms were revised to adopt them for their use in different circumstances. Many were connected with David as a way to give psalms a context in Israel's emerging scriptures. Psalms began to be composed out of the resources of the extant scriptures. Psalm study has, of course, always been aware of this history, but, currently, its effect on the psalms is receiving much more attention.

Examples of such attention include the following: Psalm 30 belongs to the genre of "the thanksgiving song of an individual" who prayed for help and was delivered from death. Its superscription identifies the psalm as "a song of the dedication of the temple." This reclassification indicates that the psalm has been reread as a thanksgiving of Israel, since its corporate salvation most likely with reference to the Exile. In its present form the psalm has two identities and may be interpreted in two related but different contexts.

Psalm 102 seems to be a case of the rereading of a psalm by the literary process of expansion and intercalation. Its superscription identifies it as the prayer of an afflicted person. The psalm begins appropriately as the lament of an individual (vv. 1-11) and resumes the genre toward its end (vv. 23-24). But in its middle (vv. 12-22) and conclusion (vv. 25-28), the psalm turns to the corporate concern of Zion's restoration. The community is personified as the afflicted one. Either an individual lament has been revised by expansion for use as a community lament or the genre of the individual lament has been used as a literary convention in the composition of a song for the congregation.

The superscription of Psalm 3 identifies this lament of one individual as "a psalm of David, when he fled from his son Absalom." Accordingly, the context in which the psalm is to be read is a portion of scripture, the story in 2 Samuel 15. The superscription provides evidence of the process by which psalms were related to scripture and by which they became scripture. There was a late stage in the course of psalm composition when psalms were apparently composed drawing on extant scripture. For instance, Psalm 103 reflects the influence of Yahweh's self-proclamation in Exodus 34 on its composer (cf. Ps 103:8 with Exod 34:6-7). Psalm 119, the great poem on the law of the Lord, contains echoes of Deuteronomy, Jeremiah, Isaiah, and Proverbs. In extolling the instruction of the Lord, it uses scripture as instruction.

A Psalm as Part of a Book

Although psalm criticism has interpreted psalms in the contexts of their genre and cultic setting, attention is also now being directed to the literary context of a psalm, i.e., its location in the book of Psalms. Some question the assumption that the order and arrangement of psalms in the book is random or accidental. The relation of particular psalms to their immediate literary context and the possible coherence of sequences of psalms are being explored to see if there is a purposive or intentional ordering of the psalms. Some readers have discerned clues of vocabulary and theme that enable reading a psalm as part of a larger, meaningful context.

Psalm 8 can exemplify the significance of a psalm's particular literary location. It is the first hymn of praise in the book, set in a sequence of prayer psalms attributed to David. Psalm 7 ends with David's resolution to "sing praise to the name of the LORD, the Most High" (v. 17). Psalm 9 begins with a repetition of the resolution (vv. 1-2). Psalm 8 opens and closes with the praise of the name of the LORD, majestic in all the earth. In effect, "David" does in Psalm 8 what he promises in Psalms 7 and 9; the two frame Psalm 8 and explain what is happening in it. In turn Psalm 8 is a meditation on the importance of the human species to God and offers one theological explanation of why the prayers in the midst of which it stands are heard by God.

Psalms 113–118 offer an example of a sequence of psalms that can be read in a mutually interpretive way. As a group these psalms have a liturgical identity; they compose the Egyptian Hallel that was used in all the joyous festivals of Judaism and played a special role in the liturgy at Passover. The sequence is composed primarily of hymns of praise for the community, but 116 and 118 feature an unidentified individual. When the group is read in order, the unidentified "I" takes on the identity of personified corporate Israel. Several themes establish continuity and create an interpretive context in this sequence. Psalm 113 praises the Lord whose majesty is combined with mercy in raising up the lowly. Psalm 114 celebrates the Exodus as a manifestation of majesty acting in mercy, whereby the topic of the sequence is set as the Lord's way with Israel. Psalm 115 identifies the congregation who sing the psalms as Israel, house of Aaron and fearers of the Lord, and the nations as the problem that threatens them. In the face of the threat, Israel is to trust the Lord. The dead, says 115, do not praise the Lord but Israel does. In Psalm 116 a singer gives thanks that the Lord in his mercy has saved him from death, and he promises to offer a sacrifice of thanksgiving and to call on the name of the Lord. Psalm 117 calls on the nations to praise the Lord because of the Lord's steadfast love shown to Israel. In Psalm 118 the promise is kept. The congregation composed of Israel, house of Aaron and fearers of the Lord, and personified as an individual who has been saved from death and who testifies that it is better to trust the Lord than human powers and nations, comes in the name of the Lord to give thanks to the Lord. By their position in the sequence, Psalms 116 and 118 are made into psalms of the community. Moreover, the theme of rescue from death that belongs to the songs of an individual is read as a metaphor for the salvation of the people of the LORD.

The Book of Psalms as a Book of Scripture

Historical criticism and form criticism paid little attention to the shaping and final shape of the book of Psalms. The opinion was held that the collection and arrangement of the psalms offer little for understanding individual psalms. That judgment was based on viewing the psalms as instances of a type and as agenda for cultic contexts. Those who also view the psalms as scripture argue that what the psalms became and how they were understood in the process of making a book of scripture have to be considered. The interest in the book as a whole and the shaping that created it is, of course, the larger dimension of the interest in the literary location of particular psalms. But it is by gaining a perspective on the whole that the various hermeneutical purposes that belong to the psalms as a book of scripture can be brought to light.

As various features of the macro-structure of the book are explored, it is becoming apparent that no one scheme comprehends the whole. The book seems to have been created by combining a succession of earlier stages. The approaches of redaction criticism, tradition-history, and canonical analysis are being used to see what can be discerned about these arrangements, the stages they represent, and their significance for the whole. Some important items on the agenda of investigation are the following: the introduction of the book by a psalm whose theme is the *torah* (law, instruction) of the LORD, and the division of the whole into five parts marked by doxologies. The appearance of a *torah* theme and vocabulary in a considerable number of psalms suggest an interest in shaping the book in analogy to the *torah* of Moses to serve as complementary scripture. The strategic location of psalms that deal with the anointed king points to a concern for the prophetic potential in texts about the Messiah. The incorporation of two collections of the prayers of David, perhaps the earliest form of a psalter, witnesses to the role the piety of the lowly played in creating the psalter as an anthology of authorized prayers for all fearers of the LORD. Study of these and similar items may well converge in a comprehensive picture of the formation of the psalter and the function of its final form as a hermeneutical context.

The Prospect

In the coming decades, the study of psalms will likely follow the trends of the present. Form-critical and cult-functional approaches will continue to be established participants. But the interest in the literary distinctiveness of individual psalms, the transmission and composition of psalms through a history of successive traditions, and the formation and final form of the psalter will enrich and broaden the perspectives in which psalms are interpreted. No single approach is likely to gain dominance. What psalm study has learned thus far is that the answer to the question, What is a psalm?, is complex. Any approach based on a single, simple answer will not be adequate to discern the rich and multilevel nature of a psalm.

Selected Bibliography

Introductions to Current Study of the Psalms:
Day, John. *Psalms*. Old Testament Guides. Sheffield: JSOT, 1990.
Seybold, Klaus. *Introducing the Psalms*. Edinburgh: T. & T. Clark, 1990.

The Form-Critical Approach:
Gunkel, Hermann. *The Psalms: A Form-Critical Introduction*. Biblical Series 19. Philadelphia: Fortress, 1967.
Westermann, Claus. *Praise and Lament in the Psalms*. Atlanta: John Knox, 1981.

The Cult-Functional Approach:
Mowinckel, Sigmund. *The Psalms in Israel's Worship*, 2 vols. Oxford: Basil Blackwell, 1962.

The Psalms in the Context of the Ancient Near East:
Keel, Othmar. *The Symbolism of the Biblical World: Ancient Near Eastern Iconography and the Book of Psalms*. New York: Crossroad, 1985.

Literary Analyses of Psalms:
Allen, Leslie C. *Psalms 101-150*. WBC, vol. 21. Waco: Word Books, 1983.

Transmission and Scripturization:
Mays, James L. "Going by the Book." In *The Lord Reigns*. Louisville: Westminster/John Knox, 1994.
McCann, J. Clinton, ed. *The Shape and Shaping of the Psalter*. JSOTSup 159. Sheffield: JSOT, 1993.
Wilson, Gerald Henry. *The Editing of the Hebrew Psalter*. SBLDS 76. Chico, Calif.: Scholars Press, 1985.

Chapter 10
PROVERBS AND
ITS SUCCESSORS

W. Sibley Towner

The Book of Proverbs

Introduction

Certain passages of the book of Proverbs are well known and a number of individual proverbs are familiar to everyone, even people who think that Benjamin Franklin wrote them. But as an entire work, Proverbs is unknown territory even for many devout readers of Scripture. Students of the Bible are sometimes surprised, then, when they find the book of Proverbs is a wonderfully rich, diverse, and lively collection of ancient wisdom.

Proverbs can be infuriating and even obnoxious to our ears, as for example, the famous text that seems to lend support to the penal system of Singapore:

> Do not withhold discipline from your children;
> if you beat them with a rod, they will not die.
> If you beat them with the rod,
> you will save their lives from Sheol.
> (Prov 23:13-14; cf. 13:24)

Worthy of modern Washington, D.C. is its apparent cynicism about access to officialdom:

> A gift opens doors;
> it gives access to the great. (Prov 18:16)

The book is male-oriented and its patriarchal view of life gets it bad press today even among some of its most serious students:

157

It is better to live in a corner of the housetop
than in a house shared with a contentious wife.
(Prov 21:9; cf. 19:13; 21:19; 25:24; 27:15-16)

When it comes to class orientation, the sages who gave us Proverbs are allied with the ruling circles. They have high praise for kings and accept their absolute authority (e.g., Prov 20:2). They urge sympathy for the poor but would rather hang around with the rich:

The poor are disliked even by their neighbors,
but the rich have many friends. (Prov 14:20)

Alongside these "politically incorrect attitudes," however, are surprisingly modern sounding insights that deserve close attention. This "psychological" observation is an example:

To get wisdom is to love oneself;
to keep understanding is to prosper. (Prov 19:8)

They teach their pupils the dangers of alcohol abuse:

Who has woe? Who has sorrow?
Who has strife? Who has complaining?
Who has wounds without cause?
Who has redness of eyes?
Those who linger late over wine,
those who keep trying mixed wines.
(Prov 23:29-30; cf. 20:1; 23:19-21; 31:4-7)

The sages also are aware of how devastating gossip can be and repeatedly warn against it with insights as fresh as the one that links trouble and gossip:

For lack of wood the fire goes out,
and where there is no whisperer, quarreling ceases.
(Prov 26:20)

It is not the task of the interpreter of Proverbs to try to release it from its moorings to the ancient culture in which it was launched and to pretend that it can be docked, without representation, in our lives. Instead, the task is to value its teachings that continue to function one way or another as they were intended to do, namely, to help provide order in society and structure for the individual psyche. This we can do with appreciation even while warts remain on the book.

Where the Book of Proverbs Comes From

The Hebrew name of the book of Proverbs, *Mišlê Šelomoh,* makes two claims about the book at once: the teachings are attributed to Solomon, and they are called *Mešalim,* "parables, proverbs." Underlying the noun *māšāl* is the verb "to be like . . . similar." Etymologically, then, the Hebrew "proverb" is a similitude. Indeed, the teachings of the book of Proverbs do consist in great part of brief aphorisms containing two clauses (distichs) in which virtuous or foolish behavior is compared to some other known phenomenon of life. A better name for the book of Proverbs might have been the "book of Similitudes." However, Jerome called it *Proverbia* in his Latin version, and Proverbs it is.

The claim that the author of the book was Solomon is neither surprising nor accurate. No doubt it is founded on Solomon's reputation as the wisest of all kings. According to 1 Kgs 4:32, "He composed three thousand proverbs, and his songs numbered a thousand and five." The Queen of Sheba came to hear his wisdom and proclaim his greatness in words like these: "Your wisdom and prosperity far surpass the report that I had heard" (1 Kgs 10:7). In short, when wisdom was in view, Solomon was the name to claim, and the wisdom teachers claimed it for their book. Two other late Jewish wisdom writings, Qohelet (Ecclesiastes) and the Wisdom of Solomon, bear the Solomonic label, as does the nuptial poem, the Song of Solomon. Outside the pale of canonical and deutero-canonical literature are the Psalms of Solomon, Odes of Solomon, and a Testament of Solomon.

The almost uniformly positive attitude toward kingship, which has already been noted, does not require royal authorship. It is just as likely to have arisen out of the patronage, which the teachers enjoyed from the ruling class, and their own social location in the retinue of the social elites.

Relevant to this discussion of the authorship of the book is discussion of its date. The book of Proverbs is notoriously difficult to date because it seldom alludes either to historical event or personage. We can neither confirm nor deny that significant portions of the book emanate from the period of monarchy in Israel, as two of those rare allusions, the superscription (1:1) and the reference to "other proverbs of Solomon that the officials of King Hezekiah of Judah copied" (25:1), would have us believe. Observation of the smaller literary genres used in the book is not conclusive, either. Modern scholars tend to divide the material found in Proverbs and other sapiental books into two broad categories, based on both form and content: (a) folk wisdom, characteristically expressed in aphorisms or ethical sentences, typically stated in two clauses or stichs; and (b) courtly wisdom, characteristically expressed in rather more elaborate, sometimes rhetorically excellent and theologically sophisticated instructional texts. (Of course,

many more smaller genres can be identified as well, e.g., the graded numerical dictum [6:16-19; 30:15-33]; similes beginning with "like" [25:11-26:26];
acrostic poetry [31:10-31]. For full discussion of these, see Murphy, *Wisdom
Literature*.) As discoveries of texts in the Egyptian sapiental tradition have
shown, both types—folk wisdom of the aphoristic variety and the more
literary and sophisticated courtly instruction—go far back into the literary
antiquity of the ancient Near East, but continue to be employed down to
Roman times.

Two considerations are most useful in giving at least a relative date for the
canonical form of the book of Proverbs: (a) the diversity of content and
genres show the present book to be the end product of a process of collection
and elaboration; (b) its authors seem to be familiar with an already extant
scripture of Torah and Prophets, and even with the other wisdom books of
Job and Qohelet. These considerations point to a date for the book, at least
in its final form, more than seven centuries after Solomon's time—as late as
the third century BCE.

Its true authors are "sages" or "intellectuals" (*hakkāmîm*). The exact profile
of this circle of functionaries in ancient Israelite life will continue to be
debated in the coming decades. It is possible that a simple village elder or
other traditional teacher might have been deemed a "sage" by the community, but there is no doubt that there were "sages" among the professionals
who attended the king, high priest, or other leadership figures in the capacity
of advisors, teachers, prognosticators, and so on. The assumption that its
authors participated in circles that had access to both written and oral texts
explains the detailed familiarity of its authors with the sacred traditions of
their people. Participation in the relatively cosmopolitan circles of the
Judean elite would also help account for the sages' awareness of certain
foreign wisdom traditions. The most famous evidence of this in Proverbs is
the section headed "The Words of the Wise" (22:17-24:22), which is self-
described as "thirty sayings of admonition and knowledge" (22:20). In these
two and a half chapters there are no less than sixteen topical similarities with
a twelfth century BCE Egyptian sapiental text, the "Teaching of Ame-
nemope," a work of thirty chapters.

An examination of the structure of the book of Proverbs will also establish
a basis for considering the stages of the growth of the book. The book
outlines itself into seven constituent parts, to which can be added two
sub-units.

(A)	1:1–9:18	"The proverbs of Solomon son of David, king of Israel" (theological wisdom)
(B)	10:1–22:16	"The proverbs of Solomon"
(C)	22:17–24:22	"The words of the wise"

(D) 24:23-24   "These also are sayings of the wise"

(E) 25:1–29:27   "These are other proverbs of Solomon that the officials of King Hezekiah of Judah copied"

(F) 30:1–33   "The words of Agur son of Jakeh. An oracle" (includes an appended collection of graded numerical dicta, vv. 15-33)

(G) 31:1-31   "The words of King Lemuel. An oracle that his mother taught him" (includes an appended poem on the virtuous wife, vv. 10-31)

This collection of teachings falls into the two major formal categories discussed above. A few chunks of the book consist almost entirely of sentence sayings or aphorisms (i.e., 10:1–22:16; 25:1–29:27; 22:17–24:22; 24:23-24). On the other side is the more literary opening section, 1:1–9:18, with its lengthy delineations of the truly wise person, the strange woman and her foil and nemesis, Woman Wisdom; and the final chapters 30–31. If "folk wisdom" has deeper roots in the clans and communities of Israel than "theological wisdom," then perhaps chapters 1–29 are the older core of the book, for which at some later stage an outer shell was provided by the more theologically sophisticated sages. That model is hypothetical, of course, and it is ill-advised to base the interpretation of the book of Proverbs entirely on such an analysis. It does suggest, however, that the book is composite, that it experienced stages of growth and editing, and that both the author and the audiences are plural.

The Purpose of the Book

The final editors of the book of Proverbs had to answer to their patrons among the patricians of Jerusalem. Though they drew upon the wisdom of more humble and popular circles of the past, they turned it all to the task of preparing the future leadership of their people for successful living. The sages discharged their responsibility unsystematically. They worked pragmatically, seeking "practical knowledge of the laws of life and of the world, based upon experience" (von Rad), that would be agreeable to the reader and effective in helping that reader cope with life.

Learning to cope with life is, in essence, the purpose of the book. That purpose is expanded in the prefatory verses of 1:2-6, which use such key "wisdom" words as instruction, insight, wise dealing, righteousness, justice, equity, shrewdness, knowledge, prudence, learning, skill, "a proverb," "a figure," and "the words of the wise and their riddles." The passage culminates in the slogan of the book:

The fear of the LORD is the beginning of knowledge;
fools despise wisdom and instruction. (1:7)

The Topics of Proverbs

One way to approach the ideological content of the book of Proverbs is to discuss the ideas of its component units one at a time, identifying differences between them along the way. This essay takes a different approach. Here the topics of the book are treated synthetically, as if the sources were essentially of a piece. This is possible because, though the book is an anthology written over many years, its ideas converge impressively, even across the major divide between popular and theological wisdom. In fact, it is impossible to limit many of the themes of the book to one section or another, although the images of Woman Wisdom and her counterpart, Woman Folly or the "strange woman," are certainly more developed in chapters 1–9. Salient ideas of the book are discussed in the following pages, therefore, without any attempt to put them into some developmental sequence. Even though Proverbs lacks plot, characterization, and other features that would make it a prime candidate for literary analysis, the topical approach used here is friendly to that type of interpretation because it reads Proverbs holistically, without depending on any critical reconstruction.

(1) *The Two Ways.* In all of its parts the book of Proverbs is consistently sanguine about the certain connection of uprightness with reward and sin with failure and death. In an optimism comparable to that of Psalms 1 and 37 and Job's friends, not to mention some modern TV evangelists, the sages promise plenty to those who fulfill their obligations to God. Riches and righteousness are twins:

Honor the LORD with your substance
and with the first fruits of all your produce;
then your barns will be filled with plenty,
and your vats will be bursting with wine. (3:9-10)

Life itself depends upon the good walk:

The upright will abide in the land,
and the innocent will remain in it;
but the wicked will be cut off from the land,
and the treacherous will be rooted out of it. (2:21-22)

(2) *Theonomy vs. Autonomy.* On this topic Proverbs would have it both ways. Sometimes the sages seem to believe that God is the hidden force behind all events. People have the impression that they are acting independently, but

God sees everything they do (15:3). People make plans, decisions, take initiatives, but in reality, "the LORD directs the steps" (16:9; cf. 20:24). A classic assertion of divine predestination is 21:30-31:

> No wisdom, no understanding, no counsel,
> can avail against the LORD.
> The horse is made ready for the day of battle,
> but the victory belongs to the LORD.

Such a high doctrine of theonomy is not unique to Proverbs in the Old Testament. Qohelet gives it strong support (Qoh 3:9-15). Many apocalyptic texts, too, suggest that God fixes the time of everything in advance (e.g., Dan 9). But the notion is seldom stated more comprehensively than in the teaching of Proverbs that every single thing, even the wicked, was made by God for a specific purpose (16:4).

What is surprising about the motif of divine predetermination in Proverbs is that it stands alongside its polar opposite, the affirmation of human autonomy. Long ago scholars pointed out that parallel to claims about the human proposal and divine disposal of events are statements that omit the divine element altogether.

> For by wise guidance you can wage your war,
> and in abundance of counselors there is victory.
> (24:6; cf. 15:22, 20:18)

In short, the sages seem to be ambivalent about the respective roles of divine predisposition and human decision making. Nevertheless, the fact that the book aims at affecting behavior by inculcating sound ethical values suggests that the sages believed their pupils could make independent and free decisions. The model suggests a universe upheld and guided by the sovereign purposes of the Lord. There is a sphere of human autonomy within which people must make independent choices and accept responsibility for their consequences. That possibility is reinforced, too, by the idea of the "destiny-producing deed" (Koch):

> Whoever digs a pit will fall into it,
> and a stone will come back on the one who
> starts it rolling. (26:27; cf. Eccl 10:8)

A human deed itself sows the seed that is eventually harvested. No divine intervention is necessary.

(3) *Personal Virtues and Vices*. In years to come we shall be seeing more and more interest in how biblical wisdom undertook to form character. Proverbs believes that true character flows from "the fear of the LORD." Indeed, the admonition to adopt that fundamental attitude is repeated some seventeen times, both in the "theological wisdom" of chapters 1–9 and in the sentences of the rest of the book.

The sages counsel *prudence,* and in the relatively lengthy teaching of 27:23-27, promise that if one takes care of one's flocks, "there will be enough goats' milk for your food, for the food of your household and nourishment for your servant girls" (v. 27). The capable wife of 31:10-31 is richly endowed with this virtue. She takes care that provisions be laid by, that the household servants have their work laid out for them, and that she make a profit with her handicrafts. Then she "laughs at the time to come" (v. 25).

Discipline is mentioned twelve times in Proverbs; only Sirach lays greater emphasis on this virtue. Often it is mentioned in connection with the folly of adultery: The "simple ones" who get involved with the "strange woman" lack discipline (e.g., 5:12-14). Discipline is more than wisdom in sexual matters, however, but it is also a way of life that knows how to keep itself teachable:

> Whoever loves discipline loves knowledge,
> but those who hate to be rebuked are stupid.
> (12:1; cf. 13:1)

Discipline is taught by father and mother, that is to say, authorities. It is also taught by experience itself. Suffering, for example, is a kind of discipline, a chastening unto perfection:

> Blows that wound cleanse away evil;
> beatings make clean the innermost parts. (20:30)

In contrast to these virtues of awe, prudence, and discipline, and their virtuous practitioners, stands the *fool* who deserves no honor, but only a whip (26:1-3). The "simple ones" who fool with adultery stand high on the list of fools (7:7), but those who are not yet instructed (1:4) and who are gullible (14:15) are also "simple ones." To be a "simple one" is not a hopeless case. A fool can be converted to prudence and wisdom by punishment (19:25), and it is the task of teachers to inculcate the etiquette and moral sophistication that are the opposites of foolishness and simplicity.

Among other vices that Proverbs identifies can be mentioned gluttony and drunkenness (e.g., 20:1; 23:19-21; 31:4-7), laziness (e.g., 26:13-16), pride (e.g., 16:18), and a loose mouth, or gossip (e.g., 11:13; 18:8; 20:19; 26:20).

(4) *Social Virtues.* The book of Proverbs is concerned for the health of the society, too, and it is here that the affinities with both the legal tradition of the Pentateuch, including the Decalogue, and with many of the cries of the prophets come to the fore. Integrity of language in the testimony in court is a social virtue of major importance:

> Whoever speaks the truth gives honest evidence,
> but a false witness speaks deceitfully.
> (12:17; cf. 14:4, 25; 19:5, 9; 21:28; 25:18)

Here is an issue as old as the ninth commandment (Exod 20:16; Deut 5:20), and older. It may have been a theme of the early wisdom of Israel for the Decalogue, that legal "creed" of Israel, may itself have been born out of the traditions of tribal wisdom.

In addition to juridical integrity and truth-telling, the sages evidence considerable concern about economic fairness. As in the case of such prophets as Amos, Micah, and Isaiah of Jerusalem, they stress the importance of honest weights and measures in the marketplace (11:1). In 16:11 they go so far as to call honest weights for the balance "the work of God." And then for good measure, they join these same prophets on the side of social justice in preference to the observance of piety:

> To do righteousness and justice
> is more acceptable to the LORD than
> sacrifice. (21:3; cf. 28:9)

(5) *Family Relationships.* To a degree surprising for an ancient text, the mother is elevated to a high role throughout the book. Whether she speaks or not is a matter of debate, but she is certainly present by the side of the father when the "child" is instructed (1:8; 6:20). The book culminates with both an oracle by the mother of King Lemuel (31:1-9), and a rhetorically excellent poem about the capable wife (31:10-31).

Consideration of wife and mother raises the question of the proper relationship of children to their parents. This was an issue of abiding concern in the covenant tradition of the Hebrew Bible, and appears even in the Decalogue itself (e.g., Exod 20:12; Deut 5:16). Wisdom offers help in this matter, too, for that sages know that:

> Foolish children are a grief to their father
> and bitterness to her who bore them. (17:25)

165

Above all the child is warned against unleashing the malevolent power of the curse against parents:

> If you curse father or mother,
> your lamp will go out in utter darkness.
> (20:20; cf. Exod 21:15, 17; Lev 20:9; Deut 21:18-21)

If readers are moved to give the name Prudence to the lady of Prov 31:10-31, they may also want to name the other great female figure of the book of Proverbs Sophia, for she is personified wisdom (*ḥokmāh*—a noun which is itself feminine in Hebrew). Woman Wisdom appears most frequently in the "theological" section, chaps. 1–9. In the remarkable presentation of the lady in chap. 8, she speaks directly and at length to the "simple ones." Beginning with v. 22 and speaking as the Lord's first creature, she characterizes her role in creation as the Lord's "master worker." (Or was she the Lord's "little child"?—see NRSV note to 8:30. The latter reading would fit well with v. 30*b*, in which the young lady appears as God's delightful, playful companion.) She serves as God's intermediary as well, for not only does she work with God in creation but she also "delights" in the human race (v. 31) and finds satisfaction in inducting them into the ways of righteousness and life (vv. 35-36).

In chap. 9, Woman Wisdom has built an earthly house with seven enigmatic pillars. She invites people in to banquet at her table. To feast with her is to lay aside simplicity or "immaturity" and live. If the list of virtues for the wise in 9:7-12 is part of her after-dinner speech, then the core of her table talk is this:

> The fear of the LORD is the beginning of wisdom,
> and the knowledge of the Holy
> One is insight. (9:10)

Woman Wisdom speaks in the public marketplace in 1:20-33, again summoning simple ones to the knowledge and fear of the Lord. In 3:13-18 she is compared to precious metals and jewels (cf. Job 28:15-19) and the tree of life (cf. Gen 2:9; Ps 1:3). In 7:4 she appears again as life-giver, so accessible that the "child" can address her as "my sister" and "intimate friend."

Over against Woman Wisdom stands the "loose" or "strange" woman (e.g., 2:16-19). The juxtaposition suggests that the latter is more than just a sexual temptress; she is the mirror image of wisdom, Woman Folly. In the theological wisdom of chaps. 1–9, she sits at the door of her house, too, and, with enticing words calls the "simple" to come in to feast with her:

> Stolen water is sweet,
> and bread eaten in secret is pleasant. (9:17)

The "child" is warned of danger from this siren. Unlike Woman Wisdom's guests, who live and walk in the way of insight (9:6), Woman Folly's "guests are in the depths of Sheol" (9:18; cf. 5:1-14).

The sexual aspect of Woman Folly is manifest, to be sure. In 6:24-35 she is more than a prostitute—she is "the wife of another," an "adulteress" (cf. 7:5). She and her "simple" paramours overrun that fencepost of social order, the Seventh Commandment (Exod 20:14; Deut 5:18). Because of her shattering of the family bond, her husband is driven to behavior that, though evidently justified in the minds of the sages, might further rend the fabric of society:

> For jealousy arouses her husband's fury,
> and he shows no restraint when
> he takes revenge. (6:34)

Concern with the strange woman is not confined to chaps. 1–9, however. As one might expect, the issues of marital fidelity and adultery come up in the "sentence" section of the book as well, for these matters were and remain a daily concern of parents, teachers, and other ordinary people. No longer juxtaposed to Woman Wisdom, in these chapters the strange woman is simply the incorrigible sexual temptress (23:26-28; 30:20).

(6) *Human Destiny.* The sages were also concerned with what lies ahead for human beings in life and in death. The book of Proverbs is keenly aware that old age impends, though it does not paint the gloomy picture that Qoh 12:1-7 does. In fact, for it:

> Gray hair is a crown of glory;
> it is gained in a righteous life. (16:31)

In the end, of course, all arrive at Sheol, the shadowy abode of the dead in the Hebrew Bible and in Sirach from which no one ever arises again. The writers of Proverbs see no exception to this sovereignty of Sheol, but they generally link it to premature death, and particularly to the folly of those who are drawn in by the seductions of the strange woman (7:27). Occasionally the sages sound as if Sheol could somehow be finessed:

167

> For the wise the path of life leads upward,
> in order to avoid Sheol below. (15:24; cf. 23:14)

But of course, there is no escaping the abode of the dead. At least Proverbs knows of one continuity between the real world and Sheol: The Lord is sovereign in both places:

> Sheol and Abaddon lie open before the LORD,
> how much more human hearts! (15:11)

The Book of Proverbs Within the Canon

The sages feel friendly toward both the Law and the Prophets. Indeed:

> Where there is no prophecy, the people cast off restraint,
> but happy are those who keep the law. (29:18)

One assumes that they were familiar with the sacred traditions of Torah and Prophets, perhaps even in some written form. As has been noted, concerns similar to some found in the Decalogue manifest themselves in the book. The instructions in 6:20-22 to keep the commandment of the "father" and the "mother," i.e., the authorities, sound almost as if they had been lifted from the Shema in Deut 6:6-9.

The teaching of the next verse, 6:23, that "the commandment is a lamp and the teaching a light," resonates with the language of Ps 119:105. In fact, many affinities exist between the book of Proverbs and the psalter, both in stylistic features used (e.g., aphorisms or short sentences, rhetorical questions, acrostic poems) and in ideas expressed. These are especially apparent in the so-called "Wisdom Psalms" (e.g., 37, 49, 73, 112, 127) and "Torah Psalms" (e.g., 1, 19, 119). In their contrast of the "two ways," psalms like 1 and 37 agree with Proverbs that reward and punishment lie within secure lines of cause and effect.

Points of opposition also exist between the book of Proverbs and other parts of the canon, particularly the other great sapiental works. Job rebukes his friends' conventionally pious notion that suffering is sent by God in order to lead a person to perfection. Many interpreters believe that Qohelet was written precisely to rebut the optimism of a closed system in which righteousness pays dividends. It would be hard to imagine more diametrically opposed viewpoints than those of Prov 10:7 and Qoh 2:16.

> The memory of the righteous is a blessing,
> but the name of the wicked will rot. (Prov. 10:17)

For there is no enduring remembrance of the wise
or of fools, seeing that in the days to come all will
have long been forgotten. (Qoh 2:16)

There are commonalities among the three canonical wisdom books, to be sure. All use similar literary conventions, draw on a common semantic repertoire, even quote from one another (compare Prov 26:27 with Qoh 10:8; Prov 30:4 with Job 38:1-7). The basic mission of the three is the same, namely, to teach that "the fear of the LORD is the beginning of wisdom" (e.g., Prov 1:7; Job 28:28; Qoh 12:13), and to help the pupil cope successfully with life.

The book of Proverbs echoes in the New Testament as well, whose writers granted it the authority of scripture. One of the most evident intertextual relationships is that between the advice against taking vengeance in Prov 24:28-29 and a clause of the Lord's Prayer ("Forgive us our debts, as we also have forgiven our debtors," Matt 6:12). Given the resonance of his Golden Rule with the Proverbs passage, Jesus might well have said (emphasis added), "In everything do to others as you would have them do to you; for this is the law and the prophets *and the wisdom of Israel*" (Matt 7:12). Paul quotes Prov 25:21-22 with great approval in his caution against taking vengeance (Rom 12:19-21).

It is somewhat difficult to know why the book of Proverbs should have been accepted in the rabbinical and early Christian communities as sacred scripture even as Sirach and the Wisdom of Solomon, the other two great Jewish wisdom books of the late Old Testament period, were being treated as at most deutero-canonical writings. After all, both of the latter renew many of the themes of Proverbs, both expand upon wisdom personified in Woman Wisdom, and both pursue the essential task of inculcating the fear of the Lord in pupils so that they might live successfully. The Wisdom of Solomon may have failed to win acceptance with the rabbinical authorities of the first two centuries CE because it was written late and written in Greek. Sirach, however, was written in Hebrew and known in that text form at Qumran at the turn of the era, though it came down through the centuries in Greek translation. In any case, the canonizing communities never gave them the full status accorded to the book of Proverbs.

Sirach (Ecclesiasticus)

The book known as Ecclesiasticus (not to be confused with Ecclesiastes of the Hebrew Bible) is the work of an intellectual of ancient Israel named

169

Joshua ben Sira, or, in hellenized form, Jesus, son of Sirach. This man was a teacher of the Jewish tradition who wrote his book in Hebrew about 192 BCE (a calculation extrapolated from the explicit date given in the Prologue to the book for the time of its translation into Greek). He was a Jerusalemite (50:27). Presumably the students of whom he speaks in 51:23 were sons of the priestly establishment and political elite that had prospered during a century of Ptolemaic rule, and were now settling into a new period of political calm created by the conquest of Palestine in 198 BCE by the Seleucid monarch of Antioch in Syria, Antiochus III. Perhaps the serene and reflective writing of Sirach reflects the security of his time and class; however, though he could perhaps not have imagined it, it was the last of its kind in Israel.

The "plot" of the book, excluding the translator's prologue, can be analyzed into six sections:

(A)	1:1–23:27	First main section, beginning with an encomium on Wisdom
(B)	24:1–42:14	The Praise of Wisdom, beginning with a hymn to the personified Woman Wisdom (24:1-22)
(C)	42:15–43:33	Nature declares the glory of God
(D)	44:1–49:16	"Let us now praise famous men," an evaluation of Israelite history (cf. Heb 11:4–12:2)
(E)	50:1-29	Praise of the High Priest "Simon son of Onias" (assumed to be Simon II, 219-199 BCE)
(F)	51:1-30	Two appendices

Ben Sira used the language and espoused the ideas of his predecessor sages who gave us the book of Proverbs. Here are familiar aphorisms and sentences like those of ancient popular wisdom; here is the repertoire of words like "prudence," "diligence," "righteousness," "understanding," and "instruction." Here is extravagant praise for the good and chaste wife:

> A wife's charm delights her husband,
> and her skill puts flesh on his bones. . . .
> Like golden pillars on silver bases,
> so are shapely legs and steadfast feet.
>
> (26:13-18)

Here are expressed concerns for the poor that seem almost transitional between the advocacy of social justice in the book of Proverbs (e.g., 31:8-9) and the call for self-giving for others in the Sermon on the Mount:

Help the poor for the commandment's sake. . . .
Lose your silver for the sake of a
    brother or a friend. . . .
Lay up your treasure according to the commandments of the Most High,
    and it will profit you more than gold.

(Sir 29:9-11; cf. Matt 6:19-20)

Right up front here is the familiar slogan, "To fear the LORD is the beginning of wisdom" (1:14; cf. 1:27; 19:20; 21:11). For Sirach the wisdom that begins with the fear of the Lord is from the very outset Woman Wisdom (e.g., 1:1-27; 14:20–15:10; 24:1-34). Her dignity is increased in Sirach; her independence is escalated. She presents herself as nearly co-eternal with God (24:9). She is the mist which, "came forth from the mouth of the Most High and covered the earth in the beginning" (24:3). She is poured out by the Lord like wine lavishly upon those who love him (1:9-10), and "she inebriates mortals with her fruits" (1:16). After searching through the whole earth for a resting place, she "took root in an honored people, in the portion of the LORD, his heritage" (24:12), and there she abides as an almost palpable presence, an indwelling spirit. Woman Wisdom is on her way toward being a true hypostasis, no longer a concept in female clothing but a holy person in her own right.

In the texts of the Israelite wisdom tradition, that trajectory will reach its apogee in the Wisdom of Solomon. What makes the role of Sirach in this development so interesting is that this "new theology" for the second century BCE comes from the pen of a conservative patrician and traditionalist. His view of class structure is fixed: masters should rule their servants with iron hands (33:24-27); society should make sure that intellectuals and scribes have necessary leisure (38:24-25); the working classes play an important community role, but "they are not sought out for the council of the people" (38:31-33). His paean of praise for the high priest Simon II (50:1-21) is the last expression of its kind in Israel. Against the belief in the resurrection of the dead that was spreading among the Jews of his day, at least in apocalyptically minded circles (Isa 26:19; Dan 12:1-3), he firmly reiterates the older Sheol expectation of Proverbs and Qohelet and the rest of the Hebrew Bible (17:27).

Yet this very same conservative patrician reveals that he too has been affected by the change he distained. In his limning of Woman Wisdom the new Hellenistic spirit whispers, tempting him to go beyond the personification employed in Proverbs to make her a Jewish counterpart of Sophia, the Greek goddess of Wisdom, through whom human beings can draw near to the very presence of God:

171

Happy is the person . . .
who camps near her house
   and fastens his tent peg to her walls;
who pitches his tent near her,
   and so occupies an excellent lodging place . . .
who is sheltered by her from the heat,
   and dwells in the midst of her glory.

(14:20, 25-25, 27)

The Wisdom of Solomon

Fortunately, a second beautiful example of deutero-canonical Jewish Wisdom literature survived its exclusion from the canon by the rabbis, Jerome, and, in later times, the reformers. Unlike ben Sira, the hellenized Jew who wrote this work cloaked himself in anonymity. However, literature, like nature, abhors a vacuum, so the ancients attributed the work to that grandaddy of all sages, King Solomon. The Greek language in which the book has come down to us appears to be the language in which it was written, and there is no evidence that there was ever a Hebrew original. Internal evidence suggests that the book was written in the large Greek-speaking Jewish community of Alexandria after the conquest of that city by the Romans in 30 BCE.

The "plot" of this book can be analyzed into two major sections, each with distinct subunits:

(A) Chaps. 1–9   The Role of Wisdom in Human Experience
    (1) Chaps. 1–5   The demands and rewards of wisdom
    (2) Chaps. 6–9   Wisdom's character and her powers
(B) Chaps. 10–19   The Wisdom at Work in Israel's History
    (1) Chaps. 10–11 Ancestors and the Exodus
    (2) Chap. 12   Canaanites
    (3) Chaps. 13–15 Digression on idolatry
    (4) Chaps. 16–19 God's differing treatment of Israel and Egypt

This book contains little or no "folk" wisdom or sentence-wisdom of the kind found in both of its sapiental sisters. From beginning to end it must be classified as "theological wisdom." In rhetoric and content alike, Wisdom stands in continuity with its predecessor in sapiental writing, Sirach. Both books openly confess that wisdom, the highest goal and greatest good of life, is a gift from God (Wis 7:7; 8:21; cf. Sir 1:1). Like Proverbs and Sirach before it, Wisdom continues to employ and develop the image of Woman Wisdom. In contrast to the book of Proverbs, which makes no significant purchase on history, both of these books contain summaries of the salvation history of

Israel written in such a way as to show the role of wisdom in the great events of the past (cf. Sir, chaps. 44–50). Wisdom, chaps. 10–19, retells the beginnings of Israel's history with special emphasis on the ten plagues of Egypt, which are taken to be appropriate punishments for ten corresponding crimes of the Egyptians. Springing off of the incident of the golden calf, he blasts idolatry, scornfully noting that kings order carved images of themselves to be placed around their realms so that "by their zeal [the subjects] might flatter the absent one as though present" (14:17). This is exactly what Roman emperors did, of course. No doubt the writer of Wisdom had seen it himself, though he probably never knew that the image Caius Caligula placed in the Temple in Jerusalem in 40 CE stirred up the riots that preceded the First Jewish Revolt (66-74 CE) and led to the destruction of the Temple.

In contrast with the interest in history shared by Sirach and Wisdom is their radical disagreement on the matter of life after death. Job, Qohelet, Proverbs, and Sirach all struggle in different ways with the question of why the righteous suffer and die, but all agree that die they must and descend into the shadowy underworld of Sheol they certainly will. Against this gloomy certainty Wisdom introduces the Hellenistic notion of blessed immortality, a doctrine unprecedented in any of the earlier Hebrew literature, not excluding the two late apocalyptic texts that touch lightly on the quite different notion of the resurrection of the dead (Isa 26:19; Dan 12:1-3):

> But the righteous live forever,
> and their reward is with the LORD;
> the Most High takes care of them. (5:15)

The twin visions of resurrection and immortality emerged in Judaism in the second and first centuries BCE as partial answers to the tragic problem of the death of the righteous. Though only the minority voices of the apocalyptists and Wisdom promoted their respective faiths at the beginning, in the teachings of Jesus and the Pharisees life in a world to come became the norm. By and large, the norm settled on resurrection, but the theme of immortality is not unknown in the later texts as well (Luke 23:42-43).

The other major innovation in the Wisdom of Solomon is the extreme to which it takes the figure of Woman Wisdom. By opening the door a crack to the possibility of deep communion, even near union, of the individual believer with the Godhead, Wisdom breaks new theological ground. The book never hints at an esoteric Jewish mystery cult, as another Alexandrian Jew, Philo, seems to do, nor does it get into gnostic denial of the physical world in favor of the spiritual. In its rendition of Woman Wisdom, however, particularly in 6:12–8:21, its new thinking can be seen.

In the first part of the book, divine transcendence is emphasized over imma-nence. The relation of God to the created order devolves onto Woman Wisdom. Now she is more than Proverbs' personification, more even than the nascent hypostasis of Sirach. Now she is preexistent, divine, nearly a person of the Godhead. In language dear to neo-Platonists and gnostics she is described as

> . . . a breath of the power of God,
>> a pure emanation of the glory of the Almighty . . .
> She is a reflection of eternal light,
>> a spotless mirror of the working of God,
> and an image of his goodness. (7:25-26)

Then, in language that is reminiscent of the Hellenistic mystery cults in which the initiates sought to mount up the light stream into unity with God, Wisdom is pictured as a true intermediary, a conduit with connections at both ends. She is both the beloved intimate of God and a friend and consort of human beings:

> She glorifies her noble birth by living with God,
>> and the LORD of all loves her (8:4)

and,

> God loves nothing so much as
>> the person who lives with wisdom. (7:28)

The imagery of Wisdom is striking when one comes to it out of the Hebrew Bible, but it is less so when one approaches it from the New Testament side. It is generally conceded that the writer of Ephesians found the Wisdom of Solomon in the Greek Old Testament that lay open before him. In Eph 6:11-17 the image of spiritual armor is used in a manner very reminiscent of Wis 5:15-20. In Gal 5:22-23, Paul's list of fruits of the spirit is interestingly comparable to the virtues of wisdom given in Wis 7:22-23. However, most debated and important is the representation of the Woman Wisdom figure in the New Testament found in the prologue to the Gospel of John. John asserts that "In the beginning was the Word" (John 1:1); Wisdom, too, is "from the beginning of creation" (Wis 6:22). John tells us that "the Word was with God (John 1:1); Wisdom, too, is with God "and an associate in his works" (Wis 8:4). "All things came into being through him, and without him not one thing came into being" (John 1:3); Wisdom, while remaining in herself, "renews all things" (7:27). In John the Word brings forth a new kind of light: "The light shines in the darkness, and the darkness did not overcome it" (John 1:5). Of Wisdom it can be said:

174

She is more beautiful than the sun,
and excels every constellation of the stars.
Compared with the light she is found to be superior,
for it is succeeded by night,
but against wisdom evil does not prevail. (7:29-30)

Three elements in the Johannine text distinguish it decisively, however, from the wisdom theology of Hellenistic Judaism exemplified in Wisdom. The first is the conversion of the feminine *hokmāh*, "wisdom," into the masculine *lógos*, "Word." The second goes to the true identity of wisdom/word. Although Woman Wisdom is an emanation from God, the writer of the Wisdom of Solomon is never quite prepared to say that she is a divine being or God herself. John says it right away: "and the Word was God" (1:1). Finally, Wisdom is the "spotless mirror of the working of God, and an image of his goodness" (7:26). Although "in every generation she passes into holy souls and makes them friends of God" (7:27), still, "nothing defiled gains entrance into her" (7:25). In the end she remains a beautiful, eternal principle. The Christian gospel plunges the Word into the scandal of incarnation. "The Word became flesh and lived among us" (John 1:14), and he did not get out of his deep involvement with the human community without bleeding and dying.

Selected Bibliography

Camp, Claudia V. *Wisdom and the Feminine in the Book of Proverbs*. Bible and Literature Series, 11. Sheffield: Almond, 1985.

Crenshaw, James L. "Book of Proverbs." In *ABD* 5:513-20.

———. "Wisdom Literature: Retrospect and Prospect." In *Of Prophets' Visions and the Wisdom of Sages*. Edited by H. A. McKay and D. J. A. Clines. JSOTSup 162. Sheffield: JSOT, 1993, 161-78.

Fontaine, Carole R. "Wisdom in Proverbs." In *In Search of Wisdom*. Edited by Leo G. Perdue, et al. Louisville: Westminster/John Knox, 1993, 99-114.

McKane, William. *Proverbs: A New Approach*. OTL. Philadelphia: Westminster; London: SCM, 1970.

Murphy, Roland E. *Wisdom Literature: Job, Proverbs, Ruth, Canticles, Ecclesiastes and Esther*. FOTL 13. Grand Rapids: Eerdmans, 1981.

Skehan, P. W., and A. A. DiLella. *The Wisdom of Ben Sira*. AB 39. New York: Doubleday, 1987.

Whybray, R. N. *The Composition of the Book of Proverbs*. JSOTSup 168. Sheffield: JSOT, 1994.

Winston, David. *The Wisdom of Solomon*. AB 43. Garden City, N.Y.: Doubleday, 1979.

Chapter 11
JOB AND ECCLESIASTES

Carol A. Newsom

Job

Someone once said that every biblical scholar wants to write a book on Job in the same way that every actor wants to play Hamlet. Scholars appear to be fulfilling their ambitions, for in the past ten years alone over a score of important commentaries and monographs have been published, along with hundreds of articles. Nor is the conversation limited to biblical scholars. Significant books and articles have been written by theologians, literary critics, philosophers, psychologists, and even political commentators. Although it is impossible to do justice to the rich variety of this body of work in a few pages, there are a number of trends that have characterized recent discussion and which will guide the direction of Job scholarship into the twenty-first century.

The most important trend in reading Job is the shift from a historical-critical to a literary paradigm. Traditionally, the standard critical questions that dominate the introduction include the issue of the ancient Near Eastern background of Job, the history of composition and redaction of the book, the difficult issues of date and authorship, and the problem of genre. It can be quite a surprise to turn to Norman Habel's 1985 commentary and discover that such classic questions are all but ignored in favor of a detailed account of the book's plot. In his discussion of the integrity of the book Habel brushes aside the long, inconclusive history of redaction criticism. He makes a case for the unity of the book using the insights of new critical literary theory. Two other important commentaries, those of David Clines and Edward Good, are even more direct in their impatience with traditional historical-critical questions. Clines dismisses issues of author, date, and redaction as of minimal importance to the question of reading the book as it now is (p. 29).

Good provocatively places those matters in what he entitles "A Dispensable Introduction," remarking that such discussions are "irrelevant to what I wish to do in this book" (1).

The commentaries of Habel, Clines, and Good are also illustrative of the variety of literary approaches being used. Habel depends strongly on new criticism, taking as axiomatic the unity and coherence of the text, and is careful to identify devices such as narrative frames, balanced formal structures, foreshadowing, structuring metaphors, and the use of verbal and dramatic irony. Habel's Job is "a literary whole integrating prose and poetic materials into a rich paradoxical totality" (9). Published only four years after Habel's, Clines's commentary reflects the impact of reader response criticism. In acknowledging the role of the reader and the reader's ideology in making meaning, Clines provocatively illustrates by suggesting what feminist, vegetarian, materialist, and Christian readings of the book might look like (48-56). Similarly, Clines does not provide just one but three alternative ways in which one might understand the shape of the book, depending on whether the reader gave emphasis to formal features, plot features, or rhetorical features of the book. Good's commentary is the most radical of the three. Whereas Clines's discussion suggested readings produced by differences in interpretive judgment or informed by different ideological commitments, Good's guiding image for reading is that of play with an open text. "This kind of reading promotes a certain purposelessness. . . . to let the text play openly on us and we openly on it—or, perhaps better, that we and the text play with each other—so that we close off no possibility" (180). It is impossible to imagine such a statement in the commentary of an earlier generation.

Even for those who do not embrace the model of free play, literary readings of Job have raised the question of whether the book can be said to have a determinate meaning. The contradictions between the prose tale and the poetic dialogues, not only in terms of style but also in terms of ethos and religious values, have long been a perplexing issue. The historical-critical approach pointed to these contradictions as traces of the history of composition, created when a traditional prose tale was combined with a poet's radical recasting of the story and its characters. If one engages in a final-form literary reading, however, the contradictions pose a more difficult interpretive problem. Habel's approach, to recognize the tensions and paradoxes within a literary unity, is widely followed. Increasingly, however, one encounters claims that the book is radically self-contradictory, perhaps deliberately so. In a recent article Clines has called the book of Job a "self-deconstructing artifact."[1] More evocatively, Alan Cooper has used the image of a tangram, a puzzle whose pieces can be fitted together in a variety of ways, none of which is exclusively right or wrong.[2] This discussion of whether the meaning of the book is determinate or indeterminate has important theological implications. If the book has a determinate meaning, then the main business is to clarify what it says about God, the world, human suffering, and the moral order. If, instead, the book is like a tangram, then attention is drawn as much to the *process* of constructing a reading, and to the analogous process by which individuals and communities construct their beliefs about such matters. How one chooses what to emphasize and what to ignore in order to achieve an interpretation and in order to construct a belief system become objects of reflection themselves. When Job is understood on the analogy of a tangram, an ineradicable pluralism of religious and moral thought is central to the experience of reading the book.

It is a mistake to suggest that literary approaches to Job have completely ousted historical-critical ones or that scholars whose approach is primarily literary do not use the insights of historical criticism in their exegesis. In fact, some of the most interesting work is being done by those who are exploring new ways of asking old questions. The issue of the contradictions within the book provides a good example. In his provocative book *Job the Silent*, Bruce Zuckerman starts with the problem of a book that "appears to be at odds with itself," resisting all homogenization (14). To account for this peculiarity of the book Zuckerman uses a redaction-critical approach. In Zuckerman's reconstruction, however, this is no dreary procession of dim-witted and clumsy editors but rather a contrapuntal history of deliberate parody and "sincere misreading," created as succeeding generations struggled with a literary heritage that often seemed inadequate to the moral and religious needs created by changing historical circumstances. The stimulus for this theory of how the book of Job came to have the odd, self-contradictory shape that it now presents is the similar process which is traced in the interpretation of Y. L. Perets's Yiddish story, "Brontsye the Silent." Whether or not one is persuaded by the details of Zuckerman's book, he succeeds in showing how a stale and unprofitable question can be revitalized by a combination of historical and literary insights.

The broader question of how the book of Job is related to history is ripe for rethinking. Even in the heyday of historical-critical scholarship Job was noted for its "universality" and treated as an ahistorical exploration of innocent suffering and the problem of theodicy. Biblical scholars are becoming increasingly uncomfortable with this kind of approach. Ideas emerge from concrete historical, social, and cultural situations, not out of the air. Texts are always imbued with elements of particular ideologies, even as they resist certain aspects of those ideologies. Some of the literary approaches used in Job studies do not have the critical resources to explore issues of social location, ideological commitment, and the subtle ways in which history enters a text. The way the book of Job presents itself as a story set in a vague time and place does not make it easy to ask such questions, but they can be asked.

A few pioneering works suggest some directions. One approach, represented by the work of Ranier Albertz,[3] has been to examine the descriptions of social types within the book, especially the model of the traditional pious aristocrat and the contrasting figure of the "wicked," understood as members of the upper class who do not share the old values of piety and social obligation. Comparison with similar texts from Mesopotamia, the historical contexts of which are better known, suggest the type of social conditions likely to produce such literature. A plausible historical setting for Job would be fifth-century Jerusalem, roughly contemporary with the social conflicts described in Nehemiah 5. Although intriguing, this analysis is based on a number of assumptions that are difficult to substantiate. Another approach attempts to combine literary analysis with theories of ideological criticism, especially those of Pierre Macherey and Fredric Jameson. In this approach, represented by David Penchansky,[4] the literary tensions and contradictions of the text are seen as traces of societal struggles. Although that approach sounds promising, when one is working with literature whose historical and social setting is not already known, it is extremely difficult to use ideological analysis to reveal precisely a concrete historical setting. Consequently, the discussion tends to remain rather circular.

It has often been the tendency to assume that the question of how Job is related to history must mean how Job serves as a response to a particular historical crisis. A work like Job, however, can also be a response to social and cultural conditions of long duration. For this sort of issue the resources of anthropology are helpful. There has already been some use of anthropological studies of honor/shame to clarify the dynamics of the divine speeches and Job's reply, but the approach could be used more extensively to explore the social assumptions of the moral world represented by Job and his friends. Although he does not use specifically anthropological methods, Karel van der Toorn[5] has attempted to show how changes in the social and economic organization of Israel are reflected in the moral language of the wisdom tradition, including Job. The type of investigation that would uncover the traces of socio-economic struggles in the language and imagery of the book is at a very early stage of formulation. Although many of these early studies seem overly speculative, they lay the groundwork for more nuanced and methodologically sophisticated work.

Another recent shift, characteristic of biblical studies in general, is a greater awareness of the way historical, social, and cultural conditions affect not only the production of a text but also the way it is read. Two results follow from this recognition. One is a greater modesty about the ability of modern critical scholarship to have discovered "the meaning" of the book of Job and consequently a much greater openness to including the precritical tradition of commentary on Job as part of the conversation. Interest in the history of interpretation is reflected both in a number of translations of medieval Jewish and Christian commentators as well as in a number of studies on particular periods and interpreters.

The second result of this increased awareness of the social location of the reader has been a lively discussion of Job from the perspectives of Latin American liberation theology, African American hermeneutics, feminism, and political dissidence. Although occasionally one hears the critique that Job is "a rich man's book" and cannot illumine the situations of oppressed and marginalized people, it is striking that most of the readings of Job from these perspectives have been quite positive. The affirmation of the book includes not only the character of Job who cries out but also of the God who speaks from the whirlwind and the reply that Job makes to God. Gustavo Gutierrez's book, *On Job: God-Talk and the Suffering of the Innocent,* is the most significant of the liberationist readings of Job. For Gutierrez, the book of Job shows how two languages, a prophetic language and a contemplative language, are required in speaking of God from the context of suffering. The prophetic language is the cry for justice to a God who has a preferential love for the poor. But the prophetic language cannot be used as a means of "gaining a hold on God" (p. 94). The language of contemplation acknowledges the freedom and gratuitousness of God's love. Gutierrez quotes the words of a murdered Bolivian priest: "Train us, Lord, to fling ourselves upon the impossible, for behind the impossible is your grace and your presence" (p. 91). That, Gutierrez says, is what Job did in his reply to God.

Such a reading contrasts sharply with the ambivalence to or rejection of the book in many post-Holocaust readings. Although Elie Wiesel's play, *The Trial of God,*[6] never explicitly mentions Job, it is a deeply disturbing exposure of the way in which the subtle theodicies of those who bring closure to the book unknowingly align themselves with the demonic, instead of leaving the rawness of its cry unassuaged. A similar perspective emerges from certain authors who read Job self-consciously from the perspective of victims. Rene Girard[7] sees in the book an exploration of the mechanism of ritualized victimization that is the nasty secret of the foundations of human community. In Job himself Girard hears a voice that resists such victimization. Terrence Tilley also has challenged many of the reading practices that produce an affirmative book at the expense of silencing the cry of the victim. The book of Job is for Tilley "not a book of answers, but a text of warning, perhaps even a text of terror."[8] Clearly there is a great deal of unfinished business in this discussion. The gulf between the understanding of Gutierrez and of Wiesel reaches the heart of the enigma of Job.

A few examples of how the interpretation of particular parts of the book is changing in relation to the issues discussed above will have to suffice. One of the most notable changes is in the reevaluation of the prose tale in chapters 1–2. Long dismissed as the boring bread wrapped around the real meat of the book, the prose tale is now recognized as a literary masterpiece in its own right. Not surprisingly, however, opinion is sharply divided as to whether it is a straightforward example of didactic storytelling or a pseudo-naive story that winks at the perceptive reader by means of ironies, parodies, contradictory perspectives, and instabilities of meaning.

By contrast, the divine speeches have long been recognized as enigmatic and have been interpreted in quite disparate ways (e.g., as a silencing of Job, as an encounter with the holy, as a subtle claim that retributive justice is not a part of the fabric of the universe). That variety of interpretation continues to characterize recent scholarship. Perhaps the most original interpretation is that of Janzen, who makes a case that the questions posed by God to Job, although ostensibly rhetorical questions, can also be heard as genuine existential questions. The divine speeches thus serve to reconstruct Job's understanding of the nature of human existence in the image of God. How differently God is understood by recent interpreters can be illustrated in two articles by Norman Habel and Tryggve Mettinger that appear side by side in a recent collection of essays.[9] Habel's article is entitled "God the Sage;" for Mettinger the central metaphor is "God the Victor." As these contrasting epithets suggest, the understanding of the divine speeches, and hence of the world they portray, is quite divergent. For Habel, the divine speeches portray a world of balance constructed by opposites, where the forces of chaos and death are present but constrained. The God of this world is not one "who intervenes or reacts, but one who modulates and constrains."[10] Mettinger, reading the same divine speeches as Habel, perceives a world with a clear moral pattern manifest in the daily overcoming of evil by God the Victor, who battles against the forces of chaos. The fact that both Habel and Mettinger are excellent exegetes and yet come to such contradictory inter-pretations points to an issue that has not received nearly enough attention, namely, the question of whether the divine speeches are not merely enig-matic but written in such a way as to make impossible any determinate interpretation. Like the book as a whole, they may be constructed in a manner that requires an interpreter to repress and exclude certain aspects of the speeches in order to achieve a particular understanding; yet what is repressed and excluded undermines the stability of that very interpretation.

At no point has the loss of certainty about what is being said become more apparent than in the issue of how Job replies to God. Although the signifi-cance of the words has long been recognized as problematic, at least there seemed to be a consensus about what Job literally said. The translation of the RSV, retained in the NRSV, is typical: "Therefore I despise myself, and repent in dust and ashes" (Job 42:6). After Dale Patrick's 1976 article raising questions about the translation and interpretation of that verse,[11] the consensus fell apart, as can be seen in this sample of translations:

"Therefore I recant and relent, being but dust and ashes." (TANAKH)
"Therefore I retract and repent of dust and ashes." (Habel)
"Therefore I despise and repent of dust and ashes." (Good)
"Therefore I recant and change my mind concerning dust and ashes." (Janzen)
"Therefore I will be quiet, comforted that I am dust." (Mitchell)[12]

The whole sense of what Job has heard and understood in the divine speeches, what effect they have had on the previously angry and alienated Job, depends in large measure on this half verse. The recognition of how ambiguous the Hebrew text of Job's reply is means that at virtually every crucial juncture—the transition from prose to poetry and back to prose, the divine speeches, Job's reply—the book resists a definitive interpretation.

To a large extent the introduction of literary criticism as a primary method has resulted in an appreciation of the book of Job as an "open text," that is, one that will not yield a single, determinate meaning. It is not that the book makes no sense but rather that the book makes many senses. This is a difficult realization for critics who have understood their task as the elimination of ambiguity and the search for a unitary truth. It is also a difficult realization for religious communities that have assumed that the Bible provides straightforward instruction. Such a claim, if it does indeed establish itself as a new consensus, would set the conversation about Job on very different terms. In part there would have to be a much greater self-consciousness about the process by which an interpreter makes meaning. But there would also have to be a change in the model by which one understands conflicting interpretations. It could no longer be a simple model of competition between right and wrong interpretations but rather of interpretations confronting one another with their complementary blindness and insight.

Ecclesiastes

It is almost irresistible to begin a reflection on recent work on Ecclesiastes with two sayings from the book: "of the making of books there is no end" and "there is nothing new under the sun." Such remarks would not be entirely fair, but they are suggestive. The scholarly conversation on Ecclesiastes is characterized by a set of perennial problems of a basic nature that are never completely resolved or transcended by a shift of paradigm. These include (1) the distinctive nature of the book's language, (2) the relation (or non relation) of the book to Hellenistic culture, (3) the structure (or lack of such) in Ecclesiastes, (4) the interpretation of the contradictions in the book, (5) the fundamental message of the book, and (6) the place of Ecclesiastes in biblical theology.

Reviewing recent publications, it is also striking that scholarly work on Ecclesiastes has remained, with very few exceptions, the province of traditional historical criticism. One would have thought that the great subversive of the Bible might have attracted attention from those who were concerned to challenge the assumptions about how one reads and interprets a text. Perhaps Qohelet is too obviously a kindred spirit and his book too evidently a "self-consuming artifact" to make deconstructive analysis very appealing.

The distinctive nature of Qohelet's language is one of the classic and most important issues in criticism. The dating of the book, and thus the realization that Solomon could not have written it, is largely dependent on the issue of language. The case for the late date of the Hebrew of Ecclesiastes was established by Franz Delitzsch in 1875, setting the grounds for the prevailing consensus that Ecclesiastes belongs to the Persian or Hellenistic period. The most common opinion is that the book comes from the mid-third century BCE. Nothing challenges scholarly ingenuity as the existence of a prevailing consensus, however, and in the last few years there have been attempts to use historical linguistics to argue on the one hand that Ecclesiastes was written precisely between 152-145 BCE[13] and on the other to argue that nothing in the language of Ecclesiastes prevents a preexilic dating of the book.[14] Neither of these attempts has been judged persuasive. The most careful and exhaustive analysis, recently published by Anton Schoors, concludes that the cumulative pattern of the evidence supports the consensus for dating the book within the fourth-third centuries BCE.[15]

It is not just time alone that makes the language of Ecclesiastes distinctive from Proverbs 1–9 on the one hand and Ben Sira or the noncanonical wisdom texts from Qumran on the other. As we know from the way we listen to the voices of writers in our own native languages, much information about where they come from, what social class they belong to, and what cultural movements have influenced them is embedded in how they talk or write. Trying to identify these aspects of Qohelet's language has been and continues to be an important issue. Although earlier attempts to argue for Phoenician influence or translation from Aramaic have not won many adherents, arguments that Qohelet uses a northern Hebrew dialect and/or a form of vernacular Hebrew continue to be made. It is very difficult with the present state of knowledge to make a strong case. Increasing sophistication in the field of dialect geography, however, and the increasing availability of comparative material give some reason to hope that the next decades will see progress in identifying the geographical, and social parameters of Qohelet's speech.

Although some of the best work on the language of Qohelet in recent years relates to the clarification of the nuances of particular particles, words, and phrases,[16] most of these studies have not addressed the socio-cultural dimensions of Qohelet's language. The earlier work by Gordis[17] on the development of a philosophical idiom in Qohelet and by Dahood[18] on the presence of commercial terms in extended senses was rich in implications for the social context of Qohelet's discourse, but the inquiry seems to have languished.

This question of the cultural context of Ecclesiastes is most often raised in the perennial question of Qohelet's relation to Hellenistic culture and specifically of the influence of Greek philosophical thought on Qohelet. Arguments for identifying Greek influence in Ecclesiastes have been made since the late eighteenth century, yet the issue remains one of the most contested. Part of the problem is methodological. What does one mean by "influence" and how does one establish its presence? Largely, this has been attempted by making lists of verbal parallels between Qohelet and Greek writers or by pointing to similarities between the content of Qohelet's thought and various Greek philosophical schools. Many of the alleged parallels do not survive close scrutiny. Moreover, parallels alone do not constitute an argument for influence, especially when the ideas or expressions in question may just as easily be traced to native Semitic wisdom traditions. A "softer" form of the argument is often made that avoids the claim that Qohelet knew specific texts and philosophical arguments. He was, rather, influenced by the "spirit of the age." This more diffuse encounter with Hellenistic culture was mediated by the soldiers, merchants, and Ptolemaic officials who, it is argued, were increasingly present in Judea during the third century.[19] Unfortunately, we know very little about the extent to which Hellenistic popular philosophy and culture was available in the mid-third century BCE, when most scholars date Qohelet.

The issue is not a peripheral one. If one wants to ask what kind of cultural work the book of Ecclesiastes performs, consciously or unconsciously, one needs to know how it is engaged in receiving, resisting, reinflecting, and recombining the various elements of cultural discourse within its social horizon. The suggestiveness of such an analysis is evident in Norbert Lohfink's recent interpretation, which begins with the assumption of a high degree of Hellenistic influence. Lohfink argues that the old wisdom tradition of Israel and the fundamental components of Torah were "formulated for a rural-provincial, 'segmentary' society," based on the tribe and local community. But changing socio-political conditions after the Exile created a class-based society that was "cosmopolitan, capital-controlled, state administered, stratified."[20] Although such a society was permeable to the individual, it was also much more isolating than the older social order. Changing social conditions created a crisis for old ways of understanding. In this context, Lohfink argues, Hellenism was not only something to be struggled against but also a resource for rethinking the world, since Greek society had already experienced an analogous process of social transformation. In Ecclesiastes one sees the attempt to appropriate what was useful in this Greek understanding of the world without giving up the distinctiveness of Israelite wisdom. Lohfink's interpretation of what happens in Ecclesiastes is fascinating, but the problem is that it begins with the controversial and unproven assumption that there was in fact strong Hellenistic cultural influence on Ecclesiastes.

Robert Harrison[21] has attempted recently to address some of the same socio-cultural issues without recourse to an assumption about Qohelet's knowledge of Hellenistic culture. Harrison attempts to show that by the third century BCE the impact of Hellenistic culture in Judea was actually minimal, but that the impact of Ptolemaic economic policy was having profound effects on Judean society. Drawing on comparative historical sociology, Harrison identifies Qohelet's work in the context of the "sociology of uncertainty" that emerges in the course of protracted, fundamental changes in social organization. The parallels with Hellenistic literature are explained as analogous responses to analogous situations. In Harrison's interpretation Qohelet emerges as the voice of a conservative critic within a rising middle class.

Grand theory, such as Harrison uses, has its own limitations. There is something of an *a priori* quality in the application of such a theoretical model to a particular case. It is just as difficult to show the connections between large scale changes in economic and social structures and ideas as it is to show the influence of Hellenistic culture on a Judean writer of the third century BCE. The issue is not one that is going away, however. Our own intellectual climate is one that is deeply concerned with the relationship between social and economic shifts and changes in the ways people understand their world. Similarly, the contemporary interest in cultural pluralism stimulates interest in exploring these same dimensions in Ecclesiastes. The developing philosophical vocabulary in Ecclesiastes, the metaphors drawn from the world of commerce, the sense of impermanence, the pessimism about human activity securing anything—there is much about Ecclesiastes that begs exploration in connection with the meeting of cultures and the deep changes taking place in the Judean economy and social structure. What methodological changes can break through some of the dead ends of the current discussion is less easy to say. The use of social scientific methods in biblical studies is increasingly sophisticated. The previous models of direct influence of one text on another are being replaced with more nuanced understandings of how discourses intermingle in contexts of cultural pluralism. Perhaps the next decades will see some genuine advances in these questions./

The third of the perennial issues listed above has to do with the problem of whether or not Ecclesiastes has an overall structure. The lack of an obvious formal or logical structure to the book has stood as a challenge to any number of scholars to demonstrate that the book in fact has such a structure, if one only looks at it properly. These intrepid critics have attempted a variety of methods for disclosing the structure. Some rely on content, others on formal features, most on a combination of both (see Whybray and Murphy for various proposals). Skeptics, who are probably in the majority, point out that no suggestion has produced a consensus. The question that needs to be asked, however, is what is at stake in this controversy. There is, of course, a pragmatic necessity in positing a provisional structure of some sort. One has to decide when to draw a breath, when to pause. What is at stake for the advocates of a total, governing structure is something more, however. A clue may perhaps be found in Addison Wright's conclusion: "If the above analysis is correct, the book speaks more clearly, but at the same time says much less, than we previously thought. The idea of the impossibility of understanding what God has done (which was always seen as a theme) is in reality *the* theme. . . ."[22] The attempts to find overall structure are attempts to control meaning in the book by establishing a sort of thematic hierarchy. Although other schemas are not quite so explicitly reductionist as Wright's, the fact that the common critique is that the overall structures and labels proposed are arbitrary and not adequate to the diversity of the material, suggests that the urge to rationalize an elusive book fuels the attempts. This persistent effort to argue for a structure governing the production of meaning shows how anxious this book makes many modernist critics. Here, perhaps, is an issue to which literary critics schooled in postmodern thought might suggest some alternative ways of thinking about the heterogeneity of the book.

The problem of unitary meaning is even more acutely raised in the classic issue of contradictory statements in the book of Ecclesiastes and the various strategies for interpreting them.[23] Overwhelmingly, the interpretive assumption has been that the contradictions must be resolved in some way. The active critical question was how. In the heyday of source criticism the contradictions were resolved and unity of meaning preserved by positing one or more editors who added counter-statements to Qohelet's disturbing aphorisms. Perhaps the most prevalent interpretive strategy for resolving the contradictions was to assume that the book is a form of dialogue or disputation, in which Qohelet cites and refutes the views of others. Even in precritical commentaries this suggestion was made, although at that time it was the skeptical perspective of the presumed voice of the "fool," which "Solomon" quoted and refuted. Later, critical scholars used the same technique to claim that the skeptical Qohelet cited conventional wisdom sayings in order to undermine them.

A variation on this interpretive strategy is the recognition of the *Zwar-aber Aussage* (the "yes, but" assertion, formulated by H. W. Hertzberg[24] and widely adopted), which produces a dialectical Qohelet. According to this way of reading, Qohelet acknowledges the truth of a particular claim, at least in general terms, but then produces an observation or reflection that seriously undercuts the initial claim. Initially, J. A. Loader appears to present a significantly different analysis in his argument for "polar structures" in Qohelet, i.e., the juxtaposition of the claims of systematized wisdom and protesting wisdom. As Loader graphically puts it, "[w]hen the two poles of doctrine and protest are counterpoised in the ancient Near Eastern wisdom, the headache is always followed by relaxation—but in Qohelet's head the migraine throbs continually."[25] *Hebel* ("meaninglessness") is produced by the unresolved tension of polar claims. Nevertheless, Loader resolves the tension more than he might realize by distributing the polarities systematically between two consistent perspectives, only one of which is represented by the voice of Qohelet. As is often noted, Loader's position is itself a variant on the quotation hypothesis.

A more radical approach to the contradictions is that of Michael Fox, who argues that where contradictory assertions appear in the book of Ecclesiastes, *both* perspectives are attributed to Qohelet. Qohelet's affirmation of contradictory truths discloses the unrelieved irrationality of life. Thus Fox's reading produces an absurdist Qohelet in the spirit of Camus. Of course, as Murphy shrewdly points out, the difference between Fox and the various formulations of the "disputation hypothesis" is merely whether the contradictions are externalized or internalized, that is whether they are contradictions that represent different perspectives within a society or whether they represent contradictions within an individual. Perhaps that is not such a small difference, however. A conflict of perspective between different schools of thought is a part of ordinary social discourse. Locating the unresolvable contradictions within the individual consciousness, however, is a way of underscoring the extent to which the ideology of the society itself is perceived to be in crisis.

Fox makes the case that this contradiction of perspectives is embodied not only in the figure of Qohelet but also in the literary form of the book. In opposition to virtually all modern commentators, Fox argues that the iconoclastic Qohelet and the conventionally minded frame-narrator are both creations of the book's author, who is not identified with either one. Fox seeks to limit the implications of this position by arguing that "[t]he distance the epilogist sets between himself and Qohelet is protective rather than polemical. . . . Qohelet, for his part, is not made into an unreliable persona; he does not self-destruct" (315-16). In my opinion, however, Fox underplays the significance of the fact that the epilogist, Fox's "implied author" of the book of Ecclesiastes, provides us with the first *mis*-reading of Qohelet.[26] The issue of contradictions is the perennial issue in the interpretation of Qohelet. The way it is perceived and addressed is an index of the intellectual assumptions made by successive interpretive communities. Although Fox is in most respects a very traditional historical-critical scholar, he has recast the issues in terms that challenge some of the assumptions generally governing historical-critical scholarship's understanding of authorship, texts, and unitary meaning.

A hallmark of Qohelet studies is the inability of readers to agree on the central message and tonality of the book. Two quotations, published in the same year, illustrate. James Crenshaw summarizes Qohelet's message as follows:

> Life is profitless; totally absurd. This oppressive message lies at the heart of the Bible's strangest book. Enjoy life if you can, advises the author, for old age will soon overtake you. And even as you enjoy, know that the world is meaningless. Virtue does not bring reward. The deity stands distant, abandoning humanity to chance and death. (23)

In Graham Ogden's opinion,

> Qohelet's purpose in writing is to be sought ultimately in the positive calls to his readers to receive thankfully from God the gift of life. . . . These calls to enjoyment are actually theological statements of faith in a just and loving God, despite many signs which might appear contrary. . . .[I]t is clear that Qohelet's focus is upon an affirmative rather than a negative view of human life. (22)

The problem posed by these radically different readings of the book is best put in context by a third quotation from Johannes Pedersen (cited by Murphy, 55):

> Very different types have found their own image in Ecclesiastes, and it is remarkable that none of the interpretations mentioned is completely without some basis. There are many aspects in our book; different interpreters have highlighted what was most fitting for themselves and their age, and they understood it in their own way. But for all there was a difficulty, namely that there were also other aspects which could hardly be harmonized with their preferred view.

Although critics argue about better and worse exegesis in particular interpretations, some attention is also given to the conditions that make such a broad range of plausible interpretations not only possible but inevitable. The lack of a systematic structure to the book as a whole (according to most scholars), the uncertainty of the extent of individual pericopes and of their relation to one another, the variety of ways in which the presence of contradictory statements is explained, the ambiguity of certain thematically central words, and the uncertain relationship between the themes of *hebel* ("vanity, absurdity") and *śimḥāh* ("joy") are all mentioned as factors that contribute to Qohelet's uncanny ability to mirror and to resist the interpreter. Since one of Qohelet's themes is the inability of human enterprise to seize and hold, to take possession of a thing, it is perhaps no accident that the book eludes the attempts of interpretive activity to fix its meaning determinately. I think that scholars have underestimated the significance of interpretive ambiguity in Ecclesiastes by seeing it as merely a problem to be solved. Perhaps it should be seen instead as another means of communicating the book's message.

Ecclesiastes is a book that makes people profoundly uncomfortable, a fact that renders its reception history particularly fascinating. Recent work in canonical interpretation, the history of interpretation, and the ever lively problem of what to do with Qohelet in relation to biblical theology illumines the various methods that have been employed to control this dangerous subversive. This activity begins even within the book itself, in the interplay between the body of the book and the epilogue, as Gerald Sheppard has shown.[27] The epilogist of vv. 13-14, using expressions that also appear in Qohelet's speech, provides the book with an "adaptive commentary" by "thematizing" or summarizing the book from the perspective of a wisdom ideology like that of Ben Sira. Sheppard stresses the legitimate but selective connection that this epilogue makes with the contents of the book. Michel, however, argues that the epilogist has simply misunderstood Qohelet and has inappropriately identified what Qohelet means by "fear of God" with what the epilogist understands by it.[28] (One wonders whether this is an innocent misreading or not.) In a rather different interpretation, Fox argues that the epilogist's remarks serve to subordinate the efforts of all sages, not only Qohelet, to a secondary status in relation to the essential claim: "Fear God and keep his commandments, for his judgment is thorough and ineluctable." Thus, "[t]he epilogist's caution is in no way a polemic against Qohelet or against Wisdom in general. On the contrary, placing Wisdom in the second rank constitutes a call for tolerance of expressions of opinion. It allows everything to be heard and considered as long as everything is finally subordinated to the proper fundamental belief" (319). Fox provides an attractive way of understanding the epilogist's stance, but underplays the agonistic relationship implicit in the containment of wisdom by the formula of piety.

Unfortunately, there has been no comprehensive recent study of the history of interpretation of Qohelet, although the last twenty years have seen a number of books and articles on specific topics, as well as translations of some of the important primary texts. It is always interesting to see where the "interpretive sweat" breaks out in dealing with such an iconoclastic book; moreover, the history of interpretation of Ecclesiastes sheds an important light on contemporary exegesis. In a brief discussion that suggests a promising line of investigation Murphy[29] has shown how formally similar techniques (e.g., selective emphasis, the assumption of a dialogical structure, an emphasis on the theme of joy) have appeared repeatedly not only in pre-critical but also in critical interpretation. Although sometimes employed to emphasize the elements of traditional piety in Qohelet and sometimes employed to eliminate them, the persistence of these techniques reflects the struggles of commentators to contain the disturbing contradictoriness of the book and to reduce it to a single, consistent perspective.

The theological scandal of the book remains an arena of contention. Among contemporary treatments one seldom finds the pious misreadings that characterized much of pre-critical scholarship, although some of the modern Jewish and Christian interpretations that emphasize the theme of joy come close to this approach (e.g., Gordis). Occasionally, in Christian writings, one still encounters the use of Ecclesiastes as a foil for the New Testament, a technique for simultaneously acknowledging and containing its disturbing presence in the canon. Much more common, especially among Protestant scholars, is the attempt to marginalize Ecclesiastes as alien to the core of biblical religion. No one has stated this position more explicitly than Michel. "[Qohelet's] 'God who is in Heaven' is not the God of Abraham, not the God of Isaac, not the God of Jacob, not the God in Jesus Christ. That, for all the fascination which comes from this thinker, one may not overlook."[30] Both Murphy and Lohfink have criticized this tendency to marginalize Ecclesiastes and so not to have to take his theological claims seriously. Yet their own apologias for Ecclesiastes mute the radicality of the book. Ecclesiastes is presented as a bracing corrective who can "serve to purify the faith and convictions of the modern reader" in danger of a too one-sided emphasis on certain aspects of traditional belief (Murphy, 69). Or selected aspects of Qohelet's views are presented as worthy of theological consideration, oftentimes restated in such a way that one can question whether one is listening to Qohelet as theologian or Lohfink as theologian.[31] Murphy has keenly indicated what is at stake in the controversy, however, when he argues "[i]t unwise to isolate an 'essential' religion within the Bible [i.e., a salvation-history perspective] and to discount the role of Ecclesiastes within the totality of biblical religion" (69). This issue is important on its own terms but also as an analogue to a contemporary issue within Christian theology, namely, the challenge posed to traditional formulations of the faith by the disturbing voices of marginalized women, African Americans, Hispanics, non-western Christians, and others whose symbols and theological expressions are often judged as beyond the bounds of what is authentically Christian.

One must give Michel and others their due, however. They have recognized the radical nature of the challenge presented by Qohelet to other discourses of faith within the Bible. The question is whether or not biblical scholarship can find a way to acknowledge the radicality of Qohelet without placing it outside the bounds of biblical theology. James Crenshaw suggests such a way in his "Plea to Readers," drawing attention to the epilogist's respect for and preservation of a work that was not at all congruent with his own perspective:

> For many years I have been fascinated with Qohelet, perhaps because he makes my own skepticism appear solidly biblical. Like him, I observe a discrepancy between the vision of a just world, which I refuse to relinquish, and reality as I perceive it. This radical absurdity gives an urgency and ultimacy to theological probings. But my reading of Qohelet is not necessarily the right one, certainly not the only possible one. I only hope readers will bestow on my understanding of Qohelet the same tolerance that his original audience extended to one whose radical ideas challenged virtually everything they cherished. (53)

Thus the model for future conversation about how to include Ecclesiastes within biblical theology is found in the earliest comment upon it by the epilogist, within the book itself.

In all likelihood the perennial questions will govern the discussion of Ecclesiastes into the foreseeable future. The changes in the way these are posed, however, are already observable in the recent works discussed above. First, the attempt to understand Qohelet's language and ideas in relation to the social, cultural, and economic conditions of his time will benefit from the increasing sophistication of social scientific and literary methods. Second, scholars will become less inclined to seek a simple but comprehensive resolution to the cluster of questions having to do with structure, composition, and message; instead, the contradictiveness and elusiveness of the book will be taken more into account as a part of its message, rather than an obstacle to be overcome. Finally, the place of Ecclesiastes in theological reflection, at least in Christian biblical theology, will be a bellwether for a larger religious situation torn between a move toward dogmatic orthodoxy and a move toward pluralism in religious discourse.

Notes

1. D. J. A. Clines, "Deconstructing the Book of Job," in *What Does Eve Do to Help and Other Readerly Questions to the Old Testament.* JSOTSup 94. (Sheffield: JSOT) 120.

2. Alan Cooper, "Reading and Misreading the Prologue to Job," *JSOT* 46 (1990) 74.

3. Ranier Albertz, "Der sozialgeschichtliche Hintergrund des Hiob-buches und der 'Babylonischen Theodizee,'" in J. Jeremias and L. Perlitt, eds., *Die Botschaft und die Boten: Festschrift für Hans Walter Wolff zum 70. Geburtstag.* (Neukirchen-Vluyn: Neukirchener Verlag) 349-71.

4. David Penchansky, *The Betrayal of God* (Philadelphia: Westminster/John Knox, 1990).

5. Karel van der Toorn, *Sin and Sanction in Ancient Israel and Mesopotamia: A Comparative Study.* SSN 22. (1985) 274.

6. Elie Wiesel, *The Trial of God* (New York: Schocken Books, 1979).

7. Rene Girard, *Job: The Victim of His People* (Stanford, Calif.: Stanford University Press, 1987).

8. Terrence W. Tilley, *The Evils of Theodicy* (Washington, D. C.: Georgetown University Press, 1991) 109.

9. Norman Habel, "In Defense of God the Sage," 21-38, 232-33, and T. N. D. Mettinger, "The God of Job: Avenger Tyrant, or Victor?", 39-49, 233-36, in L. G. Perdue and W. C. Gilpin, eds., *The Voice from the Whirlwind* (Nashville: Abingdon, 1992).

10. Habel, 35.

11. Dale Patrick, "The Translation of Job 42.6," *VT* 26 (1976) 369-71.

12. Stephen Mitchell, *The Book of Job* (San Francisco: North Point Press, 1987) 88.

13. Charles F. Whitley, *Koheleth: His Language and Thought* (Berlin and New York: Walter de Gruyter, 1979).

14. D. C. Fredericks, *Qoheleth's Language: Re-evaluating Its Nature and Date* (Lewiston, Maine: Mellen, 1988).

15. A. Schoors, *The Preacher Sought to Find Pleasing Words: A Study of the Language of Qoheleth* (Leuven: Peeters, 1992) 222.

16. In addition to the work of Schoors, see Fox (general bibliography) and Diethelm Michel, *Untersuchungen zur Eigenart des Buches Qohelet* (Berlin and New York: Walter de Gruyter, 1989).

17. Robert Gordis, *Koheleth: The Man and His World,* 2 ed. (New York: Schocken Books, 1968).

18. M. Dahood, "Canaanite-Phoenician Influence in Qoheleth," *Bib* 33 (1952) 30-52, 191-221.

19. So, for example, Martin Hengel, *Judaism and Hellenism* 1 (Philadelphia: Fortress, 1974) 115-30.

20. Norbert Lohfink, *Kohelet* (Stuttgart: Echter Verlag, 1980) 8.

21. Robert C. Harrison, Jr., "Qoheleth in Social-historical Perspective," Ph.D. Diss., Duke University (Ann Arbor, Mich.: University Microfilms, 1991).

22. Addison G. Wright, "The Riddle of the Sphinx: The Structure of the Book of Qoheleth," *Catholic Biblical Quarterly* 30 (1968) 334.

23. For examples, see James Crenshaw, "Qohelet in Current Research," *HAR* 7 (1983) 43.

24. H. W. Hertzberg, *Der Prediger* (Guttersloh: Gerd Mohn, 1963).

25. J. A. Loader, *Polar Structures in the Book of Qohelet* (Berlin and New York: Walter de Gruyter, 1979) 123.

26. So Michel, 286.

27. Gerald Sheppard, *Wisdom as a Hermeneutical Construct* (Berlin and New York: Walter de Gruyter, 1980) 124-27.

28. Michel, 286.

29. Roland Murphy, "Qohelet Interpreted: The Bearing of the Past on the Present," *VT* 32 (1982) 331-37.

30. Michel, 289.

31. See Lohfink, 15-17.

Selected Bibliography

Job

Clines, D. J. A. *Job 1-20*. WBC, 17. Dallas: Word Books, 1989.

Good, E. M. *In Turns of Tempest*. Stanford, Calif.: Stanford University Press, 1990.

Gutierrez, G. *On Job: God Talk and the Suffering of the Innocent*. Maryknoll, N.Y.: Orbis Books, 1987.

Habel, N. C. *The Book of Job*. OTL. Philadelphia: Westminster, 1985.

Janzen, J. G. *Job*. *Int*. Atlanta: John Knox Press, 1985.

Zuckerman, B. *Job the Silent*. New York: Oxford University Press, 1991.

Ecclesiastes

Crenshaw, J. *Ecclesiastes*. OTL. Philadelphia: Westminster, 1987.

Fox, M. V. *Qohelet and His Contradictions*. Bible and Literature Series 18. Decatur, Ga.: The Almond Press, 1989.

Murphy, R. E. *Ecclesiastes*. WBC, 23A. Dallas: Word Books, 1992.

Ogden, G. S. *Qoheleth*. Sheffield: JSOT, 1987.

Whybray, N. *Ecclesiastes*. NCB Commentary. Grand Rapids: Eerdmans, 1989.

Chapter 12
SHORT STORIES: THE BOOK OF ESTHER AND THE THEME OF WOMAN AS A CIVILIZING FORCE

Susan Niditch

"I married beneath me. All women do."
—saying attributed to Nancy Astor in The Oxford Dictionary of Quotations, ed. Angela Partington, 4th ed. (Oxford and New York: Oxford University Press, 1992) 32:11.

Safely sequestered among the writings, Esther makes public appearances at Purim time. Scholars, of course, take Esther out more often and yet even they tend to underestimate her centrality to major issues in political and gender ethics, issues important not only in understanding a slice of late Israelite and early Jewish culture but also in assessing recurring themes in Western culture as well.

Traditional Scholarly Approaches

Studies of Esther have covered certain issues with consistency. (1) *Date:* Is Esther Maccabean, Hellenistic, or Persian? (2) *Historicity:* Scholars have paid attention to the possible accuracy of details of name and place and asked larger thematic questions. Is a historical kernel preserved in the tale of Jews' escape from a persecution in diaspora? (3) *Genre:* Is Esther a historical novel, a wisdom tale, a festal legend, or midrash? (4) *Matters of source criticism and redaction history:* What is the relationship between the versions, for Esther is found in the Hebrew Masoretic text, in a Septuagintal Greek version and in another Greek version, the so-called A text. (5) *Theology:* Is Esther a religious work at all, for the Hebrew version lacks direct reference to God.[1]

In the past decade, an important and exciting area of inquiry has increasingly come to inform the study of Esther, feminist questions rooted in the field of women's studies. In what ways, for example, does Esther reflect and affect attitudes to women among Jews of particular periods and places? Is the character Esther to be understood as "something of a proto-feminist"[2] or as an unfortunate icon of female passivity taking her place with Disney's Snow White and Perrault's Cinderella? Do our scholarly readings of the woman Esther provide insights into aspects of Jewish culture in fifth century BCE diaspora or reveal more about various contemporary intellectual trends and social contexts?

To ask such questions of Esther is, in fact, to touch upon the older questions of provenance, genre, theology, and redaction history, which has become a special focus of recent studies of Esther,[3] and to raise larger issues about biblical tales of women.

Feminist Approaches with Special Relevance to Esther

Varying approaches to women in the Bible have been outlined and charted by Carolyn Osiek, Kathleen Corley, and others.[4] These stances or responses to the ancient literature strongly reflect our own orientations, a spectrum of worldviews through time and at any one time. My own set of categories with relevance to questions about Esther is as follows.

Traditionalist Acceptance

The traditionalist approach is the approach of my Hebrew school in the suburban U.S. of the 1950s, one that takes pride in Esther's beauty and bravery without critique or guilt. This approach valorizes the "feminine mystique" described by Betty Friedan and embodied in Bert Parks's "Miss America" and admits of no concern that Esther prostitutes herself to an uncircumcised oaf. Every little girl wants the role of Esther in perennial Purim plays and to "enjoy being a girl." Esther wins a beauty contest, marries the king, saves her people, and lives happily ever after. Who could ask for anything more?

This point of view while at home in a particular American setting is also found in the portrayal of Esther presented in *Esther Rabbah,* a medieval compilation of interpretations of the book in the particular exegetical style of classical rabbinic Judaism. Many such midrashim on individual verses or segments of the biblical book existed, interpretations that cast varying lights on the heroine. The particular combination chosen by the compilers of *Esther Rabbah* creates an image much like the one I inherited in synagogue: Esther is noble (*Esth. Rab.* 6:11); it is assumed that she was involved in a full conjugal relationship with Ahasuerus, although the rabbis debate whether she bore him children (8:3); it is considered no shame to have married the king of the Persians while he is portrayed as in love with her (9:1); and she dresses for success and hides her anxieties behind a radiant smile (9:1).

This approach to Esther is a seductive one that supports a particular androcentric status quo. It remains powerful in the U.S. even today although not among scholars and biblicists.

Rejectionism and Substitution

The rejectionist position points to the negative effects such views of Esther have upon young women and gender relations. Mary Gendler writes:

> What about Esther do I find objectionable? In most ways she sounds like an ideal woman—beautiful, pious, obedient, courageous. And it is just this which I find objectionable. Esther is certainly the prototype—and perhaps even a stereotype—of the ideal Jewish woman—an ideal which I find restrictive and repressive. . . .
>
> Sociologically it is no secret that men were seen distinctly as the masters of their homes and of the society in general, not only at the period of history during which the story might have taken place, but throughout all of recorded Jewish history. Men were the leaders, the scholars, the rabbis, the authorities, [w]omen tended the home and the babies. In this sense, Ahasuerus can be seen not only as an Ultimate Authority who holds vast power over everyone, but more generally as male, patriarchal authority in relation to females. As such, Vashti and Esther serve as models of how to deal with such authority. And the message comes through loud and clear: women who are bold, direct, aggressive and disobedient are not acceptable; the praiseworthy women are those who are unassuming, quietly persistent, and who gain their power through the love they inspire in men. These women live almost vicariously, subordinating their needs and desires to those of others. We have only to look at the stereotyped Jewish Mother to attest to the still-pervasive influence of the Esther-behavior-model.[5]

Esther Fuchs[6] and Alice Laffey[7] share Gendler's position and see Esther as contributing to a portrait of woman as a passive sex object, able to succeed only by pleasing men and by conforming to a male-centered view of women. Esther so understood is ultimately destructive of women's own self-esteem while justifying a particular power structure and treatment of women in Western culture, which continues to be informed by and even shaped by scriptural models.

Gendler goes so far as to suggest that Vashti provides a better model than Esther for young women in her defiance of the piggish king and his entourage. In this way, Gendler is able to find some redeeming features within the biblical story and Jewish tradition. Others faced with similar self-realization about the impossibility of accepting biblical models and the symbolic structures to which they belong have turned to alternate traditions, e.g., Carol Christ's communion with Greek goddesses,[8] or have sought to create new traditions altogether, e.g., Naomi Goldenberg's suggestions for women's sharing and interpreting their own dreams in the formation of new meaningful combinations of symbols.[9]

The rejectionist/substitution position thus finds a place in the larger field of women and religion, as feminist studies inform women's capacity to appropriate or identify with a character such as Esther.

Selective Appropriation and Adaptation

Between those who uncritically accept the tradition and those who espouse reasoned rejection are those who retain a certain sympathy for aspects of Esther's character while being made uncomfortable by others. Aspects accepted or rationalized or adjusted will differ from period to period and author to author, but all in this category want to find their worldviews in scripture and find the portrayals of Esther wanting. Apologies and adaptations must be made.

Benno Jacob's 1930s article on biblical women in a volume of Leo Jung's *Jewish Library* reveals a strongly apologist and in many ways typical older position concerning woman in the Hebrew Bible. For example, Jacob acknowledges women's exclusion from a variety of religious duties but sees this exclusion as a positive means of defining "her individuality." While "all the tragedy in the existence of woman" may lie in God's pronouncement concerning motherhood in Gen 3:16, "all her happiness" derives from the mother's role as well. While the woman's value in monetary terms is lower than a man's, "it is of deeper significance that the Bible gives its special protection to woman when she is in danger—as the weaker party—of being defrauded or injured."[10]

Louis Ginzberg's narrative midrash, in which the erudite scholar retells the biblical story through a particular selection and arrangement of rabbinic midrashim, discloses discomfort with the theme of Esther's marriage to the gentile monarch. Thus Ginzberg includes the midrash from the Zohar stating that Esther herself never actually had sex with Ahasuerus, but a spirit image of herself would descend to go to him in her place.[11]

The ancient Esther tradition, in fact, reveals a fascinating process of appropriation and adaptation. In the Greek versions, Esther prays to God, eats only kosher food, and specifically addresses the issue of marriage to a foreigner.

Fox, Clines, and others who have explored the various ancient stories of Esther posit complex histories behind each extant version and suggest various lines of relationship between them. Such an approach has significance for our study of Esther from a feminist perspective, for in the case of each extant version and each hypothesized precursor to those texts we could ask, how is Esther portrayed; how do different authors and audiences respond to her and reveal their own worldviews in portrayals of the heroine?[12]

There is considerable debate, of course, concerning the pre- or proto-form of these variants and my own interest in this essay is in the actual extant Masoretic version. What we can say at least is that even the extant versions indicate that various groups make the tale of Esther their own, appropriating and selecting motifs in their versions of the tradition. The composers of the final form of the Greek versions like Louis Ginzberg address the issue of intermarriage. In these accounts Esther's marriage to the heathen becomes an act of self-sacrifice and martyrdom that allows Esther to save her people. [See the language in so-called Addition C of the Apocryphal version C 5:25-28 (NRSV 14:11-19).] Such tellings in effect tone down the theme of woman as a civilizing force prominent in the canonical Hebrew version to be explored below.

Modern Hebrew teachers no doubt find their own means of appropriating and adapting Esther, emphasizing her courage, her intelligence, her capacity to adapt to changing circumstances, her ultimate success in saving her people over her more passive and seemingly obedient traits, and her use of physical beauty as a means of succeeding.

The story as a whole retains power for Jews in that it raises issues relevant to the survival of a frequently persecuted minority population. What is the most efficacious stance towards the establishment: overt violent resistance, passive resistance, lobbying by placing one's own people in positions of power, full-scale collaboration? The same question could be asked about women's stance toward men's power in a culture in which men dominate the public realm.

In any event, most modern scholars worry less about relevance and appropriation than about understanding Esther in the context of early Judaism. After Ninian Smart, I refer to their approach as "structured empathy."[13]

Structured Empathy

The phrase *structured empathy* implies the scholar's desire to understand the way others believe—others who lived before us or who live in contemporary cultures different from our own. Such scholars seek to comprehend the way other human beings, set in social groups, make sense of the world. They approach this search with openness and the capacity to identify with the subjects of study but with no need to appropriate their worldviews or to make sense of our lives in terms of their "sacred canopy."[14]

The investment in this sort of study of sacred texts is thus different from the investment of appropriators. This, of course, is not to claim absolute objectivity for those who approach a work such as Esther with structured empathy. Our selves and our contexts always intrude and influence our interpretation. Thus when I explore Esther I do so as a female Jewish academician in her forties with interests in comparative literature. The gender of the scholar and other issues of identity and context will influence the scholarship that emerges. When feminist scholars urge us to read suspiciously they refer not only to primary texts but to the commentaries as well.

Examples of Structured Empathy

In the category of structured empathy are studies by Sidnie White, Michael V. Fox, David J. A. Clines, André LaCoque, Claudia Camp, Lee Humphreys, and myself.[15] After briefly exploring and expanding upon some of the themes emphasized by scholars who approach Esther with "structured empathy," I will examine some themes that have been overlooked.

One useful recurring observation is that the tale of Esther is a Bildungsroman of sorts in which the heroine develops and matures.[16] Her passive beauty, her acceptance of guidance under Mordecai and then under the chief eunuch, her capacity to be molded by men—her helpers in the traditional narrative pattern of the underdog—characterize the young Esther described as *bĕtûlāh,* a term frequently translated "virgin" or "maiden." As Peggy Day has shown, however, this term has chronological significance. For Day, the *bĕtûlāh* is generally an adolescent, a young woman who has reached puberty but who is not fulfilling the adult role as mother that will transform her status. The Canaanite goddess Anat thus is the eternal *bĕtûlāh* not because of virginity per se but because she is not Mother, tied down to parental, adult-rendering obligations.[17] The second-century rabbis of the Mishnah, in fact, define *bĕtûlāh* as prepubescent, a girl just about to undergo physical maturation but possibly already married (*m. Niḍ* 1:4). At Esth 4:15-16 comes the transformation of Esther's character, her passage into adulthood and psychological maturity as she takes responsibility for the lives of her people and actively takes control of the situation. She orders Mordecai (note the use of the imperative)[18] to instruct all the Jews of Susa to hold a fast on her behalf. She then holds the banquets[19] cleverly wooing Haman into unsuspecting and hubristic complacency while reminding her husband of her charms, finally climatically revealing her ethnic identity and convincing the king of Haman's villainy. The Jews' fortunes are reversed because of Esther's intervention. In chap. 8, Esther has the power to place Mordecai over the house of Haman (8:2), power to see that Haman's edict is reversed and that the Jews may defend themselves (8:11), and in 9:23-32 she is declared to lend her authority through letters to the celebration of Purim.

This process of Esther's coming into her own has been nicely traced by Marvin Fox, Sidnie White, and others.[20] Esther's seeming passivity before the transformation in chap. 4 is essential to understanding one theme of the work dealing with maturation, the acceptance of responsibility and moral autonomy, and matters essential to the successful development of men and women. However, we need to ask further what this mature and active Esther, successful within the parameters of the narrative, indicates about its creator's attitudes to women, about woman as a component of this cultural and symbolic map. Where does structured empathy lead in dealing with these questions, in seeking to understand the worldview of Esther's author, the cultural context of the composition, and the views of women it reflected and helped to shape? How was Esther's audience of men and women expected to react to Esther? What aspects of her characterization as a mature heroine would be sources of identification and empathy for early Jewish women? What themes does the tale reinforce?

Sidnie White points to Esther as an excellent example of the way the weak in a culture manage to achieve "basic survival." "They must adjust to their lack of immediate political and economic power to learn to work within the system to gain what power they can."[21] Esther's strength and wisdom are in her capacity to adjust to changing and insecure fortunes of the marginal, to use anything that enhances one's advantage including beauty, sex appeal, and men's susceptibility to women's emotion.[22] In a similar vein, I describe Esther's "collaboration with tyranny" as a necessary expedient for the powerless, the author's view of what it is to be wise for Jews in the setting of exile, and for women in the workaday world of gender relations as she understands them.[23]

Michael V. Fox's treatment of the material shares much with White's and mine—the emphasis on the wisdom of expediency, for example. Fox makes an additional important point, that on many levels the book of Esther is a satirical critique of the male power structure. Ahasuerus is portrayed, Fox notes, as "erratic" and "despotic." The author "is aware of female subservience and is cynical about the masculine qualities that require it."[24]

Fox, however, circumscribes this description of a key theme in Esther by suggesting that:

The satire is not, however, directed at male dominance in and of itself, but at male dominance as manifested in the Persian court and, by extension, throughout the gentile realm.[25]

In fact, Fox has pointed obliquely to a fascinating theme found not only in Esther, but in the larger Israelite tradition and in traditional literatures all over the world, the notion of woman as the civilizing force in culture and the frequently accompanying related social critique of the male-dominated worlds in which both men and women find themselves.

Woman as Culture Bringer

The wider mythological background to the theme of woman as civilizing force is the theme of woman as culture bringer. I have discussed this theme in detail in relation to the biblical Eve who helps to bring about reality with its distinctions of status and gender roles and in relation to the courtesan of the Gilgamesh Epic who transforms Enkidu from hairy wildman at home with the animals to wine-drinking, bread-eating man, the friend and alter ego of the hero, Gilgamesh.[26] As Phyllis Trible originally argued, Eve is the protagonist of the biblical tale of creation in Genesis 2–3, the active seeker of knowledge who makes the decision to eat from the tree while Adam passively accepts the fruits, a follower.[27] I have also pointed to women's strong roles in family settings in tales such as Genesis 27 and Judges 13, in which the women know more about, oversee, or help to effect the careers of their sons, while their husbands appear passive, powerless, or foolish.[28]

Less cosmogonic than the woman as culture bringer and less family-bound than images of woman as knowing mother, the theme of woman as civilizing force relates in complex ways to portrayals of gender in the Hebrew Bible and to questions of author's intent.

Woman as Civilizing Force

A host of wise biblical heroines are described in scenes with powerful male characters. The women change the heroes' minds so that the course of events is altered and the women's situation or the status those whose cause they advocate is improved. Frequently, danger to them or to those they represent is averted. Even more important for the theme of civilizing, they tame the men whom they address, powerful men who are not using their power wisely but who appear foolish, violent, willing to destroy innocent victims or unable to show mercy.

Esther is in this category as is Abigail (1 Samuel 25), who convinces David in the bandit period of his career not to take vengeance on her husband's household; for Nabal, an apparent Saul loyalist, has refused to pay David with food and supplies for the uninvited "protection" he and his band had provided to Nabal's shepherds (1 Sam 25:1-13). Also in the category of civilizing force are the woman of Tekoa hired by David's general Joab to perform an act of mediation via *mashal* between David and his estranged son Absalom (2 Samuel 14), and the wise woman of Abel Bethmaacah who intervenes between her townsmen and Joab concerning an enemy of David's state who has taken refuge in her city (2 Sam 20:4-22). Claudia Camp has explicitly or implicitly taken stock of many of the ways of these wise women.[29]

The women present themselves in stereotypical biblical feminine roles that are regarded as positive in the ancient Israelite tradition. They are appealingly ripe with non-threatening sexuality or are mother-like. Esther and Abigail are beauties and offer the men food and drink, symbols of fullness, fertility, and the woman's role as provider in the private realm.[30] The tale of the woman of Tekoa involves her self-presentation as concerned and suffering mother while the wise woman of Abel Bethmaacah begs Joab not to destroy this ancient town which is "a mother in Israel." As White notes, the men are expected to respond to emotional appeal and women expected to rouse emotions and so they do.[31] Moreover, the women convince with words carefully and cleverly chosen to enhance the self-esteem of those they address, while they place themselves in the background even as they speak. A good example in Esther is found at 8:5:

> If it pleases the king . . . and if I have won his favor, and if the thing seems right before the king. . . .

Esther Fuchs nicely describes Queen Esther's language as "placatory" and "ingratiating."[32] Abigail falls at David's feet (1 Sam 1:24), begs forgiveness for her foolish husband diplomatically by taking the blame upon herself (v. 28),[33] speaks of David as a future victor who will receive from God a sure house, addresses him as "my lord," and assures him that all his enemies will be defeated thereby conveying blessings in her very prediction. [Note the wonderful imagery "sling out as from the hollow of a sling" and the artful use of wordplay (25:25), alliteration (25:29) and other poetic devices throughout her speech.] Finally Abigail cleverly manages to tell David that he will feel better if he does not shed innocent blood (vv. 30-31). Telling David exactly what he wants to hear about his own future success softens the bandit chief to accept Abigail's plea that he spare Nabal's household and resheathe his manly sword.

The woman of Tekoa is similarly disarming in her ingratiating choice of formulas of address, in the way she frames her case ["Pray let your handmaid speak . . . (2 Sam 14:12)], and in her building up of the king's sense of his own power and his capacity to set things aright: "My lord the king is like the angel of God . . ." (2 Sam 14:17). In similarly diplomatic fashion, the wise woman of 2 Sam 20:14-22, uses a saying, a mode of making or introducing noninflammatory criticism indirectly, to approach the man of power. She thus speaks diplomatically without unnecessarily triggering his potentially violent and aggressive power (2 Sam 20:18-19).[34]

The women succeed by making themselves seem small, dependent, and unimportant while flattering the men to make them feel as if all power resides with them. The women's rhetoric also suggests that the men are fair, good men of self-discipline who know how to control their power and use it properly which is, in fact, precisely not the case for Ahasuerus, David, or Joab. The Persian king has abused his power in accepting plans to destroy good and loyal citizens; David later grabs Bathsheba's sexuality contrary to accepted mores and kills her husband, Uriah the Hittite, to cover up the woman's pregnancy; Joab kills his brother's slayer, but whereas Abner kills unavoidably in war, Joab takes vengeance in an ambush and perhaps not only to avenge his brother but also to remove a rival general who now vies for David's patronage. Each of these men exemplifies a particular sort of macho arrogance and displays an undisciplined and unbridled aggressiveness, undertaking action not circumscribed by proper thought or consideration of consequences, and evidencing, in short, a lack of wisdom.

In an excellent study of 1 Samuel 25, Jon Levenson suggests, in fact, that the tale of Abigail is an overt critique of David meant to adumbrate the rash actions concerning Bathsheba in which no wise Abigail intervenes to teach him moderation.[35] As noted in discussing Michael V. Fox's point about the way in which the book of Esther critiques Ahasuerus and his cronies, the theme of woman as a moderating, civilizing force is a popular one.

All four representations of interactions between powerful men and the women who influence them are rooted in notions of mother as teacher even, a Freudian would say, as the mother-teacher sometimes mixes with the mother-as-lover. Claudia Camp has explored these boundaries in representations of Woman Wisdom[36] who is the archetypal civilizing force of Israelite classical literature, at God's side even in creation, drawing the young man to her with words of love, nurturing, and encouragement, helping him to avoid the impetuous adolescent side of himself prone to violence, illicit sex, and other harmful aggressive activities.

Stith Thompson has outlined a number of traditional international tale types that invoke similar motifs: aggressively foolish men in power and the sensible women figures who bring the men to their senses through beauty, diplomatic and frequently manipulative speech or actions, emotional appeal, and flattery. These tale types include no. 874 "The Proud King is Won" and no. 875 "The Clever Peasant Girl." In the latter a peasant girl becomes the king's wife after performing various difficult tasks successfully because of her good sense or by solving difficult riddles. The king becomes angry when the queen helps one of his poor subjects win a dispute by using a *reductio ad absurdum* that reveals the king's lack of wisdom. He banishes her, but she wins him back when he allows her to take her dearest possession into exile, and she manages to take the sleeping king himself, moving him to forgive her.[37]

The question, of course, is why would one want to win such men over. Why not assassinate them in the case of Ahasuerus or flee from them in the case of David? What does the desire somehow to co-opt them say about the authors and worldviews behind these stories?

Social Critique, Cultural Model: Whose Voice?

On the one hand all of these images of the way that men and women interact are reactionary, for true power arrangements are not altered and the women achieve their objectives by working within that system—one might say by helping to build up the confidence of those in power so that they can be helpful to the woman's objectives at least this time.

On the other hand, these scenes, stories, and characterizations have a subversive underside. As women hear or create such typological scenes they learn that they can be wise, wiser than the men and that on one level they can take some measure of control. Even more subversive, these women's words and deeds may serve as powerful social critique, perhaps a self-critique and a critique of their culture by men when they are the composers of one or another of the tales. One thinks of the Iliad in which the words of women might be interpreted as questioning the agonistic, male-dominated ethos of their warrior husbands. (See, for example, the exchange between Andromache and Hektor in 6:406-65.)

These various complaints of women who "marry beneath them" are complex markers of cultural attitudes towards the accepted or proverbial ways of men and women, for while the critiques in the women's voice stand, the ways of the world and the ways of men—be they violent, foolhardy, or reckless—are not expected to change. And yet in individual situations and upon individual men—apart from the culture at large—the influence and therefore the responsibility of the woman can be deemed to be considerable.

In one of the many homilies on the creation of woman in Genesis 2, the rabbis attach to Gen 2:21 the following tale:

> There is a story about a pious man who was married to a pious woman, but they did not produce children with one another. They said, "We are not accomplishing anything for the Holy One Blessed Be He." They took action and divorced one another. He went and married an evil woman and she made him evil. She went and married an evil man, but made him righteous. This proves that it all depends on the woman. (*Gen. Rab.* 17:7)

This midrash suggests that women are sources of moral power and persuasion, a positive civilizing force while the men are malleable and immature, lacking moral autonomy. Images of mother as teacher and model again come to mind.[38] Such an image of women is potentially empowering, but also tends to shift responsibility for immorality away from men and somehow to leave the blame at the women's feet. If women are society's civilizing forces and men act in uncivilized ways, women must have failed.

Thus the negative counterpart of Woman Wisdom in Proverbs 1–9, so much like her wise sister in use of persuasive speech and sex appeal, draws forth from young men not their best selves, but their worst, pulling them toward the very depths of Sheol.[39]

Jezebel, the wife of Ahab, is portrayed by biblical writers as the quintessential woman as evil influence, her husband as morally weak and childlike. When Ahab petulantly desires Naboth's vineyard, his inherited family holdings, and Naboth refuses the king, Ahab pouts, lying down and refusing food. Jezebel comes to him mother-like, concerned in a nurturing way that her husband does not eat (1 Kgs 21:5). She urges him to cheer up, assures him that she, Jezebel, will fix everything and she does by seeing to Naboth's murder. Paradoxically, the woman portrayed as vicious murderer, is wife and mother who cares for her husband-son and who shapes him. Indeed Elijah and Jezebel compete for Ahab's soul like a father and mother in a bad divorce. Shakespeare's Lady Macbeth is another such wife-mother, who negatively influences her weak husband. Woman thus appears both as man's "better half" and his "worst self." In either case, it is most accurate to see these images of women not simply as representations of men's or cultures' ambivalent attitudes towards women, but rather as projections of men's views of themselves, their good and evil inclinations.

Esther, Abigail, and the wise women of 2 Samuel are ultimately ways in which men can express their conscience and their best side but through these women the superego prods in a non-threatening and non-intrusive way. Ancient Israelite women, while not encouraged to feminist liberation by these models, were no doubt reinforced in their belief in the truth of Nancy Astor's saying, but paradoxically the inner self-esteem lent by this belief to women tends to reinforce the outer status quo.[40]

Notes

1. A review of the debates concerning each of these issues and relevant bibliography is found in S. Niditch, "Legends of Wise Heroes and Heroines," in *The Hebrew Bible and Its Modern Interpreters*, eds. Douglas A. Knight and Gene M. Tucker (Chico, Calif.: Scholars Press, 1985) 445-51.

2. Michael V. Fox's phrase in *Character and Ideology in the Book of Esther* (Columbia, S.C.: University of South Carolina Press, 1991) 209.

3. See Michael V. Fox, *The Redaction of the Books of Esther*, SBLMS 40 (Atlanta: Scholars Press, 1991); David J. A. Clines, *The Esther Scroll: The Story of the Story*, JSOTSup 30 (Sheffield: JSOT, 1984).

4. See Carolyn Osiek, "The Feminist and the Bible: Hermeneutical Alternatives," in *Feminist Perspectives on Biblical Scholarship*, ed. Adela Yarbro Collins (Chico, Calif.: Scholars Press, 1985) 97-105; Katharine Doob Sakenfeld, "Feminist Uses of Biblical Materials," in *Feminist Interpretation of the Bible*, ed. Letty M. Russell (Philadelphia: Westminster, 1985) 55-64; Kathleen E. Corley, *Private Women, Public Meals: Social Conflict in the Synoptic Tradition* (Peabody, Mass.: Hendrickson, 1992) 3-8.

5. Mary Gendler, "The Restoration of Vashti," in *The Jewish Woman*, ed. Elizabeth Koltun (New York: Schocken, 1976) 242, 245.

6. Esther Fuchs, "Status and Role of Female Heroines in the Biblical Narrative," in *The Mankind Quarterly* 23 (1983) 149-60.

7. Alice L. Laffey, *An Introduction to the Old Testament: A Feminist Approach* (Philadelphia: Fortress, 1988) 216-17. For a recent rejectionist treatment see Itumeleng J. Mosala, "The Implications of the Text of Esther for African Women's Struggle for Liberation in South Africa," in *Semeia* 59 (1992) 129-37.

8. Carol P. Christ, *Laughter of Aphrodite: Reflections on a Journey to the Goddess* (San Francisco: HarperCollins, 1987).

9. Naomi R. Goldenberg, *Changing of the Gods: Feminism and the End of Traditional Religions* (Boston: Beacon, 1979).

10. Benno Jacob, "The Jewish Woman in the Bible," in *The Jewish Library*, ed. Leo Jung (London and New York: Soncino, 1970) 1, 3, 4.

11. Louis Ginzberg, *The Legends of the Jews*. Vol. 4 (Philadelphia: Jewish Publication Society of America, 1913) 387-88.

12. Michael Fox, *The Redaction of the Books of Esther*, 172-33; David J. A. Clines, *The Esther Scroll*, 144, 168-74.

13. Ninian Smart, *Worldviews: Crosscultural Explorations of Human Beliefs* (New York: Scribner's, 1983).

14. Peter L. Berger's term. *The Sacred Canopy: Elements of a Sociological Theory of Religion* (Garden City, N.Y.: Doubleday, 1967).

15. Sidnie White, "Esther: A Feminine Model for Jewish Diaspora," in *Gender and Difference in Ancient Israel*, ed. Peggy L. Day (Minneapolis: Fortress, 1989) 161-77; Michael V. Fox, *Character and Ideology*; David J. A. Clines, *The Esther Scroll*; André LaCoque, *The Feminine Unconventional Four Subversive Figures in Israel's Tradition* (Minneapolis: Fortress, 1990) 49-83; Claudia V. Camp, *Wisdom and the Feminine in the Book of Proverbs* (Sheffield: JSOT, 1985) 134-35; "The Three Faces of Esther: Traditional Woman, Royal Diplomat, Authenticator of Tradition," in *Academy: Journal of Lutherans in Professions* 38 (1982) 20-25; Lee W. Humphreys, "A Life-style for Diaspora: A Study of the Tales of Esther and Daniel," *JBL* (1973) 211-23; Susan Niditch, *Underdogs and Tricksters: A Prelude to Biblical Folklore* (San Francisco: Harper and Row, 1987) 126-45.

16. S. Niditch, *Underdogs and Tricksters*, 135, 138; S. Talmon, "Wisdom in the Book of Esther," *VT* 13 (1963) 449; S. White, "Esther," 169-72; Michael V. Fox, *Character and Ideology*, 196-204.

17. Peggy L. Day, "From the Child Is Born the Woman: The Story of Jephthah's Daughter," in *Gender and Difference*, ed. Peggy L. Day, 59-60. On Anat, see Neal H. Walls, *The Goddess Anat in Ugaritic Myth*, SBLDS 135 (Atlanta: Scholars Press, 1992) 154-59.

18. Michael Fox, *Character and Ideology*, 199.

19. On the banquet motif see Sandra B. Berg, *The Book of Esther*, SBLDS 44 (Missoula, Mont.: Scholars Press, 1979) 31-35; Claudia V. Camp, *Wisdom and the Feminine in the Book of Proverbs* (Sheffield: JSOT, 1985) 133-36.

20. White, "Esther," 169-72; Michael Fox, *Character and Ideology*, 196-204.

21. "Esther," 166-67. See also S. Niditch, *Underdogs and Tricksters*, 141-45.

22. White, 167-68; 171.

23. S. Niditch, *Underdogs and Tricksters*.

24. *Character and Ideology*, 107, 109. On the caricature of Ahasuerus see also S. Niditch, *Underdogs and Tricksters*, 133-34.

25. *Character and Ideology*, 209.

26. S. Niditch, *Chaos to Cosmos: Studies in Biblical Patterns of Creation,* (Chico, Calif.: Scholars Press, 1984) 36-38, 40-43.

27. Phyllis Trible, "Depatriarchalizing in Biblical Interpretation," in *The Jewish Woman,* ed. Elizabeth Koltun (New York: Schocken, 1976) 226-27.

28. S. Niditch, *Underdogs and Tricksters,* 96, 99-101; "Samson as Culture Hero, Trickster, and Bandit: The Empowerment of the Weak," *CBQ* 52 (1990) 610-12.

29. Camp, *Wisdom and the Feminine,* 42, 85-87, 90-96, 120-24, 133-36, 143-45.

30. Camp, *Wisdom,* 80-81.

31. "Esther: A Feminine Model," 171.

32. "Female Heroines," 156.

33. See Jon Levenson on the rhetorical style of 1 Samuel 28 and especially on Abigail's comments on her husband. "1 Samuel 25 as Literature and History," *CBQ* 40 (1978) 19-20.

34. On the wise women in 2 Samuel and the use of sayings as a diplomatic means of criticism, a way in which the weaker can approach the stronger, see Claudia V. Camp, "The Wise Women of 2 Samuel," *CBQ* 43 (1981) 21, 23. See also S. Niditch, *Folklore and the Hebrew Bible* (Minneapolis: Fortress, 1993), 69-70.

35. Levenson, "1 Samuel 25 as Literature and History," 23-24.

36. Claudia V. Camp, *Wisdom and the Feminine.*

37. For an outline of tale type 875 and examples see Antti Aarne and Stith Thompson, *The Types of the Folktale* (FF Communications no. 184; Helsinki: Suomalainen Tiedeakatemia, 1973) 293-95.

38. In this context one might consider Nancy Choderow's suggestion concerning men's and women's social maturation. Whereas girls grow into women and can in a sense become their mothers, boy children never will. This, she suggests, leads men to "remain psychologically defensive and insecure" even while "guaranteeing to themselves sociocultural superiority" ["Family Structure and Feminine Personality," in *Women, Culture, and Society,* Michelle Zimbalist Rosaldo and Louise Lamphere (Stanford, Calif.: Stanford University Press, 1974) 51, 66]. On mother as teacher see Fokkelien Van Dijk-Hemmes, *On Gendering Texts: Female and Male Voices in the Hebrew Bible* (Leiden: Brill, 1993) 128.

39. For a detailed discussion see Camp, *Wisdom and the Feminine,* 112-20, 125-26; and Carol Newsom, "Woman and the Discourse of Patriarchal Wisdom: A Study of Proverbs 1-9," in *Gender and Difference in Ancient Israel,* ed. Peggy L. Day, 142-60.

40. For an interesting and thoughtful discussion of women's voice and the implicit ambivalences in the portrayal of wise women see Athalya Brenner and Fokkelien Van Dijk-Hemmes, *On Gendering Texts,* 129. Professor Brenner's comments dovetail nicely with the discussion above although she and I reach somewhat different conclusions.

Selected Bibliography

Berg, Sandra Beth. *The Book of Esther.* SBLDS 44. Missoula, Mont.: Scholars Press, 1979.

Brenner, Athalya, and Fokkelien Van Dijk-Hemmes. *On Gendering Texts: Female and Male Voices in the Hebrew Bible.* Leiden: Brill, 1993.

Camp, Claudia V. "The Three Faces of Esther: Traditional Woman, Royal Diplomat, Authenticator of Tradition." In *Academy: Journal of Lutherans in Professions* 38 (1982) 20-25.

———. *Wisdom and the Feminine in the Book of Proverbs.* Sheffield: JSOT, 1985.

———. "The Wise Women of 2 Samuel." *CBQ* 43 (1981) 14-29.

Clines, David J. A. *The Esther Scroll: The Story of the Story.* JSOTSup 30. Sheffield: JSOT, 1984.

Fox, Marvin V. *Character and Ideology in the Book of Esther.* Columbia, S.C.: University of South Carolina Press, 1991.

Fuchs, Esther. "Status and Role of Female Heroines in the Biblical Narrative." In *The Mankind Quarterly* 23 (1983) 149-60.

Gendler, Mary. "The Restoration of Vashti." In *The Jewish Woman.* Edited by Elizabeth Koltun. New York: Schocken, 1976, 241-47.

LaCocque, André. *The Feminine Unconventional Four Subversive Figures in Israel's Tradition.* Minneapolis: Fortress, 1990.

Levenson, Jon. "1 Samuel 25 as Literature and History." *CBQ* 40 (1978) 11-28.

Newsom, Carol. "Woman and the Discourse of Patriarchal Wisdom: A Study of Proverbs 1-9." In *Gender and Difference in Ancient Israel.* Edited by Peggy L. Day. Minneapolis: Fortress, 1989, 142-60.

Niditch, Susan. *Underdogs and Tricksters: A Prelude to Biblical Folklore.* San Francisco: Harper and Row, 1987.

White, Sidnie. "Esther: A Feminine Model for Jewish Diaspora." In *Gender and Difference in Ancient Israel.* Edited by Peggy L. Day. Minneapolis: Fortress, 1989, 161-77.

Chapter 13
RESHAPING CHRONICLES AND EZRA–NEHEMIAH INTERPRETATION

Kent Harold Richards

First and 2 Chronicles and Ezra and Nehemiah are the primary biblical documents that help us understand the Persian or Achaemenid period (sixth–fourth centuries BCE). (This period was once described as a dark age, but now the metaphor of a fertile field, giving rise to new ideas and conflicting hypotheses, is much more appropriate.) These documents, along with Esther, form the "secondary history." It tells through borrowed and reinterpreted sources, partially from the "primary history" (Genesis–2 Kings), a story of individual leaders and people, communities fighting for a renewed identity, rebuilding a temple, and gathering around God's word. We are often most impressed by the endless lists in these books, forgetting that the Mishnah reminds us that Chronicles was one of the books read before the high priest to keep him alert prior to the Day of Atonement!

This essay will discuss, first, the remarkable fact that the interpretation of Chronicles and Ezra–Nehemiah, until the last quarter of the twentieth century, has been shaped by the demand to interpret them together and not separately. Second, we need to look at Persian period studies in order to comprehend the ways they are reshaping the interpretation of these books. Third, a scenario regarding the study of these documents in their Persian period context is envisioned. Identifying the trajectories within these books and the Persian period will better help us to understand transitions in the social, religious, and political dynamics of this formative time.

Dissolution of a Consensus

No factor in the history of the interpretation of 1 and 2 Chronicles or Ezra–Nehemiah has remained more constant than the conviction that these books must be interpreted together. Individual books of the Pentateuch, even in precritical work, could be easily interpreted as separate; not so with 1 and 2 Chronicles (hereafter Chrons) and Ezra–Nehemiah (hereafter EN). One could read Genesis focusing on the primeval history or patriarchs and, not necessarily, reflect on Moses' last will and testament in the book of Deuteronomy. But only in the last quarter of the twentieth century has the interpretive disengagement of Chrons and EN become the dominant scholarly stance.

The interpretation of these books as bound together has depended on perceptions of their authorship. In precritical times, Ezra was thought to have been the author of this entire corpus. He is an obvious candidate given his characterization of scribe and priest. These features have been expanded outside the Hebrew canon in rabbinic traditions. There, he is characterized as a second Moses; writer and interpreter of laws; primary priest of the exilic community, and even high priest in Jerusalem; founder of a school; and the restorer of Torah. However, apart from the so-called Ezra "memoir" (Ezra 7:27–9:15; Nehemiah 8), neither Chrons nor EN provide evidence of Ezra as their author. Moreover, twentieth-century scholars have rarely maintained that Ezra was the author of these books (cf. Clines 6, 12 for the exception).

During the twentieth century various hypotheses have emerged that address the character of the first-person reports of Ezra, and, for that matter, the first-person Nehemiah accounts within Nehemiah (1–7; 12:27-43; 13:4-31). The Nehemiah "memoirs" have generally been thought to contain authentic elements, developing over time and representing a combination of genres (i.e., various types of temple or votive inscriptions, report of activities, prayer of the accused). The authenticity of the Ezra "memoirs" has been questioned more frequently. However, scholars have identified genres similar to those in the Nehemiah accounts, though also viewing the Ezra material as a midrash on the Artaxerxes edict. In no case have these discussions supported a single author hypothesis that would draw EN and Chrons together as a unitary work.

Since the mid-nineteenth century and until nearly the last quarter of the twentieth century, scholars have named the author of Chrons and EN the Chronicler. Instead of Ezra or Nehemiah each having an individual author, this Chronicler was understood to have authored/edited both EN and Chrons. Some time after the events themselves, the Chronicler constructed this history. The Chronicler has been depicted in diverse ways, as an original author, as an editor, or even a school of writers who produced several editions of the work over a number of years, maybe even several centuries. The Chronicler has been designated the author/editor not only of Chrons and EN, but also 1 Esdras (see Eskenazi, *Age*).

The development of the Chronicler hypothesis in the nineteenth century stemmed in part from the inability to attribute authorship of this sizable corpus of Chrons and EN to Ezra or any identifiable eyewitness. The argument for the Chronicler as author/editor of both Chrons and EN was bolstered by similarities in language, ideology, thematic development, and point of view throughout these books. Blenkinsopp, a recent EN commentator and incisive interpreter of the Persian period, still argues on behalf of the Chronicler hypothesis. He suggests that Chrons and EN have a common authorship because of similarities in: (1) conceptions of temple building for the First and Second Temple; (2) views of leadership for the temple, namely, by the "head of an ancestral house"; (3) liturgical interests, descriptions of cult objects, and formulaic elements of prayers; and (4) the structural movement in each corpus from periods of "religious infidelity" to "renewal and reform" (53-54).

However, there are significant differences that reach beyond the priestly and ritual foci implicit in Blenkinsopp's enumerations. These include EN's identification of Israel with Judah as opposed to Chrons' identification of Israel with the twelve tribes; EN's use of exodus motifs and Chrons' lack of interest in early traditions; EN's non use of Davidic tradition as compared to Chrons' emphasizing the Davidic and Solomonic monarchy; EN's anti-Samarian ideas and Chrons' positive view of the North; EN's lack of prophetic dimensions as compared to Chrons; and the list might be expanded. The themes and theological perspectives are very different, which leads one to have serious reservations about common authorship of Chrons and EN.

Linguistic arguments on behalf of common authorship for these books have long been made. However, advances in linguistic analysis of Hebrew in general, and Late Biblical Hebrew in particular, have revealed flaws in such arguments. A more refined diachronic understanding of Late Hebrew has emerged, in part, based on studies of Chrons. A number of scholars (e.g., Japhet, Polzin, Throntveit, Williamson) have, in the last quarter of the twentieth century, presented analyses of the linguistic data (e.g., syntax and morphology) that challenges the notion of common authorship. Even a supporter of the Chronicler hypothesis such as Blenkinsopp notes the problems of the linguistic arguments for common authorship. The current debate is whether or not linguistic arguments can prove separate authorship in these books.

Despite the longstanding view of Chrons and EN as one entity, no manuscript tradition treats them as a single work. The manuscript tradition holds Chrons together as a single book, and EN as a single book. They were divided into four books: 1 Chronicles, 2 Chronicles, Ezra, Nehemiah, much later in their history of transmission, i.e., in the Septuagint the division existed, but not in Hebrew editions until the fifteenth century CE.

There is an obvious connection between Chrons and EN, since the Cyrus edict that concludes 2 Chronicles (36:22-23) is repeated, nearly verbatim, in the first lines of Ezra (1:1-4). Some have regarded this connection as indicative of common authorship. However, common authorship is not demanded or even implied by what might be regarded as an intentional compositional technique of the author. From this perspective, if one reads these books in the order that they appear in English Bibles, the repetition of these lines invites the reader to continue reading EN once having completed Chrons.

Arguments identifying this repetition of lines in Chrons and EN have been used to bind together the interpretive history of these books in the West. After all, almost all of the translations into Western languages have retained the order Chrons and then EN. While this order does exist in some Hebrew traditions, it is not the dominant one. The most prevalent order in Hebrew manuscripts and printed editions is to place Chrons at the conclusion of the Writings, with EN coming before it. In the Greek Bible, one finds a chronological arrangement of books. Hence, Ruth follows Judges and Chrons follows Kings with EN and then Esther. The majority of Greek traditions have 1 Esdras situated between Chrons and EN. This placement would lend some support to the hypothesis that the Chronicler is the author of Chrons and 1 Esdras.

The repeated lines, when not placed "end to end" as in the English Bible, do not lead the reader from one book to the other, let alone suggest the same author for both works. Some commentators have suggested that the aforementioned repetition of the Cyrus edict was accomplished precisely because it served to unite two originally disparate books. Whenever diverse authors are suggested, the lines in Chrons are usually thought to have been borrowed by Chrons from EN, since Chrons is regarded, frequently, as the later document.

The separation of Chrons from EN has influenced yet another hypothesis that has arisen in the last decade of the twentieth century, namely, that Ezra and Nehemiah represent books each with its own autonomy. However, it has been difficult to make strong arguments for autonomous thematic, structural, and linguistic tendencies in Ezra and Nehemiah (Kraemer). Nehemiah's concern with the Torah and Ezra's interest in the more priestly matters reflect major issues of Persian period Judah, but not necessarily, distinct literature.

Literary problems do exist in Ezra and Nehemiah. The fact that Nehemiah has a portion of what seems to have been a part of the first-person Ezra account (Nehemiah 8) has generated numerous debates. In Ezra, the Aramaic sections framed by Hebrew present another set of problems. Still, numerous thematic and theological motifs and structures hold the texts together. In addition, the manuscript evidence for understanding Ezra and Nehemiah as separate Hebrew books emerged only when printed editions became available; in other words, long after authorship was determined. No concomitant hypothesis regarding the separation of 1 Chronicles from 2 Chronicles has emerged or is likely to evolve.

Literary critical analysis of EN has added support to other arguments for interpreting Chrons and EN as separate literatures. For example, Eskenazi uses characterization, point of view, and literary structure to demonstrate the way the themes of community, city-temple, and sources hold EN together as one book. In addition, Throntveit focuses on the way such literary conventions as concentricity, parallel panels, and repetitive resumptions provide the "literary architecture" of EN. And, though explicitly literary critical, other work has identified conventions that hold Chrons together. Far more prevalent in Chrons research is the identification of the genres within that corpus, and the identification of a genre for the entire work (history, commentary, theological essay, collection of sermons, historical midrash). Attention to the literary design of these forms, coupled with a growing interest in the canonical shape of biblical books, has had enormous influence in the last quarter of the twentieth century.

In sum, the common interpretive history of Chrons and EN has been significantly challenged in the last quarter of the twentieth century. This interpretive disengagement gains impetus from more than the manuscript and textual traditions. In addition, the thematic, theological, and ideological differences between Chrons and EN add further weight to the separate interpretation of these literatures. Understanding Chrons as representing one set of themes and theological perspectives and EN another set affords a new opportunity to identify the diverse perspectives that existed during this formative period of Judaism.

It is important to distinguish two books within this period, a time when the "book" was gaining enormous importance for the emerging identity of Judaism. Chronicles and EN, along with the Pentateuch, which was being codified during the Persian period, help interpreters understand the ways the written word gained authority.

Shifts in scholarly focus during the last quarter of the twentieth century have not been based on new literary, or for that matter material, evidence. Some extrabiblical literary remains have emerged, but no Elephantine type cache has been unearthed. The discoveries in the Judean desert have produced virtually no new texts or fragments of texts of these books (six lines with four legible words from Chrons). The map of Chrons and EN interpretation is being redrawn, but not because of significant new literary data. Rather the map is shifting, in part, because of the deployment of literary methods and the interpretive disengagement of Chrons and EN. Another element influencing the redrawing of this map reflects the impact of Persian period studies.

KENT HAROLD RICHARDS

The Impact of Persian Period Studies

Peter Ackroyd, who helped set the stage for reshaping the study of Chrons and EN, observed in 1982 that there was a need to review the material remains of the Persian period as well as to determine the connections with data from the preceding and following historical periods. This review continues today, with many more questions and no clear consensus. Moreover, some longstanding puzzles in Chrons and EN studies remain.

First, the view that Chrons is historically unreliable dates from rabbinic times. Perpetuation of the position that Chrons' history was arbitrary was supported by a comparison with parallel material in Samuel–Kings. But, when the examination of Chrons' additional material—material not included in Samuel–Kings—was considered, interpreters suggested that some material may derive from reliable sources, despite their slight distortion. This positive evaluation of nonsynoptic material led to a reconsideration of both synoptic and nonsynoptic materials.

Second, while there is still no consensus regarding Chrons as an historical work, there has been a shift away from the reliability issue. Though some still search Chrons for "facts" unique to it, the far more dominant issue involves its historiography. Since the mid-twentieth century, scholars have attempted to describe the various historiographies within the Hebrew Bible, namely, comparing Chrons' history to the Deuteronomistic History (see the essays of Knight and Wilson).

Chrons certainly relies on the earlier Deuteronomistic History, as well as on sections of the Pentateuch. Genesis is adapted by scouring the genealogies to focus on the direct connections from Adam to Israel in order to substantiate an election ordained from the foundations of the earth and conferred on Israel by God. No mention is made of extraneous individuals such as Cain. Covenants are unnecessary because of Israel's special place. The slavery-exodus-wandering traditions recede into the shadows. The laws of the Pentateuch are paraphrased, woodenly repeated, or not even mentioned. Certainly we hear more about priestly legal issues. The period of the judges seems unimportant in the telling of Chrons history. The Deuteronomistic historical framework is almost slavishly followed, but without any efforts to synchronize between Israel and Judah during the period of the divided kingdoms. After all, Chrons is interested only in "Israel" and, of course, in their God. Direct communication from God comes not only through the prophets, but also to David and Solomon who charter the royal dynasty. Prophets take on expanded roles, including the establishment of religious music. As one contemporary interpreter has said, Chrons was always making an effort to elevate the traditions for a new generation, to bridge the gap between a dead past and a newly legitimated present. Chrons "is a

216

comprehensive expression of the perpetual need to renew and revitalize the religion of Israel . . . affirm the meaningfulness of contemporary life without severing ties . . ." (Japhet, *I* and *II Chronicles*, 49).

Chronicles presents the bringing together of story and history, not simply neutral history writing. When interest in Chrons or EN focused on historical veracity, the sources (edicts, letters, "memoirs," etc.) used by Chrons and EN were evaluated for their reliability. One could ask whether the first-person source or the third person account was more reliable (e.g., one could compare Neh 12:44–13:3 and 13:44-31). As interest in historiography increased, it became more crucial to examine the way these sources, or one might say the diverse genres, were woven together in the story told by Chrons or EN. Identification of the genres of the sources themselves became increasingly significant. The comparison, for example, of the ways lists or letters are used and with what intent they are employed becomes crucial. The comparison of genres and their use is important for determining the way the themes and ideas were developed in the larger work. In addition, scholars are currently contextualizing the biblical historiographical tendencies with extrabiblical history writing. More careful attention to historiographical works from Judah's neighbors in Mesopotamia, Egypt, and Greece will further illuminate the interpretation of Chrons and EN.

Third, despite these new directions, attempts to date the composition of Chrons remain complicated. Dates all the way from ca. 525 to 200 BCE have been proposed, with some interpreters bracketing the issue and offering no judgment. Moreover, there is no correlation between dating alternatives and authorship hypotheses. In other words, those holding the diverse authorship of Chrons and EN do not opt for either an early or a late date for the composition of Chrons.

Fourth, the chronology developed in EN has always presented problems for the interpreter. Earlier attempts to correct the garbled chronology of EN's 100-150 year history in order resulted in some significant rearrangement of the text. One needed to bring a portion of Nehemiah (7:73*b*–8:18) between Ezra 7 and 8, and then Nehemiah 9–10 after Ezra 10. These changes enabled the modern interpreter to impose the "correct" history on the text. Then interpretation could proceed. Given the new impetus to examine the text as it exists, and without thinking of the text as an objective reporting of events, the interpreter is forced to look for the reasons the story is told in the way it is. Historiographic concerns now focus on the extant literature. The decision on whether to rearrange the text and then interpret it is directly related to discussions about the historical order of the figures of Ezra and Nehemiah. The relationship of these figures constitutes another persisting problem. The pendulum seems to have swung back to preserving the traditional, "biblical" order of Ezra, then Nehemiah. The actual dates of the figures and whether or not their work overlapped or remained virtually without mutual recognition, as EN seems to imply, has evoked numerous theories (Suiter). Questions about whether or not Ezra even existed or was a necessary literary invention are still being raised.

Fifth, the most significant historical advances regarding the Persian period have not come from new material evidence. Rather, they have come from an enormous burst in research on almost every dimension of the Persian period. Some helpful cataloguing of the existing material evidence (Stern) has been undertaken. The reevaluation of data in concert with archaeology's new ties to social scientific methods (Carter, Hoglund) have produced important new understandings about this period.

We are now able to reflect more carefully about the population size and borders of the postexilic Persian province of Judah. Ezra 2 and Nehemiah 7 suggest a sizeable population of returnees (around 40,000), and estimates, based on biblical texts, of a total population have ranged as high as 200,000. However, apart from the literary recollections of size, there are new methods of estimating populations long after they have disappeared. These estimates use ethnographic data in conjunction with archaeological material. With these newer methods, some have suggested that in the late sixth century a low population of around 11,000 existed with a population high of 17,000 in the early fourth century BCE (Carter). The geographical boundaries of Judah have been estimated to be roughly half the size of the state of Rhode Island (about 620 square miles). The picture in Neh 11:25-36 certainly suggests a larger region. This picture, however, was not designed to provide a descriptive geography, but one that indicated the ancestral attachments of returnees.

Despite the tendency to see a smaller, poorer, and less stable Judah in the sixth-fourth centuries, there remains the growing awareness that this population was in no way disconnected from the international exchanges between East and West. One merely needs to read EN to see the references to Persian rulers and the use of diverse dating procedures for events. Judah existed in a massive Persian empire. The Persian Empire stretched from Greece across Turkey just below the Black Sea and Caspian Sea and beyond Afghanistan. Circling around the Mediterranean Sea, the empire included Syria, Lebanon, Israel, across the delta of the Nile as far as Libya. Dropping down deeper into Egypt, the empire went at least as far south as Elephantine and across the Red Sea, including portions of Saudia Arabi, Jordan, Iran, Iraq, and beyond the Indus River. It has been said that a decision in Susa altered the destiny of Athens and reverberated in Jerusalem.

Not only was Judah embedded in a vast geographical landscape, so too its literature sits in a literary landscape of incredible scope. The libraries of Greece contained books of authors from approximately the same time as

Ezra and Nehemiah, i.e., Herodotus, Thucydides, Xenophon, Sophocles, Aeschylus, Euripides, Aristotle, and Demosthenes. The names of Egyptian authors, while less well known, constitute an impressive list. Interpreters of Chrons and EN will be well served by remembering that the context for understanding this literature is not merely the deuteronomistic historian or genealogies in Genesis.

Understanding the Judahite society that gave rise to Chrons and EN, and other canonical literature, within the vast Persian Empire (Davies, Eskenazi, and Richards) is of extraordinary significance. Answers to the questions of who wrote, when and why, need conceptual refinement. Understanding the way a society works helps us to determine a range of potential authors. Groups do not write, specific individuals within groups write. Furthermore, the range of individuals with appropriate skills and knowledge to write history in any culture is limited, and especially so in Persian period Judah given its small size. When Chrons seeks to revitalize an understanding of Israel, how is the interpreter to relate the material (earlier and later) Israel to the Israel of the text? The question can only be answered when one has adequately understood the sociology of the period, as well as the individual author's social stance. Greater clarity is needed in understanding and identifying the ways in which Crons and EN are related to the social terrain of Persian period Judah.

Finally, the area of most significant research in recent Persian period studies focuses on the so-called civic-temple community. The data we have gained regarding temple-cities.from various historical periods has led to the conclusion that the civic-temple community is the best way to understand the Second Temple. This new temple community of returning exiles, who no doubt closely associated with certain issues in EN, were not merely a religious body who gathered in public for the reading of the Torah. They were a socio-political organization made up of the privileged, self-managing elite who controlled the agriculture, ran the bank that was housed in the temple, collected voluntary and mandatory contributions, had a workforce, and were grouped by ancestral houses headed by an elder. The priest was an administrator for the distant Persian rulers, as much as a religious figure. The returnees used the city-temple for identifying religious space and place, but also for reclaiming a political and economic place and space.

Situating the study of Chrons and EN in the broader context of the Persian period demands knowledge of classical Greek sources, studies of the Persian Empire, geographical and archeological data, and interdisciplinary socio-economic analysis. Many loose ends exist in trying to tie these broader studies to the individual problems and solutions of Chrons and EN interpretation. This agenda will occupy a good portion of the concluding years of the tweitieth century and the beginning of the twenty-first century.

KENT HAROLD RICHARDS

A Scenario for Study

Problems, and solutions to them, are usually predicated on the realities of the present. This is the case whether one is examining the judicial system in twentieth-century America or suggesting ways to advance our understandings of biblical literature. We are more comfortable relying on the observable present rather than leaping beyond it. We avoid looking over the rim. We look into the future too often through a rearview mirror. It may seem out of place to borrow from the futurists as we consider looking toward the twenty-first century in the study of Chrons and EN. Yet, much of the most creative historical, literary, and social scientific research devoted to these books, and to the Persian period out of which they emerge, have derived from imaginative ventures.

A number of years ago when the venture into space began, there was much discussion about simulation. Future astronauts were given various scenarios with expected, sometimes unexpected, factors, to which they needed to respond. The simulation provided opportunities to anticipate various conditions and develop more appropriate responses. As a result of that interest in simulating what it might be like when landing on the moon, some biblical interpreters began to write biblical simulation games. A story or situation from the Bible was taken, such as the garden of Eden or the story of Job, and people were given parts to play.

Inevitably groups that used these simulations went back to the text prior to acting out the story. Upon completing the simulation through a debriefing, I was always struck by how the imaginative act, a kind of role playing, drove the students to imagine what might have been. They filled in some of the silence in the texts. However, more strikingly, the play drove them back to the text, urged them to reexamine the data, helped them see imprecise formulations in the way they played the scene, and most importantly imbedded in them the importance of using diverse methods and tools when interpreting texts.

I will attempt very briefly to provide a scenario that might cause certain shifts in our understanding of Chrons and EN, as well as of the Persian period. I have imagined the discovery of a civic-temple community archive. Since we have discovered such archives from closely related periods, this is not an outlandish possibility. Just imagining such a discovery will not make it a reality. But the simulation does make it possible for an interpreter to reexamine creatively a hypothesis and formulate new responses.

The discovered archives are from a site just outside Judah near Gezer. The archives include many of the expected documents that deal with loans, rental of farmlands, lists of persons who were members of the community, as well as one that listed various administrative responsibilities of priests. A copy of the Cyrus edict is present in both Aramaic and Hebrew. In addition, there are letters exchanged between Ezra and Nehemiah, brought to this archive in what appear to be copies of the originals that must have been in the Jerusalem Temple. Two points, among the diverse data, emerge from this discovery.

First, the data seems to imply that Chrons and EN represent closely related, but diverse understandings of leadership and community from the same basic period of time: Ezra arrived 458 BCE and Nehemiah about twenty years later in 445 BCE. EN's author says in a newly discovered letter to one of his close associates, that he, the author of EN, wanted to place his focus on the extremely important role the entire community played in the return and rebuilding. He understood the events to represent a more populist perspective. Furthermore, this author of EN says in the letter that he has been in Judah twenty years longer than the author of Chrons. The EN author wants the reader to understand that his views were more closely related to the actual occurrences of return and rebuilding. The EN author's more populist perspective than the one found in Chrons, avoids emphasizing heroic leaders. In fact, in that one letter he explicitly criticizes Nehemiah.

The new archival findings clearly indicate that there was enormous dependence on Persian authority among the returnees as well as reliance on the social, religious, and political patterns that worked in the Exile. There is a hint in one of the letters from a senior military officer, possibly a Persian convert to Judaism, that even the figures of Ezra and Nehemiah were not characters of unambiguous heroic dimensions. All of the correspondence found in the archives indicates that much confusion existed in leadership. The confusion seems to have resided in the growing tendency not to separate scribal and priestly roles. The diversity of views concerning who represented the faithful was hard to detect. Moreover, the place of several indigenous groups worshiping Yahweh remained unclear.

The archives indicate, that while Nehemiah wanted to be looked upon as a more decisive leader, he, too, failed miserably. Letters from an attaché of Nehemiah indicate that Nehemiah was called back to the Persian court and asked to justify his failures despite all the reports he had filed on a regular basis with Persian authorities in Susa.

Further documents among the archives suggest that the author of Chrons, while highly respected for having held up the Davidic and Solomonic traditions, presented a hope too late for a Judah near extinction. The reinterpretation by Chrons of the Davidic and Solomonic leadership found so explicitly in earlier sources provided a patina over the real political and economic interests that Chrons wanted to revive during the Persian period. In fact, in one letter written by the author of Chrons, he hints to a fellow historian that he is concerned about the variations he is using in his telling of the "biblical story."

Second, within the new archives there are documents from a debate among the various factions claiming true faithfulness to the tradition. The debate centered on the meaning of the temple, about which there seems to have been an extraordinary diversity of views. A group from Elephantine had been at odds with a group of exiles who decided not to return to Judah, and hence advanced the cause of their temple in Susa. The issue of the ability to worship Yahweh in a foreign land continued to threaten the very fabric of various Jewish communities.

From all the correspondence in these newly discovered archives, the fight over who really represented the faithful seems not just to have been a battle of religious differences. It was that too, but at the center it was a battle over power within and without the communities. Every document found in the temple archives suggests that any separation of religion and politics was foreign to the competing factions.

One of the most important pieces of documentation from the archives was an exchange between the authors of Chrons and EN. There seems to have been some disagreement about the interpretation of the meaning of the Cyrus edict. They believed that they would be able to put their own "spin" on the edict. The author of EN suggests, that while he has made available to Chrons the copy of the edict, he also concedes that both will no doubt end up using it in their works. The author of EN does receive a concession from the Chrons' author that although the Chrons' author will use the edict, he will not carry his history any further into time. Therefore, the one promises to conclude his work with the edict, while the other begins his story with it.

This tactic of imagining the discovery of an archive scenario, and reporting the tendencies from the archival documents, enables the interpreter to propose solutions to old problems. Naturally, it would be easy to point out new problems that emerge from interpreting data from the new discovery. It would be a fortunate set of circumstances to find such an archive, even if it were an archive that would demonstrate the inaccuracy and impossibility of the civic-temple community concept for the Second Temple, or even that, indeed, the figure of Ezra never existed.

The material and textual evidence from the past will never be complete. Additional evidence may suggest the resolution of one issue or another, but interpreters are always faced with the incomplete information about the completed past. A more explicit effort to engage diverse scenarios will enable interpreters to understand the importance of their own role in the interpretive process, as well as the context out of which they interpret. So, even the discovery of an ancient document that suggested that the figure of Ezra most likely preceded Nehemiah would not once-and-for-all solve the meaning of

EN. Nor would the confirmation that two authors agreed to disagree on the importance and role of the Cyrus edict settle the issue of the meaning of Chrons or EN.

Explicitly placing the interpretation of Chrons and EN at the intersection of a tiny Judean province and the vast reaches of the Persian empire has made the interpretive task more complex. On the other hand, such a placement seems necessary for two documents that refer to numerous external sources, demonstrate the reconfiguration of older traditions, contain bilingual materials, refer to leaders known outside these documents, and reflect upon such classic issues as the relationship between leader and community, book and sacred place-space.

Selected Bibliography

Ackroyd, P. *The Chronicler in His Age.* JSOTSup 101. Sheffield: JSOT, 1991.

Blenkinsopp, J. *Ezra-Nehemiah: A Commentary.* OTL. Philadelphia: Westminster, 1988.

Carter, C. *A Social and Demographic Study for Post-Exilic Judah.* Ph.D. Diss., Duke University, 1991.

Clines, D. *Ezra, Nehemiah, Esther.* NCB. Grand Rapids: Eerdmans, 1984.

Davies, P., ed. *Second Temple Studies. 1. Persian Period.* JSOTSup 148. Sheffield: JSOT, 1992.

Eskenazi, T. "Current Perspectives on Ezra-Nehemiah and the Persian Period." In *Currents in Research: Biblical Studies* 1 (1993) 59-86.

———. *In an Age of Prose: A Literary Approach to Ezra-Nehemiah.* SBLMS 36. Atlanta: Scholars Press, 1988.

———, and K. Richards, eds., *Second Temple Studies 2. Temple Community in the Persian Period.* JSOTSup 175. Sheffield: JSOT, 1994.

Hoglund, K. *Achaemenid Administration in Syria-Palestine and the Missions of Ezra and Nehemiah.* SBLDS 125. Atlanta: Scholars Press, 1992.

Japhet, S. *I and II Chronicles.* OTL. Louisville: Westminister/John Knox, 1993.

———. "The Historical Reliability of Chronicles," *JSOT* 33 (1985) 83-107.

Klein, R. "Chronicles, Book of 1–2," *ABD* 1. New York: Doubleday, 1992, 992-1002.

———. "Ezra-Nehemiah, Books of," *ABD* 2. New York: Doubleday, 1992, 731-42.

Kraemer, D. "On the Relationship of the Books of Ezra and Nehemiah," *JSOT* 59 (1993) 73-92.

Noth, M. *The Chronicler's History.* JSOTSup 50. Sheffield: JSOT, 1987.

Polzin, R. *Late Biblical Hebrew: Toward an Historical Typology of Biblical Hebrew Prose.* HSM 12. Missoula, Mont.: Scholars Press, 1976.

Stern, E. *Material Culture of the Land of the Bible in the Persian Period 538-332 BC.* Warminister: Avis and Phillips; Jerusalem: Israel Exploration Society, 1982.

Suiter, D. *The Contribution of Chronological Studies for Understanding Ezra-Nehemiah.* Ph.D. Diss., Iliff School of Theology/University of Denver, 1992.

Throntveit, M. *Ezra-Nehemiah.* IBC. Louisville: John Knox, 1992.

Williamson, H., *Ezra, Nehemiah.* WBC 16. Waco, Tex.: Word Books, 1985.

Chapter 14
BEFORE THE CANON: SCRIPTURES IN SECOND TEMPLE JUDAISM

John J. Collins

The so-called "intertestamental" literature occupies a pivotal place in the history of Western religion. It documents the period that saw the Hebrew Bible and Christian Old Testament take shape, the birth of Christianity, and the early formation of rabbinic Judaism. Yet it is only in recent years that this literature has begun to emerge from the shadows of the biblical and rabbinic canons. Only a small selection of apocryphal Jewish writings was known in the West before the Enlightenment. The corpus of Pseudepigrapha gradually came to light in the nineteenth century. This literature had been preserved in Eastern Christian churches, in such languages as Ethiopic and Old Church Slavonic, and there was often doubt as to whether it accurately represented ancient Judaism. The standard treatments of Judaism in the late nineteenth and early twentieth centuries, by such scholars as Emil Schuerer and G. F. Moore, fitted this "marginal" literature into a framework drawn from the "normative" rabbinic sources. Only with the discovery of the Dead Sea Scrolls at mid-century did we obtain a corpus of extracanonical Jewish literature in the original languages, including, in some significant cases, works already known from the Pseudepigrapha, such as 1 *Enoch* and *Jubilees*. But only with the final publication of the microfiche edition of the Scrolls in 1993 did the extent of this extracanonical literature become clear. On one estimate, approximately one thousand documents had been hidden in the caves by the Dead Sea. Unfortunately, only fragments survived. More than half the original text is preserved in fewer than a dozen cases, but over six hundred can be reconstructed to some degree.[1] It is now clear that the traditional Apocrypha and Pseudepigrapha contained only a fraction of the rich Jewish religious literature that was excluded from the canon.

This treasure trove of new material will dominate the study of early Jewish literature well into the twenty-first century. It will be some time before its full implications for the understanding of ancient Judaism become clear. In this essay, I wish to focus on a narrower topic, which bears on the fate of this literature for nearly two millennia. This topic is the closing of the canon of the Hebrew Bible. The canon has been a topic of great theological interest in recent years, mainly because of the influential work of B. S. Childs. My primary interest here is historical rather than theological. From the view-point of the historian of pre-rabbinic Judaism, the closing of the canon was a disaster of catastrophic proportions, as it led directly to the abandonment of so much of the literature from this period. The historical study of this development is not, however, without theological implications, as it gives us a glimpse of the all too human process by which the limits of the canon were established.

The Debate About the Closing of the Canon

Jewish tradition ascribes the fixing of the canon and its division into three sections to Ezra and the "Men of the Great Assembly." This view has been discredited in scholarly circles for more than a century. In the late nineteenth century, however, a new orthodoxy arose. On this view, the Torah was canonized in the time of Ezra (fifth century BCE), the Prophets were complete by the time of Ben Sira at the beginning of the second century BCE, and the Writings were closed at the Council of Jamnia, about 90 CE. The larger canon of the Christian Church was believed to have originated as the canon of Alexandrian, and more broadly Diaspora, Judaism. But this consensus too has eroded in the last third of the twentieth century. A. C. Sundberg conclusively demonstrated that "there was no 'Alexandrian canon' of Hellenistic Judaism that was distinct from and different in content from a 'Palestinian canon.'" Rather, he argued, "in addition to closed collections of Law and Prophets, a wide religious literature without definite bounds circulated throughout Judaism as holy scripture before Jamnia."[2] More recently, Jamnia itself has come under scrutiny and the hypothesis of a Council of Jamnia has been widely rejected. There has also, however, been a reaction against Sundberg, in favor of a more traditional view. A Jewish scholar, Sid Leiman, argued in 1976 that the Hebrew canon was closed by Judas Maccabee in the second century BCE. This thesis has won support from some Christian scholars, who find reassurance in the belief that Jesus knew the canon later adopted by the Protestant churches. However, it is far from commanding a consensus in the scholarly community.

The Council of Jamnia

Virtually all scholars agree that the number of books in the canon of Hebrew Scripture was fixed by the end of the first century CE. The word "canon" is admittedly anachronistic in this context. It is first applied to a definite list of scriptural books in fourth century Christianity, and carries the connotation "rule of faith" as well as "fixed number." The kind of authority ascribed to these books in a Jewish context was somewhat different. Nonetheless, for the sake of convenience we may follow standard usage and use the term "canon" to mean that a specific number of books is recognized as qualitatively different from other literature and endowed with a normative status for a religious community. In the case of Scripture, the authority of the literature derives from divine inspiration.

The standard view for the last century or so has been that the number of canonical books was fixed at a "Council of Jamnia" about 90 CE. The evidence for this "Council" is as follows. Before the fall of Jerusalem in 70 CE, R. Johanan ben Zakkai established an academy at Jamnia (Yavneh), which proceeded to function like a Sanhedrin in the period between the Jewish revolts (70-132 CE). Johanan was succeeded by R. Gamaliel II. Somewhere between 80 and 117 CE Gamaliel was deposed for a time, and Eleazar ben Azariah was installed as head of the academy. The Mishnah reports that on the day of the installation of Eleazar, the sages ruled that both Song of Songs and Ecclesiastes "make the hands unclean," that is, are holy books. The same passage states that "all the Holy Scriptures render the hands unclean," and so it is clear that the point at issue was whether Song of Songs and Ecclesiastes ranked among the Holy Scriptures. This passage is followed by a series of enactments introduced by the phrase "on that day" (*m. Yad* 3:5-4:4). Later tradition (*b. Ber.* 28*a*) claimed that every ruling introduced by the phrase "on that day" was made on that occasion. Consequently, the impression arose that there was a single session that made definitive decisions in the manner of the later Church Councils. This impression is misleading. The deliberations at Jamnia were closer to the character of a school, academy, or court. The celebrated discussion of Ecclesiastes and the Song of Songs, in *m. Yad* 3:5, only records that there was some dispute about the status of these books, and in fact such disputes were not terminated by the decisions at Jamnia. Some later rabbis, notably R. Meir (135-70) denied that Ecclesiastes defiled the hands. There is no evidence that the status of other writings was debated, or that a final decision regarding the canon was reached at Jamnia.

The notion of a Council of Jamnia, on the analogy of the Church Councils, is properly discredited. The Jamnia hypothesis, however, admits of a looser formulation. Sundberg, who defended the hypothesis, used the "Council" as "a loose term designating the decisions of the Pharisaic schools that gathered at Jamnia and gained ascendancy in Judaism following the fall of Jerusalem" (113). He also recognized "that the actions of the schools of Jamnia were not official decisions. Probably there was no body in Judaism that functioned in an 'official' capacity after the destruction of Jerusalem in AD 70" (127). While the term "Council" is unsatisfactory, the deliberations at Jamnia in the period between the revolts had an important bearing on the emergence of the biblical canon.

A Fixed Number of Books

The delimitation of a fixed number of biblical books is in fact first attested at the end of the first century, when the academy at Jamnia was in session. In his tract *Against Apion,* written in the last decade of the first century CE, the Jewish historian Josephus sets out to refute the detractors of his people. The first point at issue is the antiquity of the Jews and the reliability of their records. After some disparaging remarks about the trustworthiness of the Greeks as antiquarians, he emphasizes the care with which Jewish records are preserved. "With us," he says, "it is not open to everybody to write the records." This privilege was reserved for prophets, guided by divine inspiration. Consequently "there is no discrepancy in what is written." He goes on:

> We do not possess myriads of inconsistent books, conflicting with each other. Our books, those which are justly accredited, are but two and twenty, and contain the record of all time. Of these, five are the books of Moses, comprising the laws and the traditional history from the birth of man down to the death of the lawgiver. This period falls only a little short of three thousand years. From the death of Moses until Artaxerxes, who succeeded Xerxes as king of Persia, the prophets subsequent to Moses wrote the history of the events of their own times in thirteen books. The remaining four books contain hymns to God and precepts for the conduct of human life. From Artaxerxes to our own time the complete history has been written, but has not been deemed worthy of equal credit with the earlier records, because of the failure of the exact succession of the prophets. (*Ag. Ap.* 1.37-41)

This passage in Josephus is most probably the earliest witness to the notion that only a specific number of books were "justly accredited" among the Jews. A similar idea is found in the apocalypse of 4 Ezra, which is roughly contemporary with the tract *Against Apion.* This apocalypse envisages a situation where "thy law has been burned and so no one knows the things that have been done or will be done by thee" (4 Ezra 14:21). Ezra is given a fiery liquid to drink, which causes his heart, and mouth, to pour forth understanding. Five scribes write down what he says, so that over a period of forty days ninety-four books are written. Then Ezra is told:

> Make public the twenty-four books that you wrote first and let the worthy and the unworthy read them; but keep the seventy that were written last, in order to give them to the wise among your people. For in them is the spring of understanding, the fountain of wisdom, and the river of knowledge. (4 Ezra 14:45-47)

While 4 Ezra differs sharply from Josephus in the claim that the hidden books contain the higher wisdom, it shares the notion of a special category of books, limited to a specific number. It is generally assumed that Josephus's twenty-two books are the same as 4 Ezra's twenty-four, though counted differently. Some later authorities, such as Origen and Jerome, count Judges–Ruth and Jeremiah–Lamentations each as one book, for a total of twenty-two, while twenty-four is the standard number in Talmudic sources. We know from the *Antiquities* (book eleven) that Josephus included the book of Esther, which has not been found in the Dead Sea Scrolls, and is also missing from the lists of Melito of Sardis in the second century and of Athanasius in the fourth. On the other hand, we cannot assume that Josephus's canon was identical with our Hebrew Bible, since he narrates the contest between Darius's guards, which is only found in the apocryphal book of 1 Esdras. This may be an issue of text rather than of canon; 1 Esdras may not have been regarded as a different book from Ezra–Nehemiah. While some uncertainty remains, however, 4 Ezra and Josephus, taken together, constitute strong evidence that a "canon," in the sense of a fixed number of authoritative books, had been established, at least in some circles, by the end of the first century CE.

The Antiquity of the Canon

What was the origin of this "canon"? The theory that it was promulgated by the sages at Jamnia has been shown to lack supporting evidence, but the same can be said of any other theory. Several recent works have argued that the Hebrew canon was closed before the turn of the era. Sid Leiman suggested that the activity of Judas Maccabee, as described in 2 Macc 2:14-15 "may, in fact, be a description of the closing of the Hagiographa, and with it, the entire biblical canon."[3] The passage in question reads:

> In the same way Judah also collected all the books that had been lost on account of the war which had come upon us, and they are in our possession. So if you have need of them, send people to get them for you.

R. T. Beckwith goes further and asks:

> What is more likely than that, in gathering together the scattered Scriptures, he and his companions the Hasidim classified the now complete collection in the way which from that time became traditional, dividing the miscellaneous non-Mosaic writings into the Prophets and the other Books?[4]

But 2 Maccabees says nothing whatever about canonization. It only says that Judas collected "all the books that had been lost on account of the war." There is no suggestion that he distinguished between books that were canonical and others that were not, much less that he introduced distinctions within a canonical corpus. In fact, all the available evidence suggests that the category of Scriptures, or authoritative writings, was open-ended down to the late first century CE.

This is not to say that there was no recognition of authoritative Scriptures. The formation of the Hebrew canon was a lengthy process, which can be traced back to the promulgation of "the book of the law" in the reform of Josiah (621 BCE). Ezra is often credited with giving the Torah, or Pentateuch, its final shape. The books of Ezra and Nehemiah, however, make no mention of the Day of Atonement, although Nehemiah 8 describes the liturgical observances of the seventh month, especially the Feast of Booths. The omission indicates that the Pentateuch had not yet reached its final form, although Ezra presupposes other priestly laws, and must have had something close to the Torah as we know it. The prophetic corpus took shape somewhere in the Persian or early Hellenistic period.

The first clear witness to a canon, in the sense of an accepted corpus of authoritative Scripture, is found in the prologue to Ben Sira. The prologue was written by Sirach's grandson, who had migrated to Egypt in 132 BCE, in the thirty-eighth year of Euergetes II. The prologue was written some time later, possibly after the death of that king in 117 BCE. It begins with the following statement:

> Many great teachings have been given to us through the Law and the Prophets and the others that followed them, and for these we should praise Israel for instruction and wisdom. . . . So my grandfather Jesus, who had devoted himself especially to the reading of the Law and Prophets and the other books of our ancestors, and had acquired considerable proficiency in them, was himself also led to write something pertaining to instruction and wisdom.

It has been widely assumed that this statement implies a tripartite canon, but in fact it is not at all clear that "the other books of our ancestors" constitute a canonical category. They are simply "other traditional writings."

The category is open-ended and, according to the grandson, Sirach himself felt free to contribute to it. The Jewish writings to which Sirach alludes are quite limited. He wrote at some time in the first quarter of the second century BCE, before the composition of most of the books we know as Apocrypha and Pseudepigrapha. But he also shows no awareness of some older writings that were eventually accepted as biblical, such as Ruth, Song of Songs, Esther or, most surprisingly, Ezra (although he praises Nehemiah in Sir 49:13). Even writings on which he draws freely, such as Proverbs, are not necessarily distinguished as qualitatively different from other religious writings. They are traditional, but not necessarily canonical in the later sense of the term. There is no doubt that the book of the Torah is of fundamental importance to him (witness his bold identification of the book of the Law with Wisdom in 24:23) and that he draws heavily on traditional Jewish literature. There is also, however, evidence of dependence on non-Jewish wisdom texts: there are numerous points of contact with the Greek gnomic poet Theognis and with the Demotic wisdom book of Phibis, preserved in Papyrus Insinger. The ideal sage not only devotes himself to the study of the law of the Most High, but seeks out the wisdom of all the ancients (Sir 39:1). There is in Sirach what we might call a "canon consciousness" with respect to the Torah, but there is no sense of a closed canon beyond the books of Moses.

It is commonly inferred that the collection of Prophets was closed by Sirach's time, and that the inference is confirmed by the fact that Daniel was not included in the Prophets in the Hebrew Bible. This inference, too, is unsafe. To be sure, Sirach knew all the prophets of the Hebrew Bible, and refers to the Twelve as such. In his review of Israelite history in the "Praise of the Fathers," however, it is not apparent that he makes any distinction between the prophetic books and Nehemiah. In the New Testament period, David was often regarded as a prophet and the Psalms as prophecy (e.g., Acts 2:30). In short we cannot tell just how much material was categorized under "The Prophets" in Ben Sira's time. Daniel, too, is often identified as a prophet in antiquity. 4QFlor (4Q174) 2:4 speaks of "the book of Daniel the Prophet," Matt 24:15 refers to "the prophet Daniel," and Josephus regards him as "one of the greatest prophets" (*Ant* 10.11.7, 266-68). While Daniel is not included in the prophets in the Masoretic Bible, it is quite possible that the book was classified as prophetic in antiquity, or that the line between Prophets and Writings was not clearly drawn.

Most of our witnesses through the New Testament period attest a bipartite rather than a tripartite division of the scriptures: so Matt 5:17; 7:12; 11:13; 16:16; 22:40; Luke 16:29-31; Acts 13:15; 24:14; 28:23; Rom 3:21. The normal reference is to "The Law and the Prophets." Luke 24:44 is exceptional in the NT in referring to "the law of Moses, the prophets and the psalms."

A similar view of Scripture is implied in Philo's account of the Therapeutae (*De vita contemplativa* 25). He says that in each house they had a consecrated room into which they took nothing but "laws and oracles delivered through the mouth of the prophets, and psalms and anything else which fosters and perfects knowledge and piety." This passage is often cited as evidence for a tripartite canon, but the last category "anything else" is clearly open-ended. As in Luke, there is recognition that the Psalms belong among the Holy Scriptures, but there is nothing to indicate how either the Therapeutae or Philo delimited the books of the Prophets. Philo's own usage of scripture is predominantly focused on the Torah, which he cites forty times as often as the books of the Prophets and Hagiographa combined. Here again there is recognition that the Torah is in a class by itself, but that prophetic and other books are also of value, without any clear demarcation of the latter categories.

The boundary between the Prophets and the other Writings remains a problem in the passage from Josephus quoted above. Josephus assigns thirteen books to the prophetic corpus and only four to the Writings. The latter four are most plausibly identified as Psalms, Proverbs, Ecclesiastes, and Song of Songs. On this reckoning, Ezra–Nehemiah, Chronicles, Esther, and Job must be assigned to the Prophets. Such an alignment corresponds neither to the Hebrew nor to the Greek Bibles as they emerged in later tradition.

Diverse Scriptures

The evidence, then, for the period before 70 CE points to a core canon, consisting of the Torah and Prophets, which was universally accepted, although the precise definition of the prophetic corpus seems to have varied, and an open-ended supplement of "other writings" was also acknowledged. It is quite possible that some group or groups delimited the "other writings" exactly as Josephus and 4 Ezra did. Already in the nineteenth century Frants Buhl argued that "we cannot possibly assume that the representation which Josephus, residing in Rome shortly after the Synod of Jamnia, gives of the contents and idea of the canon must have been influenced by the decisions of the Synod." Instead, "it is highly probable that Josephus in his Apology reported simply the teaching of the Pharisees of his times."[5] More recently Frank Cross has also argued that Josephus was drawing on Pharisaic tradition. He has further suggested that both text and canon were fixed under the auspices of Hillel, in the early first century CE. He cites a saying from the Talmud (*Sukk.* 20*a*) that "When Israel forgot the Torah, Ezra came up from Babylon and reestablished it; and when Israel once again forgot the Torah,

Hillel the Babylonian came up and reestablished it." However, the point of this saying is usually taken to refer to the interpretation of the Torah, rather than to the canon.[6] A more weighty consideration can be found in the account of the dispute about Ecclesiastes and the Song of Songs in the Mishnah: "Ecclesiastes is among the lenient decisions of the School of Shammai and among the stringent decisions of the School of Hillel" (*m. Yad* 3:5; cf. *Meg.* 7a). The ruling at Jamnia affirmed the teaching of the house of Hillel. This would seem to suggest that the status of particular books had been discussed in the disputes between the houses of Hillel and Shammai before 70 CE, and that the sages at Jamnia only needed to address a few outstanding disputes.

Hillel, however, did not speak for all Judaism. There is good evidence that other strands of Judaism had a wider body of Scriptures than did the Pharisees. One corpus of evidence in this regard is constituted by the Greek Bible inherited by early Christianity. There is considerable variation in the manuscripts and in the lists cited by the Church Fathers, and so it is inappropriate to speak of an Alexandrian canon. The most frequent additional books are those that came to be designated Apocrypha after the Reformation: Tobit, Judith, Sirach, Wisdom of Solomon, 1–2 Maccabees, Baruch, Letter of Jeremiah, 1–2 Esdras, Prayer of Manasseh, and the additions to Esther and Daniel. Others that are sometimes included are 3–4 Maccabees, Psalm 151, and the Psalms of Solomon. While 2 Esdras and possibly 4 Maccabees were composed after 70 CE, the others had presumably won status in Jewish circles before they were adopted by Christians. It is difficult to see why books such as Judith or 1 Maccabees should have been accepted as Scripture by Christians if they were not so recognized in some Jewish circles. Presumably these were the books that enjoyed scriptural status in the Diaspora, even if they were never formalized as a canon.

New light has now been shed on the Scriptures of the land of Israel by the publication of the Dead Sea Scrolls. The evidence of the Scrolls for the canon has often been discounted on the grounds that they only represent a sectarian view. There is indeed compelling evidence that the collection as a whole has a sectarian character. It has a predilection for sectarian rule-books (twelve copies of the Community Rule, seven of the Damascus Document) and books of a Hasmonean or Pharisaic stamp (the books of Maccabees, Judith, Psalms of Solomon are conspicuously absent). Nonetheless, as the extent of the collection becomes clear, it is apparent that not all the writings were distinctively sectarian. While this corpus is not a random sampling of the literature of the time, much of it was surely known beyond the confines of the sect that preserved it.

JOHN J. COLLINS

The Evidence of the Scrolls

The most explicit comment on the authoritative writings of the day is found in the so-called Halakic Letter, 4QMMT. This document is addressed to a religious leader of Israel, most probably a high priest, and it sets out the reasons why the community had separated itself from the majority of the people. It appeals to the leader to consider the validity of the sectarian interpretation of Scripture: "For on account of [these things] we have [written] for you that you may perceive in the book of Moses [and in the words of the pro]phets and in Davi[d. . . .] from generation to generation." The statement refers to the familiar categories of the Law and the Prophets. David was widely regarded as a prophet, but he is singled out as the author of a special category (Psalms). These were the Scriptures that were presumed to be common to all Jews.

The canon that the sectarians shared with the authorities was basically a bipartite canon, with the addition of Psalms. The fundamental importance of the revealed Torah at Qumran is beyond doubt. According to the "Well midrash" on Num 21:18 in the Damascus Document, "the Well is the Law, and those who dug it were the converts of Israel who went out of the land of Israel to sojourn in the land of Damascus. . . . The Stave is the Interpreter of the Law. . . ." (CD 6:2-11). Similarly, the Community Rule instructs the sectarians to prepare in the wilderness the way of the Lord, and specifies that "this is the study of the Law which He commanded by the hand of Moses" (1QS 8:14-15). In 1QS 8, the fundamental revelation of the Law is supplemented by "all that has been revealed from age to age" and by what "the Prophets have revealed by His Holy Spirit." The authoritative status of the Prophets and the Psalms is confirmed by the fact that they are subject to a special form of interpretation in the pesharim which apply the words of the prophets to the experiences of the community at the end of days. The pesher mode of interpretation could be applied to prophetic passages in the Torah as well as to the prophetic books, as can be seen from the pesher on Genesis 49 in 4Q 252. There is also a pesher on Psalms, and Daniel is interpreted in pesher-like manner in the *Florilegium* and in the *Melchizedek,* but none of the other Writings is interpreted in this way. This suggests that Psalms and Daniel were regarded as prophetic books, even if Psalms was understood to constitute a special category in 4QMMT. This view of the emerging canon corresponds with what we know from other sources for the period between the Maccabees and the fall of Jerusalem in 70 CE.

The common view of authoritative Scriptures, however, is modified in a number of ways by the Scrolls. First there is the existence of variant texts. Examples include a text of Exodus that corresponds to the Samaritan recension, except that it lacks the distinctively Samaritan mention of Mount

Gerizim at Exod 20:17 and a text of Jeremiah that agrees with the short recension found in the Septuagint. The most controversial example is provided by the Psalms Scroll from Cave Eleven. This scroll contains most of the last third of the Psalter but in an unconventional arrangement. It also includes a poem identical with 2 Sam 23:1-7 ("the last words of David") and several apocryphal psalms: Psalm 151 (a variant of the corresponding Psalm in the Greek psalter), Psalms 154-55, which are also extant in Syriac, and a poem related to Sir 51:13-19, 30. There are also three psalms that were previously unknown: "A Plea for Deliverance," "Apostrophe to Zion," and a "Hymn to the Creator." There is also a prose catalogue of David's compositions, placed neither at the beginning nor at the end (it is followed by Pss 140:1-5, 134:1-3 and Psalm 151)./

The editor of this scroll, James Sanders, regarded it as a portion of the Davidic Psalter. The inclusion of "the last words of David" and the prose catalogue suggest that the entire collection was regarded as Davidic. There is no distinction in the scroll between canonical and noncanonical material. Sanders infers that the content and order of the Psalter had not yet been finalized in this period. This conclusion was vigorously disputed by such scholars as M. Goshen-Gottstein, S. Talmon, and P. Skehan, who suggested that it was merely a collection for liturgical use, without implications for the canon. It is difficult to see, however, why a catalogue of David's works should be included in a liturgical collection. It is probably true that the scroll was not viewed as definitive or canonical; the question is whether any collection of Psalms was so viewed in this period. Whatever use was made of the Psalms scroll, no distinction was made between canonical and apocryphal compositions. Sanders has had the better of the argument: the Psalter was still fluid at Qumran. It should be noted that the Psalms Scroll shows no signs of distinctively sectarian interests. Since some of the additional material is also found in other manuscript traditions (Psalms 151, 154–55) we must conclude that variation in the Psalter was not peculiar to Qumran.

Another more perplexing kind of variation is presented by the Temple Scroll. This document weaves together related but different legal texts, mainly from Deuteronomy and Leviticus, often with new interpretations. It is presented as a first-person address of God to Moses, so that it becomes in effect a new Torah. The status of this document vis-à-vis the traditional Torah remains one of the puzzles of the Dead Sea Scrolls. In view of the first-person divine speech, one assumes that if the document was accepted at all it was accepted as divine revelation. The divine name is written in square script, as it is in biblical books (e.g., Isaiah), not in paleo-Hebrew script as in the pesharim. Yadin took this as evidence that the Temple Scroll enjoyed the status of Scripture at Qumran. Ben Zion Wacholder goes farther and argues that the author of the Temple Scroll "set out to rival Moses, hoping to succeed where his predecessor had failed." He infers that it was the Torah of the Qumran community.[7] It does, in fact, emphasize matters that are highlighted elsewhere in sectarian documents, such as sexual impurity, the purity of the Sanctuary, and sinful wealth. It presupposes the sectarian 364 day calendar. Yet there is no clear reference to it in the other sectarian literature, in contrast to the abundance of references to the traditional Torah. Yadin's suggestion that the Temple Scroll is "The Book of Meditation" referred to in the Damascus Document and 1QSa is not compelling:[8] the book in question is more likely to be the traditional Torah. Some scholars have argued that the Temple Scroll is not a product of the Qumran sect at all, but is rather a traditional pseudepigraphon like *Jubilees* that shares some common traditions with the sect. Larry Schiffman makes the noteworthy observation that "whereas the other texts from Qumran see the extrabiblical material as derived from inspired biblical exegesis, the author of the Temple Scroll sees it as inherent in the biblical text."[9] It makes no reference to a *yaḥad* (commune) or distinct sectarian organization. Given the extensive correspondence with the sectarian scrolls on halakic issues, however, the Scroll should be regarded as sectarian, at least in a broad sense. While it was not necessarily produced in or for the community of the Community Rule, it represents the reformist strands of Judaism from which that community emerged.

It has been suggested that the Temple Scroll is a new Torah for the New Age. On this view, the hidden sense of the Law was partially disclosed in such documents as 1QS and CD, but would be available to all surviving Jews in the endtime in a new Torah. This suggestion is unsatisfactory, however. The endtime in the Scrolls is associated with the coming of the Messiah, but the king envisaged in the Temple Scroll is conspicuously lacking in messianic traits. The Scroll presents a law for this age rather than for the end of days. It is a reformist proposal. We do not know whether its author hoped that it would replace the traditional Torah. If he did, he was disappointed. Those who preserved the Scroll presumably read it in conjunction with the Torah, perhaps interpreting the Torah in its light.

The problem presented by the Temple Scroll is extreme, because of the use of divine speech, but analogous problems are presented by a number of other documents. One, known long before the discovery of the Dead Sea Scrolls, is the book of *Jubilees*. Here we have a document, supposedly revealed to Moses by an angel, which covers the same ground as the book of Genesis but is often at variance with the biblical text. The variation may be understood as making explicit what was thought to be implicit in the text (e.g., the 364 day calendar), but nonetheless it involves an amazing freedom. Some of the novel elements, such as the role of Mastema or Satan, have really no exegetical basis in the biblical text. *Jubilees* does not challenge the traditional

Torah. Rather it provides a complementary revelation, which could serve as a guide for the interpretation of the older document, to which it refers as "the first law" (*Jub.* 6:22). Yet it is presented as an independent revelation, not as a midrash or commentary. In this case we have evidence that it was accepted as an authoritative document by some Jews in antiquity. CD 16:2-4 says that the exact determination of the times is strictly defined in the book of the Divisions of the Times into their *Jubilees* and Weeks, and this is surely none other than the book of *Jubilees*. It is cited as an authoritative source, and there are no grounds for the claim that its authority is less than that of other scriptures. Fragments of at least fourteen copies of *Jubilees* have been found at Qumran. Only five biblical books (Genesis, Exodus, Deuteronomy, Isaiah, and Psalms) are represented by more manuscripts. Jubilees later became part of the canon of the Christian Church in Ethiopia.

Various parts of *1 Enoch* are also represented in multiple copies at Qumran. It has been argued that the books of *Enoch* and *Jubilees* must have been regarded as Scripture by those who accepted them, since they claim to be divinely inspired. *First Enoch* is cited in the New Testament in Jude 14–15, is cited as Scripture in *Barn.* 16:5 and, like *Jubilees*, was later canonical in the Ethiopian Church. The fact that Enoch and Jubilees survived in Christian circles suggests that they were known more widely than most of the writings found at Qumran.

Beckwith has argued that apocryphal books are not cited with such formulae as "it is written" in the Scrolls, but the argument is tendentious. The Damascus Document cites a Levi apocryphon with the phrase "of which Levi son of Jacob spoke," but it also introduces biblical citations with the phrases "Moses said" and "Isaiah said." The so-called *Testimonia* (4Q175) draws passages not only from Deuteronomy and Numbers, but also from the apocryphal *Psalms of Joshua*. The evidence is sporadic and incomplete, but it is apparent that at least some apocryphal compositions could be cited as authoritative sources.

In addition to the few cases where documents are cited, the Scrolls contain a huge corpus of previously unknown writings. Many of these writings are not distinctively sectarian. Some, such as the *Genesis Apocryphon* or the Pseudo-Ezekiel text are adaptations of a biblical prototype. Others, such as the *Testaments of Amram and Qahat,* are independent pseudepigrapha. In some cases, such as the Pseudo-Daniel literature, it is uncertain whether the fragments represent a reworking of a biblical text or independent compositions that happen to share common themes and figures with the more familiar Scriptures. At least some of this literature is presented in the form of divine revelation.

While we cannot be sure whether or how far these compositions were regarded as authoritative, we must bear in mind that some of the biblical writings are poorly attested at Qumran. All the books of the Hebrew Bible except Esther have been found among the scrolls, but Chronicles is represented by a single scrap. If Ecclesiastes, Song of Songs, or Ruth were not known to us as part of the traditional Bible, there would be no reason to think that they were Scripture at Qumran. We have seen that the Writings generally carried less authority than the Torah and the Prophets. There is no evidence that there was a clear distinction between canonical and non-canonical writings at Qumran.

Jamnia Revisited

Most of the writings hidden in the caves near the Dead Sea disappeared from the scene of history and played no further part in Jewish or Christian life. Most of the Apocrypha and all the Greco-Jewish literature vanished from the tradition passed on by the rabbis. Ben Sira is the only one of the traditional Apocrypha cited in the rabbinic corpus, although mention is made of the otherwise unknown works of Ben La'aga (j. *Sanh* 28*a*) and Ben Tagla (*Koheleth Rab.* 12:12). Origen, in his *Letter to Africanus* 13, acknowledges the currency of the book of Maccabees outside the canon, but adds that the Jews not only do not use Tobit and Judith, but also do not even have them "in the Hebrew apocrypha." We need not infer that the Hebrew Apocrypha was a well-defined category. The point is simply that Tobit and Judith were not current in Hebrew (or Aramaic) in Origen's time. Origen also mentions a "letter" that appears as part of Jeremiah in the Hebrew but is usually found separately in the Greek. The reference is presumably to the *Epistle of Jeremiah*. Apart from these cases, however, there is remarkably little controversy about the status of apocryphal writings in the rabbinic tradition.

In this shrinking of the corpus of religious literature we discover the true significance of Jamnia for the formation of the canon. Shaye Cohen has argued that Jamnia marked the end of Jewish sectarianism:

> "Pharisaic triumph" is not a useful description of the events at Yavneh. Perhaps many, if not most, of the sages there assembled were Pharisees or the descendants of Pharisees, but they made little of their ancestry. . . . Yavneh was a grand coalition of different groups and parties, held together by the belief that sectarian self-identification was a thing of the past.

But even this inclusive vision had its limits: "Those who refused to join the coalition and insisted on sectarian self-identification were branded *minîm* and cursed. Those rabbis who could not learn the rules of pluralism and mutual tolerance were banned."[10] The strand of Judaism that is most prominent in the Dead Sea Scrolls could find no place at Jamnia, since it relied on claims of revelation that were not accepted by the rabbis. Moreover, if most of the rabbis at Jamnia were Pharisees, it was inevitable that Pharisaic opinions would prevail. So it was with the canon. If the twenty-two or twenty-four book canon had taken shape before 70 CE, as seems likely, it was the canon of a party, not of all Jews. After 70, through the influence of Jamnia, other Scriptures were ignored and lost.

The rejection of other Scriptures cannot be entirely explained as benign neglect. A saying attributed to R. Akiba proclaimed that one who reads the outside books would have no share in the world to come (*m. Sanh* 10:1). The Talmud explains that "this means the books of the heretics" (*b. Sanhedrin* 100*b*), which presumably included Christian literature. There is other evidence that Christian writings were specifically rejected: "The Gospels (*haggilyônîm*) and the books of the heretics do not defile the hands" (*Tosefta Yadaim* 2:13) and "the Gospels and the books of heretics are not to be rescued but allowed to burn where they are, names of God and all" (*Tosefta Shabbath* 13). Reasons can be imagined for excluding some of the Pseudepigrapha and sectarian writings. Most obviously, books that had been composed in Greek, such as the Wisdom of Solomon, did not qualify for consideration. Books such as *Jubilees, 1 Enoch,* and the Temple Scroll would have been unacceptable to the rabbis because of their calendrical teachings. There is no clear evidence that books were excluded because of apocalyptic content. R. Akiba, who pronounced the most severe ban on the "outside books" is credited with an ascent to Paradise (*Hag* 14*b*) and with endorsing Bar Kokhba as the Messiah (*j. Taànit* 4.8), and so he at least cannot have been too negatively disposed toward apocalyptic speculation. Yet the fact that the apocalypses relied on special revelations, the virtual equivalent of a voice from heaven, may have made them less than congenial to the rabbis, although Daniel was too well established to be questioned. Compare the famous story in b. *Baba Metzia* 59*b*, which cites Deut 30:12 ("it is not in heaven") and concludes "we pay no attention to a heavenly voice, because Thou hast long since written in the Torah at Sinai 'after the majority must one incline'" (Exod 23:2).

To a great degree, decisions on canonicity may have been determined by pragmatic rather than ideological considerations. The only reason given in the rabbinic texts for the exclusion of books other than the books of the heretics is a late date of composition. *Tosefta Yadaim* 1:13, after pronouncing on the books of the heretics, adds "the books of the son of Sirach and all books that have been written since his time do not defile the hands." This point is related to the widespread, though not universal, view that prophetic inspiration had ceased in the Persian period. At least it suggests that the rabbis were aware of a difference between the age of Scripture and their own time. Such considerations may help explain the omission of a relatively recent book like 1 Maccabees. A more weighty concern, however, may have been the need to limit the number of books: "whoever brings into his house more than the twenty-four books introduces confusion into his house" (*Eccl. Rab.* 12:12). The books included were simply those that were most firmly established in the circles of the sages who made the decisions.

By restricting the number of "properly accredited" books the sages provided a common frame of reference for their debates and reduced the risk of sectarian division. Their strategy played its part in ensuring the survival of Judaism in a time of crisis. Yet it also involved a goodly measure of loss. The writings retrieved in scraps from the caves of the Dead Sea many not quite contain "the spring of understanding, the fountain of wisdom and the river of knowledge" like the hidden books of 4 Ezra 14. But they do contain a rich and variegated picture of Jewish practices, beliefs, and hopes in a period before Judaism and Christianity went their separate ways and sealed their identities in their different conceptions of the canon.

Notes

1. So Hartmut Stegemann, *Die Essener, Qumran, Johannes der Täufer und Jesus* (Freiburg: Herder, 1993) 115.

2. A. C. Sundberg, *The Old Testament of the Early Church* (Cambridge, Mass.: Harvard University Press, 1964) 102-03.

3. S. Z. Leiman, *The Canonization of Hebrew Scripture* (Hamden, Conn.: Archon, 1976) 29.

4. R. T. Beckwith, *The Old Testament Canon of the New Testament Church and Its Background in Early Judaism* (Grand Rapids: Eerdmans, 1985) 152.

5. F. Buhl, *Canon and Text of the Old Testament* (London: MacMillan, 1892) 25.

6. F. M. Cross, "The Text Behind the Text of the Hebrew Bible," in *BibRev* 1 (1985) 13-25.

7. B. Z. Wacholder, *The Dawn of Qumran* (Cincinnati: Hebrew Union College Press, 1983) 228.

8. Y. Yadin, *The Temple Scroll* (Jerusalem: Israel Exploration Society 1, 1983) 394.

9. L. Schiffman, *Sectarian Law in the Dead Sea Scrolls* (Chico, Calif.: Scholars Press, 1983) 17.

10. S. J. D. Cohen, "The Significance of Yavneh: Pharisees, Rabbis, and the End of Jewish Sectarianism," in *HUCA* 55 (1984) 50.

Selected Bibliography

Barton, J. *Oracles of God: Perceptions of Ancient Prophecy in Israel after the Exile.* Oxford: Oxford University Press, 1986.

Beckwith, R. T. *The Old Testament Canon of the New Testament Church and Its Background in Early Judaism.* Grand Rapids: Eerdmans, 1985.

Ellis, E. E. *The Old Testament in Early Christianity.* Tubingen: Mohr, 1991.

Leiman, S. Z. *The Canonization of Hebrew Scripture.* Hamden, Conn.: Archon, 1976.

———. *The Canon and Masorah of the Hebrew Bible: An Introductory Reader.* New York: Ktav, 1974.

Lewis, J. P. "Jamnia (Jabneh), Council of." In vol. 3 of *ABD*. New York: Doubleday, 634-37.

Sanders, J. A. *The Psalms Scroll of Qumran Cave 11 (11QPsa)*. In DJD 4. Oxford: Oxford University Press, 1965.

Sundberg, A. C. *The Old Testament of the Early Church*. Cambridge, Mass.: Harvard University Press, 1964.

Tov, E., with S. Pfann. *The Dead Sea Scrolls on Microfiche*. Leiden: Brill, 1993.

Wilson, H. "The Qumran Psalms Scroll Reconsidered: Analysis of the Debate." In *CBQ* 47 (1985) 624-42.

PART FOUR
CONTEXT

Chapter 15
THE ANCIENT NEAR EAST
AND ARCHAEOLOGY

J. Maxwell Miller

The Old Testament, timeless as it is, nevertheless emerged from a particular geographical, cultural, and historical context. The geographical setting was the Near East, with the central hill country of Palestine[1] as center stage. The cultural and historical setting was what archaeologists working in Syria-Palestine refer to as the Iron Age, beginning with the rather sudden decline of the Egyptian and Hittite Empires, approximately 1200 BCE, and ending with Alexander the Great's conquest of the East shortly before 300 BCE. The Old Testament's narratives and poetry are full of references to specific mountains, valleys, cities, and villages. They take for granted that the reader is familiar with the various peoples and cultural patterns of the day. Almost any passage from the Old Testament illustrates the necessity of becoming familiar with its context. Let us consider the following three texts.

Genesis 12–13 narrates the immigration of Abram and his family from Mesopotamia to Palestine. The central theme is Abram's unquestioning willingness to follow God's command wherever it led, and even the most casual reader observes that he built altars at three different places as he passed through Palestine. More attentive readers will note further that the three places where he built the altars (Shechem, Bethel, and Hebron) also figure prominently in other Old Testament passages. Yet the narrative is even more specific. We are told the very spots in the vicinities of Shechem, Bethel, and Hebron where Abram worshiped.

Abram passed through the land to the place at Shechem, to the oak of Moreh. . . . From there he moved on to the hill country on the east of Bethel, and pitched his tent, with Bethel on the west and Ai on the east. . . . So Abram moved his tent, and came and settled by the oaks of Mamre, which are at Hebron. . . . (Gen 12:6, 8; 13:18)

A particular tree on the outskirts of Shechem, a particular hill between Bethel and Ai, a grove of trees near Hebron—this kind of detail presupposes a firsthand knowledge of the Palestinian hill country. The narrator could presuppose this because his original audience lived in the land and knew these places. Many no doubt would have worshiped at one or other of these spots, and these geographical details would have added a sense of immediacy to the narrative for them.

The second text, Deuteronomy 13, provides instruction in case one of the Israelite cities were to go astray by worshiping other gods.

> . . . you shall put the inhabitants of that town to the sword, utterly destroying it and everything in it—even putting its livestock to the sword. All of its spoil you shall gather into its public square; then burn the town and all its spoil with fire, as a whole burnt offering to the LORD your God. It shall remain a perpetual ruin, never to be rebuilt. (Deut 13:15-16)

Already in Old Testament times the Near East was dotted with mounds of debris, stratified ruins of ancient cities that had flourished during the preceding Bronze Age (ca. 3200-1200 BCE) but for various reasons had become ghost towns during the Iron Age. These mounds of debris were, and still are today, known as "tells"; and it is the Hebrew word *tel* that is translated "ruin" in the passage above. This phenomenon of "tells" figures in several Old Testament passages, and would have conveyed a strong visual image of destruction and desolation to people living in Palestine.

The third passage, the account of the Israelite conquest and destruction of Ai in Joshua 7–8, uses the tell image. The account concludes:

> So Joshua burned Ai, and made it forever a heap of ruins [tel], as it is to this day. And he hanged the king of Ai on a tree until evening; and at sunset Joshua commanded, and they took his body down from the tree, threw it down at the entrance of the gate of the city, and raised over it a great heap of stones, which stands there to this day. (Josh 8:28-29)

"To this day" refers to the time that the story was being told. The narrator was inviting his contemporaries to see the "tell" and look specifically for the heap of stones that marked the king's burial.

These passages illustrate the rich geographical and archaeological detail in the Old Testament. These details elicited visual images and added a sense of immediacy for the earliest readers (or hearers) who still lived in the land. It is not surprising that later generations of readers living in distant lands would want to come to Palestine and visit the biblical places. Thus the practice of pilgrimages to the Holy Land on the part of Jews and Christians began during late Roman times and continues today with commercially prepackaged Holy Land tours. Neither is it surprising that attempts to understand and clarify obscure place names, terminology, and customs has been central to biblical scholarship until today.

Indeed, even in the Old Testament itself there are occasional clarifying notations that explain place names, customs, and terminology. These clarifications were inserted by redactors, late editors of the Old Testament material before it reached final canonical form. They realized that these place-names, customs, and terms were no longer familiar and thus required explanation. In this regard consider Genesis 14, which recounts an invasion of Palestine by a coalition of kings led by Amraphel from the land of Shinar. According to the account:

> . . . these kings made war with King Bera of Sodom, King Birsha of Gomorrah, King Shinab of Admah, King Shemeber of Zeboiim, and the king of Bela (that is, Zoar). All these joined forces in the Valley of Siddim (that is, the Salt Sea). (Gen 14:2-3)

The names "Sodom," "Gomorrah," "Admah," and "Zeboiim" would have been generally familiar to the readers living about the time of the Babylonian exile when the story was edited to its present form. "Bela" and "the Valley of Siddim" apparently required explanation. It is explained, namely, that Bela is the same as Zoar and that the Valley of Siddim is the Salt Sea. A modern commentator would need to explain further that the Salt Sea is what we generally refer to in English as the Dead Sea. Other biblical passages that include similar clarifying notations pertaining to place names are Gen 23:1-2, 18-20 and Josh 15:8-10; 18:13-14.

Still other passages, such as 1 Samuel 9, include notations that explain cultic practices of earlier times and clarify the terminology of neighboring peoples. First Samuel 9 recounts an occasion when Saul and a servant set out in search of some asses and, as a last resort, went to a local "seer" for help. This local "man of God" turned out to be none other than Samuel. Even the earliest readers of the story would have known Samuel as one of Israel's great prophets, yet this particular story never actually refers to him as a prophet. Thus a note has been added to explain that prophets were called "seers" in earlier times:

> The boy answered Saul again, "Here, I have with me a quarter shekel of silver; I will give it to the man of God, to tell us our way." (Formerly in Israel, anyone who went to inquire of God would say, "Come, let us go to the seer"; for the one who is now called a prophet was formerly called a seer.) Saul said to the boy, "Good; come, let us go." (1 Sam 9:8-10)

Gen 43:31-32 explains why Joseph, while still playing the role of an Egyptian official, did not eat with his brothers when he served them in his home:

> Then he washed his face and came out; and controlling himself he said, "Serve the meal." They served him by himself, and them by themselves, and the Egyptians who ate with him by themselves, because the Egyptians could not eat with the Hebrews, for that is an abomination to the Egyptians. (Gen 43:31-32)

Notations in Deuteronomy 2, part of Moses' last address to the Israelites before his death, seek to clarify some ethnic terminology that apparently was confusing even in biblical times.

> "Today you are going to cross the boundary of Moab at Ar. When you approach the frontier of the Ammonites, do not harass them or engage them in battle, for I will not give the land of the Ammonites to you as a possession, because I have given it to the descendents of Lot." (It also is usually reckoned as a land of Rephaim. Rephaim formerly inhabited it, though the Ammonites call them Zamzummim, a strong and numerous people, as tall as the Anakim. But the LORD destroyed them from before the Ammonites so that they could dispossess them and settle in their place. He did the same for the descendants of Esau, who live in Seir, by destroying the Horim before them so that they could dispossess them and settle in their place even to this day. As for the Avvim, who had lived in settlements in the vicinity of Gaza, the Caphtorim, who came from Caphtor, destroyed them and settled in their place.) (Deut 2:18-23; see vv. 10-12)

If already in biblical times there was a recognized need to clarify obscure place-names, ancient customs, and confusing terminology mentioned in the Old Testament materials, all the more is this the case for the twentieth-century readers. Not only are we far removed from ancient Palestine in time and space, we live in a radically different cultural environment. Our context has been shaped by the Enlightenment, the Industrial Revolution, and the amazing technological advancements of the twentieth century. Three over-lapping branches of modern scholarship help clarify the obscure and figure prominently in contemporary Old Testament studies—historical geography, epigraphy, and archaeology. In effect, the techniques and findings of historical geography, epigraphy, and archaeology continue a tradition of bringing the obscure to clarity already begun in the biblical texts.

Historical Geography

Gen 14:2-3 and several other passages were cited above that illustrate that some of the place-names mentioned in the Old Testament narratives were not generally familiar even in antiquity. This became more the rule than the exception during Hellenistic and Roman times. For the next thousand years following Alexander's conquest of the East, until the expansion of Islam in the seventh century CE, Greek (and to a lesser degree Latin) served as the official language of the Near East. Consequently, many of the old Semitic place-names, the ones used in the Old Testament, were replaced with new names based on Greek and Latin. For example, Old Testament Acco was renamed Ptolemais (compare Judg 1:31 with Acts 21:7), Samaria became Sebastos, Shechem was superseded by Neapolis, Jerusalem was renamed Aelia Capitolina, and so on. Fortunately, writers from Hellenistic and Roman times often noted the name changes. This enables modern scholars to make the appropriate connections between the older Semitic names and the later ones of the classical periods. Eusebius, for example, bishop of Caesarea ca. 264-340 CE, prepared extensive Bible study aids for the clergy of his day, a portion of which has survived and is known as the *Onomasticon*. This work was essentially a list of the most important place-names mentioned in the Old Testament with notes correlating names and locating them in relation to the Roman road system. Eusebius' *Onomasticon* was regarded as valuable enough for Jerome to annotate and translate it from Greek into Latin almost a century later. This was the information source for a famous mosaic map on the floor of a sixth century CE church at Madaba, a town in the region east of the Dead Sea. This map, which unfortunately has not survived in its entirety, depicts the lands of the Bible from the Egyptian delta to Syria and indicates places where important biblical events occurred. In effect, the Madaba Mosaic Map is the predecessor of modern Bible atlases.

Jewish and Christian pilgrims were arriving in Palestine already by the end of the second century CE and have continued until the present. Many of the earlier pilgrims' accounts were collected, translated, and published between 1887 and 1897 by the Palestine Pilgrims' Text Society, which was organized for that purpose. These pilgrims often were rather gullible, believing whatever the local guides told them. Early on in the Ottoman period, however, there began to appear a new kind of traveler in the Near East, scholar-explorers who exhibited the spirit of the dawning age of scientific exploration—travelers such as Leonhard Rauchwolf and Johann Zuallart in the late-sixteenth century, Pietro della Valle in the mid-seventh century, and Henry Maundrell and Richard Pococke in the eighteenth century. However, the event that marked the real beginning of the modern exploration of Palestine was Napoleon's invasion of Egypt in 1798. In addition to the discovery of the Rosetta Stone (see below), Napoleon's engineers prepared the first trigonometrically based (1:100,000 scale) map of Egypt and the Palestinian coast. This is the so-called Jacotin Map, the Palestinian portion of which was prepared under the difficult circumstances of Napoleon's march up the coast and unsuccessful attempt to take Acre (i.e., Old Testament Acco, later Ptolemais, now Acre).

Characteristic of the first half of the nineteenth century were individual travellers such as Ulrich Seetzen and Ludwig Bruckhardt, the first westerners to penetrate the region east of the Dead Sea (ancient Moab) since the Crusaders were expelled from their castle at Kerak seven centuries earlier. Scholar-explorers increased in numbers during the mid-nineteenth century, an especially important figure being Edward Robinson. Robinson pioneered the study of biblical geography, made two extended trips to Palestine in 1838 and 1852 as part of his research, and published a three-volume work, *Biblical Researches in Palestine, Mount Sinai and Arabia Petraea* (1841), which remains one of the classic studies. In 1865, the Palestine Exploration Fund was established in London for the purpose of fostering the systematic exploration of Palestine. One of the major accomplishments of this society was a systematic survey of the region west of the Jordan River. The resulting map in twenty-eight sheets (1" to 1 British mile scale) and six-volumes of notes on such matters as local topography, archaeological remains, and contemporary Arabic place names served as the basic source for a large fold-out Bible map published by the society in 1890 and two excellent Bible atlases that appeared soon after the turn of the century—H. Guthe's *Bibelatlas* (1911) and G. A. Smith's *Atlas of the Historical Geography of the Holy Land* (1915).

These nineteenth-century travelers and explorers were aware that the present-day Arabic names often correspond to or preserve elements of the ancient biblical names. Robinson, for example, recognized that the Arabic name of the village "Beitin" corresponds to the old Hebrew name "Bethel." Not until the century drew to a close, however, did it gradually dawn upon these scholar-explorers that the "tells" scattered throughout the land were stratified ruins of ancient cities. Again Robinson serves as an example. Standing on a prominent tell east of Beitin, known locally as et-Tell ("the tell"), Robinson observed that the old biblical city of Ai should have been located at precisely that spot. Since he saw nothing that he recognized as archaeological remains, he continued his search for biblical Ai elsewhere. We know now, of course, that et-Tell itself represented the archaeological remains of ancient Ai.

In addition to recognizing the significance of "tells," biblical scholars during the present century have had at their disposal increasingly accurate and more detailed maps of Palestine. Important mapping projects were undertaken during the British Mandate period. Then, especially during the 1950s and 1960s, even more accurate and detailed topographical maps were produced with aerial photography. The latest developments include satellite imagery. Already a Bible atlas based on satellite imagery has appeared.[2] Ten years ago, when the author conducted a survey of archaeological sites in the region of ancient Moab, the process of establishing exact map coordinates for each ruin was time consuming. Today, with field instruments that combine satellite and computer technology, it is possible to determine the exact location of any spot on the globe within minutes. With aerial photography it is possible to recognize archaeological features from above that cannot be seen on the ground. Now, with sophisticated satellite imagery, it is possible to "see" to some extent even below the ground.

Epigraphy

Epigraphy has to do with deciphering ancient inscriptions, which brings to mind stone monuments with texts literally "inscribed" in the stone. A more inclusive definition that includes the study of written documents of any sort recovered from ancient times is more useful for our purposes. Also it is useful to distinguish between epigraphical and archaeological evidence, defining the latter as nonverbal material remains such as city ruins, wall lines, pottery, etc.

The recovery of thousands of documents from the peoples of the ancient Near East, and the decipherment of most of the languages in which these documents are written, has produced one of the most exciting developments of modern times to impact biblical studies. Earlier readers had tended to think of the Old Testament as an essentially unique document from the dawn of time. By the end of the nineteenth century, however, it had become apparent that the Israelites were preceded by two thousand years of advanced civilization. The Old Testament texts have close parallels in the literature of ancient Israel's neighbors.

The decipherment of ancient Egyptian writing was the first major breakthrough. Jean Francois Champollion, working with the trilingual Rosetta Stone (Greek, Egyptian demotic, and hieroglyphics) discovered during Napoleon's invasion of Egypt, managed to work out the basics of Egyptian hieroglyphics in 1822. Hundreds of hieroglyphic inscriptions were already visible on the ancient Egyptian temples, tombs, and various other monuments. Now for the first time they could be read and understood. Beginning in 1846, came the decipherment of two major Mesopotamian languages, Akkadian and Sumerian, in their cuneiform scripts. Henry C. Rawlingson, working with the Behistun Inscription, another trilingual (Persian, Median, and Babylonian), gets the credit for this breakthrough. By the end of the nineteenth century, archaeologists excavating in the ruins of ancient Mesopotamian cities had turned up several archives of Akkadian and Sumerian tablets. Also, in 1887, an archive of Akkadian letters was discovered in the el-Amarna district of Egypt. These letters, representing correspondence between pharaohs of Dynasty XVIII and various Syro-Palestinian rulers, provide a glimpse of socio-political circumstances in Palestine during the late fifteenth and early fourteenth centuries BCE—i.e., shortly before the people of Israel appeared on the scene.

In 1915 came the decipherment of Hittite documents discovered at Boghazköy (ancient Hattusas) in central Turkey. An ancient Canaanite archive was discovered at Ras Shamra (ancient Ugarit) on the Syrian coast in 1929 and deciphered that same year. These Canaanite (or, more specifically, Ugaritic) texts date from the mid-fourteenth to the early twelfth centuries BCE. These important texts in a language closely related to Hebrew include royal and commercial records, as well as mythical texts concerning the Canaanite god, Baal. Recovery of a major archive of Bronze Age records at Tell Hariri (ancient Mari) in 1933 was the next major epigraphical discovery. Tell Hariri/Mari is situated on the middle Euphrates, just on the Syrian side of the modern Syrian/Iraqi boundary. Most of the Mari texts are in Akkadian, and they are an especially important source for understanding socio-political circumstances in Syria-Palestine during the Middle Bronze Age. The most recent, major archival discovery of significance was made at Tell Mardikh (ancient Ebla) in 1975. Scholars are still in the early stages of studying and publishing the Ebla texts, but already it is clear that they are in an ancient language related to Akkadian and that they will be extremely important for understanding the Early Bronze Age.

Epigraphical evidence from Palestine is meager compared to the extensive royal archives that have been discovered in Egypt, Mesopotamia, Syria, and Asia Minor. Especially noteworthy from Palestine are the Mesha Inscription, the Siloam Inscription, and several groups of ostraca. The Mesha Inscription, discovered in 1868 at the site of the ancient Moabite city of Dibon, reports the royal accomplishments of King Mesha who ruled Moab from Dibon in the ninth century BCE. Clearly Mesha regarded as his major accomplishment a successful struggle to rid Moab of Israelite domination, and the inscription identifies Omri as the Israelite king who had subjected Moab in the first place. This same King Mesha is mentioned in the narrative of 2 Kgs 3:4-28, which reports how Jehoram, Omri's grandson, attempted unsuccessfully to restore Israelite control over Moab. The Siloam Inscription was discovered at Jerusalem in 1880 in a tunnel hewed out of solid rock for the purpose of transferring water from the Gihon Spring to the Siloam Pool. Although intended to commemorate the completion of the tunneling project, the inscription was vandalized soon after its discovery and the remaining legible portion does not name the king who commissioned the project. Most scholars associate it with Hezekiah (cf. 2 Chr 32:30). Discovered among the ruins at Sebastiyeh (ancient Samaria) were approximately sixty ostraca bearing administrative records concerning dispatches of wine and oil. While the ostraca include no references to known persons or events that would enable scholars to date them, the archaeological context of their discovery, the script, and certain clues from their content, suggest that they derive from the time of Jehu's dynasty (late ninth-early eighth centuries BCE). Two other important ostraca groups have been uncovered at Tell Arad (ancient Arad) and Tell ed-Duweir (ancient Lachish). Both groups contain letters apparently sent to military commanders at these two places in the seventh and sixth centuries BCE.

The above is not an exhaustive list of the epigraphical discoveries, but enough to make the point that the recovery and decipherment of ancient texts has revolutionized our understanding of the ancient world from which the Old Testament emerged. Indeed, this rich store of ancient documents in languages with varying degrees of similarity to Hebrew has shed light on virtually every aspect of Old Testament scholarship—Hebrew philology and literary forms, ancient Israel's cultic practices and institutions, the role of prophets in Israelite society, and legal traditions. Moreover, since the ancient Egyptian, Assyrian, and Babylonian rulers often can be dated, the occasional references to Israelite and Judean kings in their royal records serve as valuable benchmarks for establishing the chronology of Israel's kings.

Usually the references to Israel or its leaders are only passing references. They typically include reports of military campaigns conducted into Syria-Palestine and records of tribute collected from the various peoples encountered there. Except for two Egyptian hieroglyphic texts, which are not very revealing, there is no mention of ancient Israel or of any biblical character or events in any of the epigraphical sources before the mid-ninth century BCE. The earliest inscription is from the reign of Merneptah, an Egyptian pharaoh of Dynasty XIX (thirteenth century BCE), which mentions Israel along with several cities that Merneptah claims to have conquered during a military campaign into Syria-Palestine. The hieroglyphic presentation of the name "Israel" in the inscription suggests that the "Israel" that Merneptah encountered was a loosely defined group of people, rather than a city or an organized kingdom. Otherwise one learns from the inscription only that Israel was located somewhere in the general vicinity of Palestine. The other exception dates from the tenth century BCE and reports an Egyptian military campaign into Syria-Palestine conducted by Pharaoh Sheshonk. Sheshonk's campaign is mentioned also in 1 Kgs 14:25-28 (where the pharaoh is called Shishak). But while Sheshonk claims to have conquered many cities in Palestine, some of which presumably belonged at that time to the separate kingdoms of Israel and Judah, his inscription conspicuously fails to mention either of these kingdoms.

It is not until the mid-ninth century, the time of Omri, Ahab, and Mesha, that the epigraphical sources yield any specific references to Old Testament characters and events. This means that the ancient documents recovered thus far do not mention Abraham, Isaac, Jacob, Joseph, Moses, the Exodus from Egypt, Joshua, the conquest of Canaan, Saul, David, Solomon, etc. These characters and deeds are known only from the Old Testament and later literature dependent upon it.

Israel, referring specifically now to the Northern Kingdom, enjoyed a period of national strength under Omri and Ahab, and the trail of epigraphical references picks up at that point. The Mesha Inscription refers specifically to "Omri king of Israel" and, as indicated above, witnesses to the fact that Israel dominated Moab during Omri's reign. Assyria was beginning to expand westward during the same century, especially under Shalmaneser III who claims (in his Monolith Inscription) to have defeated a coalition of Syro-Palestinian kings that included "Ahab of Israel." The battle, fought at Qarqar on the Orontes River in Syria, is reported to have taken place during Shalmaneser's sixth year, around 853 BCE. Other inscriptions from later on in Shalmaneser's reign report that he conducted several more western campaigns and, in 841 BCE, collected tribute from "Jehu the son of Omri." Adad-nirari III (753-745) claims in one inscription to have received tribute from "the land of Omri" and in another to have received tribute from "Joash of Samaria." Tiglath-pileser (744-727) reports tribute from Menahem of the land of Omri and claims to have confirmed Hoshea on the throne in Samaria after the people of that city overthrew Pekah (compare 2 Kgs 15:29-31). Sargon II (722-705) claims to have conquered Samaria, exiled much of its population, and resettled the city with exiles from other places (compare 2 Kings 17, which seems to credit Shalmaneser V with the deed).

Judah, the Southern Israelite Kingdom, turns up for the first time in Tiglath-pileser's records with "Jehoahaz of Judah" listed among those who paid him tribute. But surely the most notable Assyrian inscriptions relevant to the history of Judah are two annalistic prisms from the reign of Sennacherib (704-681). They provide almost duplicate accounts of his invasion of Palestine and siege of Lachish in 701 BCE (compare 2 Kgs 18:9–19:37). Assyria held a firm grip on all of Syria-Palestine during the reigns of Esarhaddon (680-669) and Ashurbanipal (668-627), and both of these rulers report tribute from Judah, Edom, Moab, etc. With the collapse of Assyria and the rise of Babylon, the local Palestinian kingdoms that had survived Assyrian domination fell into Babylonian hands. One of the Babylonian Chronicles reports Nebuchadnezzar's conquest of Jerusalem in March of 597 BCE. We know from the biblical account of this event that Jehoiachin was on the throne in Jerusalem when the city fell (2 Kgs 24:1-17) and that he was taken captive to Babylon. Babylonian lists of food rations mention Jehoiachin along with other exiles resident in Babylonia during Nebuchadnezzar's reign (604-561).

Under the Persians, Palestine belonged to the fifth satrapy known as "the land beyond the river" (i.e., beyond the Euphrates). Coins were struck in the province of *Yehud* (Judah), and a group of papyri from Elephantine Island in the upper Nile witness to the existence of a Jewish military colony living there during the fifth century BCE. But there are no specific references to either the province of Samaria or of Judah in the surviving Persian records.

There is every reason to expect that the future will bring more epigraphical discoveries, including more texts from Syria-Palestine. Since the earliest epigraphical discoveries were made in Egypt and lower Mesopotamia, there has been a tendency to think of these areas as the active centers of civilization during ancient times, with Syria-Palestine as a kind of "empty quarter." Already Syrian sites are yielding texts, which demonstrate that this is not true, however, that the cities of Syria in any case (Ebla, Mari, Ugarit, etc.) were very much in the mainstream. What we really need are more texts from Palestine in order to paint a fuller picture. An inscription fragment discovered recently at Tell Dan revives hope that sooner or later one of the Palestinian tells will produce archives.[3]

Archaeology

The term archaeology often is used rather loosely for any sort of research, discovery, or speculation that involves either digging in the ground or antiquity. A narrower definition was proposed above, whereby archaeology has to do specifically with the artifactual remains of human civilizations—things made by human hands. According to this narrower definition, the work of an archaeologist would be distinguished from that of a geologist (who studies the earth's crust), a paleontologist (who attempts to trace the evolution of biological forms), and an epigrapher or philologist (who studies ancient written documents). While it is useful for our purposes to make these distinctions, obviously this "academic" definition of archaeology cannot be rigidly maintained. It was field archaeologists who discovered most of the epigraphical archives discussed above. Moreover, all artifactual evidence must be studied in relation to its physical and historical context. In actual practice, therefore, archaeological research is interdisciplinary; it necessarily involves geology, paleontology, epigraphy, historical-geography, and a host of other related disciplines and subdisciplines.

As seen above, the nineteenth century was a period of increasingly intentional and systematic exploration of the Near East. The last four decades of that century were especially active in terms of archaeological exploration with much of the important work in Palestine conducted under the auspices of the Palestine Exploration Fund. By the end of the century, western Palestine and much of the region east of the Jordan had been surveyed and mapped with careful attention to local Arabic names and visible archaeological remains. Also by the end of the century, "tells" had come to be recognized for what they were, and one of them had been excavated—Tell el-Hesy, by Flinders Petrie in 1890 under the auspices of the Palestine Exploration Fund.

Beginning with Petrie's work at Tell el-Hesy, Palestinian archaeologists turned their attention increasingly to the major tells of the region. By the outbreak of World War I, several of them (including Gezer, Tanaach, Megiddo, Samaria, Beth Shemesh, and Shechem) had been excavated to some degree by British, German, and American archaeologists employing a wide variety of techniques. Many more were examined during the postwar years, which also saw significant advances in excavation and dating techniques. Perhaps the most important of these advances was ceramic dating. Petrie, in addition to understanding that tells were stratified ruins with the successive strata corresponding to successive occupational phases, recognized that the pottery found in each stratum would be the key for dating the corresponding occupational phases. It took some years to work out the basics of ceramic dating for the Palestinian region, a task that was pioneered by W. F. Albright and essentially accomplished by the late 1920s. Carbon-14 dating, introduced in 1933, serves as a check on ceramic dating, but is less useful for the day-to-day work of an archaeologist because it applies only to organic remains and requires a specialized laboratory. Every stratum of a tell typically will yield basket loads of potsherds, and trained archaeologists usually can get a fairly accurate reading of the period(s) represented in a basket of pottery simply by visual examination.

Archaeological research during the latter half of the present century (aftermath of World War II and the establishment of modern Israel) has witnessed increasingly rapid changes. First, there have been major improvements and increased consensus in excavation techniques. Virtually all archaeologists working in Syria-Palestine now use some variation of the so-called Wheeler-Kenyon method of excavation, pioneered by Kathleen Kenyon at Samaria and Jericho. Second, rather than attempting to dig the largest and most impressive tells, archaeological projects today usually are designed with rather specific goals in mind. This means, among other things, fewer long-term excavations and more attention to one-period sites. Third, there has been a noticeable shift of interest away from historical towards anthropological kinds of questions. Archaeologists working in Palestine today tend to be less concerned to correlate their findings with the political history of ancient times. They are more interested in learning what sort of communal configurations existed among the people who lived in the region and how they utilized or exploited their environment. This, in turn, has led to more regional surveys, as opposed to concentration on individual sites. Fourth, archaeological teams are being drawn now from an increasingly broad range of disciplines, and more now from the sciences than from the humanities. Archaeological teams may include geologists, botanists, zoologists, or hydrologists. Also, especially in Israel, more of the actual work is done now by student volunteers than by hired laborers. Thus a broad variety of data is collected, collected more carefully, and more completely understood. Finally, the practice of field archaeology has been and continues to be significantly influenced by computers. Recording the excavated evidence and subsequent data management is as important a part of archaeology as the digging. Computers already have had a major impact on archaeology and the possibilities seem endless.

With systematic analysis of the archaeological evidence surviving in a given area (ancient city and village ruins, architectural remains, remnants of tools, potsherds, etc.), archaeologists can learn a great deal about the settlement patterns and life-styles of the people who lived there in times past. It is important to keep in mind, however, that archaeology by itself—i.e., the nonverbal artifactual evidence—usually is neither ethnic specific nor very useful for clarifying matters of historical detail. If the people who lived in the cities, used the tools, and produced the pottery are to be identified in terms of their ethnic identity, the artifactual record must coordinate with the written documents. Artifacts themselves occasionally bear inscriptions, as observed above. But whatever the source, any extensive use of artifactual evidence toward understanding the specifics of the history of a particular people depends ultimately on textual information.

The point to be made here is that archaeology alone really tells us very little about ancient Israel. Indeed, were we entirely dependent on the archaeological evidence narrowly defined, we would not even know that ancient Israel existed. Only when this evidence is interpreted in the light of the Old Testament and the epigraphical evidence is surveyed can archaeology be brought to bear on the ancient Israelite culture and history. The following are some examples of how that works.

Merneptah's inscription indicates the presence of a group known as Israel on the scene in Palestine near the end of the thirteenth century BCE. This seems to "fit" with the biblical narratives in the books of Judges and 1 Samuel, which have the Israelite tribes settled in the central Palestinian hill country on the eve of the establishment of the monarchy under Saul and David (i.e., before ca. 1000 BCE). The thirteenth century also marked the end of the Late Bronze Age in archaeological chronology, and one of the features of the artifactual record that leads Palestinian archaeologists to distinguish between the Late Bronze (usually dated ca. 1550-1200 BCE) and the subsequent Iron Age (ca. 1200-332 BCE) has to do with the population density of the central hill country as reflected in the settlement patterns from these two ages. Specifically, archaeological field surveys indicate that the central Palestinian hill country was very sparsely occupied during the Late Bronze Age, but as indicated by the remains of numerous Iron I settlements, received a noticeable population increase early in the Iron Age. Thus it is reasonable to associate the Israelites, known from the Merneptah Inscription to have been in Palestine during the thirteenth century, and from Judges narratives to have been settled in the hill country before ca. 1000 BCE, with the emerging Iron I hill country settlements.

Nothing has been discovered at any of these settlement sites which, of itself, identifies any of them specifically as Israelite. Moreover, while it seems reasonable on the basis of the Merneptah Inscription and the Judges narratives to connect the Israelites with the Iron I settlements, the nature of the connection is not entirely clear. For one thing, we do not know exactly what the term "Israelite" would have meant at that early stage of Israel's history. Furthermore, the same Judges narratives that associate the Israelites with the central Palestinian hill country prior to the monarchy also name other people living in the same area (Hivites, Jebusites, etc.). This brings us back to the observation made above that archaeological evidence normally is not ethnic-specific. At least to this point, archaeologists have no way of distinguishing from the settlement remains themselves which villages were inhabited by Israelites and which were inhabited by Hivites, Jebusites, or whatever.

In the instance discussed above, there seems to be a reasonable "fit" between the archaeological evidence, Merneptah's inscription, and the implied geographical and chronological setting of the narratives in the book of Judges. There seems to be an unavoidable conflict, on the other hand, between the archaeological evidence and account of the Israelite conquest of Canaan presented in the book of Joshua. Archaeologists have excavated several of the cities that are reported in the Joshua account to have resisted the Israelites. The archaeological results—specifically Tell Arad (biblical Arad), Tell Hesban (Heshbon), Tell es-Sultan (Jericho), and et-Tell (Ai)—produced little or no evidence to suggest that the cities in question were even occupied when the conquest occurred, much less that they were major fortified cities as the Joshua account implies.

Other times there is a possible "fit," but the connection is open to question. For example, excavations at Tell Qedah (biblical Hazor), Tell es-Mutesellim (Megiddo), and Tell Jezer (Gezer) reveal remains of relatively impressive fortifications of similar architectural design dated to roughly 1000 BCE. First Kgs 9:15 reports, on the other hand, that Solomon levied forced labor "to build the house of the LORD and his own house the Millo and the wall of Jerusalem, Hazor, Megiddo, and Gezer." Again, there is nothing in the archaeological evidence itself from any of these three sites, no inscriptions and nothing about the architectural design, to identify the builder of the excavated fortifications. Nevertheless, in view of the biblical record that credits Solomon with building activities in these three cities at a corresponding time, it seems reasonable to many scholars to attribute the fortifications to him. Other scholars are not convinced.

To summarize, archaeology is relevant to biblical studies primarily in that it helps us understand the material culture and, to some extent, settlement patterns of the ancient Near East from which the Old Testament emerged. Archaeological evidence is less useful, especially when defined as referring specifically to nonverbal artifactual evidence, for dealing with the specifics of Israelite history. The widespread notion that archaeology has "proved" the accuracy of the Bible is misleading. There are some convincing "fits" between archaeological findings and the Old Testament texts, but there are also some glaring conflicts. Moreover, in instances where archaeological evidence and the Old Testament record are brought together, the Old Testament record invariably plays a major role in interpreting the archaeological evidence.

Notes

1. The term "Palestine" is used here and below in its traditional geographical sense with no intended implications regarding the current political conflict.

2. R. Cleave, *The Holy Land Satellite Atlas—Student Map Manual Illustrated Supplement, Volume I* (Nicosia, Cyprus: Rohr Productions Ltd., 1994).

3. Avraham Biran and Joseph Naveh, "An Aramaic Stele Fragment from Tel Dan," in *IEJ* 43 (1993) 81-98.

Selected Bibliography

Aharoni, Y. *The Land of the Bible: A Historical Geography.* Translated by A. F. Rainey. Philadelphia: Westminster, 1967.

Ben-Arieh, Y. *The Rediscovery of the Holy Land in the Nineteenth Century.* Jerusalem and Detroit: Magnes and Wayne State University Press, 1989.

Cleave, R. *The Holy Land Satellite Atlas—Student Map Manual Illustrated Supplement, Volume I.* Nicosia, Cyprus: Rohr Productions Ltd., 1994.

Drinkard, J. F. , G. L. Mattingly, and J. M. Miller, eds., *Benchmarks in Time and Culture: An Introduction to Palestinian Archaeology.* Atlanta: Scholars Press, 1988.

Edelman, D., ed. *The Fabric of History: Text, Artifact, and Israel's Past.* Sheffield: JSOT, 1991.

Hoerth, Alfred J., Gerald L. Mattingly, and Edwin M. Yamauchi, eds., *Peoples of the Old Testament World.* Grand Rapids: Baker Books, 1994.

Mazar, A. *Archaeology of the Land of the Bible: 10,000-586 BCE.* New York and London: Doubleday, 1990.

Moorey, P. R. S. *A Century of Biblical Archaeology.* Louisville: Westminster/John Knox, 1991.

Pritchard, J. B., ed. *Ancient Near Eastern Tests Relating to the Old Testament,* 3d ed. with supplement. Princeton: Princeton University Press, 1969.

Robinson, E. *Biblical Researches in Palestine, Mount Sinai, and Arabia Petraea,* 3 vols. Boston: Crocker and Brewster, 1841.

Silberman, N. A. *Digging for God and Country: Exploration, Archaeology, and the Secret Struggle for the Holy Land, 1799-1917.* New York: Knopf, 1982.

von Soden, W. *The Ancient Orient: An Introduction to the Study of the Ancient Near East.* Translated by D. G. Schley. Grand Rapids: Eerdmans, 1985.

Thomas, D. W. ed., *Archaeology and Old Testament Study.* Oxford: Clarendon, 1967.

Chapter 16
THE RELIGION AND INSTITUTIONS OF ANCIENT ISRAEL: TOWARD A CONTEXTUAL THEOLOGY OF THE SCRIPTURES

Erhard S. Gerstenberger

Old Testament research during the past decades has been considering ever more seriously the social implications of faith and liturgy, prophetic speech, and theological reflection. The Word of God, formerly understood as a rather self-sufficient theological entity, has been rediscovered, by means of form-critical and social-historical approaches to biblical texts, firmly rooted in historical and social contexts. There is necessarily a "carnal" (cf. John 1:14) quality to the messages of the law and the gospel that makes them tangible and understandable. Social structures and group interests are tied to and interwoven with even the most refined articulations of faith and theology. The intricate interrelationships between them is by no means deterministic. But when doing exegesis and theology, we have to take into account the social and institutional roots of all communication and every type of text.

Quite frequently, religious texts are considered as free-floating works of zeal or art that have lost their *Sitz im Leben* and turned into spiritual nourishment for anybody who cares to consume them. A number of differing structuralist and literary hypotheses have led to such a lofty appreciation of traditional texts. There certainly is good reason to point to shifting uses especially of texts in the biblical tradition. Without a doubt, the words of Torah and Prophets have been formed and reformed in changing historical and social situations, repeatedly interpreted, and adapted to new circumstances and undergoing substantial modifications. But, as soon as any "Word" is taken over into a new social environment, it in fact sinks down new roots immediately, becoming part of a new contextual situation. When we recognize that human discourse of any kind necessarily belongs to some sort of communication, we already have conceded its social moorings. All the more urgent will be the exegetical and theological task of recognizing the changing institutional affiliations of changing discourse about God.

The notion of change is of special importance, especially in Old Testament literary tradition. After all, we are dealing with a rich and varied body of material accumulated and formed during centuries of conscious application to freshly emerging situations. In terms of social perspectives, Israel, during its long and painful history, had to undergo transformations of considerable severity and speed. If our estimations are correct, the people of Yahweh emerged in an environment of political strife and unrest as a rather loose association of clans and tribes. Thereafter, external pressures forced the tribal people into the bureaucratic, patriarchal, and militaristic patterns of a near eastern monarchical system, which in turn soon broke down under increasing aggression of neighboring world powers. Finally, the tiny Judean province lost its political autonomy and Israel arose as a new people united by faith and lineage rather than political-military organization. All these developments took place in relatively brief periods. For the most part they were enforced and not voluntary, and the social implications were felt through all layers of society. We must look at these social transformations in order to gain more insight about the growth of Old Testament literature and the articulations of faith and creed within Israelite traditions. Naturally, the results of modern social studies in various fields (cultural anthropology, ethnology, social psychology, sociology) are invaluable in assessing Israelite institutions.

Religion Within the Lineage System

The smallest social unit in human history has always been the family, organized around procreative relationships of women and men, bound together by productive, life-sustaining work, legitimated by descendent and firm rules of marriage, and bent on guaranteeing the individual's well-being inside the shell of the primary group. The family of old may have consisted of ten to thirty members; aside from its nucleus, it sheltered members of the older generation as well as sons and their in-laws and offspring, unmarried women, unfree servants, and, possibly, sojourners. Excavated city dwellings suggest family sizes towards the lower end of the scale. In the countryside we may expect larger numbers. The family was, through blood-relationships, tied into a network of kin groups; together they made up a clan. While the family was responsible for basic needs in the economic, juridic, educational, and religious fields, the clan provided other means of assistance to the smaller social units.

Although the family has persisted in humankind since time immemorial and continues to exist even under very adverse conditions in an industrial and postindustrial age, family patterns and functions shifted throughout the turbulent history of ancient Israel. In the earliest period (twelfth century BCE), proto-Israelites and early Israelites were presumably seminomadic people living at the fringes of arid zones, supported by livestock, occasional crop cultivation, and artisan-trade. They may have been, in part, lower class urban refugees who looked for survival in less inhabited areas. Lack of larger social organization made these early groups autonomous by sheer necessity. The individual could survive only inside this solidary group of kinspeople. Hence, religion was geared almost exclusively to the necessities of this form of group-life.

Significant changes in Israelite history certainly affected family life and structures. The first involved the transformation of Israelite family clans into an agrarian society organized into tribes and tribal alliances. Rain-farming in the hill country of Canaan as well as irrigation-farming along the rivers called for special skills and experiences, just as the expansion of herding (cows, poultry and, sometimes, swine are added to goat and sheep), with different religious rites and beliefs developing in accordance with them. During the time of the monarchies, the agrarian society remained basically the same, enjoying the protection of the state or suffering its defeats, and paying heavily for the military and administrative expenses of the government. Urbanization also continued due to the strengthening of central and military power. This political superstructure brought a new kind of religion with it. There had been tribal systems of belief, connected with the requirements of tribal functions, but the idea of a monarchical state fostered different expectations and theological legitimation. A second deep alteration in family status occurred after the final defeat of Judah in 587 BCE. Family and clan again proved their strength: they became the backbone of the new faith-community system. With the absence of strong government and under the weary eyes of occupational forces, the Israelites organized as followers of Yahweh, the first known confessional, or even parochial, entity. Still some families, especially in the farmers' villages, proved the least powerful in society's chain. They had to bear the burden of taxes and contributions, apparently receiving only low payment for their products. Small wonder that signs of impoverishment, class struggle, and concomitant theological reflection began to appear (cf. Nehemiah 5; Psalm 37).

Potentially, all of life, each individual day or moment, held religious significance. There was no hard and fast division between realms of holiness pertinent to the gods and areas of the profane in which the heavenly hosts took no interest. Yet, people knew from their own experience that the gods did not actively interfere in the same fashion with all things going on in the world. Therefore religious ceremonialism concentrated on the most important events in everyday life, while much other human business was endowed with only latent religious interest.

Yet another feature requires self-critical reflection. We are accustomed, at least in Europe, to depreciate family religion because we usually pretend to live out of those resources provided by society at large, be it state or denomination (creed, ethos, or worldview). Yet, the Old Testament at times places a very strong emphasis on the "creed of the fathers" and its peculiarities. We may surmise, furthermore, that family creeds in contrast to state religion never died out in Israel, even after the Exile.

Faith and rites of the small kinship group revolve around the well-being of its members and that intimate community. Especially important are *rites de passage* (A. van Gennep) from birth to grave, concerning procreation and fertility, on the human plane as well as in the fields and with the livestock. Because families, as such, do not produce literature, there are only slight traces of family religion left in the Old Testament. We occasionally read about birth and name giving (Gen 30:1-6; 35:16-18; Ruth 4:13-17), events of deep religious significance and family worship. At times (perhaps because of high infant mortality), the weaning of the three-year-old was the occasion for feasting and thanksgiving (cf. Gen 21:8; 1 Sam 1:24–2:11). Circumcision of the male child originally may have occurred at the time of puberty or even shortly before marriage (cf. Gen 17:25; Exod 4:25). In later times it became one of the central marks of identification and happened on the eighth day after birth (Gen 21:4), thus determining in the long range the baptismal date of (Catholic) Christianity. Puberty, in one way or another, was the next important date for family religion, both in its male and female branches (cf. Gen 17:25; Judg 11:37-40). Marriage followed in due course (cf. Judges 14), with careful rules to be obeyed by families and fiancées (Gen 24:29, 9-30). We do not know about other regular ceremonies during a person's mature life, but religious customs were connected with death and burial at least for the chief of family (cf. Genesis 48–50).

There were many more occasions in the family to keep up a harmonious relationship with the deity, some tied to seasonal events like sowing, harvesting, lamb season, others prompted more by noncalendrical events like building a new house, digging a well, clearing ground for a field. Naturally, families also were very much concerned about health and security, internal peace, education, and punishment of crimes against family members. Mothers would look for a holy person to cure their sick children; fathers were responsible for chastising disobedient sons or executing revenge against murderers. Families obeyed sexual and other taboos that helped to preserve harmony. Contracts with other groups beyond marriage liaisons had to be ratified in solemn procedures. In short, there were many occasions beside daily life and the work of the small group that required religious action and ritual.

Unfortunately we are not informed thoroughly about religious life on the family level. The reason is obvious. Families seem to be subservient structures as soon as some secondary social organization has been formed. Tribe, nation, and postexilic community in Israel drew heavily on family traditions. This fact is obvious in the extant literature, which has been produced only by people benefitting from the larger society, not by family institutions themselves. Thus, we have to reconstruct religious patterns, customs, and structures of the family, which are so basic to Israel's faith, especially in postexilic times.

In early Israel, father and mother played the decisive religious roles of family life. While the male leader was responsible for various kinds of bloody sacrifices (there seems to have been an archaic taboo, probably deriving from hunting practices, preventing females from slaughtering animals), annual family reunions, and pilgrimages to distant sanctuaries (cf. Judg 13:19-23; 1 Sam 1:3; 20:28), the housewife, at least part of the time, took care of the family shrine with its well attested figurine of the deity (*tĕrāpîm*) venerated by the particular group (cf. Gen 31:19, 30-35; Judg 17:3; 1 Sam 19:13). Discussion about the range and function of the "family-cult" in Israel is still under way; it has been enhanced significantly by archaeological discoveries of large quantities of small figurines and private ceremonial equipment in Israelite cities. We now know that women in early Israel, at a minimum, took active roles in family worship. This may be true also for healing and thanksgiving ceremonies as we can correctly surmise from the evidence of complaints and thanksgivings for individuals in the Old Testament psalter and narratives of curing, incantation, divination, and praise (cf. 1 Samuel 28; 1 Kgs 4:18-21).

No matter how much family religion with its particular rites and concepts of the divine was superseded by later secondary organizations and their different faiths, the values and visions of small-group theology did persist in the Old Testament. They, in fact, constitute the firm base of all religious thought in the Scriptures. Of course, tribal, state, and community structures provided their specific theological perspectives and concepts that infiltrated family rites. However, new names and "higher" gods hardly changed the innate qualities of family faith. For instance, the creation of the world or the election of Israel were hardly meaningful for the *rites de passage* of a person and that individual's primary group. Or vice versa: Wherever the name of Yahweh and his great acts of salvation for his chosen people were implanted into texts of familial concerns, these borrowings from secondary social organization clearly have been subordinated to private theological expectations and concepts. Thus we may say that small-scale faith, limited by the horizons of intimate groups, throughout the history of Israel and in some ways to this very day has remained the solid basis of all Western religion.

(This assertion, of course, runs counter to official and popular belief that the large values and visions of the extended society are the only valid norms to live by.) Future Old Testament research has to take into account this fact, which has been lost since the Middle Ages: Christian enthusiasm for imperial designs of faith and church for the most part ignored and buried those humble origins of the family and its "god of the father." The paternal god, however, who existed in close contact with his client-group, never was forgotten in the tradition of Israel. In fact, that deity remained faithful to the weak and the poor.

Religion in Village and Tribe

Social organization of human beings all over the world developed in similar patterns. Early bands of hunters and gatherers proliferated and formed tribal networks. They settled down to agrarian life and organized in local communities. Basic needs had to be taken care of on the family level, but common interests were delegated and developed within the larger society. Among these, protection against external enemies probably held a very high ranking. Defense mechanisms grew out of such joint endeavors. Other interests of secondary social organizations always include the cultivation of internal harmony and culture, religion, and well-being. Obviously, such common objectives will result in appropriate institutions involving political, economic, and religious dimensions.

The Old Testament gives us some information about the fabric of village and tribal life after the settlement or the formation of the first larger organizations (approximately the eleventh century BCE). Ethnological and anthropological studies of tribal societies in our times are of great help in illuminating the situation in Canaan. We clearly realize in the ancient texts that social and political ties between tribes normally were quite loose and limited to a few common interests and joint ventures. Even petty conflicts could result in deadly confrontations (cf. Judg 12:1-6; Genesis 49). Inhabitants of one and the same (agrarian) township, however, must have gone further in uniting to meet challenges and common responsibilities.

The extant literature of Israel reflects some outstanding secondary social structures of the tribal level. Foremost it points to the "elders" of a given tribe (later redactors claim "of Israel") who apparently came together in a sort of "tribal (or town) council" to talk over and decide important issues. We are led to assume that they actually were heads of family or clan who acted as an egalitarian leadership conference in all matters of war and peace, right or wrong, custom and property. Again, all problems of common concern had, in principle, their religious implications. Yet we do not exactly know what kind of spiritual authorities were invoked, if necessary, by those councils of elders, granted that each family or clan was autonomous in its religious affiliation. Possibly the local (fairly independent) sanctuary, well attested in Old Testament sources, emerged at this point. We receive the impression that each village had its own "high place" (cf. 1 Sam 9:12:22) either without a continuous priestly service (but perhaps attended by "free-lance" men of God?) or with a small temple kept up by a hereditary priesthood and possibly endowed with regional functions (cf. Nob, 1 Sam 22:6-19; Shilo, 1 Samuel 1–3). Thus we may imagine a loosely knit tribal society with a secular council of elders as leading body and with some spiritual guidance by local or regional priesthoods whenever special advice seemed necessary. Sociologists often employ the terms "segmentary" and "acephalous" indicating the non-centralized character of tribal societies.

Biblical tradition gives some more ideas about tribal times. On one side, we find confirmation of minimal authority and considerable clan independence ["everyone did what was right in his own eyes" (Judg 17:6)]. On the other side, later historians suggest that even before the time of monarchy Israel had been unified under the rule of "judges," who served as charismatic war-chiefs and/or administrators of Israelite customary law. We have to take into account later, (i.e., exilic), deuteronomistic views of the past. Therefore the "all-Israelite" aspects of the tradition are not to be trusted too much as historical claims. However, it is quite possible that a tribal society in a transition to monarchy may have witnessed local rulers like Abimelek (Judges 9) who tried to overthrow the mild rule of tribal councils and elders. Also, charismatic war-chiefs, who would claim divine inspiration and call for resistance (cf. Gideon; Jephthah), may have emerged during military attacks. In the same vein other intertribal "offices" are conceivable: prophets who transmitted messages to a whole region, men of God who cured and worked wonders, and mantics and wise people whose fame transcended tribal limits. All in all, the main interests of a society that had developed beyond the family level were centered on protection against hostile interference, preservation of custom and law, and—as far as possible—in a common production of livelihood, as well as in commercial exchange. All of these endeavors were charged with religious meaning and rituals.

All evidence suggests that Yahweh came to be known in Israel during its tribal period. Most likely, Yahweh had been a god connected to the southern mountainous region (Midianite or Kenite domains), the locale mentioned in the oldest sources being Mount Sinai or Seir. Even much later he is being called "mountain god" (1 Kgs 20:23, 28). There is broad agreement on the fact that Yahweh was not a family but a tribal god principally tied to the larger group by means of war-rituals and war-symbols (i.e., the ark). Very possibly one particular group of proto-Israelites (the Moses-group?) met and adopted the mountain-god, taking him along into Canaan (the Exodus from Egypt may have been attached to this group from a different tradition) and introducing him to the tribes there. Yahweh, although not different in essence from other deities, made himself known through "mighty deeds" of salvation in favor of those groups who adhered to him. Old tales of the beginnings of Israel (even if edited later, like Judges 4–5) clearly show the victorious divine warrior who fights for his clients and convinces by his power.

We have to ask whether and how institutions of Israel changed under the influence of Yahweh, or, vice versa, which new social structures came into being under the theological image of the tribal deity. Basically, tribal Israel, after accepting the leadership of Yahweh, seems to have continued her political existence along the previous lines. Former academic theories of very particular institutions like "amphictyony," "covenant," "apodictic law," etc., hotly discussed until the seventies, have altogether proven to be wishful thinking and no longer hold their ground. What we are able to ascertain is the affinity of early Yahwism to wars of liberation and defense against superior enemies. Apparently, a genuine institution of this type of society was charismatic leadership with adherents in battles of liberation. Quite often, the leader is "seized by the spirit of Yahweh" (cf. 1 Sam 9:5), and his ecstatic behavior in battle may be supposed to lie behind many a tale (cf. Judg 15:14; 16:17; Numbers 6). Much later still, the "zeal for Yahweh" is a trademark of firm believers within Israel (cf. 2 Kings 10; Jeremiah 35). The centralized legal functions of those leaders representative of Yahweh-religion, however, are very likely later systematizations.

If we initially consider Yahweh as a tribal warrior god, and if we assume that families, clans, tribes, and villages remained autonomous in their religious beliefs, we have to search further for a possible cult or shrine to the new deity. Tradition tells us that, in the beginning, there was no centralized and exclusive place of worship. Rather, the ark (before it became the receptacle of the tablets), possibly housed in a tent, served as portable sanctuary. It went into battle with the army (Num 10:35; 1 Samuel 4) and apparently required neither temple nor priesthood.

Religion and Monarchy

The tribal system did not last very long in Israel. It was threatened by better organized neighboring states. According to tradition, the wars against the Philistines laid bare the weaknesses of tribalism, pressing the people of Yahweh to adopt the more tightly knit organization of an oriental monarchy. To be sure, this goal was not reached in one leap. The kingship of Saul still bears all the signs of a charismatic tribal affair (although we do not have complete information about Saul's reign). In any case, the transition to monarchy implied or brought about a profound alteration of the social system. Old tribal independence could not last under a centralized and almost absolute government. It was replaced by a bureaucratic administration, a system of taxation and forced labor, a well-organized professional army, a considerable shift of power towards urban centers (predominantly to the capital), a centralization of the main branches of foreign commerce, and similar newly created administrative institutions.

What changes were wrought in religious belief and traditional institutions by the installation of monarchical governments? There are traces of early resistance to change of such enormous proportions. However, the pressures of the tenth century imbalance of power was such that the tribes could not and would not avert the "reform" of their own liberal system, which for all practical purposes ceased to exist. Instead, monarchy made its way in different modes and shades into the northern and southern provinces of Israel with different effects on "private" faith. We limit ourselves to identifying some major lines of development.

The most important religious innovation was the establishment of a state-cult administered at a central temple (Jerusalem, and soon after the secession of the northern tribes, Dan and Bethel). David was the first king to respond to the challenge of the new statehood. He transferred the ark, old symbol of tribal Yahwism, into his royal capital, an old Jebusite city with marked Canaanite traditions of its own. The new king thus incorporated the old faith into his new system, probably in a conscious effort to legitimate the monarchical structure he was setting up in defiance of former tribal liberalism. The Yahwistic tradition, one may argue, served more or less as a rationale to cover up totalitarian features inherent in monarchical models of society. To be sure, Yahweh continued to be the warrior god; but he was no longer fighting together with or in favor of oppressed and inspired tribesmen against better equipped and trained professional urban armies. Now Yahweh became the ally of an established kingdom like all the other kingdoms around bent on hegemony, expansion, and self-glorification. David's empire was built on a stately thirst for power. It thrived and vibrated with aggression and occupied all habitable territory between Egypt in the south and the Euphrates River in the north. Yahweh of Jerusalem had to bless this imperialistic enterprise throughout. No wonder that his charismatic presence was not sufficient to fulfill this task. In fact, it proved rather counterproductive (prophecy!). To stabilize monarchical centralism, the deity had to move into a stable sanctuary to be attended day and night by a professional priesthood controlled by the government. The temple itself and the holy place where it had been constructed, Mount Zion, became the center of the empire—even of the world (cf. Psalms 46; 48). As the abode of the highest God, both were clothed with myths and legends of absolute invulnerability.

The king of Israel (or better, Israel and Judah) became the center of the state with considerable consequences for the social texture and its theological legitimation. There are shades and grades of difference between the two states as well as between individual monarchs. However, a common element remains: The king wanted to keep or assume full control over all relevant proceedings likely to serve the interests of the state, as well as those consistent with his personal and dynastic goals. Therefore he appointed state secretaries that were fully responsible only to him. There are only minimal references to councils of elders (cf. 1 Kings 12) and state-employed counselors (cf. 2 Sam 16:15), and prophets (cf. 2 Samuel 24; 1 Kings 22) or priests who really did not possess any authority of their own.

The structure of the state was hierarchic, and any such structure needs strong divine support to be able to subsist against "segmentary" interests and traditional rights. Therefore, the king had to imbue himself with divine legitimation. The Old Testament preserves overwhelming evidence that at least the Judean king dared call on the firm promise of Yahweh to maintain the Davidic dynasty without end (2 Sam 7:12-16). This guarantee did imply a very special relationship with the former tribal God. Similar to some neighboring kings and pharaohs, the successors of David declared themselves as "sons" of God and his "vice regents" (cf. Psalms 2; 45; 110). Centralized, authoritarian states need to glorify their head as semidivine, with all the consequences this may have for theological conceptualizations (an authoritarian deity!). This is exactly what happened in the Davidic dynasty of Jerusalem, in considerable contrast to earlier contemporary and later theological movements attested in the Scriptures.

What do we know of institutionalized and ritualized religion during the time of the monarchies? Our sources seem to be richer in comparison to the earlier period of the tribes. However, the material of Samuel and Kings (with minimal authentic additions in the Chronistic work) was heavily reworked during its final composition in exilic times. So we have to be quite careful in reconstructing the monarchical religion. Presumably, the temple-service in Jerusalem served state purposes only. Regular sacrifices were offered by royal officials, recruited in the beginning from the local, Jebusite priesthood (i.e., Zadoq). This fact (proved by archaeological findings) immediately suggests that local sanctuaries were relatively autonomous as long as they did not interfere with or rebel against state interests. Family religion, in the same vein, must have gone on unchallenged, although we have little evidence for it (cf. 1 Sam 19:13; Jer 44:15-19). The rites and services of the temple served the state's and its overlord's well-being, including the defeat of possible enemies. Bits and pieces of royal liturgies include texts referring to enthronement (cf. Psalms 2; 110), wedding (Psalm 45), victory (Psalm 18), and lament (Psalm 89). Yahweh-kingship hymns (Psalms 93, 96–99) are ambiguous. They may have at one time given glamour to his earthly vice regent, but at other times then may have been intoned by the postmonarchical community and in defiance of earthly kingship.

Opposition to institutionalized hierarchy has been mentioned before: In the beginning it came from the ranks of tribal elites who were deposed by the king. They more or less disappeared as political agents during the time of the monarchies. Critique arose, even during the Exile, when people realized that the kings "had done evil in the sight of Yahweh," had over-reached themselves and usurped powers reserved to God alone, leading their people astray and causing the downfall of the state. These are stereotyped accusations waged against royal heads (with the exception of David, Hezekiah, and Josiah, who remained heroes of Israelite dreams of greatness) by the deuteronomistic writers. Still we must consider the phenomenon of prophecy promoting apparent archopponents of monarchy.

Again, caution is advisable in reading our sources. Tradition has it that prophets followed each other in a sequence, starting either with Elijah/Elisha in the ninth or Amos/Hosea in the eighth century, and forming a continuous opposition against the ruling classes and/or against Israel as a whole until the final defeat inflicted by Babylonian troops in 587 BCE. On the one hand, there seems to have been a coherent and continuous warning by Yahweh through his special envoys, but Israel never heeded their message for long and, therefore, was punished by the disaster of deportation and exile. Old Testament scholarship has, by and large, maintained this biblical picture in spite of curious gaps of evidence. The deuteronomistic historian clearly creates the overall view of Yahweh's calling his people in vain through the monarchic period, but he ignores the concrete names and actions of those prophets assembled in the prophetic canon (the notable exception being Isaiah in 2 Kings 19, cf. Isaiah 37). On the other hand, the array of prophetic books themselves betray little knowledge of such continuous activity of these messengers of Yahweh; there are few if any direct cross-references among the prophets, even if they are supposed to be contemporaries. For the most part (excluding Jeremiah) historical details and attributions to reigning monarchs are to be found in redactional superscriptions. Furthermore, a thorough analysis of prophetic collections is resulting more and more in deep historical skepticism regarding the authenticity of various prophetic sayings and admonitions. Also, the prophetic behavior is being investigated on the basis of comparative materials throughout the world, ancient and modern. The decisive question for us is: To what extent are we justified in presupposing a prophetic "office" of any kind during the time of the monarchies? What type of institution could it have been and where in

Israelitic society could it have been rooted? Two things seem to be plain based on anthropological research. First, prophets in themselves do not constitute a closed and well-marked professional group but have to be classified according to their varying specialities in mediating between humans and their deities. (The biblical "prophet" as the divine messenger who transports the "Word of God" already seems to be a later theological construct.) Second, prophets as divine messengers, although appearing haphazardly at odd times and unforeseeable junctions of the political history, nevertheless needed a "support group," which would put its own voice and interests into the prophetic message. Judging from the critical stances of those prophetic sayings considered most authentic, the ad hoc opposition against royal politics in Israel must have come from minority groups that had been superseded and subdued by the monarchical structures and institutions. Amos and Micah may be the best examples of texts representing the lower class, while Isaiah and Jeremiah seem to have grown out of marginalized elite families. In any case prophetic opposition must also be investigated in regard of its social moorings. Royal officials entrusted with telling the fortunes for the dynasty (Nathan? Gad?) may have existed, but they were not prophets in the strict sense. There may have been popular healers, mantics, and incantators, but they were not prophets. There may have been ecstatics, wandering priests, and men of God in various capacities using different methods of mediation, but they were not prophets. Chance opponents against the kings like Uriah and Micah (Jer 26:18, 20) or Amos (Amos 7:10) were the original prophets. Later tradition transformed them into preachers and interpreters of the Torah (Zech 7:7-10), letting the social background of their protest disappear, adding a great amount of legal and liturgical material to their collections, and extending the title "prophet" to many a real or fictitious person who could be made into a spokesman of Yahweh.

Religion in the Early Jewish Community

After the major institutions of Israel, e.g., state, central temple, army, were wiped out or severely damaged during the Babylonian disaster, the people of Yahweh had to reorganize. One may easily wonder whether the institutional break of the Exile was worse than the ones experienced in transitions from seminomad to sedentarian or tribal to state life. The shock of losing national and, to a large extent, also religious autonomy, was deeply felt in Israel. Services of lamentation were held, and deported parts of the population developed a rather nostalgic and rigid theology filled with notions of guilt and repentance. Voices of doubt and accusations against Yahweh himself also arose (cf. Isa 40:27; Jer 44:17; Psalm 44). Israel lived through extremely difficult times, and the danger of Israel loosing its own identity and disappearing among the ethnic groups of the empire, similar to what happened to the northern tribes deported by the Assyrians in 722 BCE, was very real. The closely knit clan system and Babylonian policy of admitting coherent settlements of exiled peoples offered the opportunity for a new beginning. Of course, older traditions had to be used along with new organizational features. To return to tribal organization was impossible. Instead they used the heritage of family faith, village structures, Yahwistic creeds, tribal council procedures, temple and Zion traditions, and nostalgic hopes for the righteous king and added the economic, legal, and religious elements required by the contemporary situation. Israel was, as a dependent people, living by the grace of Babylon and later the Persians—and yet it succeeded, perhaps miraculously so, in building a new community.

The remaining decades of Babylonian rule and the first half-century of Persian dominance were decisive for the reconstitution of Israel as a spiritual nation of Yahweh. Civil organization both in the homeland of Canaan and in the diaspora apparently followed old family, village, and clan concepts with elders taking the lead. More important were the new religious institutions, a conglomerate of traditional and pioneering features. Faith in Yahweh turned out to be the overarching determinant of Israelite/Jewish community life. Up to the Exile, Yahweh had been the tribal and state god, with room for other deities especially on lower levels of society. Now, Yahweh increasingly became, although against some opposition, the only and exclusive God of his people, down to the last household and family shrine. Outward pressures and the need for the people to have a clear identity were responsible for this outcome.

After the catastrophe of 587 BCE, Israel compiled, edited, and used the Scriptures. As far as we know, the composition of the Hebrew Scriptures was the first tentative act to build a whole community around the written "Word of God." This fact does not preclude the use of writings in religions and cultures for liturgical and theological purposes throughout the Near East, Persia, and India. In Israel, the sacred writings, brought together from various ancient traditions, served the exclusive end of building and strengthening the new faith community. These writings really constituted the centerpiece of common life. This statement implies, however, that Scripture did not come about by itself. Rather it resulted from the collaboration of a class of scribes and interpreters of ancient tradition, who, by virtue of their closeness to the "Word," became the main spokesmen and leaders of the community. The guardians of Scripture were therefore the most important social institution in Israel. Priests and their descendents certainly maintained some traditional influence, but on the whole the scribes, the wise men, and the rabbis, as experts in Scripture, proved to be the leaders of the community.

The various collections of writings (deuteronomic/deuteronomistic, "priestly," prophetic, chronistic, liturgical, etc.) represent different times, locales, or groups of Israelite society. They were brought together, however, in the process of forging one community under one God, which would include Jewish people from all the known world. Tensions and conflicts among the different groups are visible everywhere in the texts, but the consciousness of unity was even stronger. The learned men of the Scriptures entrusted with the collections and interpretation of the tradition were educated in schools from Egypt to Mesopotamia. Their spiritual "genealogy" lives on in rabbinic tradition. And they succeeded, to a considerable measure, in ordering Jewish life in both home and community, whether in Syria-Palestine or the most distant places of their sojourn. The network of popular customs and feasts became an important means for achieving cohesion, with circumcision and Sabbath, dietary rules and synagogue worship standing out as supreme realizations and symbols of Jewish identity.

Conclusion

Analysis of the growth and change of Israelite religious institutions should not be understood as an antitheological task. To the contrary, this kind of evaluation of Scripture and society should liberate contemporary theologians to take over full responsibility for their concepts and systems of doing theology in the present. To recognize the historical, social, and institutional conditioning of every assertion about and communication on behalf of God means that we must abandon claims of absolute, timeless truth, valid for all people and through the ages. God must be different in varying historical and social situations, even if the deity's name should remain the same. The deities of family, clan, tribe, nation, or religious community are manifestations of the one "ground of being," unrecognizable to us in its true essence. Individual theological configurations consequently are as particular and limited as the groups who used them. At best they may serve as road signs to the Absolute. Jewish and Christian traditions have long offered this insight to their followers: Who may draw near to God's presence and grasp God's fullness of life, truth, justice? No human can do so. Rather, each manifestation of the eternal occurs only in the temporary world, i.e., within its historical and social conditions. Human beings simply do not have the capacity to grasp or express the absoluteness of God. They have to be content with the relativity of human existence (cf. 1 Cor 13:12). The analysis of Israel's institutions and its varying expressions of faith through the ages leads us to give up the idea of being called to do a mining job in Scripture and history. There is no way of finding pure, unchangeable truths like gold nuggets in the biblical past. What we do find are conglomerates of religious faith and social dynamics—a faith that is born anew at each juncture of social and historical turmoil.

Since new junctures of history neither fall from heaven nor are born out of hell, but arise from confluences of tradition and chance developments and their unexpected challenges, the theological task in general will be a contextual one. It will consist in evaluating the parameters of the present world, the emergence of a world society, intertwined economically and culturally, with a common fate for all humankind and the world of nature. This world is the place for doing of theology. The richness of biblical traditions teaches us where and how decisions for good and bad developments have been made. It comforts us with the message that none of our modern problems are unheard of, and it makes available to us alternatives for doing and thinking the right things at the right time. The contribution of Old Testament scholarship continues to be the special awareness and the extraordinary thankfulness for this monotheistic faith, which resulted from Israel's suffering. To discover its liberating force anew in the context of this postindustrial, postrationalistic, postmodern world may be the main challenge of the decades to come.

Selected Bibliography

Ahlstrom, G. *The History of Ancient Palestine from the Palaeolithic Period to Alexander's Conquest.* JSOTSup 146. Sheffield: JSOT, 1993.

Albertz, R. *A History of Israelite Religion in the Old Testament Period.* OTL. Louisville: Westminster/John Knox, 1994.

Causse, A. *Du groupe ethnique à la communauté religieuse.* Paris: Felix Alcan, 1937.

Crüsemann, F. *Der Widerstand gegen das Königtum: Die anti-Königliche Texte das Alten Testament und der Kampf um den frühen israelitischen Staat.* WMANT 49. Neukirchen-Vluyn: Neukirchener Verlag, 1978.

Gerstenberger, E., *Jahwe- ein patriarchaler Gott? traditionelles Gottesbild und feministische Theologie.* Stuttgart: Kohhammer, 1988.

———. *Das dritte Buch Mose, Leviticus.* ATD 6. Göttingen: Vandenhoeck and Ruprecht, 1993.

Gottwald, N. *The Tribes of Yahweh: A Sociology of the Religion of Liberated Israel, 1250-1050 BC.* Maryknoll: Orbis Books, 1979.

Kippenberg, H. *Religion und Klassenbildung im antiken Judäa, Eine religionssoziologische Studie zum Verhältnis von Tradition und gesellschaftlicher Entwicklung.* SUNT 14. Göttingen: Vandenhoeck and Ruprecht, 1978.

Lemche, N. *Early Israel: Anthropological and Historical Studies on the Israelite Society before the Monarchy.* VTSup 37. Leiden: Brill, 1985.

Meyers, C. *Discovering Eve: Ancient Israelite Women in Context.* New York: Oxford University Press, 1988.

Ribeiro, D. *The Civilization Process.* Washington: Smithsonian Institution, 1968.

Smith, M. *The Early History of God: Yahweh and the Other Deities in Ancient Israel.* San Francisco: Harper & Row, 1990.

Thiel, W. *Die soziale Entwicklung Israels in vorstaatlicher Zeit.* WMANT 52. Neukirchen-Vluyn: Neukirchener Verlag, 1985.

van Gennep, A. *The Rites of Passage.* Chicago: University Press of Chicago, 1960.

Vaux, R. *Ancient Israel, Its Life and Institutions.* 2 vols. New York: McGraw Hill, 1961.

Wilson, R., *Prophecy and Society in Ancient Israel.* Philadelphia: Fortress, 1980.

Chapter 17
THE FUTURE OF SOCIAL JUSTICE RESEARCH IN THE HEBREW SCRIPTURES: QUESTIONS OF AUTHORITY AND RELEVANCE

Norman C. Habel

The aim of this essay is to explore some directions for future research into the issues associated with social justice and the Hebrew Scriptures. The massive array of literature on justice and social justice in recent biblical scholarship cannot be surveyed. Rather, the focus will be on those issues where the future of biblical interpretation in this field is likely to be concentrated. The problem of appropriating the biblical tradition for addressing contemporary social and ethical issues will be included. The underlying question is whether the Hebrew Scriptures can still make a serious contribution to any future debates on contemporary social justice questions.

Social Justice and Hermeneutics

Basic to any future research into social justice and the Hebrew Scriptures is the need to clarify the specific hermeneutical approach being employed in a given investigation. There are at least three distinct ways in which the question of social justice has been and will be investigated. While there may be some overlap in the way scholars use these approaches, they can be identified as discrete ways of interpreting the text.

Social Injustice/Justice and History

This approach involves an investigation of the social processes, groups, and forces at work in the historical world behind the text. By the use of sociological and historical tools of analysis, the scholar seeks to reconstruct social developments within the course of Israelite history. The location of concepts of social justice functioning in a given social order depends on the reconstruction of that order and the evidence cited to support that reconstruction.

This approach is illustrated by Norman Gottwald and others in a collection of essays entitled *The Bible and Liberation,* and subtitled *Political and Social Hermeneutics* (Gottwald, 1984). Gottwald's sociological model for reconstructing ancient Israel is well known. A central feature of this interpretation involves reconstructing a peasant revolt against the oppressive rulers of Canaan as the impetus for the emergence of Israel as a people with a distinctive religious orientation. Gottwald's reconstruction of Israel's origins has been accepted by many liberation exegetes because it is sympathetic to their theology. Some go so far as to claim that ancient Israel established a genuinely egalitarian society.

Whether or not one agrees with Gottwald's reconstruction, it remains a reconstruction, and therefore problematic. Is it possible to reconstruct, with any degree of certainty, the specific social orders that developed in Israel's history, especially in Israel's early history? Is it possible to determine the actual concepts or practice of social justice that existed in these social orders? These are some of the challenges facing those who pursue this approach to analyzing the text as the source of ancient history and social ethics.

Social Injustice/Justice and the Text

This approach recognizes that the biblical texts we seek to interpret represent a range of documents from an alien time and culture. These texts are themselves the products of social groups and forces at work in ancient society. The aim of this approach, however, is not to reconstruct the social history behind the text, but to ascertain the social order and ideals being promoted within the text.

Typical questions posed by exponents of this approach are: What kind of social model is being represented in the text? How is social injustice understood within the parameters of the social order being represented? What social group, according to the text, seems to be promoting this position?

An important feature of this approach is its focus on larger literary complexes as social products rather than focusing on isolated references dealing with particular social justice topics. Social justice is therefore interpreted in the light of the total ideology of the largest literary unit. For example, the numerous allusions to caring for the stranger, the widow, and the orphan in the book of Deuteronomy are interpreted in terms of the total book, and the ideology being promoted in that book. An issue for future research in the case of this book is whether its ideology actually promotes social justice or a form of social control.

This approach is illustrated by the work entitled *This Land Is Mine: Six Biblical Land Ideologies* (Habel, 1994). This study seeks to ascertain the distinctive land ideology being promoted in a given literary complex. Within each ideology, the question of land rights is raised: Who claims entitlement to land and who is denied access to the land? The question of right to land is only one of the social justice questions that could be explored in these literary complexes.

A challenge to both of the preceding approaches can be mounted by those who argue that while the first has a vested interest in uncovering history and has a particular sociological bias, the second is influenced by particular literary theories of textual analysis. Interpreters today therefore tend to identify their particular bias before proceeding with their analysis. This is particularly desirable in future social justice research where people are likely to hold strong opinions that precede the reading of the text.

Social Injustice/Justice and the Reader

There are at least two major approaches that focus on the centrality of the reader in the hermeneutical task. The first tackles the reality that every reader, in one way or another, has a particular worldview, intention, and set of interests that will influence what he or she reads. According to this approach, the reader can be viewed as constructing the text from the stuff on the page. The text is like a mirror, reflecting to the reader the reader's own world of interests. A less extreme version of this approach views the text as another voice with which the reader is in dialogue. The meaning discerned is a result of that dialogue.

A clear example of how people find in the text what they want to find is the fact that last century the curse of Canaan in Genesis 9 was read as the curse of Ham, and interpreted as referring to the black peoples of Africa. This was used as justification for enslaving black peoples.

This awareness that we are likely to construct the meaning we want to find in the text moves contemporary scholars to identify where they are coming from as they proceed to interpret the text. So, in the case of social justice research, the interpreter is likely to be asking, "Does the ethical position reflected in the text agree or conflict with my own?" "Does the text promote or negate the principles of social justice I espouse in the contemporary world?"

The second approach that focuses on the reader is represented by feminists and liberationists who consciously identify their position as readers with a particular orientation and bias. These approaches are extremely important in connection with social justice research because they claim to reflect the critical stance of those who are socially oppressed. They are readings of the text from the bottom, from the perspective of those who have experienced gross injustice.

The force of these approaches means that future studies in social justice will never be the same. The reader of the future will be forced to ask whether he or she is reading the text as one of the oppressors, one of the oppressed, or someone seeking to identify with the oppressed and shed the history of oppressive behavior associated with his or her social group. The experiences associated with being one of these three groups will be recognized as a part of the interpretative process.

In the following analysis the focus shall be on future research in terms of the second approach—social justice and the text—and the third approach—social justice and the reader. The starting point will be the way the text seems to portray a given aspect of social justice.

Definition and Diversity

The second major issue that demands further clarification and closer scrutiny is the broad question of the definition of social justice, and the allied question of diversity in biblical approaches to the subject. What is meant by social justice in biblical research? Are the features of social justice in the Scriptures determined by contemporary theories of justice such as those articulated by Karen Lebacqz in her book, *Six Theories of Justice* (Labacqz, 1986 cf. Frey 1992)? Do scholars make any general assumptions about the elements of social justice when they approach a biblical text?

An important work by Leon Epsztein, entitled *Social Justice in the Ancient Near East and the People of the Bible* (Epsztein, 1986), illustrates the problem. Epsztein does not, at the outset, seek to define or outline the elements of social justice. He traces laws and statements of concern for the less privileged in Babylonian and Egyptian documents and the Hebrew Scriptures, but does not provide a composite outline of the elements of social justice. His orientation is the text rather than a contemporary reader's view of social justice.

Epsztein, after surveying many scholarly works, maintains that *mišpāṭ*, usually rendered "justice," "represented something obligatory and necessary, a set of religious rules in conformity with the divine will" (Epsztein, p. 47). The term *ṣedāqāh*, usually rendered "righteousness," and regularly paired with *mišpāṭ*, "comes more and more to be approached as a social phenomenon concerning relations between parties" (Epsztein, p. 47). In the final analysis, however, one gets the impression from this work that social justice means social obligation to live according to ideals of justice given by God, whatever the social order.

A major contribution to the understanding of social justice in documents of the ancient Near East, and especially in the Hebrew Scriptures, has been made by Moshe Weinfeld in his article, "Justice and Righteousness," in which he deals with the meaning of *mišpāṭ* and *ṣedāqāh* as a word pair. He argues that this word pair is not primarily concerned with judicial matters, but with social justice. According to Weinfeld:

> We must therefore conclude that the word *mišpāṭ*, and especially the phrase *mišpāṭ ûṣdāqāh*, does not refer to the proper execution of justice, but rather expresses in a general sense, social justice and equality, which is bound up with kindness and mercy. (238)

Weinfeld demonstrates that central to this concept of social justice are both kindness for the weak and deliverance of the oppressed (e.g., 1 Kgs 8:1-6). The divine ideal is summarized by Micah who clarifies the expression "doing *mišpāṭ*" by the idioms "loving kindness" (*ḥesed*) and "walking humbly with God" (Mic 6:8), both of which imply demands of a moral and social rather than legal nature.

Weinfeld's enlightening analysis provides an excellent basis for clarifying the patterns of social justice in the Hebrew Scriptures even further. One may be tempted from Weinfeld's analysis of the word pair justice/righteousness as a idiom meaning "social justice" to assume that (a) all texts use the idiom in the same sense and with the same intention, and (b) that a study of this pair will provide a uniform and clear portrait of social justice in the Hebrew Scriptures. But this is unlikely.

One of the important tasks for the future, therefore, is to research the precise way in which matters of social justice are interpreted, promoted, and expressed in diverse textual complexes. The following are typical of research questions that need to be asked. Is, for example, the ideology or theology of social justice, reflected in the law codes, different from that espoused in the prophets? Is the ideology or theology of social justice, promoted as the responsibility of the just king under a monarchy, different from that espoused in texts that reflect or endorse a different social order? How uniform, then, are the ideals and practices of social justice across the wide range of texts preserved in the Hebrew Scriptures?

God's Option for the Poor

One of the solutions to the problems of diversity of theologies relating to social injustice/justice in various texts of the Hebrew Scriptures is to take the liberationist approach and opt for a "governing center" within the Scriptures. In this approach, the experience of the reader as part of the community of the oppressed leads to the choice of this center as the perspective from which to interpret and judge the text. This center is variously defined as "the God of justice takes sides with the poor and oppressed," "doing justice is liberating the poor and oppressed" or "God identifies with the poor and oppressed" (McGovern, 1983).

In the light of this governing center, all texts, including those referring to matters of social justice, can be interpreted as further evidence of God at work on behalf of the poor. Thus even the conquest and attempted genocide of the Canaanites, portrayed in Joshua, can be reinterpreted as evidence of liberation from Canaanite oppression. But does this approach do justice to the text of Joshua?

It is a common axiom of many approaches to social justice that only those who have experienced injustice can understand social justice as genuine hope. Those who have experienced oppression have insights into the text that may be hidden from the oppressor or even the sympathetic reader. According to this approach, the poor who have experienced God on their side are the best interpreters of the text; they read the text from their posture and bias.

Yet sympathetic readers who, with liberation exegetes, acknowledge the Exodus event as a bold portrait of God taking sides with Israelite slaves, point to other texts and traditions that offer an alternative perspective. The story of Solomon seems to be one where God takes sides with the rich and powerful. On numerous occasions, God is presented as showing none of the mercy that is said to typify God's very nature as a God of *mišpāṭ ûṣdāqāh*. Is God always on the side of the oppressed according to the text? And if God is not, then how is such a text to be judged? Or do we end up arguing that whatever side God is on must be the side of the poor?

Epsztein maintains that, in Jewish interpretations of the Hebrew prophets, God is not necessarily identified with the poor as a social class involved in a class struggle:

> On the other hand, in conformity with the basic principles of Judaism which consists in not a priori favouring the poor in the face of the rich, as we have already seen, the prophets attack the wicked rich, not the rich without distinction. They are the defenders of the poor, the weak, the oppressed; they turn against the privileged, the kings. Not, however, as partisans of the class struggle so much as those with a concern for a lifestyle, a type of culture, in which violent confrontations will be lessened, if not eliminated. (101)

Future research, focusing on social justice and text approach, will need to examine those texts that seem to challenge the axiom that God is on the side of the poor, and come to terms with the possibility that the biblical texts reflect the interests of numerous groups, each of which claims God is on its side. This raises the further question of whether social justice within the text is viewed from the perspective of those in power or of those being oppressed.

As Epsztein has pointed out, social justice in the ancient Near East was a weapon of propaganda in the hands of the monarch. Hammurabi declares himself to be "the shepherd bringing salvation" (255), the legislator "to bring the orphan and widow their rights" (257). He addresses "the oppressed man who has a cause," and invites him to come into the presence of the king so as to understand his cause, and be at ease (261). Thus:

> The principle of protection of widows, orphans and the poor appears in different prologues of the Mesopotamian laws, but is formulated in an almost stereotyped way and probably served primarily for the propaganda of the sovereign, who sought to satisfy popular opinion. (Epsztein, p. 16)

Further research is required on the relevant biblical texts to determine the extent to which laws, oracles, or stories about social justice matters serve the interests of those in power. Do these texts reflect an attempt to control and maintain the existing social order with social justice ideals that uphold the status quo? Or do these texts reflect the pains and hopes of those who are suffering injustices? Are any of the biblical texts actually the work of the oppressed, a group who normally would not have the resources to record their experiences?

Feminist exegetes have made us acutely aware that most of the biblical texts reflect a patriarchal orientation; they are the work of men in power. If this is so, are all biblical texts the products of the powerful elite? Have they been preserved in a manner that is acceptable to the elite? If so, where can the genuine voice of the oppressed be heard in the biblical text? Or is the voice of the oppressed explicitly that of the reader, which exposes the various biblical texts as the work of those in power to be interpreted accordingly?

Who Are the Poor and Oppressed?

The terms "poor" and "oppressed" are often used as general terms to refer to a range of social groups that experience social injustices. Historically, certain social groups have frequently experienced the various forms of social injustice. These groups include women, blacks, widows, orphans, immigrant aliens, slaves, laborers, landless poor, people with disabilities, and conquered and indigenous peoples.

The various texts of the Hebrew Scriptures reflect a number of social systems, each of which assumes a social hierarchy of some kind. Within these systems, particular social groups are regularly located at the lower levels of the social order and are consequently disadvantaged. Some of these are favored in various law codes while others are excluded. A brief consideration of selected examples will illustrate some future directions for this field of study where the focus is on the text.

The role of slaves in Israelite society has long been a crucial topic in biblical ethics. There were at least two categories of slaves: non-Israelites who were taken captive in wars or bought as foreign slaves, and Israelites who were forced into slavery because of their debts or for some other reason. Both Canaanites and Israelites could be conscripted as slave or corvée labor, but Israelites were not to be considered permanent slaves of the king (1 Kgs 9:20-22).

By contemporary standards, there is no social justice for slaves in Israelite law. Every Israelite slave is to be released after six years; in the Hammurabi code, a slave is to be released after three years. But for non-Israelite slaves, there is no release. In the law codes, the slave is reckoned as property (Exod 21:21; Lev 25:45). In cases of death or injury, the worth of the slave is clearly much less than that of an ordinary citizen (Exod 21:28-33). The memory of Israel's slavery in Egypt provides a basis for not enslaving its own people permanently (Lev 25:42-43). This same experience, however, does not prevent Israel from making permanent slaves of aliens or foreigners (Lev 25:44-46). In Deuteronomy escaped slaves are to be given asylum and freedom, and not to be oppressed (Deut 23:15-16). These examples illustrate that social justice is clearly selective in certain texts; it is this selective dimension of Israel's social justice ideals that is likely to demand attention in future research.

Considerable research has been done on the poor as a social group. The various terms rendered "poor" or "needy" are first and foremost those who are economically and socially deprived, even though in some contexts the term "poor" may assume religious or spiritual dimensions (e.g., Ps 140:12-13). The poor are those who have no land, property, or sustained source of sustenance. The poor apparently lack the power to change the social situation in which they are classed as marginal.

Social justice for the poor, of whom the widow and the orphan are classical symbols, is understood in several ways within the Hebrew Scriptures. According to the ideology of Deuteronomy, for example, charity ought to be part of the social structure in the polity of the land. The poor (*'ebyôn*) are a given component of society, and ought to be provided with liberal gifts (Deut 15:7-11; cf. 26:12). This is confirmed by a divine edict to "Open your hand to the poor and needy neighbor in your land" (Deut 15:11). Social concern for the poor, however, seems to remain at the level of organized charity. The poor are cared for, while at the same time, it seems, are kept in their place. There is no suggestion that the social structure should be modified to enable those who are poor to obtain land, property, or resources to be self-support-ing. The question then arises whether the humanitarian concern for the poor in Deuteronomy can be legitimately considered social justice or whether it is closer to enlightened social control. Detailed research is required into the relative status of the poor in the social order being promoted or reflected in texts like Deuteronomy.

Special attention needs to be drawn to the plight of resident aliens, and the original inhabitants of the land. In works like Deuteronomy, the resident aliens or strangers are classed with the widows and orphans as worthy of welfare assistance (e.g. Deut 10:19; 26:12). Yet, some foreigners, like the Moabites, are excluded from any social concern (Deut 23:6), while others, including the Egyptians (Deut 23:7), are not to be despised.

The Canaanites, however, have absolutely no rights and no mercy is extended to them. No social justice is even considered as appropriate for Canaanites. In Deuteronomy, the holy war regulations allow submissive Canaanites to become slave labor (Deut 20:10-11), but elsewhere no mercy whatsoever is to be shown to the original inhabitants of the land. No respect is to be shown Canaanite women by stooping to marry them (Deut 7:3; Josh 23:12).

The grounds given for this apparent lack of social justice for the Canaan-ites is their worship of gods other than YHWH. Future research is needed to identify the extent and nature of the exclusion of social justice for this group in biblical texts. This exclusion is significant in these texts, since the books of Samuel and Kings provide ample evidence that Canaanites played an active part in Israelite society. Why is one group so forcefully excluded from experiencing the *mišpāṭ ûṣdāqāh* that is said to typify the God of Israel?

Victims or Agents of Resistance

Recently, Basil Moore, a colleague of mine, interviewed Archbishop Desmond Tutu, who asserted, most forcefully:

> We are not victims of apartheid. We are fighters against apartheid. It makes all the difference in the world how you see us. If you see us as victims, you will offer us charity. But if you see us as resisters, you may offer us solidarity in our struggle for freedom. (Moore, 1994)

Contemporary social justice research is moving away from analyzing those subjected to social injustice as victims to an appreciation of their role as human beings courageously resisting these evils. By classifying the oppressed as innocent sufferers, we perpetuate their social status as powerless victims.

But by recognizing their part in the struggle to overcome injustice, we acknowledge their humanity, their dignity, and their courage.

James Limburg has written an excellent study entitled *The Prophets and the Powerless* (1977). But does the use of the term "powerless" perpetuate the concept of the victim? Are the poor and oppressed of the biblical text actually powerless? Are they deliberately or unconsciously represented as powerless victims and objects dependent on the goodwill of others in society? How does a resistance-conscious reader analyze texts dealing with the poor and oppressed?

The biblical law codes clearly recognize the existence of groups in Israelite society who need appropriate forms of charity and care. The poor and the resident alien are free to collect the grapes that fall to the ground during the harvest (Lev 19:10). Every third year there is a tithe on the harvest for the benefit of the resident alien, the widow, and the orphan (Deut 24:19-20). These social groups are accepted as part of society and worthy of welfare. But are they viewed as helpless victims?

The text of Deuteronomy 14 can be interpreted as a document that seeks not only to care for but also to curb the poor. The reason given for not withholding the daily wages of the poor laborers is that they need them for their daily livelihood (Deut 15:9). But the rider is added that they may also "cry to the LORD against you, and you would incur guilt."

The "crying out" of the poor is clearly a mode of resistance. The Israelites knew this "crying out" to YHWH as part of their resistance against slavery by the Egyptians (Exod 2:23). To what extent does the biblical text reflect traditions of resistance as integral to the process of social justice? What biblical narratives demand attention as indicators of these resistance traditions within the Hebrew Scriptures? To what extent has the resistance voice of the Israelite people been suppressed in the interest of those who preserved the text?

Bastian Wielanga, writing from the social context of India, highlighted the resistance tradition against the introduction of the monarchy. In addition to the opposition of Samuel, Wielanga points to the Jotham fable of the bramble offering shade. In the words of Wielanga:

> The point of the fable is to say that the institution of kingship is utterly useless. It is as unproductive as a bramble in comparison to an olive tree, fig tree and vine. To realise its subversive power, we have to imagine peasants sitting in the shade of their trees after some state officials have been visiting their village, and one starts telling, you know the fable which Jotham told of the trees who wanted to anoint a king . . . (Wielanga, 170-71)

The orientation of Wielanga is that of a reader who has experienced the resistance of the oppressed in India. The lead of Wielanga deserves to be explored more fully in the future, focusing on the resistance elements in popular proverbs, narratives, laws, and prophetic oracles. The narrative of Ruth and Naomi is an excellent example of how two widows resisted the system, and moved from being gleaners on the fringe of society to being incorporated into the mainstream. Ruth gains a husband who is a respected landowner, and Naomi, through the resident alien Ruth, gains a son and posterity.

Similar resistance stories, like the trickery of the Gibeonites (Joshua 9), also deserve attention. It is the prophets, however, who actively represent the struggle of the oppressed. The prophets personify resistance.

Amos, for example, is a rural herdsman who takes the case of the oppressed to the centers of power. He even lobbies for justice in the royal sanctuary, explaining to Amaziah the priest that he is not a typical member of the prophetic guild. Amos's action on behalf of the oppressed leads to Amos being accused of conspiracy against the king (Amos 7:10-15).

In the writings of prophets like Amos, social justice seems to be more than a concern to provide welfare for those in need and to ensure their legal rights in the city gate. Are the voices of the oppressed crying to God and demanding an end to the ugly injustices associated with the affluence of their age, or has their voice too been domesticated by those in power who have preserved the prophetic record?

Research into resistance activities and ideals in the Hebrew Scriptures is a major field for future investigation. Especially important will be the clarification of ways in which the biblical text portrays the prophets as resisters, and the ways in which they are viewed as accommodating the system. So, for example, are many of the judgment oracles of the prophets expressions of resistance, examples of how the oppressed used divine oracles to subvert the system?

Rights and Relevance

Given the preceding discussion, we are faced with the question of whether the Hebrew Scriptures can make any serious contribution to the current debates on social justice. Are any of the biblical ideologies relevant to the current social justice context?

Scholars like Bruce Birch have sought to articulate the relevance of the Hebrew Scriptures for contemporary Christian ethics and avoid a Marcionite view that "relegates the Old Testament to a second-class status" in relation to the New Testament (Birch, 29). Birch speaks of the Old Testament as a moral resource, but not in terms of the particular "reconstruction of the actual popular morality or moralities of ancient Israel" (Birch, 37). Rather, Birch views the Old Testament in its present canonical form as a broad witness to the total character, activity, and will of God.

Given this broad vision of love and justice, scholars such as Birch can tolerate a diversity of socially unacceptable practices reflected in the biblical text. It is the existence of the canon as a whole and its broad moral vision which, according to Birch, guards against developing a canon within the canon, or reducing our analysis to a critical examination of parts of the text without considering them in their wider canonical context. Birch wants to prevent his own experience or ideology as a modern reader from becoming normative and to make the text decisive.

Does Birch avoid the very pitfall he sees in other approaches? Is not his "broad moral vision" itself a canon within the canon that judges the various social justice orientations presented in the text? What precisely are the components of this moral vision, and to what extent is it a reflection of his own tradition or experience? Future interpretations of the Hebrew Scriptures that seek to determine relevance will need to ascertain more clearly the central criterion or principle by which the question of relevance is being decided. As some indigenous theologies suggest, it may be the specific cultural practices of the Hebrew Scriptures with which the third world peoples find kinship and relevance rather than the broad moral vision that is often seen through Western eyes.

One test of relevance is to use a contemporary set of social justice principles as the touchstone for determining continuity or discontinuity with the biblical heritage. Central to such contemporary concepts of social justice are certain principles and ideals of what is socially just. These principles might include freedom, equal worth, equal voice, equal opportunity, or equal rights for all peoples and individuals.

Many of these principles are enshrined in the United Nations' *Universal Declaration of Human Rights,* which assumes that all human beings, by virtue of being human beings, have equal and inalienable rights. The list of rights given in the documents formulated by the United Nations is promoted as the norm for judging whether a society, group, or individual is maintaining and fostering justice.

One model for determining the relevance of the Hebrew Scriptures would be to use the social justice principles of these United Nations documents as a critical hermeneutic to ascertain the degree of fit. A number of scholars have recently sought to determine whether the biblical text has a concept of human rights in the modern sense and whether there is any dimension of universality embedded within its laws and ideals. As has long been recognized, rights in the Hebrew Scriptures are not portrayed as intrinsic to the human condition but as coming from God. James Barr, however, contends that "a concept similar to that of 'rights' does exist and is visible even on the surface of the Hebrew Bible text" (25). As part of his evidence, he cites particular usages of the term *mišpāṭ*, which as we saw earlier can also designate something similar to our concept of "social justice." The most relevant cases cited by Barr are those that talk of the *mišpāṭ* or the "right" or "rights" of someone as that to which he or she has a right, which belongs to him or her (e.g., Deut 21:17; Jer 32:7-8).

Barr also seeks to bridge the gap between the culture-specific demands of biblical justice and the universal claim of contemporary human rights. He argues that the biblical laws, while presented as divine revelation, are "there because they were already common practice and generally accepted from ancient times" (29). The rule that stealing is wrong can be learned from a number of sources, but the commandment not to steal is powerful because God endorses this as an ethical principle. According to Barr:

> This perception does something to bridge the apparent gap between an ethic of divine command and ideas such as natural law which in turn leads us toward a concept of human rights. (31)

In spite of the efforts of Barr and others to demonstrate a connection, the gap between the principles of social justice reflected in contemporary models of human rights and the practice of social justice represented in the Hebrew biblical text remains wide. While the biblical text recognizes the relative worth of social groups, there is no concern for the ideal of equal worth. And while the biblical laws recognize the relative rights of social groups, including widows, orphans, and resident aliens, there is no concept of equal rights. Future research into social justice will need to take this disparity between contemporary and biblical principles into account.

Conclusion and Challenge

This essay has considered some of the options for future interpretation of the Hebrew Scriptures in relation to the issue of social justice. It has posited the need for greater clarity in describing the components of social justice as embraced, for example, by the idiom *mišpāṭ ûṣdāqāh*, and the need for determining how this basic concept is variously understood within the diverse ideologies reflected in the various biblical texts.

In connection with the now popular hermeneutical norm summarized as "God's option for the poor," the essay has challenged a simplistic application of this norm, and posed again the question of whether the text portrays God just as frequently on the side of the powerful, especially if, as some exegetes suspect, the text itself is a product of those in power, and propaganda for those in authority rather than a commitment to social change.

It argues also that there is a policy of selective justice for the various marginalized social groups represented in the Hebrew Scriptures. Slaves and Canaanites have virtually no social rights or expectations. Where, in a work like Deuteronomy, the poor are identified as the object of social concern, the outcome seems to be more like social welfare or social control than social justice.

We need to clarify the degree to which the biblical tradition promotes a model of charity for the poor who are depicted as powerless victims. Are there not also suppressed traditions of the oppressed as agents of resistance? Future research will want to explore the resistance tradition and resistance narratives of the Scriptures, especially through the voice of prophets like Amos or Micah.

Ultimately we are led back to the hermeneutical approaches with which we began. The issue of how we interpret social justice in the Hebrew Scriptures raises not only the question of relevance but also of the authority accorded these Scriptures in contemporary ethics and theology.

This challenge derives not only from the diversity of ideologies and theologies of social justice that the text itself presents, but also, and most significantly, from the various reader-oriented approaches to the text. The question these approaches pose is where the primary source of authority lies—in the text or outside the text in the values or experiences of the reader?

If, as we explored above, we focus on human rights, then the United Nations' *Declaration of Human Rights* can be used as an external ideal. By this norm, the social justice principles and practice of the Hebrew Scriptures seem to fall far short. Using this approach, the source of authority appears to lie in the progressive explication of natural law rather than in the biblical text.

If we take the more radical approach and acknowledge that the meaning of social justice is only really known by those who have experienced social injustice and the struggle for justice, then the challenge is even greater. The source for authority in relation to social justice lies not in the text of the Hebrew Scriptures but in the experience of the suffering reader. And the reader may not be the highly trained scholar or cleric, but the oppressed community whose suppressed voice may be heard in some limited way through the scholar.

The final challenge, then, for future research into social justice in the Hebrew Scriptures is the question of relative authority. If sources outside the text are normative for reading and judging the text, what is the role of the text in the explication of ethics or theology in society today? What, then, are the limits of social justice as depicted in the Hebrew Scriptures for consideration in the contemporary debate?

Selected Bibliography

Barr, James. *Ancient Biblical Laws and Modern Human Rights*. In Knight, 1989.

Birch, Bruce C. *Let Justice Roll Down*. Louisville: Westminster/John Knox, 1992.

Epsztein, Leon. *Social Justice in the Ancient Near East and the People of the Bible*. London: SCM, 1986.

Frey, Christopher. *The Impact of the Biblical Idea of Justice on Present Discussions of Social Justice*. In Reventlow, 1992.

Gottwald, Norman, ed. *The Bible and Liberation: Political and Social Hermeneutics*. Maryknoll: Orbis, 1983.

———. "Sociological Method in the Study of Ancient Israel." In Gottwald, 1983.

Habel, Norman. *The Land Is Mine Six Biblical Land Idealogies*. Minneapolis: Fortress, 1994.

Knight, Douglas and Peter Knight, eds. *Justice and the Holy: Essays in Honor of Walter Harrelson*. Atlanta: Scholars Press, 1989.

Lebacqz, Karen. *Six Theories of Justice*. Minneapolis: Augsburg, 1986.

Limburg, James. *The Prophets and the Powerless*. Atlanta: John Knox, 1977.

McGovern, Arthur. *The Bible in Latin American Theology*. In Gottwald, 1993.

Moore, Basil. Unpublished interview with Archbishop Desmond Tutu in Adelaide, 1994.

Reventlow, H. G. and Yair Hoffman. "Justice and Righteousness: Biblical Themes and Their Influence." Sheffield: JSOT, 1992.

Weinfeld, Moshe. *Justice and Righteousness—mišpāṭ ûṣdāqāh—*"The Expression and Its Meaning." In Reventlow, 1992.

Wielanga, Bastian. *It's a Long Road to Freedom*. Madurai: Tamil Nadu Theological Seminary, 1981.

Chapter 18
OLD TESTAMENT THEOLOGY

Brevard S. Childs

In any effort to project the discipline of Old Testament theology into the next generation, it is important to carefully distinguish between the prescriptive agenda of an individual writer and a descriptive analysis of the most likely direction that the field will take. It is this latter task that I shall attempt to undertake.

Methodological Problems Within the Discipline

The field of Old Testament theology first emerged as an independent discipline apart from both New Testament study and dogmatic theology at the end of the eighteenth century. However, right from the beginning there remained many problems respecting methodology that evoked great controversy. The debate as to what exactly is intended by a theological approach to the Hebrew text has persisted to this very day. Some of these methodological issues can be briefly summarized:

(1) Many Old Testament scholars remain critical of describing Israel's religion as a theology. Does not the concept of theology entail introducing modern systematic and philosophical categories that are alien to these ancient texts?

(2) Others wonder whether in the light of the great diversity of content one can ever properly speak of a single theology. Would it not be more reasonable to speak of various theologies without assuming a unity at the outset?

(3) Many scholars are convinced that there is something innately static in a theological approach that cannot properly do justice to the concept of historical development that was established by the literary criticism of the nineteenth century.

In spite of the lack of any consensus on these critical issues, most writers of Old Testament theology during the nineteenth and early twentieth centuries came down firmly on the side of those affirming the priority of the historical, descriptive task. They sought to describe the various forms of Israel's religious reflection, which they then sought to correlate with specific historical periods. Nevertheless, even the most historically oriented presentation also tended to introduce some larger literary, developmental, or theological categories by which to provide some semblance of continuity among the various expressions of historical Israel's religious faith.

Two Classic Old Testament Theologies

Because the history of Old Testament theology has been reviewed frequently,[1] only a few broad strokes are necessary to provide a historical context from which to reflect on future developments. Several impressive Old Testament theologies were produced in the last quarter of the nineteenth century, but increasingly the forces exerted by the new source-critical concerns and by Wellhausen's reconstruction of the history of Israel's religion brought the writing of Old Testament theologies virtually to an end by the close of the nineteenth century. The genre was replaced by histories of Israel's religion, usually cast within an evolutionary schema. The last major Old Testament theology in the English language was that of A. B. Davidson, which was published posthumously in 1904, but it was really a nineteenth-century book in outlook.

Beginning in the 1920s, interest in Old Testament theology began to revive, largely because of a rebirth in confessional theology in Germany following World War I. The period from 1930 to 1960 can well be called the golden period of Old Testament theology. Two major Old Testament theologies appeared, each of which employed very different approaches. It is worthwhile reviewing the distinctive methods represented because in the decades that followed only different variations of these two basic directions appeared.

The first volume of W. Eichrodt's[2] ground-breaking Old Testament theology appeared in 1933. Eichrodt was much concerned with defending the legitimacy of the discipline of Old Testament theology against its nineteenth century opponents, and to construct an approach that would avoid many of the pitfalls of the older traditional theological presentations. He projected a method that combined a historical dimension with a systematic structure that centered in a concept of covenant. According to Eichrodt, Old Testament theology could be studied phenomenologically by contrasting, on the one hand, Israel's faith with other Semitic religions and, on the other hand, with that of the New Testament and rabbinic Judaism. The great strength of Eichrodt's approach lay in his comprehensive treatment of the subject matter. However, in spite of an appeal to objectivity, Eichrodt's agenda emphasized the superiority of the prophetic faith over all such forms as law, wisdom, and apocalyptic, and he envisioned a *Heilsgeschichte* (redemptive history) culminating in Christianity that proved to be a position increasingly vulnerable to attack. His concept of the role of the covenant also appeared to many unable to support the great diversity within the Old Testament.

In the post-World War II era the Old Testament theology of G. von Rad [3] was by far the most creative attempt to combine the recently developed form critical and history-of-traditions approaches to Israel's faith. Von Rad sought to hear Israel's changing response to God's intervention in history by carefully analyzing the growth of the varying levels of Israel's tradition and by reading off of these complexes the growth of Israel's self-understanding. The brilliance of von Rad's traditio-critical analysis, which was combined with a profound grasp of Israel's theological witness, succeeded in dominating the field for well over two decades. However, by the early 1970s, if not before, cracks began to appear in the many critical hypotheses on which von Rad had constructed his system. Moreover, his inability to hold together a critically reconstructed history with Israel's own confessions raised serious questions of method. Finally, a general cultural shift in Western Europe and in America in the late 1960s also resulted in a growing alienation from many of von Rad's traditional Christian assumptions.

In the period since the writing of these two classic theologies there have appeared a number of serious newer theological attempts. Most recently, H. D. Preuss[4] has produced a very competent Old Testament theology that is remarkably comprehensive. Yet in a real sense there have been no new major advances in these latter works. Perhaps equally important is that it is very doubtful whether the way of the future lies in more attempts at such comprehensive summaries of the Old Testament material. Because the older syntheses that emerged in the 1950s and 1960s have largely come apart, scholars in the coming decades will probably focus their energy on fresh, more limited analytical investigations in order to reconstitute the field. Some of the different directions for Old Testament theology that are now being explored can be briefly sketched.

Future Directions for Old Testament Theology

First, it seems probable that the study of Old Testament theology will tend to focus on specific topics with a limited scope rather than attempting to produce works that will rival Eichrodt or von Rad. It is characteristic of the new spirit of tentative probing that a popular modern series is entitled "Overtures to Biblical Theology."

At times Old Testament scholars have returned to traditional biblical topics such as creation, election, and eschatology, but even here the newer works have tended to seek strikingly different perspectives on these familiar topics such as one finds in T. E. Fretheim's *The Suffering of God*.[5] Another example of seeking a fresh avenue into traditional subject matter is Jon Levenson's *Creation and the Persistence of Evil*,[6] which brings to the investigation a rich Jewish tradition of interpretation. Finally, one sees in James Barr's *The Garden of Eden and the Hope of Immortality*[7] a conscious attempt to radically alter traditional thinking on the subject of the soul and immortality. These works are mentioned as representative of concerns and interests that will continue into the next decades.

Another characteristic newer trend is the attempt to rework the problems of critical exegesis by concentrating on a particular biblical book or literary strand in order to provide a new but agreed upon basis for subsequent theological reflection. Thus H. D. Preuss[8] assesses the critical problems associated with the book of Deuteronomy in order to support a return to theological reflection on the deuteronomic theology of God, people, land, and law. One sees such similar works focusing on the Priestly source or the apocalyptic writings within postexilic Israel. In every case critical testing of older literary theories is seen as the necessary grounding for fresh theological reflection. The great advantage of limiting one's study to a smaller and discrete unit of subject matter is that one can concentrate on new analytical research rather than simply assuming an older synthesis on which to base theological reflection. The danger is of losing oneself in technical minutiae of critical research and never being able to construct a larger synthesis on which to reflect theologically.

Second, it is very likely that future works of Old Testament theology will attempt to exploit the insight of the social sciences in opening a new vista into the biblical material. From an earlier period books like Mary Douglas's *Purity and Danger*[9] have been taken up as a model for a fruitful use of critical anthropological data in reflecting on the complex purity and ritual laws of Leviticus.

Within American scholarship credit goes, above all, to N. K. Gottwald's provocative book, *The Tribes of Yahweh*,[10] for aggressively exploiting in a fresh way a sociological approach to Israel's early settlement traditions. He has stimulated a whole new generation toward expanding his approach into other areas of research. Although Gottwald tended to contrast sharply his sociological approach with that of a theological perspective, any who followed in his footsteps have attempted to combine Old Testament theology and sociological research. The many recent works of W. Brueggemann[11] on prophets, kings, and sages are representative of this effort to join sociology and theology into a positive configuration. Moreover, a host of new Old Testament dissertations offer convincing evidence of the enduring interest in reconstructing Israel's social history in order to provide new perspectives on well-worked material.[12] Although at first the area of Old Testament prophecy provided the most attractive area for applying a sociological perspective, it is now fair to observe that no area of the Old Testament is immune to the newer sociological methods including the study of law, wisdom, and psalmody.

Perhaps a word of caution should be registered in regard to future work. Since biblical scholars often come to the sociological approach late in their training and do not control the full range of sociological methodologies, there is a danger in attaching oneself to a single, narrowly conceived sociological school of thought without adequate attention to the full and complex diversity within this cognate discipline. It is ironical to note that some highly critical biblical scholars who are fully aware of the diversity and tensions within the biblical disciplines often view sociology in a flat and monolithic manner, an approach sharply repudiated by the specialists within the fields of the social sciences.

Third, one of the more promising areas of current research in Old Testament theology has been that of narrative theology. There is every indication that this interest will continue and even be expanded in the next generation. Initially the simple application of the concept of story to the Old Testament material had the effect of freeing the investigation from the heavy ballast of historical referentiality that had come to dominate much biblical work.

More recently the study of narrative theology has grown in sophistication and interest in narrative theology has developed hand-in-hand with the modern hermeneutical debate. Such a book is G. W. Stroup's *The Promise of Narrative Theology*,[13] which served both to popularize and stimulate the use of insights from the complex hermeneutical debate for a new generation of seminary and divinity school students. One of the more attractive features of narrative theology has been its insistence that the content of biblical theology not be detached from the story itself, and that the activity of exegesis consist in the particular rendering of the story to a given audience by an interpreter. Moreover, it was not a large step to expand the interest in transmitting stories by individuals to that of a communal role of a worshiping group for whom these particular stories function as religiously normative literature. In this sense recent writers have assigned to the story within a faith community the role of shaping reality or of forming moral character. Here the link between Old Testament theology and the contemporary ethical discussion is obvious.

Fourth, another relatively recent development within Old Testament theology has been the flowing contributions of previously marginalized groups within the scholarly guild that have now aggressively sought a hearing. Among these various advocacy groups the most significant is the emergence of feminist theology, which undoubtedly will continue to develop in the next generation. In terms of Old Testament theology credit goes to P. Trible in first alerting the scholarly guild to the emergence of a new set of issues for debate through her important essay "Depatriarchalizing in Biblical Interpretation,"[14] shortly to be followed by *God and the Rhetoric of Sexuality*.[15] Within the last decade there has been a virtual explosion of literature in Old Testament studies that has sought to explore the full range of the biblical material from a feminist perspective.[16] Few will doubt that this movement will increase in influence in the next decades.

Another advocacy group, which is only in part linked with feminism, consists of the defenders of the various forms of liberation theology. The central role of the Old Testament for many liberation theologians was apparent from the outset with the use made of the Exodus theme and prophetic eschatology by J. Moltmann in his *Theology of Hope*.[17] The seminal work of G. Gutierrez, *A Theology of Liberation*,[18] also sought to exploit the Old Testament as a major biblical warrant for the concept of political and social liberation. Unfortunately, very little of the technical Old Testament work that has been done by Latin American scholars has been translated into English. Fortunately, within the last decade E. Gerstenberger[19] has sought to make known in Europe and in North America the work of some of these South American Old Testament scholars. From the English-speaking world the veritable flood of books on liberation theology from the perspective of both the Old and New Testaments is a good indication that interest in this field will only grow in the coming decades.

While the proponents of all the different advocacy groups correctly insist that the traditional claim of pure scholarly objectivity among biblical scholars was patently untrue, troubling questions remain when the passion for a particular ideological cause tends to run roughshod over the biblical text itself. It is to be hoped that the dialogue among the various communities will be such as to develop critical corrective measures against egregious distortion and trivialization of the Bible.

Fifth, there is a significant theological perspective represented by some current Old Testament scholars which, although far from being a major voice, nevertheless shows enough life that its influence will extend into the next decade. I have in mind those set of interests that are summarized under the rubric of Canon and Scripture.

The interest in the subject of canon has always been a part of Old and New Testament introductions, but the subject remained largely dormant until it was joined to the larger hermeneutical issues of exegesis and biblical theology. Beginning some twenty years ago a number of scholars began to shift their interest away from the form-critical problems of oral tradition and literary genre and turn to the effect of the textualization of the tradition into collections of authoritative religious writings. Very soon the subject of normative writings moved the discussion to the communities who received, shaped, and transmitted these writings and the development of a concept of sacred Scripture within Israel.

The new interest evoked by the reference to communities of faith in the process of canonization was especially welcomed by those who were training for an ecclesiastical office. Many sought a way by which to join ancient Israel's liturgical use of its Scriptures with the modern church's continued use of the Bible in worship. The discussion over canon appeared for many to provide a new means of access to some of these theological concerns. The study of the Old Testament as canonical literature also raised the issue of the Scripture's unity and diversity as well as posing the theological issue of the Scripture's continued ability to shape the lives of its modern readers. Within the last two decades a variety of books have sought to focus attention on various parts of the Old Testament in relation to a concept of canon, such as that of J. Blenkinsopp's *Prophecy and Canon* [20] or D. F. Morgen's *Between Text and Community: The Writings in Canonical Interpretation*.[21] In these books traditional problems of Old Testament introduction as well as Old Testament theology have been given a fresh perspective when linked with the development of the Jewish canon.

Finally, in the context of the debate over the development of the canon, new insights have emerged affecting the larger theological and hermeneutical issue of recovering a holistic reading of Scripture that is a modern concern arising as a strong reaction to the widespread fragmenting of the biblical text in the previous generation. Because the focus on canon holds together a received text with a community of faith that is in historical flux, it is able to mediate theologically between the legitimate roles of the diachronic and synchronic dimensions of the biblical texts. For these reasons it appears likely that the discussion over canon will continue to be an approach that will have its adherents well into the next century.

Postscript

After one has attempted to describe some of the future directions that the discipline of Old Testament theology might take, it is well to be reminded of how frequently in the past such predictions have proven to be grossly in error. At the turn of the nineteenth century when cultural Christianity envisioned an unlimited era of progress, Old Testament theology almost died as a discipline. Conversely, in the early 1930s when the German church fought a life and death struggle to preserve faithful Christian identity, Old Testament theology gained new life. In a word, because all genuine theology is closely tied to the events of world history, its future is equally unpredictable. Perhaps the wisest guide to the ways of God in our world is still that offered by the prophet Isaiah:

> For the LORD will rise up
> . . . to do his deed—strange is his deed!
> and to work his work—alien is his work! (Isa 28:21).

Notes

1. B. C. Ollenburger, E. A. Maartens, G. F. Hasel, eds. *The Flowering of Old Testament Theology: A Reader in Twentieth Century Old Testament Theology, 1930-1990.*

2. W. Eichrodt. *Theology of the Old Testament,* 2 vols., (Philadelphlia: Westminster/John Knox, 1961, 1967).

3. G. von Rad. *Old Testament Theology,* 2 vols. (San Francisco: Harper, 1965).

4. H. D. Preuss. *Theologie des Alten Testaments,* 2 vols. (Stuttgart 1991, 1992).

5. T. E. Fretheim. *The Suffering of God: An Old Testament Perspective. OBT.* (Philadelphia: Augsburg Fortress, 1984).

6. Jon Levenson. *Creation and the Persistence of Evil: The Jewish Drama of Divine Omnipotence* (San Francisco: Harper, 1988).

7. James Barr. *The Garden of Eden and the Hope of Immortality* (Minneapolis: Augsburg Fortress, 1993).

8. H. D. Preuss. *Deuteronomium* (Erträge der Forschung 164), Darmstadt 1982.

9. Mary Douglas. *Purity and Danger: An Analysis of the Concepts of Pollution and Taboo* (London: Routledge, 1966).

10. N. K. Gottwald. *The Tribes of Yahweh: A Sociology of the Religion of Liberated Israel* (Marykoll, N.Y.: Orbis Books, 1979).

11. Cf. the bibliography in Ollenburger's volume, 504.

12. Cf. R. H. Lowery. *The Reforming Kings, Cult and Society in First Temple Judah,* JSOTSup 120 (Sheffield: JSOT, 1991).

13. G. W. Stroup. *The Promise of Narrative Theology* (London: SCM, 1981).

14. *JAAR* 41, J 1973, 30-48.

15. P. Trible. *God and the Rhetoric of Sexuality. OBT.* (Minneapolis: Augsburg Fortress, 1978).

16. Cf. the bibliography on feminist biblical theology in Ollenburger, 448 ff.

17. J. Moltman. *Theology of Hope* (New York: Harper & Row, 1967).

18. G. Gutierrez. *A Theology of Liberation: History, Politics, and Salvation* (Maryknoll, N.Y.: Orbis Books, 1973).

19. VTSup 36, 1985.

20. J. Blenkinsopp. *Prophecy and Canon: A Contribution to the Study of Jewish Origins* (Notre Dame: University of Notre Dame Press, 1986).

21. D. F. Morgen. *Between Text and Community: The Writings in Canonical Interpretation* (Minneapolis: Augsburg Fortress, 1990).

Selected Bibliography

Childs, B. S. *Biblical Theology of the Old and New Testaments: Theological Reflection on Christian Bible*. London and Minneapolis: Augsburg Fortress, 1993.

Eichrodt, W. *Theology of the Old Testament*. English Translation 2 vols., London and Philadelphia:Westminster, 1961, 1977.

Goldingay, J. *Approaches to Old Testament Interpretation*. 1st ed. Leicester and Downers Grove, Ill.: InterVarsity, 1981; 2nd ed., Downers Grove: InterVarsity, 1990.

Ollenburger, B. C., E. A. Martens, and G. F. Hasel, eds. *The Flowering of the Old Testament Theology: A Reader in Twentieth Century Old Testament Theology, 1930-1990*. Winona Lake, Ind.: Eisenbrauns, 1992.

von Rad, G. *Old Testament Theology*. ET 2 vols. San Francisco: Harper, 1966.

LIST OF ABBREVIATIONS

Abbreviations of the Names of Biblical Books (with the Apocrypha)

Gen	Exod	Lev	Num	Deut	Josh	Judg	1–2 Sam	1–2 Kings
Isa	Jer	Ezek	Hos	Amos	Mic	Ps (*pl.*: Pss)		Job Prov
Ruth	Eccl (*or* Qoh)			Lam	Esth	Dan	Ezra Neh	1–2 Chr 4 Ezra
1–2–3–4 Macc	Sir		Wis	Matt	Mark	Luke	John Acts	Rom 1–2 Cor
Gal	Eph	1–2 Tim		Heb	Jude			

Abbreviations of the Names of Pseudepigraphal and Early Patristic Books

Ep. Arist.	*Epistles of Aristeas*
Jub.	*Jubilees*
Barn.	*Barnabas*

Abbreviations of Names of Dead Sea Scrolls and Related Texts

CD	Cairo (Genizah text of the) *Damascus (Document)*
1QS	*Serek hayyahad (Rule of the Community, Manual of Discipline)*
1QSa	Appendix A *(Rule of the Congregation)* to 1 QS
4QFlor	*Florilegium* (or *Eschatological Midrashim*) from Qumran Cave 4
4QMMT	*Miqsat Ma'aseh Torah* from Qumran Cave 4

Abbreviations of Flavius Josephus' Works

J.W.	*Jewish Wars*
Ag. Ap.	*Against Apion*
Ant.	*Antiquities*

Abbreviations of Orders of Tractates in Mishnaic and Related Literature

m.	Mishna
t.	Tosepta
b.	Babylonian Talmud
y.	Jerusalem Talmud
'Abot	*'Abot*
Ber.	*Berakot*
B. Mes.	*Baba Mesi'a*
Meg	*Megilla*
Nid.	*Niddah*
Sanh.	*Sanhedrin*
Sukk.	*Sukka*
Ta'an.	*Ta'nit*
Yad	*Yadayim*

Abbreviations of Other Rabbinic Works

Gen. Rab.	*Genesis Rabbah*
Esth. Rab.	*Esther Rabbah*
Qoh. Rab.	*Qohelet Rabbah*
Eccl. Rab.	*Ecclesiastes Rabbah*

Abbreviations of Commonly Used Periodicals, Reference Works, and Serials (with additions to the SBL abbreviation list noted with an asterisk)

AB	Anchor Bible
ABD	*Anchor Bible Dictionary**
ARBL	Anchor Bible Reference Library*
ANET	J. B. Pritchard (ed.), *Ancient Near Eastern Texts*
AOAT	Alter Orient and Altes Testament
ATD	Das Alte Testament Deutsch
ATDan	Acta theologica danica
BAR	*Biblical Archaeologist Reader*
Bib	*Biblica*
BibRev	*Bible Review*
BZAW	Beihefte zu *ZAW*
CBQ	*Catholic Biblical Quarterly*
CBQMS	Catholic Biblical Quarterly Monograph Series
DJD	Discoveries in the Judean Desert
FOTL	The Forms of Old Testament Literature
FRLANT	Forschungen zur Religion und Literatur des Alten und Neuen Testaments
HAR	Hebrew Annual Review
HBC	J. L. Mays, et al. (eds.), *Harper's Bible Commentary*
HKAT	Handkommentar zum Alten Testament
HSM	Harvard Semitic Monographs
HTR	*Harvard Theological Review*
HUCA	Hebrew Union College Annual
IBC	Interpretation: A Bible Commentary for Teaching and Preaching
IDB	George Buttrick (ed.), *Interpreter's Dictionary of the Bible*
IEJ	*Israel Exploration Journal*
JAAR	*Journal of the American Academy of Religion*
JBL	*Journal of Biblical Literature*
JSOT	*Journal for the Study of the Old Testament*
JSOTSup	Journal for the Study of the Old Testament—Supplement Series
NCB	New Century Bible
ORO	Orbis biblicus et orientalis
OBT	Overtures to Biblical Theology
OTL	Old Testament Library
RB	*Revue biblique*
SBLDS	SBL Dissertation Series
SBLMS	SBL Monograph Series

SBLSP	SBL Seminar Papers
SBLSS	SeL Semeia Series
SBT	Studies in Biblical Theology
SHANE	Studies in the History of the Ancient Near East*
SJOT	*Scandinavian Journal of Theology**
SSN	Studia semitica neerlandica
SUNT	Studien zur Umwelt des Neuen Testaments
TUMSR	Trinity University Monograph Series in Religion*
VT	*Vetus Testamentum*
VTSup	Vetus Testamentum, Supplements
WBC	Word Biblical Commentary
WMANT	Wissenschaftliche Monographien zum Alten und Neuen Testament
ZA	*Zeitschrift für Assyriologie*
ZAW	*Zeitschrift für die alttestamentliche Wissenschaft*

Abbreviations of Books Cited Often in this Work

Blenkinsopp, *Pentateuch*

Blenkinsopp, Joseph. *The Pentateuch: An Introduction to the First Five Books of the Bible*, ARBL. New York: Doubleday, 1992.

Childs, *Introduction*

Childs, Brevard. *Introduction to the Old Testament as Scripture*. Philadelphia: Fortress, 1979.

Clines, *Theme*

Clines, David J. A. *The Theme of the Pentateuch*, JSOTSup 10. Sheffield: JSOT, 1978.

Cross, *Canaanite Myth*

Cross, Frank More. *Canaanite Myth and Hebrew Epic: Essays in the History of the Religion of Israel*. Cambridge: Harvard University Press, 1973.

Hayes, ed., *Form Criticism*

Hayes, John. *Old Testament Form Criticism*, TUMSR 2. San Antonio: Trinity University Press, 1974.

Knight/Tucker, eds., *Hebrew Bible*

Knight, Douglas, and Gene Tucker, eds. *The Hebrew Bible and Its Modern Interpreters*. Chico, CA: Scholars Press, 1985.

Mann, *Torah*

Mann, Thomas W. *The Book of the Torah: The Narrative Integrity of the Pentateuch*. Atlanta: John Knox Press, 1988.

Polzin, *Moses*

Polzin, Robert. *Moses and the Deuteronomist: A Literary Study of the Deuteronomic History, Part I: Deuteronomy, Joshua, Judges*. New York: Seabury, 1980.

Polzin, *Samuel*

Polzin, Robert. *Samuel and the Deuteronomist: A Literary Study of the Deuteronomic History, Part II: 1 Samuel*. San Francisco: Harper & Row, 1989.